New Covenant, New Community

*The Significance of Biblical
and Patristic Covenant Theology
for Current Understanding*

To Dale Fredrickson,

With all my best wishes!

Peter Gräbe
St. Andrews, July 2006

New Covenant, New Community

*The Significance of Biblical
and Patristic Covenant Theology
for Current Understanding*

Petrus J. Gräbe

PATERNOSTER

Copyright © 2006 Petrus J. Gräbe

First published in 2006 by Paternoster Press

12 11 10 09 08 07 06   7 6 5 4 3 2 1

Paternoster Press is an imprint of Authentic Media,
9 Holdom Avenue, Bletchley, Milton Keynes MK1 1QR, UK
and
129 Mobilization Drive, Waynesboro, GA 30830-4575, USA

www.authenticmedia.co.uk/paternoster

Authentic Media is a division of Send The Light Ltd, a company
limited by guarantee (registered charity number 270162).

The right of Petrus J. Gräbe to be identified as the Author of this Work has been asserted by
him in accordance with the Copyright, Designs and Patents Act 1988.

*All rights reserved. No part of this publication may be reproduced, stored in a retrieval system,
or transmitted in any form or by any means, electronic, mechanical, photocopying, recording or
otherwise, without the prior permission of the publisher or a licence permitting restricted copying.
In the UK such licences are issued by the Copyright Licensing Agency,
90 Tottenham Court Road, London W1P 9HE.*

British Library Cataloguing in Publication Data
A catalogue record for this book is available from the British Library

ISBN 1-84227-248-9

Unless otherwise stated, Scripture quotations are taken from the
HOLY BIBLE, NEW INTERNATIONAL VERSION
Copyright © 1973, 1978, 1984 by the International Bible Society.
Used by permission of Hodder and Stoughton Limited. All rights reserved.
'NIV' is a registered trademark of the International Bible Society.
UK trademark number 1448790.

Cover Design by fourninezero design.
Typeset by WestKey Ltd, Falmouth, Cornwall
Print Management by Adare Carwin
Printed and Bound by J.H. Haynes & Co., Sparkford

I dedicate this book to my dear wife, Rachel,
and my daughters Alice and Catharina.

Contents

Contents

Acknowledgements

As I look back over the time of research on the new covenant motif I want to express a special word of gratitude to the following people: to Prof. Dr. Karl Kertelge who suggested this theme to me; to Prof. Dr. Ferdinand Hahn who guided my research during my visit to the University of Munich in 1995 and who continued to be interested in the project; and to Prof. Dr. Alexander Wedderburn for his critical and constructive help and guidance in the final phase of this project. Deep thanks are due to Professor Wedderburn for agreeing to write the foreword to this English edition. I am also grateful to Prof. Dr. Christoph Levin and Prof. Dr. Hans-Josef Klauck for insightful and helpful conversations, and to Prof. Dr. Thomas Söding, editor of the series *Forschung zur Bibel*, for his advice and encouragement.

An important part of my research was done during a six-month sabbatical in Cambridge (U.K.). While I was there, Prof. Dr. Graham Stanton shared valuable suggestions related to the covenant concept in the patristic and apologetic literature.

I am deeply appreciative of the Association of Commonwealth Universities and the German Academic Exchange Service for enabling my research in Cambridge and in Munich, and to Regent University for a research grant.

The outcome of my research was first published by Echter Verlag (2001) in the series "Forschung zur Bibel" (volume 96) under the title *Der neue Bund in der frühchristlichen Literatur unter Berücksichtigung der alttestamentlich-jüdischen Voraussetzungen*. I want to express my sincere appreciation to Katharina Penner, who assisted me in the translation process, and to Skip Horton-Parker for his eloquent and theologically perceptive editing of the manuscript.

Petrus J. Gräbe
February 2005

Foreword

Dr. Petrus Gräbe is one of those rare talents, a scholar who can write with equal fluency in either English or German. Thus, while his Pretoria doctoral dissertation on "power" in the main Pauline letters was published in English, his second monograph appeared in German – although it was based on research conducted not only in Germany but in England as well. Yet it was evident that a work in German would not reach as wide an audience, and so it is more than welcome that Dr. Gräbe has now produced a revised version of his study in English, the language of the land in which this thoroughly international young scholar is now teaching.

Moreover, the theme of this monograph is a central one. For a start, the concept of God's covenant, or covenants, is one that is integral to that enterprise which in various forms is labelled "Biblical Theology." And yet the very concept of a "new covenant" highlights a fundamental problem, for the reference to a "new covenant" stresses the discontinuity between the former covenant and the new one every bit as much as the continuity, as the use of this motif in Hebrews shows. Talk of a "new covenant" underlines the oldness of the former covenant, even if for the *auctor ad Hebraeos* this does not mean that it had already been done away with completely, but merely that it was on the point of disappearing (Heb. 8:13).

It is true that the term "covenant" does not appear as often in the New Testament as one might expect and that one must therefore beware of reading it into contexts where it is absent. (And, as I recall, my main function in discussions of his work with Dr. Gräbe during his time in Munich was essentially that of an *advocatus diaboli*, adopting the stance of a minimalist approach to the role of the covenant in the writings of the New Testament.) And yet where it does occur in the writings of the New Testament, it is sometimes to be found in key passages within that corpus. I have already alluded to its important role in Hebrews, in that somewhat neglected work that is nevertheless one of the theologically most important New Testament documents, but nowhere does the covenant play a more important role than in the various accounts of Jesus' last meal with his disciples, with the exception of the Fourth Gospel and the shorter version of Luke's text. It is thus central to early Christian reflection on that meal, even if it may be asked whether its presence in the "words of institution" goes back to Jesus himself, who does not otherwise seem to have spoken explicitly in terms of "covenant." Nonetheless, the very action of Jesus in eating and drinking together with his disciples on this occasion, one fraught with ominous forebodings, may have a certain "covenantal" quality and function, binding them together with one another and with their Lord as well as committing them to solidarity with him and his service of God's rule, even if they were to fail him so dismally immediately afterwards (Mark 14:50).

In other texts of the New Testament the stress on discontinuity is plainer. That is true of Hebrews, but it is also true to a lesser extent of 2 Corinthians 3. For the "letter" of the former Mosaic covenant "kills" (3:6–7), even if that dispensation nevertheless possessed a certain "glory" (3:9–10) that is then surpassed by that of the new dispensation. For even if the contrast is softened by the talk of a greater and a lesser glory, the opening contrast between killing and giving life remains, and it could hardly be phrased more strongly without lapsing into a gnostic or gnosticizing denigration of the God who had given the former covenant. Indeed, one may ask whether even these statements of Paul and of the writer of Hebrews do not implicitly pose the question as to how one can properly speak of God giving a covenant that "kills" or that is unable to achieve its purpose and must be replaced by another one. Does that not raise awkward theological questions at least regarding God's competence and wisdom? Or must one rather view all "covenant" language from a human perspective, not as a matter of divine giving but of an (imperfect) human perception and awareness of the divine and of the appropriate human relationship to the divine?

It was also a particularly welcome and impressive feature of Dr. Gräbe's study that he did not confine himself to the New Testament nor even to the New Testament together with its Old Testament and early Jewish precursors. He also found room to trace, albeit succinctly, the theme of the "new covenant" in second-century early Christian writings, in the Syrian Christian tradition and in the later history of the Christian church and Christian theology up to and including Karl Barth. That part of the work is in itself a helpful reminder of how influential "covenant" language has been at various times and in various traditions, including those of my native land, even if Dr. Gräbe's treatment of this theme in more recent times could not be more than a couple of samples drawn from a whole plethora of possibilities.

Such is the importance, then, of this theme that the appearance of this learned, wide-ranging, carefully and thoroughly researched study in a more generally accessible version can only be welcomed. It will assuredly be frequently consulted by any who wrestle with this theme and its implications, and both the theme and its ramifications are theologically so important that relatively few who concern themselves with issues such as the relationship between the two Testaments or between Judaism and the Christian church can sidestep this challenge. Those concerned with such issues will find here a valuable contribution to, and basis for, their own discussion of them.

A. J. M. Wedderburn
Munich 2005

Introduction:
A "Renaissance" of Covenant Theology

The last decade has seen a renaissance[1] of interest in covenant-related theology, following a period during which interest in the subject had all but disappeared from the agenda of biblical studies.[2] Covenant theology has again become an important topic of discussion. Erich Zenger (for example) represents an influential group of scholars, asking questions such as: Are Israel and the church members of one covenant? Is the new covenant reserved for Christians, or do the covenants belong only to Israel as the people of God?[3]

Covenant theology, as it was developed in the Old and New Testament periods, is once again being seen as the foundation of the nexus of biblical literature. When Judah faced extinction with the abdication of the king and the destruction of the temple in 587 B.C., it found new hope and new life through the preaching that the covenant that was seemingly annulled by Judah's infidelity would be renewed (Jer. 31:31–34). Later the followers of Jesus would find, in the Lord's Supper tradition, an interpretation of Jesus' death as the establishment of this new covenant – a covenant which Paul interprets fundamentally in terms of the Holy Spirit (2 Cor. 3; cf. Ezek. 36:27). The concept of this eschatological new covenant became the foundation of early Christian literature, rooting the new gospel in Jeremiah, Ezekiel, and Deutero-Isaiah's original vision of a divine action that grants new life and hope and triumphs over human weakness and despair.

---

[1] See Avemarie and Lichtenberger (eds.), *Bund und Tora: Zur theologischen Begriffsgeschichte in alttestamentlicher, frühjüdischer und urchristlicher Tradition* (Tübingen: J. C. B. Mohr [Paul Siebeck], 1996), V.

[2] Cf. Zenger, "Die Bundestheologie – ein derzeit vernachlässigtes Thema der Bibelwissenschaft und ein wichtiges Thema für das Verhältnis Israel – Kirche," in E. Zenger (ed.), *Der Neue Bund im Alten: Zur Bundestheologie der beiden Testamenten* (Freiburg: Herder, 1993), 13–15.

[3] Cf. Backhaus, "Rezension: Manuel Vogel, Das Heil des Bundes. Bundestheologie im Frühjudentum und im frühen Christentum," *BZ* 41 (1997), 149.

The motif of the (new) covenant remains a key motif shedding light on three of the most important theological questions of the twenty-first century:

(i)   What is the relationship between Jews and Christians?
(ii)   What is the relationship between the Old and the New Testaments?
(iii) What is the self-understanding of Jews and Christians?

1. An overview of recent contributions

The closing decades of the twentieth century saw significant scholarly advances in the area of covenant theology. Ernest W. Nicholson (1986) and Eckart Otto (1998) both provided comprehensive overviews of Old Testament research on this topic. *Der Neue Bund im Alten* collects papers read at the society for German-speaking Catholic Old Testament scholars ("Arbeitsgemeinschaft deutschsprachiger katholischer Alttestamentlerinnen und Alttestamentler") in September 1991 in Augsburg. These papers address the "covenant deficit,"[4] which had developed during the 1970s, and provide new impetus for a multi-layered concept of covenant.[5]

Questions and conclusions gleaned from this conference were the focus of a meeting of the society of German-speaking Catholic New Testament scholars ("*Arbeitsgemeinschaft deutschsprachiger katholischer Neutestamentler*") in 1997. These questions included:

- How are terms such as "covenant" and "new covenant" understood in the First Testament?
- How do New Testament scholars interpret the covenant motif?
- How does the covenant theme in contemporary systematic theology reflect the early Jewish and biblical findings?[6]

The fourth issue of the *Theologische Quartalschrift* (1996) was also dedicated to the theme of covenant. This volume attempts to analyze the validity of theological understanding regarding the new covenant in delineating the relationship between the church and Israel.

Susanne Lehne (1990) advanced an understanding of "covenant" in the Epistle to the Hebrews which was closely analyzed by Kurt Backhaus (1996). Under the title "Bund und Tora" ("Covenant and Torah"), ten studies from a

---

[4]   See Chapter 1.1, below.
[5]   Cf. Zenger, *Der Neue Bund im Alten*, 7.
[6]   Results of this conference are published in the helpful volume 172 of the series Quaestiones disputatae by Frankemölle (ed.), *Der ungekündigte Bund? Antworten des Neuen Testaments* (Freiburg/Basel/Wien: Herder, 1998).

Tübingen 1994 seminar[7] on this topic have also been published. In her 1995 dissertation on "Ritual Boundaries as Identity Markers," Ellen Juhl Christiansen analyzes the use of the term "covenant" in Judaism and by Paul.[8] Manuel Vogel offers an overview of pre-second-century postbiblical covenant theology in Jewish and Christian literature in his monograph *Das Heil des Bundes* ("The Salvation of the Covenant"). Walter Brueggemann published a collection of essays entitled *The Covenanted Self: Explorations in Law and Covenant* in 1999, in which he reflects on key covenant-related themes and their significance for contemporary life and thought.

Steven McKenzie's *Covenant* appeared in the series "Understanding Biblical Themes" in 2000. Stanley Porter and Jacqueline de Roo edited an insightful volume of essays in 2003 entitled *The Concept of the Covenant in the Second Temple Period*. Contributions to this volume address, among other issues: covenant and the Old Testament, covenant and the Dead Sea scrolls, covenant and the Pseudepigrapha and Targumim, covenant and Hellenistic Jewish literature, and covenant and the New Testament. Our knowledge of the covenant theme is further enriched by a 2003 volume of essays in honor of E. W. Nicholson, *Covenant as Context*, edited by A. D. H. Mayes and R. B. Salters.

2. The goal of this study

Our present study analyzes the concept of the *new covenant*[9] in early Christian literature (with special attention to Old Testament and Jewish presuppositions) and observes the influence of covenant understanding in early Christian theology. We shall focus particularly on how the motif of the new covenant has been interpreted and reinterpreted in different theological contexts.

Theology has been defined as "reflection on faith under the 'signs of the times.'"[10] This study, therefore, will investigate the role that the notion of the new covenant plays in important contemporary theological issues. Such issues

---

[7] Cf. Avemarie and Lichtenberger, *Bund und Tora*, VII.

[8] Cf. also Hahn, "A Biblical Theological Study of Covenant Types and Texts in the Old and New Testament" (DPhil Dissertation, Marquette University, Milwaukee, WI. UMI Microform 9600849, 1995).

[9] Although this study begins with a discussion of the meaning of the word ברית, it must be pointed out that it is not a simple word that is under consideration, but an entire *semantic field*. The covenant term is also closely connected with other motifs (cf. 1.2.1) and can be alluded to even when the words ברית / διαθήκη do not appear, cf., e.g., the covenant formula (cf. 1.3.6).

[10] Zenger, "Thesen zu einer Hermeneutik des Ersten Testaments nach Auschwitz," in Dohmen and Söding (eds.), *Eine Bibel – zwei Testamente: Positionen biblischer Theologie* (Paderborn: Ferdinand Schöningh, 1995), 143.

include the meaning of a *new* covenant, Christian identity and the Jewish–Christian dialogue. The reception of the concept of the new covenant in the history of theology will be discussed from two perspectives: that of early federal theology and that of the theology of Karl Barth.

The historical and theological complexities that attend any attempt to plumb the meaning of concepts as profound as (new) covenant are, of course, daunting. But the abiding importance of maintaining a dynamic appreciation of these ideas, which have played such an important role in both Judaism and Christianity, overshadows these difficulties. Indeed, theology is called to engage in an ongoing process of transmitting and reinterpreting the meaning of our "theology of the covenant." This study, therefore, will provide some suggestions for formulating a theology of "new covenant" for the present day.

1

The Old Testament Background for Understanding the Covenant Concept in the New Testament

1. Introduction

The relationships between the Old and New Testaments and between the church and Israel are at the center of scholarly debate once more. The nature of covenant in both Testaments is crucial for understanding both issues.[1] One cannot, of course, comprehend the meaning of the covenant motif in the New Testament without reference to the rich traditions of the Old Testament and the intertestamental literature.[2]

The history of research on the covenant theme reveals it to be arguably one of the most controversial terms in theology. At times, the criticism leveled at covenant theology is so radical that one wonders if it is possible to speak meaningfully of the nature of covenant at all![3] In the earlier Reformed context of "federal" theology, however, covenant was used to describe the unity and continuity of God's salvific activity in its totality.[4]

"Covenant theology" was not a focus of exegetical discussion for some years during the latter half of the twentieth century. There was, however, a turning point in Old Testament Studies in the 1970s. Josef Haspecker's 1962 article in the *Handbuch theologischer Begriffe* described covenant as *the* constitutive historical, cultic and theological reality in Israelite theology. The 1991

---

[1] Cf. the discussion between Seebass and Zenger in *Theologische Revue* 90.4 (1994), "Bemerkungen zur 'kleinen Antwort'."

[2] Cf. Seebass, "Hat das Alte Testament als Teil der christlichen Bibel für christliche Theologie und Kirchen grundlegende Bedeutung?," *TRev* 90.4 (1994), 267.

[3] See the many contributions written by Ernst Kutsch on this topic, e.g., *Neues Testament – Neuer Bund? Eine Fehlübersetzung wird korrigiert* (Neukirchen-Vluyn: Neukirchener Verlag, 1978). See also 1.2.3, below.

[4] The beginnings of this theology, in the earliest historical sources, go back to the time of the Reformation in Zürich and the debate with the emerging Anabaptists (cf. Goeters, "Föderaltheologie," in *TRE* XI, 246). See also 10.2, below.

revised edition of the handbook edited by Peter Eicher,[5] however, drops the entry on covenant altogether – the term does not even appear in the indices of the five-volume handbook.

There have been several attempts to address this covenant "deficit" since the late-1980s (cf., for example, E. W. Nicholson, *God and his People* [1986][6] and the 1993 volume from the series Quaestiones disputatae *Der Neue Bund im Alten: Zur Bundestheologie der beiden Testamente*).[7] During the last decade it has become obvious that attempts to achieve a consensus regarding the meaning of covenant have failed due to a number of open questions. These attempts include work done by Ernst Kutsch on the semantics of ברית and by Lothar Perlitt on covenant theology. The time is ripe to readdress the topic of covenant in a comprehensive manner.[8]

2. The meaning of the word ברית

2.1 Not a simple term, but a semantic field

In his 1995 study on the "covenant formula," Rolf Rendtorff made a significant contribution to the interpretation of "covenant" in the Old Testament by highlighting its interrelationship with other Old Testament motifs.[9] The term "covenant" exists in the same semantic field with other expressions, especially with the "covenant formula," the "knowledge formula," the "introduction formula" and the notion of "election." Rendtorff especially underscored the meaning of the covenant formula, demonstrating that covenant formula language is consciously used throughout the Hebrew Bible. Such language succinctly describes the relationship of God toward Israel and vice versa.[10] In many

---

[5] *Neues Handbuch theologischer Grundbegriffe: Erweiterte Neuausgabe in 5 Bändern* (München: Kösel-Verlag, 1991).

[6] The 2003 volume of essays in honor of E. W. Nicholson, edited by A. D. H. Mayes and R. B. Salters, also deals with the covenant theme and is titled *Covenant and Context* (Oxford: Oxford University Press).

[7] Cf. also Lohfink, "Kinder Abrahams aus Steinen: Wird nach dem Alten Testament Israel einst der 'Bund' genommen werden?" and Groß, "'Rezeption' in Ex 31,12–17 und Lev 26,39–45: Sprachliche Form und theologisch-konzeptionelle Leistung," both in Frankemölle, *Der ungekündigte Bund?*, pp. 17–43 and 44–63, respectively.

[8] This is what Seebass, "Hat das Alte Testament," 267, suggests.

[9] Cf. also Lohfink, "Kinder Abrahams aus Steinen," who does not perceive the term "covenant" to be the shibboleth for his exposition of the covenant theme, because the covenant theme does not depend exclusively on the word ברית.

[10] Rudolf Smend thoroughly analyzed this formula in 1963 (*Die Bundesformel*, ThSt 68 [Zürich: EVZ-Verlag, 1963]). Through his contribution, the phrase "covenant formula" has become widely used.

instances the covenant formula connects election, knowledge and the introduction formula. These connections give a broader context for interpretation
that yields new theological correlations and contributes to the expansion of
"covenant theology."[11] Rendtorff's study thus methodologically advanced our
understanding of the term ברית ("covenant") in the Old Testament in significant ways.[12]

2.2 Usage and shades of meaning of ברית[13] ("covenant")

In *Deuteronomy*, ברית describes what goes on between Yahweh and Israel in
three primary ways:[14]

(i) ברית describes Yahweh's gracious *promise* to the patriarchs: Deuteronomy
4:31; 7:9, 12; 8:18.

(ii) ברית is related to the revelation at Horeb and points to the Decalogue,
especially to the first commandment, in two different ways. First, there are
positive covenant references and, secondly, there are references to covenant breaking. The covenant is broken through forgetting (שׁכח, 4:23),
transgressing (עבר, 17:2), leaving (עזב, 29:25) or breaking (פרר, 31:16, 20)
the first commandment, as when the Israelites worshiped "other gods"
(17:3; 29:25; 31:16, 20). Deuteronomy 4:23 prohibits idols or false gods,
and chapter four avoids the expression "other gods."

(iii) ברית is connected to the stay in the land of Moab. Israel's ceremonial *commitment* to the whole Deuteronomic code of law is the context implicit in
"covenant" (28:69a; 29:8, 11, 13, 20). "Oath" is an important component of
the meaning of ברית in these texts.

ברית describes similar phenomena in Joshua – 2 Kings:[15]

---

[11] Rendtorff, *Die "Bundesformel:" Eine exegetisch-theologische Untersuchung* (Stuttgart:
Verlag Katholisches Bibelwerk, 1995), 93.

[12] See 1.3.6, below, on the significance of the covenant formula for the meaning of the
covenant concept.

[13] Neef, "Aspekte alttestamentlicher Bundestheologie," in Avemarie and
Lichtenberger, *Bund und Tora*, 3–5, offers a full overview of appearances of ברית in
the Old Testament.

[14] Cf. Braulik, "Die Ausdrücke für 'Gesetz' im Buch Deuteronomium," in Georg
Braulik (ed.), *Studium zur Theologie des Deuteronomiums* (Stuttgart: Verlag
Katholisches Bibelwerk, 1988), 1–17. (This was first published in *Biblica* 51 [1970],
39–66.) See also Lohfink, "Bundestheologie im Alten Testament: Zum
gleichnamigen Buch von Lothar Perlitt," in Lohfink (ed.), *Studien zum
Deuteronomium und zur deuteronomistischen Literatur I* (Stuttgart: Verlag Katholisches
Bibelwerk, 1990), 338–40.

[15] See Lohfink, "Bundestheologie," 338.

(i) The connotation *"promise"* is also implicit in covenant references here. In Judges 2:1 and 2 Kings 13:23 Yahweh gives a promise to the forefathers (or to the Exodus generation). David receives a promise in 2 Samuel 23:5, and possibly also in 1 Kings 8:23.[16]

(ii) The term ברית usually refers to the *Decalogue* or to the first commandment (Josh. 3:3, 6, 8, 11, 14, 17; 4:7, 9, 18; 6:6, 8; 8:33; 23:16; Judg. 2:20; 20:27; 1 Sam. 4:3, 4, 5; 2 Sam. 15:24; 1 Kgs. 3:15; 6:19; 8:1, 6, 21; 11:11; 2 Kgs. 17:15, 35, 38). It is possible that the term includes not only the Decalogue, but also the whole Deuteronomic law (cf. Josh. 7:11, 15 and 2 Kgs. 18:12; possibly also 2 Kgs. 17:15). This expanded use of the term becomes more obvious in the Deuteronomistic texts of Jeremiah.

(iii) 2 Kings 11:17 and 23:21, 22, 23 point to a specific *commitment* ritual, to which Joshua 24:25 also refers. There Joshua places the tribes of Israel under the obligation to worship Yahweh alone. This commitment results in the Torah book. 2 Kings 11:17, therefore, deals with the relationship to God as described in the covenant formula.

The idea of covenant as God's merciful *promise* to the forefathers (usage i) seems to have been introduced into Deuteronomistic thinking from outside and achieves a central position only in certain late literary layers of OT literature. The reference to the Decalogue or to the first commandment (usage ii) is probably not originally Deuteronomistic either.

The third category (iii) is directly analogous to the profane, interpersonal usage of the word "covenant" as a binding legal agreement. This usage is found in contemporary literature as well as in the Deuteronomistic material.

This connection between covenant terminology and the Decalogue, which was only later introduced into the Sinaitic context, would not have been possible if the Decalogue did not have an affinity with covenant terminology. One cannot exclude the possibility that the Deuteronomic usage of covenant may refer to a previous commitment to the exclusive worship of Yahweh, exercised either in the context of the Decalogue or even apart from this concrete text.[17]

---

[16] This could also be a general predication (Lohfink, "Bundestheologie," 338).

[17] See Lohfink, "Bundestheologie," 340. He points out that, in connection with the Decalogue and with the exclusive worship of Yahweh, a semantic study of the word ברית possibly also offers some arguments in favor of the view that one does not need to encumber the Deuteronomist with having introduced the word ברית.

2.2.1 Components of meaning of the word בְּרִית ("covenant"): A table (see comments below)

	Law/ obedience	Promise	Sign of covenant	Solemn ceremony	Comments
Gen. 9		x	x		God's covenant with Noah: Rainbow in the clouds
Gen. 15		x		x	God's covenant with Abraham: numerous descendants, land
Gen. 17		x	x		Descendants, land; circumcision as sign of covenant; eternal covenant
Exod. 19:5	x	x			
Exod. 24:7, 8	x			x	The meal of the covenant
Exod. 31:16, 17			x		Celebration of Sabbath
Exod. 34:28, 29	x				
Num. 25:13		x			Covenant of eternal priesthood
Deut. 4:13, 23; 9:9, 11, 15; 17:2; 28:69; 29:8, 11–12, 24; 31:16; 33:9	x				
Deut. 10:8; 31:9, 25, 26	x				Ark of the covenant
Deut. 4:31; 7:9, 12; 8:18		x			In Deut. 7:9, 12 obedience to the laws/regulations is required for the covenant
Josh. 24:25	x				
2 Sam. 23:5		x			Covenant with David; cf. also Ps. 89:4; eternal covenant
Jer. 11:6, 8	x				
Jer. 31:31–34	x	x			New covenant: law in the hearts of Israel; forgiveness of sins

2.2.2 Comments on the shades of meaning of ברית *("covenant")*

The table in section 2.2.1 above sets out the "components of meaning" of ברית in different contexts in which this theme is used in a theological sense. This schematic presentation requires some explanation:

(i) *The relationship with Yahweh*

Relationship with Yahweh is fundamental in each of the above contexts.[18] We see this dynamic present throughout the lives of the patriarchs. Genesis 6:9 speaks of Noah as a "righteous man" who "walked with God." God made a covenant with him (v. 18) and Noah did everything exactly as God had commanded him (v. 22). In Genesis 15:1 we read that God encourages Abraham: "Do not be afraid, Abram, I am your shield …" God promises him numerous descendants, and the words that follow this promise will have a determinative effect on New Testament theology: "Abram believed God, and it was credited to him as righteousness."

The passage dealing with circumcision as the sign of the covenant (Gen. 17:1–27) begins with God's words to Abraham: "I am God Almighty, walk before me and be blameless." Verse 7b promises: "to you and your descendants after you I will be their God." This chronological expansion of the scope of covenant intimacy corresponds to the intention expressed by the Priestly writer throughout chapter 17, and indeed acts as the chapter's center.[19]

The relationship with God is also the focus of the report about the sealing of the covenant at Sinai (Exod. 19:5): "… if you obey me fully and keep my covenant, then out of all nations you will be my treasured possession …" Yahweh,

---

[18] Cf. Dyrness, *Themes in Old Testament Theology* (Downers Grove, IL: InterVarsity Press; Exeter: Paternoster, 1979), 125. Lohfink, "Kinder Abrahams aus Steinen," 19–20, also underlines the importance of the relationship between Yahweh and his people in the framework of the covenant theme. He entitles the first passage of his exposition of the covenant theme "God's commitment to Israel": "That Israel is Yahweh's people and Yahweh is Israel's God, that this notion in itself makes and further advances history, that, even when this history will once include the world of the nations, Zion will still remain at the centre of it, this notion is omnipresent in the narrative writings of Israel."

[19] See Westermann, *Genesis*, II (Neukirchen-Vluyn: Neukirchener Verlag, 1981), 316.

The promise that God, the Almighty, will be the God of Abraham and of his descendants indicates that making a covenant is God's exclusive activity. P underlines the reciprocity of the relationship with God through the way in which chapter 17 is structured: vv. 9–14 are located between vv. 3b–8 and 15–23 (cf. Westermann, *Genesis*, 316).

who owns the whole earth, and thus all nations also, will make Israel his special personal possession.[20]

In Jeremiah 33:20–22, Yahweh underlines the eternal, steadfast nature of his covenant with David and with the Levites, "who minister before me" (vv. 21b, 22b).[21] At the end of his life David opines: "when one rules over men in righteousness … he is like the light of the morning at sunrise … Is not my house right with God? Has he not made with me an everlasting covenant, arranged and secured in every part?" (2 Sam. 23:3–5). The priest Pinehas and his descendants receive a covenant of lasting priesthood because *he was zealous for his God* and has made atonement for the Israelites (Num. 25:13).

The center of Deuteronomic covenant theology is, therefore, the relationship to God. The very goal of covenant keeping is to serve, and thus remain close to, the one God. When the covenant is discussed in Deuteronomy in parenetic contexts, it usually relates to the prohibition of images, as in 4:23: "Be careful not to forget the covenant of the LORD your God that he made with you; do not make for yourselves an idol in the form of anything the LORD your God has forbidden." Breaking the covenant means rejecting Yahweh, and this happens when people turn to other gods. The *parallelismus membrorum* in Deuteronomy 29:25 and 26 is striking:

> v. 25 … because *they abandoned the covenant* …

> v. 26 … because *they have worshipped other gods* …[22]

In Joshua 24, God's prophet calls the tribes of Israel to make a decision: whom shall they serve? Will they worship only the true God, and reject the gods that Abraham rejected and that seduced Israel when they were slaves in Egypt?[23] The narrative ends with a covenant ceremony sealing the peoples' decision (v. 24): "We will serve the Lord our God and obey him."

(ii) *"Law" as a component of meaning*

"Law" is an important component of the meaning of ברית ("covenant") in many contexts in the Deuteronomic and Deuteronomistic literature, as in

---

[20] Noth, *Das zweite Buch Mose: Exodus* (Göttingen: Vandenhoeck & Ruprecht, 1959), 126.

[21] Cf. Weiser, *Das Buch des Propheten Jeremia: Kapitel 25,15–52,34* (Göttingen: Vandenhoeck & Ruprecht, 1955), 315; Lamparter, *Prophet wider Willen: Der Prophet Jeremia* (Stuttgart: Calwer Verlag, 1964), 331–32.

[22] Cf. Deut. 17:2; 31:16 as well as Judg. 2:20; 1 Kgs. 11:11; 19:10,14; 2 Kgs. 17:15; 18:12.

[23] Gutbrod, *Das Buch von Lande Gottes: Josua und Richter* (Stuttgart: Calwer Verlag, 1985), 183.

Exodus 19:5 "... if you obey me fully and keep my covenant."[24] In Joshua 7:15; 2 Kings 18:12; Jeremiah 34:18; Hosea 6:7; 8:1 ברית ("covenant") is connected with עבר (transgress) in the sense of "transgressing the *covenant*." This usage is similar to that in Daniel 9:11, where עבר (transgress) is connected to the תורה (torah) in the sense of transgressing the *law*.

We must, however, resist the temptation to equate "covenant" (ברית) with "law" (תורה). In numerous contexts where the motif of law/obedience plays an important role, "covenant" is supplemented with a second term: Exodus 24:7 has "the *book* of the covenant" (ספר הברית); Exodus 34:28; Deuteronomy 28:69; 29:8 and Jeremiah 11:6, 8 use "the *words* of the covenant" (דברי הברית). Thus ברית is *more* than a "book/document" or the "words/terms" of the covenant. Jeremiah 34:18 is noteworthy in this regard, as this verse further explains the violation of the covenant by pointing to the *terms* of the covenant:

> ".... the men who have violated *my covenant*
> and have not fulfilled the *terms of the covenant* ..."

2.3 ברית – covenant?

During the 1960s and 1970s, theological discussion focused on the question of the meaning of ברית. In 1962, Jepsen[25] asked if the time had come to abandon the translation "covenant," at least in the scientific theological usage, since "covenant" carries the connotation of a legal agreement. Wouldn't it be truer, Jepsen argued, to describe "covenant" as a "promise" between persons, and the divine "covenant" more specifically as a combination of "promise and command" (*Verheißung und Geheiß*)?

Kutsch has also fiercely challenged the translation of ברית as "covenant." While the term "covenant" has traditionally been interpreted as describing the relationship between God and individual persons, or the people of Israel in Old Testament theology, Kutsch[26] argues that, in contrast to the legalistic, profane usage of the term, Yahweh and people are never mentioned together as subjects of one ברית. The word ברית does not describe a relationship but is the "regulation"; it signifies an "obligation" which is accepted by the subject of the ברית. It is, therefore, close to a "promise" or a "pledge."[27] If we choose to

---

[24] Cf. also Deut. 4:13: "The Lord declared to you his covenant, the Ten Commandments, which he commanded you to follow."

[25] Jepsen, "Berith: Ein Beitrag zur Theologie der Exilszeit," in Kuschke (ed.), *Verbannung und Heimkehr: Beiträge zur Geschichte und Theologie Israels im 6. und 5. Jahrhundert v. Chr. Festschrift für Wilhelm Rudolph* (Tübingen: J. C. B. Mohr [Paul Siebeck], 1962), 178–79.

[26] Kutsch, "Bund," in *TRE* VII (Berlin: Walter de Gruyter, 1981), 399.

[27] Kutsch, "ברית Verpflichtung," in Jenni and Westermann (eds.), *THAT* I (München: Chr. Kaiser, 1971), 342.

refurbish the traditional concept of "covenant" as contract, says Kutsch, two alternative concepts implicit in ברית are likely contenders for replacement: God's promise and his law; his giving and his demanding; his encouragement (*Zuspruch*) and his claim (*Anspruch*). Kutsch stresses that the translation of ברית must in every case proceed from the "*root meaning*" (*Grundbedeutung*) "regulation, obligation."[28]

Kutsch's thinking was very influential, especially in German language scholarship. Claus Westermann even speaks of achieving a "full consensus" regarding the understanding of the word ברית based on Kutsch's suggestion.[29] Although Westermann grants that in its earliest usage ברית describes the making of a solemn binding assurance (which, if God is the subject, is the equivalent of an oath, or a pledge), he nevertheless concurs that in a text such as Genesis 17, ברית has the meaning of "covenant" – a binding commitment, affecting both parties and establishing the lasting status of the covenant.[30]

Current research in semantics questions Kutsch's methodology, however, and therefore his conclusions.[31] The "word study" approach can be misleading because of historical changes in the meaning of the term under consideration.[32] To base one's understanding of a term on a "root meaning" (*Grundbedeutung*) is problematic, as the meaning of words can change over time. The early meaning of a word may not be present in later contexts.[33]

The question of the etymology of ברית has been discussed extensively in the literature. There are two separate issues at the heart of such a consideration, however: (i) the correctness of the general etymology of the Hebrew word; (ii)

---

[28] Kutsch, *Verheißung und Gesetz: Untersuchungen zum sogenannten "Bund" im Alten Testament* (Berlin: Walter de Gruyter, 1973), 206 (italics mine: PJG).

[29] Westermann, *Theologie des Alten Testaments in Grundzügen* (Göttingen: Vandenhoeck & Ruprecht, 1978), 35.

[30] One cannot speak of "consensus" at all – even though Westermann partly agrees with Kutsch, he does not deny that ברית can also mean "covenant," a notion that Kutsch rejects in principle.

[31] Cf. Breytenbach's criticism, "Verbond en verbondstekens in die Ou Testament – 'n terreinverkenning," *HTS* 38 (1984), 6–7.

[32] Herrmann, "'Bund' eine Fehlübersetzung von 'bᵉrit': Zur Auseinandersetzung mit Ernst Kutsch," in Herrmann (ed.), *Gesammelte Studien zur Geschichte und Theologie des Alten Testaments* (München: Chr. Kaiser, 1986), 210. It is not right, as Kutsch insists, to always take the basic meaning of a word as a starting point in translation, cf. Barr, *The Semantics of Biblical Language* (Oxford: Oxford University Press, 1967), 100: "One of the types of argument which I shall criticize in this study is that which places excessive emphasis on the meaning of the 'root' of Hebrew words … This belief I shall for the sake of brevity call 'the root fallacy.'"

[33] Louw, *Semantics of New Testament Greek* (Philadelphia: Fortress Press, 1982), 31.

whether such an etymological explanation is relevant to our understanding of the meaning of the word in biblical Hebrew. The semantic function of בְּרִית in the Old Testament is far removed from the meaning that can be derived from a general etymology.[34]

Barr[35] offers the following observations regarding the way בְּרִית functions as a linguistic unit in the Old Testament:

Opacity: Barr differentiates between *transparent* words (for example, the German word *Handschuh*[36]) and *opaque* words (for example, the English *glove*). He concludes: "In transparency of this kind 'bᵉrīt' seems to be completely lacking." The biblical authors were probably completely unaware of connections to the etymology of this word.

Idiomaticity: בְּרִית appears in a specific idiomatic construction – eighty times in connection with the word כָּרַת ("cut") (about eleven times with הֵקִים [establish]; and sporadically with נָתַן ["give"], שִׂים ["set" and other terms). In the context of such idioms, the meaning of the phrase cannot be deduced from its constituent parts. Barr concludes: "This idiomaticity seems to reinforce the impression of the opacity of bᵉrīt already remarked on."

Non-pluralization: No plural forms can be found for בְּרִית from biblical and early postbiblical times. This is strange, considering the many reports of covenant making in the texts. Barr observes: "The absence of the plural does not imply inability to think in a certain way: what it suggests rather is the existence of unusual restrictions on the range within which the term bᵉrīt was used."

Shape of semantic field: When seen from one perspective, the semantic range of בְּרִית is very broad; from a different perspective it seems *very narrow*.

(i) Broadly speaking, בְּרִית can be rendered "agreement, contract, commitment, promise." Such usage occurs in the Old Testament in the context of festive or solemn religious rites.

---

[34] Cf. Gertz, "Bund, II: Altes Testament," in *RGG* I (Tübingen: J. C. B. Mohr [Paul Siebeck], 1998), 1862: "The etymology of the word is not clear, in spite of intensive debates. But in any way it would help only little to define its meaning. The meaning discloses itself primarily out of the exegetic, semantic and theological context." (Translation mine, as are all quotations from foreign language works throughout this volume, unless otherwise noted.) Neef, "Alttestamentliche Bundestheologie," 2–3, also points out that it is difficult to establish a definitive etymological derivation for the noun בְּרִית if the exegetical, semantic and theological context of the noun is not taken into account. He nevertheless describes four different derivation attempts (see p. 2).

[35] Barr, "Some Semantic Notes on the Covenant," in Donner, Hanhart and Smend (eds.), *Beiträge zur Alttestamentlichen Theologie: Festschrift für Walther Zimmerli zum 70. Geburtstag* (Göttingen: Vandenhoeck & Ruprecht, 1977), 24–34.

[36] Literally, "handshoe" – a shoe to cover one's hands. The meaning of the word can be gleaned from its constituent parts, which may reflect its origin or etymology (cf. the English word "postbox").

(ii) More narrowly, ברית appears in contexts such as the following, according to Barr:

1. The making, keeping, breaking, leaving, remembering and forgetting of the bᵉrît;

2. The material or visible signs, vehicles, or embodiments of the bᵉrît: the ark, the book, the tables, the blood;

3. The duration of the bᵉrît – in fact always … 'for ever'… .

The *limitations* of the semantic field of ברית become particularly apparent when we note how the term is *not* used. As we saw above, there is no plural for ברית, it is not numerically counted; no one seems to "think about" covenant, to love it, or be happy about it; no one announces or offers commentary about covenant – what are announced or commented upon are God's mighty deeds, his praise and so on.

We must clearly differentiate between the meaning, reference, implication and usage of a word in a context.[37] Johannes Louw (following Eugene Nida) defines *meaning* as "a set of relations for which a verbal symbol is a sign."[38] The meaning of a word is its minimal contribution toward the understanding of a statement.[39] While Kutsch notes that the meaning of ברית must be derived from its context, Barr's critique is nevertheless justified:

> … it seems to me that his [Kutsch's] basic material comes from *the words spoken* on the occasion of making each bᵉrît, *the effects promised* or *undertaken, the effects* that actually follow: and from this we come to promises, the undertaking of obligations, the laying of obligations upon others, and so on as the case may be. But it does not seem to me to prove that the character of these things must be *identical* with the character of the bᵉrît itself, so that the bᵉrît is *no more than these things* and *these things exhaust the semantic content* of the bᵉrît.[40]

The covenant is a central metaphor for the relationship between God and his people.[41] Therefore, contra Kutsch, I shall translate ברית as "covenant," which

---

[37] Cf. Louw, *Semantics of New Testament Greek*, 47–66.

[38] "Verbal system," according to Louw, does not only point to individual words but can also mean a speech or a discourse.

[39] Louw, *Semantics of New Testament Greek*, 52, draws attention to the fact that "… features associated with words which are used in conjunction with other words are (often) transferred from one to the other."

[40] Barr, "Semantic Notes," 37 (italics mine).

[41] Cf. Mendenhall and Herion, "Covenant," in *ABD* (New York/London/Toronto: Doubleday, 1992), 1201. Lohfink, "Bund," in Görg and Lang (eds.), *Neues Bibel-Lexikon* (Zürich: Benziger, 1988), 344, also defines "covenant" as the usual word for a central Old Testament and New Testament concept describing the relationship between God and his people.

we shall define as a general comprehensive term for a *fellowship enabling relationship*.[42] This relationship does not exclude differentiations appropriate to different contexts, such as "agreement, contract, mutual understanding, and promise."[43]

2.4 Translation of ברית in the Septuagint, Vulgate and in recent translations

As a rule, the Septuagint translates ברית with διαθήκη (approximately 267 times). Aquila, however, who is known for his literal translation, uses συνθήκη in at least twenty-six instances. Symmachus also quite often uses συνθήκη. Theodotion's translation, on the other hand, is closer to the Septuagint in that it uses συνθήκη in only four instances.[44]

Philo uses διαθήκη and, in three instances, also the noun συνθήκη (in the plural): (i) in the text of a Greek fragment which alludes to Genesis 26:28 (or 21:32?) and originates from the *Quaestiones in Genesin*; (ii) *Legatio ad Gajum* 37; (iii) *De Congressu Eruditionis Gratia* 78.[45]

The use of διαθήκη as a translation of ברית across the board follows the tendency of the Septuagint translators to employ only one Greek equivalent for key terms. The result of this practice is that the translation term comes to serve as a semantic loanword that, while evoking some of the connotations associated with the Hebrew original, does not convey its full semantic spectrum.[46]

---

[42] Clements, *Old Testament Theology: A Fresh Approach* (Atlanta: John Knox Press, 1978), 96, points out that the term covenant "stands as the most widely used of the concepts ... to express the *nature of the relationship* between them" (Yahweh and Israel, italics mine). Mendenhall and Herion, "Covenant," 1179, render ברית as an "oath-bound promise and relationship."

[43] See Herrmann, "Bund," 220. Lohfink, "Bund," 46, also notes that covenant is a term which *points*, depending on usage, once to this and once to that reality. To what exactly it points becomes evident *only from the context*. Lohfink, "Kinder Abrahams aus Steinen," 32, draws attention to "metonymy," which may be helpful for understanding the word ברית ("covenant") and the idiomatic expression כרת ברית (make a covenant). *Metonymy* is the description of a comprehensive (difficult) notion by one of its characteristic parts. Could it therefore be that the expression "to cut a ברית," opaque in itself, means an act of commitment (usually designed as a ritual), but at the same time is also used metonymically for the whole relationship, most often a legal relationship, to which the act of commitment obliges the parties? Depending on the context, either the developed relationship or the act itself is emphasized.

[44] See also Kutsch, "ברית," 352.

[45] Kutsch, *Neues Testament*, 83. Cf. also Hughes, "Hebrews IX 15ff. and Galatians III 15ff.: A Study in Covenant Practice and Procedure," *NovT* 21 (1979), 92–93.

[46] See Lichtenberger and Stegemann, "Zur Theologie des Bundes in Qumran und im Neuen Testament," *KuI* 6/1.91 (1991), 139–40. Silva, *Biblical Words and Their*

Louw[47] points out that διαθήκη and συνθήκη are basically synonyms.[48] Διαθήκη, like συνθήκη, can therefore mean a secular "agreement" or "contract."[49] Διαθήκη, however, may also carry the connotation of "last provision, last will" that differs from a generic agreement in that it can only be made *by one party*.[50] In the papyri, where διαθήκη means "last will, last provision" throughout, this aspect of the meaning shows up very clearly.[51] Therefore the Septuagint's preference for διαθήκη over συνθήκη is underscoring the fact that the initiative for establishing the covenant relationship comes from one person, and is not the consequence of some negotiation or compromise between two parties.[52]

Already in the Vulgate one finds a certain difference in terminology between the Old and New Testaments. The New Testament consistently uses the Latin equivalent *testamentum* for διαθήκη, while Hieronymus renders the Hebrew ברית primarily with *foedus* or with *pactum*.[53] Contemporary Bible translations generally translate διαθήκη as "covenant," with the exception of Galatians 3:15 and Hebrews 9:16–17, where it is translated "last will" or "will" (see RSV, NAB). Older Bible translations render διαθήκη as "testament"; the Hebrew word ברית in the Old Testament has, however, consistently been rendered "covenant."[54]

---

[46] *(Continued) Meanings: An Introduction to Lexical Semantics* (Grand Rapids: Zondervan, 1983), 79, 90, points out that semantic changes occur when words are used in new situations. As an example he lists διαθήκη ("covenant"), which as a translation for the Hebrew ברית does not mean "last will" anymore in the Septuagint but refers to God's covenant.

[47] In a personal conversation.

[48] This notion is confirmed by Sophocles, *Greek Lexicon of the Roman and Byzantine Periods*, I (New York: Frederick Ungar Publishing, 1887), 360.

[49] Cf. Aristophanes, *Aves*, 440: ἣν μὴ διαθῶνται διαθήκην ἐμοί. See Liddell and Scott, *A Greek-English Lexicon* (Oxford: Clarendon Press, 1968), 395.

[50] Cf. Bauer, Arndt and Gingrich, *A Greek-English Lexicon of the New Testament and Other Early Christian Literature* (Chicago: University of Chicago Press, 1957), 182; Van Aarde, "Die 'verbondstruktuur' in die Nuwe Testament – 'n terreinverkenning met die oog op die debat oor die verhouding kinderdoop-verbond," *HTS* 38.4 (1984), 48.

[51] Moulton and Milligan, *The Vocabulary of the Greek Testament Illustrated from the Papyri and Other Non-Literary Sources* (London: Hodder and Stoughton, 1930), 148.

[52] Louw and Nida, *Greek-English Lexicon of the New Testament Based on Semantic Domains* (New York: United Bible Societies, 1988), 452.

[53] Lichtenberger and Stegemann, "Zur Theologie des Bundes in Qumran," 139.

[54] Lichtenberger and Stegemann, "Zur Theologie des Bundes in Qumran," 139, draw attention to the fact that the Zürcher Bibel of 1531 and Luther's 1522 "Septembertestament" render only two instances (Luke 1:72; Acts 7:8) with "covenant." The same is true in earlier English language Bibles – the King James Version almost always uses "testament," while various later translations have "covenant."

The New Testament word διαθήκη, therefore, has two possible mean-ings:[55] "covenant" and "last will." Louw and Nida (*Greek-English Lexicon*) include διαθήκη as "covenant" in the semantic field "establish or confirm a relation"; διαθήκη as "last will" is situated in the semantic field "give." Recent translations correctly indicate that διαθήκη is normally used in the New Testa-ment for "covenant," while in Galatians 3:15 and Hebrews 9:16, 17 it means "last provision, last will."[56]

3. "Covenant" in Old Testament theology: A research overview[57]

3.1 Introduction

A coherent study of the covenant concept in the Old Testament will certainly not require extensive justification. Since it was deposed by recent criticism from its cen-tral position in biblical theology, there has been a strange insecurity about its mean-ing and the position it can be given in the context of Israelite history of religion.[58]

---

[55] Louw, *Semantics of New Testament Greek*, 40, emphasizes that a word does not have a meaning in itself outside of a context; it has only "possibilities of meaning." In a cer-tain context, the word then receives a clear meaning.

[56] Van Aarde, "Die 'verbondstruktuur,'" 49, rightly points out that an exegete cannot assume that διαθήκη will in all instances mean covenant as well as last will. Barr, *Semantics*, 218, calls this mistake an "illegitimate totality transfer." See Swetnam, "A Suggested Interpretation of Hebrews 9,15–18," *CBQ* 27 (1965), 373–90, and Hughes, "Hebrews," 27–96, for an explanation of the meaning of διαθήκη in Hebrews 9:15.

[57] Our consideration here is the various ways that "covenant" has been evaluated and interpreted. See Nicholson, *God and His People: Covenant and Theology in the Old Testament* (Oxford: Clarendon Press, 1986), 1–117, for a detailed survey of research during the last hundred years. Under the heading "A Time of Controversy" he notes that Wellhausen and his contemporaries considered covenant to be a late notion. He notes in his second chapter that covenant was later interpreted as an insti-tution of the early period. In the third chapter Nicholson demonstrates how scholars then related covenant to ancient Near Eastern suzerainty treaties. With the discus-sion of "Covenant as a Theological Idea" Nicholson shows Kutsch and Perlitt returning to a consideration of covenant as a late notion. Preuß, *Theologie des Alten Testaments: Band 1. JHWHs erwählendes und verpflichtendes Handeln* (Stuttgart/Berlin/ Köln: W. Kohlhammer, 1991), 77–84, also presents a short but well-informed his-tory of research. The sketch in Otto, "Die Ursprünge der Bundestheologie im Alten Testament und im Alten Orient," *ZABR* 4 (1998), 2–37, is also quite informative.

[58] Kraetzschmar, *Die Bundesvorstellung im Alten Testament in ihrer geschichtlichen Entwicklung* (Marburg: N. G. Elwert'sche Verlagsbuchhandlung, 1896), 1.

These words seem to reflect the current situation quite accurately – even though they were written more than a hundred years ago. Although the criticisms of Wellhausen, Stade[59] and Kraetzschmar marginalized the concept of covenant, the concept has once more returned to the center of Old Testament theology. Walther Eichrodt insisted in his 1933 (trans. 1961) *Theology of the Old Testament*: "The concept in which Israelite thought gave definite expression to the binding of the people to God and by means of which they established firmly from the start the particularity of their knowledge of him was the covenant."[60]

In Eichrodt's opinion, the covenant – not as a dogmatic term, but as the description of a living process – comprises the center of the Old Testament. Starting with this term, he offers an extensive and nuanced presentation[61] of the theology of the Old Testament. The confidence with which scholars deemed it possible to postulate a center of the Old Testament has dwindled during the last years.[62] It remains true that caution must be exercised regarding any attempt at such a unification that is not supported by the Old Testament corpus as a whole.[63]

It is remarkable to see how the term "covenant" has functioned in some influential theologies of the Old Testament. We shall examine the theologies of Gerhard von Rad (1957), Walther Zimmerli (1972), Claus Westermann

---

[59] Wellhausen and Stade have defended the view that only under the influence of the prophets had the covenant notion developed over a period of time out of simpler, more naïve notions about the relationship with Yahweh and had originated only shortly before the exile (see Kraetzschmar, *Die Bundesvorstellung im Alten Testament,* 1). Wellhausen, *Grundrisse zum Alten Testament* (ed. Smend; München: Chr. Kaiser, 1965), 73–74, underlines that the relationship between Yahweh and his people was originally perceived to be natural – not defined in a contract and not considered to be soluble. Only later was this relationship explained as going back to a certain covenant making act. Sinai at first had nothing to do with law giving – the real significance of Sinai must be defined absolutely independently from the law-giving process (see also Wellhausen, *Prolegomena zur Geschichte Israels* [Berlin: Druck und Verlag von Georg Reimer, 1899], 349; Preuß, *Theologie des Alten Testaments,* 79; Nicholson, *God and His People,* 3–4).

[60] Eichrodt, *Theology of the Old Testament,* I (London: SCM Press, 1961), 36.

[61] Cf. Barr, *The Concept of Biblical Theology: An Old Testament Perspective* (London: SCM Press, 1999), 335: "Thus Eichrodt, far from imposing a unitary view of the covenant on all the material, expressly included a significant 'History of the Covenant Concept' (I, 45–69) over several historical stages. In this respect one of the most serious objections levelled at Old Testament theologies, namely that they produced a rigid systematic pattern, has not been generally justified."

[62] Cf. Smend, *Die Mitte des Alten Testaments* (Zürich: EVZ-Verlag, 1970), 7.

[63] Cf. Barr, *Concept of Biblical Theology,* 337–44; von Rad, *Old Testament Theology,* II (London: Oliver and Boyd, 1965), 376; Hasel, *Old Testament Theology: Basic Issues in the Current Debate* (Grand Rapids: Eerdmans, 1972), 49–63.

(1978), Ronald Clements (1978) and Walter Brueggemann in the next section (1.3.2). We will also interact with the contributions of Norbert Lohfink and Walter Groß at several points. Two themes that are important for analyzing these ideas are the plurality of theologies of covenant (1.3.3)[64] and the function of the term "covenant" in defining the relationship between Jewish and Christian religious communities (1.3.4).[65]

The relation of the Old Testament term "covenant" to ancient Near Eastern state treaties remains an important research topic (cf. 1.3.5). Researchers such as George Mendenhall and Klaus Baltzer have identified similarities between Akkadian and Hittite treaties and Old Testament literature. More recent research (cf. Steymans and Otto) has emphasized the significance of neo-Assyrian treaty forms. Rudolf Smend has pointed out the significance of the covenant formula (1.3.6) for understanding covenant terminology. Rendtorff also addressed this topic in his 1995 monograph. Finally, I would like to mention the authoritative work of Lothar Perlitt and also of Christoph Levin, who revises and develops Perlitt's thesis with reference to the notion of the "new covenant" (1.3.7).[66]

3.2 The covenant concept in Old Testament theology

3.2.1 Gerhard von Rad

Von Rad draws special attention to the fact that the theology of covenant divides canonical salvation history into several periods.[67] He begins by demonstrating that the word "covenant" is an incomplete translation of the Hebrew ברית. The term can describe an agreement (in its ritual dimensions), but also the relationship, or communal fellowship, between two parties that is inaugurated by such an agreement. A covenant is often an agreement that is forced onto the weaker part by the stronger counterpart (cf. Josh. 9:6–26; 1 Kgs. 20:34; 1 Sam. 11:1–11). Only the more powerful has autonomy with regard to the covenant in such a case.

A covenant is also a legal relationship that contains guarantees that create community. The relationship instituted by the sealing of a covenant can be

---

[64] Cf., e.g., Lohfink's article about the covenant, "Bund," in the *Neues Bibel-Lexikon*, as well as his contribution to the QD 172 volume ("Kinder Abrahams aus Steinen").

[65] Cf. Groß's 1998 monograph *Zukunft für Israel: Alttestamentliche Bundeskonzepte und die aktuelle Debatte um den Neuen Bund* (Stuttgart: Verlag Katholisches Bibelwerk, 1998).

[66] It should be pointed out that this review of the history of research does not follow chronological lines. Perlitt's work has influenced the research of many of those Old Testament scholars mentioned above. However, I attempt to underline certain emphases in the history of research in order to orient the reader.

[67] Cf. von Rad, *Old Testament Theology*, I (London: Oliver and Boyd, 1962), 127–35.

described with the word "shalom" (שָׁלוֹם) (cf. Gen. 26:30–31; 1 Kgs. 5:26; Isa. 54:10; Job 5:23).

Von Rad asserts that one must be very careful not to assume that there was something like a common, unified understanding of covenant in the biblical period. Von Rad contrasts "form" with "content" – this formal term can be filled with a different content depending on the situation.

Two strands of the ancient traditions of Israel, originally separated, preserve the recollection that Yahweh invited her into a covenant relationship – that of the covenant made with the forefathers, and that of the Sinai tradition. The Yahwist presents both as narrative "climaxes." Both traditions view the covenant as initiated by Yahweh and the human partner as the passive receptor.

The Elohist differs from the Yahwist in setting forth clear duties for God's human covenant partners (Exod. 24:3–8). Although the establishment of the covenant was not dependent on Israel's obedience, the receptors of the covenant had to affirm their responsibility in participating in it. This mutual correlation is so primary in Deuteronomistic theology that the word "covenant" almost becomes a synonym for laws and regulations. The Ten Commandments are written on the "tablets of the covenant" (cf. Deut. 9:9, 11, 15).

In considering the historical outline of pentateuchal sources, von Rad emphasizes that the two covenants of Yahweh – the Abrahamic and the Mosaic – provide the profile for the whole Yahwist work. The Abrahamic and the Mosaic covenants are correlated with each other and with the whole of salvation history, from Genesis through Joshua.

When considered from the point of view of covenant theology, the Priestly literature is structured differently. Here the two covenants are the Noahic and the Abrahamic (Gen. 9:11–17; 17:1–14). Covenant theology is not bound to the Law but encompasses Yahweh's voluntary and salvific care.[68]

In the final form of the Hexateuch, according to von Rad, the following periods are delineated:

> God created the world and man. After the destruction of the corrupt human race by the Flood, God gave to a new human race laws for its self-preservation, and, in the covenant with Noah, guaranteed to it the outward continuance of the world and its orders. He then called Abraham, and in covenant which he made with him, promised him a great posterity, a special relationship to God and the land of Canaan. The first promise was fulfilled in Egypt, when the patriarchs grew into a people; the second was fulfilled at Sinai, when with a fresh covenant (JE) Israel received the

---

[68] Cf. Rad, *Old Testament Theology*, I, 134, n. 10, believes that the original thinking on the covenant surfaces exactly in the expressions of the Priestly work: God will "establish a covenant" (הֵקִים), he grants the covenant (נָתַן), Gen. 6:18; 9:9, 11f., 17; 17:2, 7, 19, 21, God speaks of "his" covenant.

regulations for her community life and her intercourse with God; and the third was fulfilled when under Joshua Israel took possession of the land of Canaan.[69]

3.2.2 Walther Zimmerli

Zimmerli[70] believes that an analysis of Deuteronomic/Deuteronomistic covenant theology allows us to discern how the idea of covenant operated in older Old Testament writings and how it influenced post-Deuteronomistic theological concepts. Questions arise concerning whether the older tradition knows of Yahweh's covenant with the forefathers, of whom Abraham is the most visible representative.

Genesis 15 stands as an example of patriarchal tradition prior to P. Genesis 15:18[71] confirms Yahweh's covenant with Abraham, including the promise that Abraham's descendants will receive the land. An extensive ceremony, involving cutting apart sacrificial animals and passing between their body parts, reinforces this promise. The outlines of such a ceremony appear in a contract from the eighth century between the kings Bar-ga'yah of *KTK* and Mati'-ilu of Arpad (*KAI* I 222 A 40).

Zimmerli points out that the source of Genesis 15 remains unclear. It may well represent a pre-Deuteronomic tradition that differs from the developed Deuteronomistic History in the same way as it does from the early Priestly literature. It is therefore probably legitimate to assume that the concept of Yahweh's covenantal promise to the forefathers did not originate with Deuteronomy, but with an older tradition. The Deuteronomic mention of the covenant at Horeb represents further evidence of an older tradition.

Of course, the concept of "covenant" played a significant role in post-Deuteronomic literature. In the Priestly literature it structures the form of Israel's history. According to Zimmerli, the term "covenant" denotes the various relational periods of Israel and Yahweh.

Exodus 24:8 demonstrates that the blood sprinkled on the altar connects Yahweh and his people ritually. In unpacking the theological significance of the long and complicated transmission process reflected in Exodus 24,[72]

[69] Von Rad, *Old Testament Theology*, I, 135. See Barr, *Concept of Biblical Theology*, 259, for an explanation of the differing opinions of von Rad and Eichrodt on the covenant concept.

[70] Zimmerli, *Grundriß der alttestamentlichen Theologie* (Stuttgart: Verlag W. Kohlhammer, 1972), 39–48. Cf. Barr, *The Concept of Biblical Theology*, 313–316, who points to the different role that the covenant plays in Eichrodt, von Rad and Zimmerli.

[71] Gen. 15:18: "On that day the Lord made a covenant with Abram and said, 'To your descendants I give this land, from the river of Egypt to the great river, the Euphrates …'"

[72] Perlitt, *Bundestheologie im Alten Testament* (Neukirchen-Vluyn: Neukirchener Verlag, 1969), 194 (following Wellhausen, *Grundrisse zum Alten Testament*, 74)

Zimmerli concludes that: (i) Israel, through its representatives, is mercifully considered worthy of a unique, intimate encounter with the "God of Israel." Yet it also seems apparent that: (ii) the unity of Israel with its God is contingent on the former obeying Yahweh's law.

Excursus: Some comments about Exodus 24:8
Due to the importance of Exodus 24:8 for the covenant tradition in the New Testament (cf. allusions to this text in Matt. 26:28 and Mark 14:24), some comments on this text seem necessary. There is a broad consensus that the ending of the Sinai passage, Exodus 24:1–11, contains two originally separated traditions: one in verses 1–2, 9–11 and the other in verses 3–8.

Old Testament scholars who follow Wellhausen consider the term "covenant" to be late and therefore see Exodus 24:3–8 as a late development also. However, it may be persuasively argued that this text represents an old tradition. This perspective is confirmed by the passage's reliance on blood ritual, which is very *un*Deuteronomic (cf. the Deuteronomic emphasis on the *words* of the law).[73] After the sacrifice (v. 6) Moses sprinkles the altar with one half of the blood and in this way "swears in" the divine partner who is represented by the altar. Like a notary, Moses then reads the deed of the covenant, and the human partner Israel accepts its authority. The human partner is then also "sworn in" by being sprinkled with the blood (v. 8), which means that the people will forfeit their own blood if they break the covenant. A *communio sacramentalis* (sacramental fellowship) is thus created between both covenant partners. The words "This is the blood of the covenant" make the covenant legally valid.[74]

---

[72] (*Continued*) asserts: "Not because these laws were proclaimed here by Moses, was Sinai holy ground, but because Sinai was holy ground did the laws come to this place – and were put in the form of a book into Moses' hands." However, Zimmerli rightly points out that Perlitt's thesis, that assumes that a link between the covenant and law developed only during the Deuteronomic period, overestimates the power of the restorative Deuteronomic movement to create new traditions.

[73] This is according to Nicholson, "The Covenant Ritual in Exodus XXIV 3–8," *VT* 32 (1982), 81–82, who opposes the view of Kutsch and Perlitt that Exodus 24:3–8 is the work of a Deuteronomic/Deuteronomistic editor.

[74] See Scharbert, *Exodus* (Würzburg: Echter Verlag, 1989), 100. Scharbert also points out how these words have been appropriated in the New Testament: "According to Mt. 26[28] and Mk. 14[24] ... Jesus professes [accepts as valid, supports] that covenant. In a substitutionary sacrifice, he offers his blood for Israel that had repeatedly become guilty of breaking the covenant. This way he atones for Israel's guilt and at the same time declares his blood to be the blood of the New Covenant between God and all humans (cf. also Heb. 9[20])."

Blood was considered holy in ancient times; therefore, the blood of sacrificial animals was dedicated to God. When the people were sprinkled with blood, they were dedicated as the holy people of Yahweh. Nicholson underscores the implications here: "Thus, in addition to whatever else it entailed … the making of the covenant here was also a matter of Israel becoming Yahweh's holy people."[75]

3.2.3 Claus Westermann

Westermann emphasizes[76] that any attempt to define the term "covenant" univocally in a way that is definitive for all of the Old Testament reflects a bias that is contrary to the Old Testament itself. In the Old Testament, God is described primarily by way of verbs, not nouns. Salvation history is a series of events, of "happenings" between God and humanity. When "covenant" is understood as a description of a static condition it is used in a manner out of keeping with the nature of the Old Testament. Westermann voices three reasons why such a reading of covenant is unworkable:

1. According to Exodus 19ff., the assertion that the foundational meaning of Old Testament theology is the covenant God established with Israel at Sinai is problematic. Exodus 19 – 24 and 32 – 34, the "Sinai passage," cannot be considered a self-contained and continuous textual unit. The actual report about the theophany at Sinai comprises only Exodus 19 (the Priestly parallel for it is Exodus 24:15b–18). This report does not mention the making of a covenant. Exodus 19:3b–8, where verse 5 speaks of "keep my covenant," is a later addition displaying Deuteronomic language. Exodus 24:3–8 explicitly depicts the making of a covenant, but it is independent of Exodus 19. The text of Exodus 24:3–8 continues in Exodus 34 where, again, Sinai is not mentioned. It also is a later text that has been added to the Sinai theophany.

2. According to Westermann, the extensive scholarly discussion about the meaning of ברית has reached the consensus that it did not originally describe a condition (state), but an action. In all earlier usage,[77] ברית indicates an act or ceremony through which someone makes a solemn binding affirmation. Such affirmations can approximate an oath or pledge, or, when God is the subject, a promise. The phrase "cut a covenant" means "make a binding promise or pledge." Following Perlitt,[78] Westermann maintains that ברית received its theological meaning only during the

---

[75] Nicholson, *God and His People*, 83.

[76] Westermann, *Theologie des Alten Testaments*, 34–37.

[77] See section 1.2.2.1, above.

[78] Perlitt, *Bundestheologie*, 55–128.

Deuteronomic period; it originally described the act of a binding affirmation.

During the late Deuteronomic period ברית was understood to mean the Mosaic law. The introduction "Yahweh, our God, made a covenant with us at Horeb ..." is followed not by the description of the act of making a covenant, but by the Decalogue. We must differentiate this later view from the early Deuteronomic layer where ברית is used in conjunction with a notion of promise. In Deuteronomy 7:9 we read: "Know therefore that the LORD your God is God; he is the faithful God, keeping his covenant of love."

During the later periods ברית was used to interpret the events at the beginnings of Israelite history. Westermann notes that the shift in meaning becomes clear in two chapters in Genesis that both speak of God's covenant with Abraham. In Genesis 15:7–12, ברית means a solemn promise, a pledge or oath (in the same way as in Deut. 7:9). These texts probably belong to a similar time period. In Genesis 17, however, which belongs to the Priestly work, ברית means a mutual agreement, binding for both parties. Genesis 17 and Deuteronomy 5:2 belong to the postexilic period. Both include regulations and laws: while Genesis 17 refers to the regulation about circumcision, Deuteronomy 5:2 mentions the Decalogue.

3. According to Westermann, the so-called covenant formula (cf., for example, Deut. 26:16–19) must be considered separately because it originally had nothing to do with the word ברית or with any covenant ritual or worship ceremony. It was intended to represent Israel's relationship to God in a way that left open a wide range of explanations and possibilities, rather than circumscribing the relationship to a fixed term or rite.

3.2.4 Ronald E. Clements

Ronald E. Clements' *Old Testament Theology: A Fresh Approach* was published at the same time as Westermann's *Old Testament Theology*. Clements[79] believes that the term "covenant" is used in the Old Testament primarily to describe the kind of relationship that Yahweh and Israel have. He notes that this term has gained its prominence primarily in the Deuteronomic tradition.

A covenant usually points to a contract between two or more parties that are related in some way. The idea of a covenant that was binding for both parties was also part of the Deuteronomic tradition (cf. Exod. 19:5–6;[80] 2 Kgs. 23:3; Jer. 11:1–8). On the other hand, there is also an Old Testament tradition in

---

[79] Clements, *Old Testament Theology*, 96–103.

[80] Exod. 19:5–6: "Now if you obey me fully and keep my covenant, then out of all nations you will be my treasured possession. Although the whole earth is mine, you will be for me a kingdom of priests and a holy nation."

which ברית represents a solemn pledge (cf. Gen. 15:18, God's promise to Abraham, and also 2 Sam. 23:5, the divine promise to David and his descendants). The question that arises, therefore, is this: how can we harmonize the alternate meaning of "covenant as unconditional promise" with "covenant as conditional contract"?

Clements argues that the people of Israel knew that their existence depended upon their obedience to the covenant (cf. Exod. 19:5–6; Deut. 4:13–14; 2 Kgs. 17:15). The emphasis, therefore, is on the conditional nature of the covenant. In Deuteronomic theology, the covenant regulations to which Israel had committed herself took on the form of a written "law" called Torah (cf. Deut. 4:4).[81] "Covenant" and Torah became synonymous, such that obeying the "law" (Torah) meant almost the same thing as obeying the "covenant" (cf. Jer. 11:6, 8).[82]

During the darkest times of Judah, when the temple was destroyed and the people lost their king, Jeremiah preached a message of hope as he predicted a future for his people (Jer. 32:1–15, esp. v. 15; cf. 31:2–9, 20). When the Deuteronomic school developed their theology in conscious dependence upon the significance of Jeremiah's message, more attention was paid to God's grace and love. The insecurity associated with the understanding of the covenant as a conditional contract with God was mitigated. The meaning of Jeremiah's promise of a "new covenant" should be understood in this light.[83] In chapter 31:31–34 Jeremiah reinterpreted the framework of covenant theology – the new covenant was no longer defined as a conditional contract with God.[84]

3.2.5 Walter Brueggemann: The Covenanted Self

> For all the vagaries of Old Testament scholarship, 'covenant' looms large in ancient Israel, and in the faith of the church. For all of our study, we still have to determine how covenant is to be understood as a theological commitment, and how it is to be enacted as a mode of shared life. I understand covenant in our own time and place to be a radical alternative to consumer autonomy, which is the governing ideology of our society.[85]

---

[81] Deut. 4:4: "... but all of you who held fast to the Lord your God are still alive today."

[82] Jer. 11:6, 8: "The LORD said to me, 'Proclaim all these words in the towns of Judah and in the streets of Jerusalem: "Listen to the terms of this covenant and follow them.... . But they did not listen or pay attention; instead, they followed the stubbornness of their evil hearts. So I brought on them all the curses of the covenant I had commanded them to follow but that they did not keep.""'

[83] See 1.4, below.

[84] Jer. 31:31: "'The time is coming,' declares the LORD, 'when I will make a new covenant with the house of Israel and with the house of Judah.'"

[85] Walter Brueggemann, *The Covenanted Self: Explorations in Law and Covenant* (Minneapolis: Fortress Press, 1999), 1.

In his collection of essays titled *The Covenanted Self: Explorations in Law and Covenant*, Walter Brueggemann reflects on different aspects of covenant theology. The first essay, "'Othering' with Grace and Courage,"[86] focuses on a key aspect of the covenant, namely, its relational dimension: "… the human self is not an independent, autonomous agent but is always and necessarily preceded by a Thou, one radically other than us, who evokes, summons, authorizes and 'faiths' us into existence as persons."[87] This dialogical principle diametrically opposes both the ancient Hellenistic and the modern Cartesian view of reality.

All of the leading biblical characters (Abraham, Moses and the psalmists) stand in awe before the presence of this Other:

> Where can I go from your Spirit? Where can I flee from your presence?
> If I go up to the heavens, you are there; if I make my bed in the depths, you are there.
> If I rise on the wings of the dawn, if I settle on the far side of the sea,
> even there your hand will guide me, your right hand will hold me fast.
> If I say, 'Surely the darkness will hide me and the light become night around me,'
> even the darkness will not be dark to you; the night will shine like the day, for darkness is as light to you. (Ps. 139:7–12)

In her covenant relationship with Yahweh, Israel was aware of God's *transcendence* and of his *intimacy*. Israel could always rely on the covenantal faithfulness of Yahweh "who engages in *mutuality* with God's people, but who is never *commensurate* with that people … this God is an endlessly live, demanding, giving, surprising … other in Israel's life."[88]

Covenanting is a process which involves dialectical responses in relation to God, the neighbor and self:[89]

> With God, covenanting requires complaint and hymn, *assertion of self* and *abandonment of self*.
> With neighbor, covenanting requires *joy and sorrow, truth in love, upbuilding* in the midst of freedom.

---

[86] This section gives a taste of Brueggemann's contribution to our understanding of covenant theology and refers primarily to the following essays; "'Othering' with Grace and Courage"; "The Daily Voice of Faith: The Covenanted Self"; and "'Placed' between Promise and Command." The other essays are: "Duty as Delight and Desire: Preaching Obedience that Is Not Legalism"; "Justice: The Earthly Form of God's Holiness"; "The Cunning Little Secret of Certitude: On the First Great Commandment"; "Neighborliness and the Limits of Power in God's Realm: On the Second Great Commandment"; "Truth-Telling as Subversive Obedience"; and "The truth of Abundance: Relearning *Dayenu*."

[87] Brueggemann, *Covenanted Self*, 1.

[88] Brueggemann, *Covenanted Self*, 6.

[89] Williamson, "Review of 'The Covenanted Self,'" *EQ* 3.76 (2004), 246–47.

With the self, covenanting requires the readiness to receive *scattering* and the freedom for *gathering* a self that is unlike the old one, a process we often term conversion or transformation.[90]

Brueggemann points out that a Jewish understanding of self vis-à-vis God is one of intense *interactionism*. In this relationship *obedience* is a practice of *freedom* that culminates in *communion*.[91] Through the influence of Descartes, Locke, Kant and Freud, contemporary Western culture has come to regard autonomy as good – and submission to authority as bad. The subject has become so fascinated with him- or herself that any reference points outside the self have completely vanished. The *other has disappeared*. There is "no other to whom to address complaint, or to whom to sing praise, or finally from whom to receive command. God has vanished … And when God has vanished, the neighbor quickly disappears."[92]

The covenant offers a significant corrective in this context, as it reveals the true character of human existence in the face of the Other who does, indeed, command. In our current social crisis society has lost sight of the fact that a "true self is a self under command."[93]

In the essay "'Placed' between Promise and Command,"[94] Brueggemann points to the interrelatedness of three key covenantal themes: namely, the *land*, the notion of God's *promises* to Israel and his *commands*. Israel understood the land, as its place in the world, primarily as a gift from God. Throughout its history and in the face of many circumstances, the people of Israel found comfort in the memory of a transcendent element in their origin and destiny, the words spoken to father Abraham: "'Leave your country, your people and your father's household and go to the land I will show you'" (Gen. 12:1). This promise was, however, intimately linked to maintaining a sound relationship with the Promise Maker.

The land promised to Israel was still inhabited by the "Canaanites." The covenant at Mt. Sinai made it clear that the society Israel was to establish in the promised land would be diametrically opposed to the Canaanite society. The book of Deuteronomy stands, therefore, "as the great covenantal alternative to 'Canaanite' modes of production and ownership."[95]

The covenant relationship with God had concrete social consequences – for example, for the relationship between creditors and debtors. "There should be

---

[90] Brueggemann, *Covenanted Self*, 16.
[91] Brueggemann, *Covenanted Self*, 20.
[92] Brueggemann, *Covenanted Self*, 22–23.
[93] Brueggemann, *Covenanted Self*, 23.
[94] Brueggemann, *Covenanted Self*, 99–107.
[95] Brueggemann, *Covenanted Self*, 100.

no poor among you, for in the land the LORD your God is giving you to possess as your inheritance, he will richly bless you, *if only you fully obey the LORD your God and are careful to follow all these commands I am giving you today*" (Deut. 15:4–5). Creditors are admonished not to be "hardhearted or tightfisted" toward their poor brothers, but to be "openhanded" and to lend them freely whatever they need (Deut. 15:7–8).

In its social institutions and practices Israel should also reflect the covenant relationship with her God. The king should not multiply for himself inordinate wealth, armaments or wives (political alliances arranged through marriage), but he should "write for himself on a scroll a copy of this law, taken from that of the priests, who are Levites. It is to be with him, and he is to read it all the days of his life so that he may learn to revere the LORD his God and follow carefully all the words of this law" (Deut. 17:18–19).

Israel drew comfort from the promise "that you may live and prosper and prolong your days in the land that you will possess" (Deut. 5:33). The people knew, however, that this assurance was set within the context of command and was, therefore, conditional. In the book of Deuteronomy Israel resolves to keep the conditions and accept the land on the terms of the covenant (cf. Exod. 24:3, 7; Josh. 24:21, 24–25).

The story of ancient Israel as recorded in the Hebrew Bible reveals that this community chose death. They found the covenantal conditions too demanding and too inconvenient. Joshua, Judges and 1 and 2 Samuel, as well as 1 and 2 Kings (the classic account of Israel's life under the monarch), all relate how disregard for the Lord's commands led to exile and displacement (cf. 1 Kings 9:4–7).[96]

Courageous prophets and daring poets of Israel pointed, however, to an alternative way, voiced most eloquently in Ezekiel 37:1–14. In the midst of the greatest despair Ezekiel points to a new possibility for life in the land by using the metaphor of resurrection:

'Then you, my people, will know that I am the LORD, when I open your graves and bring you up from them. I will put my Spirit in you and you will live, and I will settle

---

[96] 1 Kings 9:4–7: "'As for you, if you walk before me in integrity of heart and upright-ness, as David your father did, and do all I command and observe my decrees and laws, I will establish your royal throne over Israel forever, as I promised David your father when I said, 'You shall never fail to have a man on the throne of Israel.' But if you or your sons turn away from me and do not observe the commands and decrees I have given you and go off to serve other gods and worship them, then I will cut off Israel from the land I have given them and will reject this temple I have consecrated for my Name. Israel will then become a byword and an object of ridicule among all peoples.'"

you in your own land. Then you will know that I the Lord have spoken, and I have done it, declares the LORD.' (Ezek. 37:13–14)

The Lord will give his people a second chance. The viability of this second chance is guaranteed by the prophecy that the Lord will put his spirit within them (v. 14). "It is the spirit-wind-power of God that blows in and through old deathly choices, that permits Israel yet again to redecide for its life in its place."[97]

Brueggemann concludes this essay by pointing out that, between the free gift and promise and the condition of command, Israel knows that its place is at the same time its very own and not its own. "To be well placed means to listen and to care. Not listening and not caring constitute a terrible alternative for Israel, or for anyone else."[98]

3.3 The plurality of covenant theologies: Norbert Lohfink

Lohfink characterizes the covenant as one of the central Old Testament and New Testament concepts describing the relationship between God and his people. This concept is analogous to privileged legal relationships[99] between persons. The relationship between God and his people is *not* to be understood according to *natural categories*, but with a *personal and historical* perspective.[100]

The Old Testament contains a plurality of covenant theologies. Although covenant is doubtless the most important category that expresses the continuity and identity of Israel as God's people, the Old Testament does not always describe covenant in the same way. The various theological concepts of covenant have followed on from one another and have influenced each other. Interpretatively speaking, the various concepts of covenant also need to be differentiated from one another.[101] Lohfink offers several points of delineation to guide us in this task:

(1) *Pre-monarchy:* Although "covenant theology" is a systematization of all the traditions of Israel, it is primarily a phenomenon of the Deuteronomic/Deuteronomistic period. It appears as though the theologians of Josiah's times took a pre-existing concept – that Israel's relationship to God was a privileged, legal one – and accentuated it. Scholars often attempt to date all instances of this theological perspective to a late period. However, Lohfink feels that the

---

[97] Brueggemann, *Covenanted Self,* 107.
[98] Brueggemann, *Covenanted Self,* 107.
[99] "Privilegrechtliche Beziehungen."
[100] Lohfink, "Bund," 344.
[101] Lohfink, "Kinder Abrahams aus Steinen," 35.

elimination of all pre-Deuteronomic privileged legal concepts of covenant is implausible. The notion of Israel being the "people of God" goes back to the early period and is visible in the ninth-century Jerusalem coronation ritual (2 Kgs. 11:17). During the premonarchic period, this self-understanding was appropriate to a tribal society that had freed itself from legal dependence on Egyptian and Canaanite dominance and that did not desire any central institutional leadership from its own people (cf. Judg. 8:23). God alone could fulfill the role of their sovereign and national king. When the monarchy began, it was the king who, representing the whole people, enjoyed this privileged legal relationship with Yahweh.

(2) Lohfink believes that this development led to the notion of the Davidic covenant (2 Sam. 7; 23:5; Ps. 89:32; Isa. 55:3; Jer. 33:17, 21). The idea of Yahweh's covenant with Abraham (or, with all patriarchs, cf. Gen. 15:18) was developed in the context of the Davidic covenant during the early Deuteronomic revision of the Tetrateuch, at the latest. The focus of this promise is dynasty – for Abraham it had been the land.

(3) In creating their covenant language, the Deuteronomic/Deuteronomistic theologians used the covenant concept of earlier times and followed the linguistic and formal aspects of Assyrian covenant language – echoing its loyalty oaths and contracts, but eschewing its hierarchical structure. They envisioned the covenant as being established at Horeb, on the basis of the Decalogue, and renewed in Moab after the proclamation of the Deuteronomic Torah. The key passage for understanding the Deuteronomic law as covenant, Deuteronomy 26:16–19, follows the covenant contract form between equals. Later Deuteronomic texts contain formal parallels to Hittite treaties with dependent vassals. During the exile, Deuteronomic covenant theology explained the collapse of Israel as a consequence of their breaking the covenant. This raised significant theological difficulties, however, as no further hope could be invested in a covenant whose curses had now come upon the people.

(4) The solution for this problem came in the form of the "Deuteronomistic" book of Jeremiah (and one layer of Ezekiel, later in date and dependent on Jeremiah) which spoke of future forgiveness, of Israel's regathering and of a "new" and "eternal" covenant in which God, through the gift of the "Spirit," would recreate the human heart in such a way that no one would break the covenant again.

(5) The foundational layer of the Priestly work changes the covenant notion in such a way that it becomes an *eternal* covenant, indestructible from God's side. The Priestly writings transfer the covenant with Israel back into the Abrahamic covenant (Gen. 17). Even before that, one finds the covenant with Noah as a covenant with all of humanity and the animal kingdom (Gen. 9:8–17). Never again will there be a flood! The Sabbath,

as a sign of the covenant, is also included in the Priestly work at a later date, as is circumcision (Exod. 31:12–17).

(6) Deutero-Isaiah, for whom the covenant is no longer a key notion, predicts a new and different act of God. The Davidic covenant will be transformed *into* God's covenant along with all of his people, who – collectively – assume the role of David toward other nations (Isa. 55:3,[102] possibly also, according to Lohfink, a key to 42:6; 49:8; cf. 61:8).

(7) *All* of these new beginnings are reflected in later layers of Deuteronomy. Deuteronomy 30:1–10 picks up the "circumcision of hearts," the core theme of the "new covenant" (v. 6).[103]

In inquiring about the possibility of a "canonical" theology of covenant, Lohfink points out that the final text of the Pentateuch permits the assumption that all of the various notions are interrelated. But, conscious of the tradition of how different textual units came into being, these transmitted units are left as they are. The real unity of these concepts is to be found apart from any attempt at formal conceptual or systematic unification. We must grasp that the Pentateuch (with its various conceptual systems) was composed for a certain and unique context, or "situation of hearing" (*Hörsituation*). It ends with the death of Moses, before the occupation of the land. The postexilic Jewish community also lived outside of the promised land, or fragmentarily in Jerusalem under occupation – a far cry from an eschatological scenario.

The various covenant theologies of the Pentateuch address this context (*Hörsituation*). The Deuteronomic covenant theology convicts of guilt and offers a Torah that will be valid even during end times. The prophetic covenant theology, reaching toward the universal (which is also present in the Pentateuch), contains the hope. The Priestly covenant theology mentions the last foundation for hope: God's eternal faithfulness which will not be annulled by any human unfaithfulness.[104]

3.4 Walter Groß's concept of the new covenant and the relationship between the Jewish and Christian religious communities

In his 1998 monograph *Zukunft für Israel: Alttestamentliche Bundeskonzepte und die aktuelle Debatte um den neuen Bund* ("A Future for Israel: Old Testament

---

[102] Isa. 55:3: "Give ear and come to me; hear me, that your soul may live. I will make an everlasting covenant with you, my faithful love promised to David."

[103] Lohfink, "Bund," 345–47. Deut. 30:6: "The Lord your God will circumcise your hearts and the hearts of your descendants, so that you may love him with all your heart and with all your soul, and live."

[104] Lohfink, "Kinder Abrahams aus Steinen," 38.

Covenant Concepts and the Current Debate about the New Covenant"), Walter Groß argued that the Old Testament theological notion that Yahweh made a covenant with his people has come to ascendancy in scholarly discourse during the last decade for the following reasons:

(1) Research on the etiology of the linguistic forms of "covenant" in Israel has come to favor Neo-Assyrian, rather than Hittite, treaties as the likely source.[105]

(2) The different variants of covenant theologies, which reveal influences of both the Deuteronomistic as well as the Priestly literary tracks, give scholars insight into the methods used by the redactors of the Pentateuch.

(3) "Covenant" has increasingly been accepted as one of the core elements of canonical exegesis.

(4) Most importantly, many have realized that "covenant" is a vital and appropriate biblical motif which may be used to help Jews and Christians develop mutually inclusive models of theology and community.

In the first part of his study Groß analyzes exilic and postexilic texts, because the interpretation of Judah's catastrophic exile was at the heart of the covenant framework. Characteristically, such texts also discuss the possibility of a new relationship between Yahweh and the people.

The second part of Groß's monograph analyzes the two perspectives emerging in the current debate about the "new covenant": (1) the perspective stressing the influence of Jeremiah 31:31–34 in ancient Hebrew thinking; and (2) the perspective of the one-covenant-theory.

In Groß's view, the Old Testament authors interpreted the postexilic relationship between Israel and Yahweh and the meaning of the exile using different concepts of "covenant." The term ברית ("covenant") proved to be so polyvalent that its implications could be adapted to the needs of the changing political situations of the authors – as well as their differing theological backgrounds. According to Groß, the richness of "covenant" lies in its "nonreducible variety."[106]

In the Old Testament, and to a somewhat more limited degree in the New Testament, "covenant" has provided a foundation for the self-understanding of the people of God. Because Christians and Jewish people view the outcome of Israel's Bible differently, it is understandable that synagogues and churches have developed different perceptions of themselves from a covenant theology

---

[105] Cf., e.g., Steymans, *Deuteronomium 28 und die adê zur Thronfolgerung Asarhaddons: Segen und Fluch im Alten Orient und in Israel* (Göttingen: Vandenhoeck & Ruprecht, 1995).

[106] Groß, *Zukunft für Israel*, 183.

point of view. Groß believes that neither the one-covenant-theory (i.e., there is only one covenant encompassing both Jews and Christians) nor the two-covenant-theory (which distinguishes between the covenant made with the Jews and the "new covenant") can successfully bridge the theological distance between synagogue and church. The *two-covenant-theory* clearly suggests a biblical dichotomy, while the *one-covenant-theory* does justice neither to Old Testament *texts* and to *Jewish self-understanding,* nor to the *New Testament characterization* of the new covenant.

Although synagogue and church can both express a theological self-understanding based on "covenant" (though with considerably different results), neither the structure of the biblical covenant concept, nor the contexts in which it is used, allow us to use this motif to clarify the problem of the postbiblical relationship between church and synagogue. "If this problem can be solved at all, one will need different conceptual frameworks and interdisciplinary cooperation."[107]

3.5 Covenant and ancient Near Eastern treaties

3.5.1 Akkadian and Hittite treaties (Mendenhall and Baltzer)
Multiple types of treaties were used in ancient history. Mendenhall, for example, points out[108] that covenantal relationships were of great importance in delineating the structures of social relationships. However, the debate regarding the extent of the influence that covenants and state treaties had in creating such structures is ongoing.

Data from the ancient Near East on the subject, including textual material, is extensive. The vulture stele of Eannatum from Lagash contains the text of one of the oldest treaties. Comparatively speaking, the state treaties of the Hittite kingdom display a more developed contractual form than the vulture stele.

There are, in total, 15 preserved treaties (9 Akkadian, 6 Hittite). These are treaties that the "great kings" – beginning with Suppiluliumas (c. 1375–35 B.C.) through Tudhaliyas IV (1250–20 B.C.) – made with their vassals in Syria and Asia Minor. We will also consider some international treaties, extant in the archives of Ras Shamra (Ugaritic), in the following overview.[109]

---

[107] Groß, *Zukunft für Israel*, 188.
[108] Mendenhall, "Covenant," in *IDB* (Nashville/New York: Abingdon Press, 1962), 714.
[109] See Baltzer, *Das Bundesformular* (Neukirchen: Neukirchener Verlag, 1960), 19. Compare also Noth, "Das alttestamentliche Bundschließen im Lichte eines Mari-Textes," in Noth (ed.), *Gesammelte Studien zum Alten Testament* (München: Chr. Kaiser, 1966), 142–54. For additional texts see Nicholson, *God and His People*,

In general, these treaties follow a certain pattern:

(i) the preamble, including the name and title of the suzerain.
(ii) the history of what led up to a treaty, narrated in a historical introduction.
(iii) a definition of the new relationship created by the treaty, including a summary of stipulations.
(iv) the complete specific stipulations that comprise the actual body of the treaty.
(v) an appeal to the gods as witnesses.
(vi) curses for disobeying and blessings for keeping the stipulations.

The partners comprising a treaty are (1) the suzerain, and (2) the dependent vassal. Treaties state repeatedly that the vassals need to know the contents of the treaty. A clause requiring that the treaty text be read regularly to the vassals emphasizes the importance of this qualification.[110] Mendenhall[111] differentiates between treaties with dependent vassals and promissory covenants. An example of the latter is the covenant made by God with Abraham. Here the one receiving the covenant was not required to make any specific commitment.

Baltzer's research demonstrates[112] that Israel's covenant formula displays a close affinity to ancient Near Eastern state treaties, although the pattern of the treaty is modified in Old Testament texts. He believes that Joshua 24, which follows the pattern of ancient Near Eastern state treaties remarkably closely in its structure and details, offers evidence of when this form of treaty started to be used in Israel.

Different kinds of covenants were made in Israel from the earliest times. The analysis of Hittite state treaties sheds light on only one kind of "covenant." ברית ("covenant") is, in fact, a general term that needs an apposition to explain what kind of ברית is being discussed. The Hittite form was used in state legislation, and Yahweh's covenant with his people can be compared to this form of ברית.[113]

---

[109] (*Continued*) 56–82. Lohfink, "Rezension: Ernest W. Nicholson, *God and His People: Covenant and Theology in the Old Testament*," *BZ* 34 (1990), 297, mentions that, beside treaties published in *Orientalia* (1968) by K. Deller and S. Parpola as well as in *Biblica* by A. F. Campbell and by P. Buis in *Vetus Testamentum* (1978), there is an additional Neo-Assyrian treaty with a historical prologue (Assurbanipal – Qedar).

[110] Cf. Baltzer, *Bundesformular*, 20–28; Zimmerli, *Theologie*, 40.

[111] Mendenhall, "Covenant," 717.

[112] Cf. Baltzer, *Bundesformular*, 96–100.

[113] Treaties dealing with legislation about private issues, such as treaties about rights to pasture and water (Gen. 21:22–34; 26:26–31; 31:43–55), must be considered separately.

While the Hittite treaty and Israelite covenant allow some comparison as to *form*, however, the difference in *content* is significant. The Israelite "pre-history," or historical introduction, describes God's activity on behalf of and among his people. Here there is evidence of Yahweh's remarkable emphasis on justice and his acts of mercy and salvation. Israel professed her relationship to her God in a plain and sober form, as compared to the religious expressions of her neighbors. She confessed that Yahweh has revealed himself in history and that Yahweh is a God of justice, not a capricious God.

Because salvation history is so foundational to the Hebrew covenant, the nation runs into problems when it no longer recognizes God's activity in history. While Israel's conquest of the land is clearly a manifestation of God's saving power, by the period of the Judges Israel has all but forgotten this historical vision, and the focus of God's activity is on judgment for Israel's sin. Biblical estimations of the monarchy display both approval and disapproval. Although David is accepted by all of Israel as God's Anointed, it becomes less and less obvious that the history of this new secular state correlates with salvation history. Nehemiah 9 and Psalm 106 clearly demonstrate how that attempt to think in terms of a historical review of Israel tended to develop into a litany of the history of her sins.

The design of Israel's covenant form insured that grave consequences would follow from forgetting the historical aspects of Yahweh's covenant with his people. As a result of the loss of the relationality that had been based on such a remembering, the law was thrust into the role of autonomous monarch. In light of a covenant structure in which history and law are so closely interrelated, the diminution of the former insured the ascendancy of the latter.

This development leads us to the consideration of a difficult issue. Is it theologically problematic that the biblical covenant imported foreign elements such as curses and blessings? The Israelites seem to have quickly come to believe that such blessings and judgments followed *automatically* as rewards and punishments for the fulfillment or non-fulfillment of the covenant regulations.[114] When the Hittite state treaty form was adapted for the covenant with Yahweh, it was the "blessings and curses" element that was modified most.

Originally and generically, "blessings" and "curses" were defined in terms of the circumstances of life – such as material prosperity or loss, success or failure in an undertaking, health or illness, fertility or childlessness and so on. In Joshua 24, the present is considered the time of salvation and blessing; the curse looms in the future. This situation is reversed in Israel's time of need – the present is the hour of curse or judgment; a period of blessing awaits in the future.

From a sociological and historical point of view it may be observed that the circle of persons addressed by the covenant has changed. The main

---

[114] Such "automatism" limits God's freedom.

demarcation of groups, progressively speaking, has been: the tribal units, the people and the cultic community. If one considers the radical changes that these stages represent, one must admit that their influence upon the covenant form remains remarkably small.

In spite of the obvious similarities between Hittite treaties and Old Testament covenantal forms, some Old Testament scholars are more reluctant to associate the two closely. They voice the following criticisms:[115]

(i)   The assumption that Israel was conversant with, and dependent upon, such treaties does not seem convincing. It is not clear how these treaty forms, used primarily by kings in Asia Minor prior to 1200 B.C., could have reached early Israel – for example, those half-nomadic tribes penetrating into Canaan from the desert.

(ii) The covenant concept became a key term in the Old Testament during the Deuteronomic period. Theories that trace Old Testament covenants back to Hittite state treaties are not helpful in explaining this development during the Deuteronomic period.

(iii) Many questions remain as to how a treaty that is understandable specifically in a political context could be appropriately generalized to represent the relationship between Yahweh and Israel.

(iv) There are differences between a contractual covenant and a promissory covenant. From the perspective of the Hittite treaties, no explanation can be offered as to why the same word is used for both forms of covenant.

(v)   The formal, detailed Hittite covenant structure cannot be found in its full form in the Old Testament. Similarities reflect correlations only between individual elements of those covenants.

In spite of these critical considerations, Hittite treaty texts do help us to understand the role that covenant played in ancient society – for covenants play almost no role in contemporary societies as a structuring principle. Although it is rare, there is evidence in the ancient world that treaty or covenant concepts were applied to relationships with deities.

Three texts seem especially important in this regard:

(i)   the reform decree of Urukagina of Lagash (twenty-fourth century B.C.), who justified his reform specifically through a treaty with the god Ningirsu;

---

[115] Cf. Clements, *Old Testament Theology*, 99–100; Zimmerli, *Theologie*, 40; also McCarthy, *Old Testament Covenant: A Survey of Current Opinions* (Oxford: Basil Blackwell, 1972), 15ff.

(ii)　the Neo-Assyrian text K 2401 in the British Museum, that reports an *adê* oath ceremony conducted with the population of Assyria by the goddess Ishtar on behalf of Esarhaddon;[116]

(iii)　a Phoenician text of the seventh century mentions the population of Arslan Tash petitioning the god Asshur, all the sons of El and the leader of the "assembly of the holy gods" to join them in an "eternal covenant" that would insure their protection against ominous demonic deities.[117]

In "covenant theology" we find an analogous transfer of interpersonal experiences from personal and legal areas onto the relationship of Israel to her God.[118] One can therefore agree with Baltzer, who notes:

> The notion of a covenant, as it is expressed in a simple literary form, has helped to apprehend in human form the relation of God to humans. The prophets' criticism demonstrates the danger of abuse even of such a form. When searching for the significance of the whole framework described by the term 'covenant' these prophetic voices must also be heard.[119]

3.5.2 Neo-Assyrian treaties (Steymans and Otto)

Walter Groß has pointed out[120] that the scholarly consensus regarding the *time* when God made a covenant with his people and the *place* where the linguistic forms for "covenant" originated has shifted from the Hittites to the Neo-Assyrians. Scholars since the 1960s have noticed the similarities between Esarhaddon's oath ceremony to secure a line of succession (VTE) and Deuteronomy (especially the curses in Deut. 28).[121]

In his monograph *Deuteronomium 28 und die adê zur Thronfolgerung Asarhaddons: Segen und Fluch im Alten Orient und in Israel*, Steymans offers conclusive evidence that VTE § 56 served as a literary model[122] for Deuteronomy

---

[116]　Cf. Otto, "Ursprünge der Bundestheologie," 45: "It is documented that a covenant between human and Godhead appears in the Ancient Near East in two instances at the same time: in Neo-Assyrian texts, especially in Neo-Assyrian prophecy, and in the Old Testament."

[117]　Zenger, "Bundestheologie," 34–35.

[118]　Cf. Lohfink, "Bundestheologie," 360.

[119]　Baltzer, *Bundesformular*, 100. Cf. Isa. 28:15; Amos 5:14; Hos. 8:1; Mic. 3:11.

[120]　Cf. 1.3.4.

[121]　See Otto, "Rezension: H.U. Steymans, *Deuteronomium 28 und die adê zur Thronfolgerung Asarhaddons*," *ZABR* 2 (1996), 214; Steymans, "Eine assyrische Vorlage für Deuteronomium 28,20–44," in Braulik (ed.), *Bundesdokument und Gesetz: Studien zum Deuteronomium* (Barcelona/Rome/New York: Herder, 1995), 119.

[122]　"*Vorlage.*"

28:20–44, to which additional curses were introduced from VTE §§ 38A–42; 63; 64 (65). He also persuasively argues that the literary unit of 28:20–44 comprises the heart of Deuteronomy 28, the chapter on blessings and curses.[123]

This text of the Pentateuch can be dated within a clearly delineated time period if VTE is accepted as a model for Deuteronomy 28:20–44. One can, according to Steymans, suggest a *terminus a quo* (a starting point) of 672 B.C., when the oath ceremonies for the throne successions were conducted. A *terminus ad quem* (a point in time when a process must have been finished) can also be secured. In 597 B.C., the Babylonian king Nebuchadnezzar II made a treaty with Zedekiah, a king appointed by him in Jerusalem. He put him under an *adê* oath (Ezek. 17:13). Ezekiel 17:19 concurs that Zedekiah's breaking of this oath was considered to be a sin against Yahweh. Steymans points out that any biblical author writing after 597 B.C. who wanted to speak of Yahweh's curses would find a natural starting point in this Babylonian oath ceremony. Accordingly, Deuteronomy 28:20–44 may have originated between 672 and 597 B.C. – the time period during which the Jewish kings Manasseh, Amon, Josiah, Jehoahaz and Jehoiakim, respectively, ruled.[124]

The Deuteronomic/Deuteronomistic authors were familiar with the conceptual world of ancient Near Eastern treaties, especially with the oath taking before the gods (*adê*). The ceremony was a special matter between those swearing the oath and the deity so, in an important parallel with Old Testament covenant language, *adê* acts as a key political term that is also used for the relationship between divinity and humanity. In the context of liberation from Assyria, the Neo-Assyrian oath commitment is applied in a specific way: the covenantal relationship granted by Yahweh is contrasted with loyalty to the Assyrian suzerains and the religious consequences of the Assyrian occupation. Obviously, the Hebrew covenant with Yahweh does not establish a vassal-like dependency that puts the political hegemony and economic interests of the suzerain first. Instead, it emphasizes the idea that Yahweh faithfully commits himself to his people.[125]

At this point we must mention Eckart Otto's paper *Die Ursprünge der Bundestheologie im Alten Testament und im Alten Orient* ("The Origins of Covenant Theology in the Old Testament and Ancient Near East").[126] He explores the deep-seated controversy in the history of research between J. Wellhausen and E. Meyer. The point of disputation is whether developmental tendencies in the religious history of Israel can be explained simply "endogenously" (from

---

[123] Otto, "Rezension: Steymans," 219.

[124] Steymans, "Assyrische Vorlage," 140–41.

[125] See Gertz, "Bund, II: Altes Testament," 1864.

[126] Cf. also Otto, "Treueid und Gesetz: Die Ursprünge des Deuteronomiums im Horizont neuassyrischen Vertragsrechts," *ZABR* 2 (1996), 1–52.

within the history of Israel) or whether the "exogenous" religious history of
neighboring cultures must be taken into account. If contemporary scholars are
ready to let go of Wellhausen's paradigm, one of the first steps will be to abandon the assumption of late dates for Old Testament books and the attempt to
reconstruct Israelite-Jewish religious history endogenously. Otto emphasizes
that Old Testament covenant theology developed with the help of Neo-
Assyrian concepts. Nevertheless, it displays a distinctive character of its own –
Yahweh is not a national god, but an autonomous God who elected his
people as a free God and was elected by his free people.[127] The theological motif
of a covenant between a Godhead and a circle of worshipers is not specific to
Judah.

The specifically Judaic feature of the Yahweh religion of this time is not
covenant theology as such, but Israel's revolt against Assyrian political power
and ideology by way of covenant theology. What is new is that the covenant
motif is used to undercut the Neo-Assyrian monarchic ideology. Yahweh, the
God of Israel, commits himself to help his people, who are under threat from
their enemy, and establishes a covenant with them. Because of this covenant,
their ritual responsibilities are henceforth to him, and not to the Assyrian
king.[128]

3.6 The covenant formula

3.6.1 Rudolf Smend

Smend poses the initial question: What is the content of the Old Testament? In
response, he refers to Julius Wellhausen's definition: "Yahweh is the God of
Israel, Israel is Yahweh's people." Although this twofold statement does not
appear verbatim in the Old Testament, it does appear in essence in several
forms. One can differentiate three progressive stages in its expression.

The first stage is the most general, but also the most important. It appears
from the outset that Yahweh simply *is* the God of Israel, and Israel *is* the people
of Yahweh – there is no need for an explanatory formula. At the second stage,
the Old Testament not only indirectly describes the fact that Yahweh and Israel
are associated with each other, but it also directly calls Yahweh the God of
Israel and Israel the people of Yahweh. The characterization "God of Israel" is
attached as an apposition to the proper name of Yahweh, resulting in the
common formula "Yahweh the God of Israel." At this stage the formula was
still so far from being stereotypical that in common religious usage it was
expressed, for example, as "Yahweh our God" and "Israel the people of
Yahweh" or, from Yahweh's perspective, "I am Yahweh your God."

---

[127] Otto, "Ursprünge der Bundestheologie," 1–2.
[128] Otto, "Ursprünge der Bundestheologie," 61.

Smend's study, however, focuses primarily on the third stage, where the relationship of Yahweh and Israel takes center stage. Yahweh as the God of Israel and Israel as the people of Yahweh are no longer mere appositions to the proper names of Yahweh and Israel; they represent predicative statements about the very natures of both entities. The fact that Yahweh is identical with the God of Israel and that Israel is identical with the people of Yahweh now defines the identities of both Israel and Yahweh. This stage evinces much deeper reflection on theological identity than the two previous stages.

The group of texts that represent the third stage have their literary origin in the period of Babylonian exile. Smend points out[129] that, with some small variations, this group of texts clearly expresses the formula "I will be your God and you will be my people." They tend to appear in the following two kinds of contexts:

(i)   As a promise for the future during the time of the prophets (cf. Jer. 24:7;[130] 30:22; 31:1, 33; 32:28; Ezek. 11:20; 14:11; 36:28; 37:23, 27; Zech. 8:8; and in part ["I will be your God"] in Ezek. 34:24).

(ii) The formula is also spoken at the beginning of Israel's relationship with Yahweh during the Exodus and later at Sinai. Evidences appear in Jeremiah 7:23; 11:4; Deuteronomy 29:12;[131] Leviticus 26:12; in the Priestly work (Exod. 6:7); and, in one instance, in a prayer of David (2 Sam. 7:24). Often the component parts appear separately, though with quite regular distribution. The Priestly material primarily stresses that Yahweh will be Israel's God (Gen. 17:7, 8; Exod. 29:45; Lev. 11:45; 22:33; 25:38; 26:45; Num. 15:41). The predominantly Deuteronomic emphasis is that Israel will be Yahweh's people (Deut. 4:20; 7:6; 14:2; 27:9; 28:9 [cf. also 26:19; Jer. 13:11; 1 Sam. 12:22; 2 Kgs. 11:17, etc.]). Among other places, the full formula appears in Deuteronomy 26:17, 18, where a mutual commitment between Yahweh and Israel appears.

The "covenant formula" "I am your God – you are my people" succinctly describes the mutuality of the relationship between two covenant partners. The context in which the expression appears is also important. The term בְּרִית ("covenant") is used explicitly three times in the context of the formula after Israel's exodus from Egypt (Lev. 26:45; Deut. 29:11–13; Jer. 11:3–4) and three times together with the formula in promises concerning Israel's future (Jer. 31:33; Ezek. 34:24–25; 37:26–27).

---

[129]   Smend, *Bundesformel*, 5.

[130]   Jer. 24:7: "I will give them a heart to know me, that I am the LORD. They will be my people, and I will be their God, for they will return to me with all their heart."

[131]   Deut. 29:12: "You are standing here in order to enter into a covenant with the Lord your God, a covenant the LORD is making with you this day and sealing with an oath."

Smend analyzes Deuteronomy 26 in the second section of his study about covenant formulae. He points out that the literary form of the formula originated during the Deuteronomic period, possibly during the covenant-making ceremony by King Josiah in 621 B.C. The institution of the covenant (cf. 2 Kgs. 11:17) was considered to be a *re-inauguration of relationship* after a serious rift in the relationship between God and his people.

In the third part of his analysis, Smend underscores that this third stage of the formula (the actual covenant formula) would not have been possible without the first and the second stage. That is, the relationship between Yahweh and Israel, and the expressions "Yahweh the God of Israel" and "Israel the people of Yahweh," must have preceded the formal covenant. The expressions "Yahweh the God of Israel" and "Israel the people of Yahweh" can be traced far back in history (cf. the Song of Deborah in Judg. 5:3, 5). Smend underlines[132] that the *full formula* was not possible before those coming from Egypt had settled in Palestine, and also that the covenant formula already presupposes the conquest of the land. The most plausible point in time for the origin of the covenant formula, then, is when the nation already settled in Canaan amalgamates with the last group of incoming Israelite immigrants. Many assume that Joshua 24 reflects this process.

With the establishment of an Israelite state, the identification of Israel with the people of Yahweh is complete. The "God of Israel" remains Yahweh's title and it appears frequently – more often than "people of Yahweh" does for Israel. During the time of the monarchy the people of Israel know Yahweh as their God and themselves as the people of Yahweh. However, the covenant formula *itself* has not yet been finalized. The unity between Yahweh and Israel is, as yet, too natural and self-evident to require such formalization. This situation provokes the criticism of the prophets because the people too easily presume the relationship and fail to adequately recognize their responsibility in light of it.

This unexamined, and therefore precarious, solidarity became evident during times of prophetic crises. The prophet Hosea's message is illustrative here. In his preaching he refers to Yahweh as Israel's God and Israel as Yahweh's people – "second stage" phraseology.[133] However, Hosea's language also transitions to the "third stage" preparatory to the full covenant formula. The third child of the prophet is called לֹא עַמִּי, "Not-my-people" (1:9a) because, Yahweh declares, "you are not my people, and I am not your God" (v. 9b).

The prophets, and especially Hosea, show how a self-evident notion is often consciously realized and named for what it is in times of *crisis*, even if only

---

[132] Smend, *Bundesformel*, 16.
[133] See Smend, *Bundesformel*, 24, for instances in Hosea.

to describe something which one had once possessed but now lost.[134] But the last word has not yet been spoken in Hosea's second stage phraseology. In a collection of promises at the climax of the book, Yahweh says: "I will say to those called 'Not my people,' 'You are my people'; and they will say, 'You are my God'" (2:23b). Yahweh indicates that "in that day" he will transform his "No" into a "Yes!"

Did King Josiah believe that "that day" had already come? Although one cannot definitively connect Josiah's understanding with Hosea 2, the expression from Hosea 1 "you are not my people, and I am not your God" certainly looms in the background. The book of Deuteronomy, noticeably influenced by Hosea's views elsewhere, also sounds after Hosea's "No" a clear "Yes" and declares Israel to be the people of Yahweh and Yahweh fully to be the God of Israel once more.

Smend[135] points out that, from the perspective of the text, historical facts suddenly became blurred at this point. The book of the law, rather than originating in the seventh century, is now attributed to Moses himself. The passage from Deuteronomy 26:16–19 is added to the book of the law. Now it is Moses who explains to the people that Israel had declared Yahweh to be her God, and that Yahweh had accepted Israel as his people. In this way the covenant formula became the foundation of all Israelite history. What the words lost in color and historical background they more than gained in terms of dignity, authority and relevance. King Josiah did not possess binding authority for all times. Moses, however, stood above changing times and circumstances; what he had done and said would never become outdated. The words of Josiah's renewed covenant, thus linked to the Mosaic legacy, became canonical.

The essential topic of Deuteronomy is the people of God. Therefore, the part of the covenant formula naming Israel as Yahweh's people predominates. In the Priestly work, however, it is the presence of Yahweh in the midst of his community that is central. Because Yahweh lives in the midst of Israel, he is their God (Exod. 29:45; cf. Lev. 26:12a). The Priestly work transfers its half of the formula to the time of the patriarchs. This covenant – the covenant with Abraham (Gen. 17:7, 8, 19, LXX) – is different than the one from the time of Moses. It is a covenant of pure grace.

In contrast, the Deuteronomic covenant formula (Deut. 26:16–19; cf. also 2 Kgs. 23:3) is embedded with regulations concerning keeping the law. Its content and requirements have to do with fulfilling the law. It is not that the people can earn salvation through these efforts – God's merciful care and devotion remain the foundation of the covenant. However, the indicative is not possible without the imperative – without the correct corresponding behavior regarding covenant stipulations, salvation can be forfeited.

---

[134] Smend, *Bundesformel*, 25.
[135] Smend, *Bundesformel*, 26.

So when the Israelites break the covenant, Yahweh brings the curse that was announced in the law upon them. The question is this: Does this also imply that the covenant loses its validity?

The book of Jeremiah does not verbally repeat Hosea's "you are not my people, and I am not your God," but it does say something very close to it. Jeremiah 31:31–33 deserves special attention here. Failure in the present is acknowledged in light of a promise for the future. A new covenant is needed to take the place of the broken old covenant. The law will be present and maintain its validity in the new covenant, but it will not be broken anymore "for men are to have the will of God in their heart, and are only to will God's will"[136] (cf. also Jer. 24:7; 32:38–40).

The covenant formula is used in a surprisingly similar way in Ezekiel (cf. Ezek. 36:26–28). Concepts already mentioned in Jeremiah are expressed here even more clearly – namely, the divine transformation of the heart and gift of the Spirit. Although the text does not state it explicitly, the covenant is the subtext here. In Ezekiel 37:26, the word "covenant" is mentioned before the covenant formula in verse 27 (as in Jer. 32:40). According to this text, the characteristic of the covenant is primarily that Yahweh's holy place is in the midst of the Israelites. The Priestly tradition becomes vividly tangible here.

Smend concludes his analysis by stating that one cannot postulate a center for the Old Testament, as one can in the New Testament. However, the assumption that the expression "Yahweh the God of Israel, Israel the people of Yahweh" is that center is well grounded. This formula has not been interpolated into the Old Testament from the outside – its elements represent genuine Old Testament thinking, and what they characterize is central to the Old Testament. The reality expressed in the formula was never static in the Old Testament. When it fell into danger of becoming so, it was annulled (see Hosea). Finally, the expression is maintained *only as a promise, not a finished reality.*

It must also be emphasized that this promise was not given simply to a fixed entity "Israel" as it existed after its foundation as a state and as the "people of Yahweh." Instead, the promise was directed to the exiles, or the "remnant" (cf. Jer. 31:7), and finally to "the nations," which Zechariah 2:15 underscores in a last modified version of the covenant formula: "and they will be my people." For a Christian, the relationship of God with Israel finds its larger fulfillment in the offer of a universal covenant through Jesus Christ.[137] "The man Jesus has fulfilled the law, with him the promised new covenant has become reality."[138]

---

[136] Smend, *Bundesformel*, 30, quotes von Rad here, *Old Testament Theology*, II, 213.

[137] Smend, *Bundesformel*, 32, who refers here to von Rad, *Old Testament Theology*, II, 363.

[138] Smend, *Bundesformel*, 32.

3.6.2 Rolf Rendtorff

In his 1995 study Rendtorff also emphasized, although from a different perspective, that the covenant formula is an important element of theological language used in pivotal sections of the Hebrew Bible to succinctly express the relationship of God to Israel and of Israel to God. The covenant formula is also semantically related to other terms, such as "covenant" and "election," as well as to other formulae such as the "knowledge formula" and the "self-introduction formula." In many instances the covenant formula connects these elements and interprets them in a new way – and through such interconnections creates new theological correlations. An analysis of the "covenant formula," therefore, makes an essential contribution to the expansion and differentiation of the topical field of "covenant theology."[139] Therefore Rendtorff significantly advances the study of the meaning of ברית in the Old Testament methodologically as well as conceptually.[140]

At the beginning of his study, Rendtorff uses Nehemiah 9:6–8 to demonstrate how, in this "late" text of the Hebrew Bible, traditions have come together that recent Old Testament research usually considers separate. Terms such as "covenant" and "election," for example, are treated in current research as two unconnected concepts, and few studies link the themes. In Nehemiah 9 the connections are, however, quite visible.

The status of recent research regarding the so-called "covenant formula" is similar. As Smend pointed out, the "covenant formula" describes the phrase "I will be your God, and you will be my people" and its variants. Research on this theme is generally unconnected from research on "covenant" and "election." But, again, relationships are visible – as in Genesis 17:7; Deuteronomy 7:6 and 14:2.[141]

Literary criticism and "Formgeschichte" (history of forms). When dealing with literary criticism, Rendtorff[142] draws attention to the misconception in Old

---

[139] Rendtorff, *Bundesformel*, 93.

[140] A short overview of how the covenant formula is used in the Pentateuch is given here. Rendtorff has pointed out that the covenant formula is also used very methodically in some of the prophetic books. We will address this issue in section 1.4, "A New Covenant."

[141] Gen. 17:7: "I will establish my covenant as an everlasting covenant between me and you and your descendants after you for the generations to come, to be your God and the God of your descendants after you."

Deut. 7:6: "For you are a people holy to the LORD your God. The LORD your God has chosen you out of all the peoples on the face of the earth to be his people, his treasured possession."

Deut. 14:2: "For you are a people holy to the LORD your God. Out of all the peoples on the face of the earth, the LORD has chosen you to be his treasured possession."

Testament research (which has shaped research on ברית ["covenant"] quite strongly!) that the primary exegetical task lies in isolating various assumed layers of tradition and "reconstructing" them separately. Each unit is then interpreted in isolation, rather than being read and interpreted contextually. The Bible, however, developed exactly through the *combination of differing traditional elements* and should therefore be read and interpreted in the same way. The exegetical task consists precisely in understanding the text in its contextual, "canonical" final form.

Analysis from the perspective of the history of forms (*Formgeschichte*) is inclined to dissociate individual, often very small, parts of the text from their contexts.[143] Hermann Gunkel spoke of singling out and defining even the "smallest literary units."[144] Larger text units were rarely considered. Primary attention was given to clearly structured expressions, "formulas" and "forms," and to their *Sitz im Leben* (situation in life, or setting). One result of this approach was that themes such as "covenant" and "election" – as well as the "covenant formula" – were isolated in research and analyzed separately. Thus recent Old Testament scholarship gives the impression that issues such as "covenant," "election" and "covenant formula" are three completely different themes.

In following the methodology described above, scholars search for the oldest "original" form of the text. "Later" developments in the texts rarely come into focus. Nehemiah 9 is a characteristic example of such a late text that has scarcely received attention (it is missing, for example, in the index in Perlitt's research on covenant theology). However, such a text demonstrates how the themes under consideration are indeed connected and integrated in Israelite tradition. It is very possible that such integration was not a "late" process, and that connections between terms and formulations expressing the mutual relationship between God and Israel were conscious at much earlier stages. Is it not likely that such formulations were an integral part of describing this most central of biblical concerns?

The task of theologically interpreting the Old Testament should, therefore, engage texts in their given contexts, unhindered either by literary criticism or *Formgeschichte*. Although one must certainly attend to literary and *Formgeschichte* related issues in the process, an understanding of the text in its final form should always be in view.

---

[143] Cf. Rendtorff, *Bundesformel*, 15–16.

[144] Cf. the way Gunkel applies this method when interpreting Genesis (Gunkel, *Genesis* [Göttingen: Vandenhoeck & Ruprecht, 1901]. The introduction to this book has been translated into English: *The Legends of Genesis: The Biblical Saga and History* (trans. W. Carruth; New York: Schocken, 1964). See also McKnight, *What Is Form Criticism?* (GBSNT; Philadelphia: Fortress Press, 1969), 10–13.

Versions of the covenant formula. According to Rendtorff, the covenant formula appears in three basic versions (with variants):[145] (i) "I will be your God," (ii) "You will be my people" and (iii) both statements united into *one* formula (the sequence of elements can change). In order to avoid the terminology of "full formula" and various "halves," Rendtorff characterizes the three versions as formula A (= i), B (= ii) and C (= iii).

Covenant formula and covenant in the context of the Priestly Pentateuch. The covenant formulation of Genesis 17:7 is consciously set at the beginning of the Abraham story and, in this way, also at the beginning of the history of Israel. God establishes his covenant as an "everlasting covenant" in order "*to be your God* and the God of your descendants after you."[146] ברית ("covenant") is virtually defined by this formula: that Yahweh is Israel's God is the content and purpose of the covenant as such. This fundamental focus is embedded in statements about other aspects of the covenant, such as: God will increase Abraham's descendants and make him a numerous people (vv. 2, 4, 6), and God will give Abraham's descendants the whole land of Canaan (v. 8). Abraham's obligation to circumcise all male descendants and household members (vv. 9–14) corresponds with God's commands to that effect. But, even so, circumcision is not a condition of the covenant, but a "sign of the covenant" (ברית אות, v. 11), which is called an "everlasting covenant" (ברית עולם) in that context (v. 13).

Statements of a diachronically earlier textual layer have been integrated into this material. For example, Genesis 15:18–21 lists only the promise of land as the covenant focus. But this statement needs to be seen in the larger context of other texts that present the exodus and the conquest of Canaan as fulfillments of the promise to the patriarchs (for example, Exod. 32:11–13; 33:1).

When Israel arrives at Sinai, a new stage in covenant history begins. The relationship of Israel with God, defined in the terminology of the covenant formula (Exod. 19:5), is now extended through Abraham to all of Israel. The "keeping of the covenant" does not hinge on one issue, such as circumcision in Abraham's case, but on "listening to my voice." The laws and regulations that God is about to announce constitute the voice to which Israel must listen; as a result of their listening God will intensify his dedication to Israel and "dwell among the Israelites" (Exod. 29:45–46).

Israel's idolatry with the "golden calf" (cf. Exod. 31:18 – 33:6) casts the covenant into doubt. Because Israel has acted this way they no longer enjoy a condition of "innocence" regarding the originally established covenant. Clearly, however, they do live under the auspice of a covenant renewed by God, which is now guaranteed exclusively by God's grace (Exod. 34:9–10). Not

---

[145] Rendtorff, *Bundesformel*, 19.
[146] Cf. Rendtorff, *Bundesformel*, 46, 59–64.

inconsequentially, Israel's "holiness," as initiated by God, now becomes a goal of the exodus (cf. Lev. 11:44–45; 22:31–33).

The tensions that arise after Israel's sin with the "golden calf" remain an issue. At the end of the law-giving process on Sinai a scenario is developed (Lev. 26) concerning Israel's future. Verses 3–13 describe the positive outcomes of a life lived in obedience to the covenant. Then, beginning with the words "But if you will not listen to me," a negative scenario describing what will happen to Israel if they disobey follows (vv. 14–39). This material in turn is followed with the injunction to change and the assurance that God remembers his covenant (v. 40) and will never break it (v. 44). He also remembers his covenant with the previous generation that he has brought out of Egypt in order "to be their God" (v. 45).

The circle that started in Genesis 17 closes here: the decisive content of the covenant is that Yahweh is and will remain Israel's God. All else receives its meaning from this and results from this.

Rendtorff concludes that the Priestly texts from Genesis 17 through Leviticus 26 employ the covenant formula in a very conscious and theologically reflective way. At important turns the covenant formula is found in conjunction with the term ברית ("covenant") (cf. Gen. 17; Exod. 6; Lev. 26:12, 45). "Covenant formula" and "covenant" are indissolubly related.[147]

Covenant formula and covenant in Deuteronomy. The connection between the covenant formula and ברית ("covenant") is at first glance much less explicit in Deuteronomy. In Deuteronomy 7:6, covenant formula and covenant are found in the same theological context. In the framework of the covenant formula and the "knowledge formula" (v. 9: "Know therefore that the LORD your God is God ..."), God is described as "keeping his covenant." This "covenant" refers back through the knowledge formula to the "oath" mentioned in verse 8, which God swore to the forefathers. In order to "keep" this oath, he brought Israel out of Egypt. Through an analysis of larger contexts it can be demonstrated that Deuteronomy 4 is related to the covenant formula in verse 20 and the term ברית ("covenant") in verses 13, 23 and 31. The connection with 29:12–13 is even closer – the covenant formula is presented as the *goal* of the covenant, as introduced by למען ("in order").[148]

The covenant formula in the Pentateuch: Summary. The covenant formula encompasses all of pentateuchal salvation history, from the moment when God spoke to Abraham (Gen. 17), through Israel's sojourn in Egypt (Exod. 6), to the entrance into Canaan (Deut. 29). One notices the appearance of Rendtorff's "two-fold covenant formula" (C = iii) especially at "turning points" in this history. When God remembers his covenant with Abraham and

---

[147] Rendtorff, *Bundesformel*, 27.

[148] Rendtorff, *Bundesformel*, 46–47.

the forefathers, he intervenes and rescues his people from Egypt – although only Moses knows this initially. At the end of their long journey, members of a new generation that anticipate entering the promised land are themselves consciously incorporated into the covenant relationship in Deuteronomy 29. The twofold covenant formula appears in both God's and Moses' speech, and in both instances it is, as it were, an explication of the very meaning of covenant. Interspersed between these two instances, the twofold formula is found also at the end of the law-giving process at Sinai in Leviticus 26. Again the formula is central to the passage (v. 12) and serves as an explanation of how God's covenant with Israel is to be demonstrated and understood (v. 9).

The covenant formula is thus essential to any comprehensive theological understanding of the Pentateuch. Its characterization *as* "covenant formula" is justified because it appears at a number of key instances in immediate relation with the term covenant, as well as serving as an explication of the meaning of "covenant."[149]

Rendtorff is therefore right when he notes: "God's covenant with Israel, interpreted by the covenant formula, encompasses and shapes the first, foundational period of the history of Israel, as it is reflected in the Pentateuch."[150]

3.7 *"Covenant" and "new covenant" in the religious history of Israel*

3.7.1 Lothar Perlitt

In order to understand the topic of Lothar Perlitt's *Bundestheologie im Alten Testament* ("Covenant Theology in the Old Testament") it is helpful to reflect first on his view of the history of Old Testament research. Behind the common characterization of the religion of Israel as a "religion of covenant" one finds frameworks based on either biblical theology, such as that given by Eichrodt, or historical reconstruction, such as the amphictyony hypotheses of Albrecht Alt and Martin Noth. These approaches were foundational in the 1930s and 1940s for the development of an overall view of the history of Israel's religion. In either case, "covenant" is considered to have decisively shaped both the early and later development of Israel's self-understanding.[151]

Perlitt criticizes any approach that makes covenant an almost universal cipher for all understanding and categorizing. He believes that Israel neither exclusively nor universally confessed or reflected upon her faith by using the term "covenant." It is his goal to explain the origin of the Israelite notion of the

---

[149] Rendtorff, *Bundesformel*, 31. However, he warns against an overemphasis on these interrelations because both the covenant formula and the discussion on ברית ("covenant") have their own profile.

[150] Rendtorff, *Bundesformel*, 71.

[151] Cf. Lohfink, "Bundestheologie," 325.

covenant with God, as well as its dominance in a certain historical and theological circle.

Perlitt believes that covenant theology is not older than the Deuteronomic movement. In other words, there was no pre-Deuteronomic covenant making or covenant theology;[152] covenant theology is the central motif of the Deuteronomic movement. Covenant theology originated not during primary monarchies (for example, during the reign of Jeroboam II, in the eighth century), but in *times of crisis* (as, for example, during the reign of Manasseh, in the seventh century). There is no central text of the Deuteronomic covenant theology that is better understood in the context of the eighth rather than the seventh century.[153]

Deuteronomic covenant theology was driven not by a book of laws but by the "greatest commandment" ("I am the LORD your God, who brought you out of Egypt, out of the land of slavery. You shall have no other gods before me" [Exod. 20:2–3]). The term "covenant" therefore sustained a theological balance in which Yahweh was both nationalistically the God of Israel, but also the one from whom all promises and gifts came, the one to whom all love was to be directed. Such love needed to find expression in concrete decisions.[154]

Although Perlitt warns against "covenant theology" becoming "a Moloch that devours all nuances of the religious richness of Israel,"[155] he also points out that Israel herself scarcely developed any theological term with such breadth as this one: "With ברית [covenant] it was possible to formulate the strictest ethical obligation, to force an unconditional religious decision and to enable insight into one's own guilt; with ברית [covenant] it was possible to revive hope and to implore Yahweh's faithfulness."

3.7.2 Christoph Levin

Levin picked up Perlitt's thesis and adapted and developed it. Levin's *Die Verheißung des neuen Bundes in ihrem theologiegeschichtlichen Zusammenhang ausgelegt* ("The Promise of the New Covenant – Explained in its Theological Historical Context") is of special importance for our study.

In his opinion, covenant theology developed at the beginning of postexilic times and was an attempt at a conscious *reinstatement* of the relationship between Yahweh and his people. The impetus for covenant theology was the breaking apart of Israel's original relationship with God, namely, a "natural synthesis of religion and patriotism" (Perlitt). The prophets challenged this synthesis in their judgment speeches and insisted on God's transcendence and

---

[152]   Cf. Lohfink, "Bundestheologie," 327.
[153]   Perlitt, *Bundestheologie*, 279, 281.
[154]   Perlitt, *Bundestheologie*, 284.
[155]   Perlitt, *Bundestheologie*, 284.

freedom. After Judah's defeat in 587 B.C., the monarchy no longer stood as the guarantor of national and religious independence. The foundation for a relationship with Yahweh – if it was to continue – needed to change from a self-evident notion to a matter of conscious decision. This pressure for a decision finds its expression in the commandment: "Listen to my voice, and I will be your God and you will be my people" (Jer. 7:23).[156] As it stands in the Exodus credo, the response to this "greatest commandment" is the basis for establishing a salvific relationship between Yahweh and Israel/Judah. It is also the foundation of the Decalogue (Exod. 20:2–3a, 5a, 13–17a), which serves as a summary of prophetic criticism (cf. Jer. 7:9; Hos. 4:2) and the oldest theological law of the Old Testament – one established to translate the greatest commandment into immediate instructions for action.

Because the commandment of love serves as the root and background of the "shema" (Deut. 6:4),[157] it is possible to understand the Deuteronomic law (Deut. 12 – 26) as essentially a practical interpretation of the greatest commandment. The drama of the giving of the Decalogue and of the scene in which the Israelites commit themselves to fulfilling it (Exod. 24:3a–b) are set in the context of the Exodus events (Exod. 12 – 15) as the nucleus of the Sinai pericope (Exod. 19 – Num. 10) and of the law codex. In parallel fashion, Deuteronomy's emphasis on covenant and obligation (Deut. 26:17–18; cf. Jer. 7:23) similarly underscores that obedience to the law is the foundation of the relationship with God (cf. the addition of Deut. 28, with the blessings and curses).

Subsequent to the third "obligation scenario" (Josh. 24:14–22), the relationship between Yahweh and his people is expressed as a "covenant," a loan word from archaic political discourse. According to Levin,[158] a complex theological and literary consolidation ensued. "Covenant" became a highly nuanced way of talking about God that could be used to address the present (Jer. 11:3b–6) or to set forth an explanation of a history that ends in a catastrophe (Jer. 11:9a, 10b–11). This development molded the book of Jeremiah, the Deuteronomistic historical works and the Tetrateuch as a whole (for example, Exod. 32 – 34) into their current forms. "In a certain sense, it is the foundation of Old Testament theology altogether."[159]

The promise of a new covenant. With the promise of a "new covenant," covenant theology returns to its original purpose: the renewal of the disrupted relationship between Israel/Judah and Yahweh. In contrast to earlier descriptions

---

[156] The New American Bible has this translation; most other English language translations render "obey my voice."

[157] Deut. 6:4: "Hear, O Israel: The LORD our God, the LORD is one."

[158] Levin, *Die Verheißung des neuen Bundes in ihrem theologiegeschichtlichen Zusammenhang ausgelegt* (Göttingen: Vandenhoeck & Ruprecht, 1985), 131.

[159] Levin, *Die Verheißung des neuen Bundes*, 129–31, here 131.

of the nature of covenant as conditional (cf. Jer. 7:23), the new covenant is understood as non-conditional (Jer. 31:27–30a; 31:31–32, 33b–34). The reason for this promise of a new covenant is summarized in Jeremiah 31:34b:

> '*For* I will forgive their wickedness
> and will remember their sins no more.'

The "no more" refers to the sins of the past, but it also points toward the future. Here we find a kind of *historical* consciousness that is lacking in early exilic thinking. From this perspective the past is considered as a history of *guilt*. The collective guilt of the nation is no longer shifted to the forefathers (31:29) but accepted by the sons as their own. Acceptance of the guilt of the past is now understood to be a precondition for experiencing the liberating presence of God in the present. God promises to leave the sins of the past in the past and cease to remember them.

Levin points out that it is almost impossible for someone reading the Bible from a contemporary New Testament perspective to recognize how such radically "good news" would have been heard and welcomed by a Jew of that period.[160]

The new covenant as renewed covenant. Through his forgiveness, Yahweh works to renew the circle of affection and protection that Israel had experienced during the time of her first love – and later rejected. He wants to create a new covenant that will recapture that epoch.[161]

In this context, Levin comments on the abstract notion of "the new" (חדשה) that appears three times in Deutero-Isaiah (Isa. 42:9 [in the plural]; 43:19; 48:6 [plural]). "The former" is always used oppositionally in this regard: "See, the former things have taken place, and new things I declare; before they spring into being I announce them to you" (Isa. 42:9; cf. also 45:21; 48:3).[162] Yes, *already* now he tells of them (48:6) and now he *creates* them, too, so that the former things will not be remembered (43:18): "See, I am doing a new thing! Now it springs up; do you not perceive it? I am making a way in the desert and streams in the wasteland" (43:19). Yahweh creates new things on earth (Jer. 31:22b), he even creates a new heaven and a new earth (Isa. 43:19; cf. 65:17a; 66:22), so

---

[160] Levin, *Die Verheißung des neuen Bundes*, 134.

[161] Levin, *Die Verheißung des neuen Bundes*, 138, here quotes Smend, saying: "'New' … is a characteristic key word for the exilic and immediate post-exilic prophecy."

[162] Isa. 45:21: "Declare what is to be, present it – let them take counsel together. Who foretold this long ago, who declared it from the distant past? Was it not I, the LORD? And there is no God apart from me, a righteous God and a Savior; there is none but me."

Isa. 48:3: "I foretold the former things long ago, my mouth announced them and I made them known; then suddenly I acted, and they came to pass."

that the former things are forgotten (43:18; cf. 65:17b). Yahweh will prove his divinity (his being Israel's God) by announcing and creating these new things as he had announced and created the former things (43:12; 45:21; 46:10; 48:5). Idols are not able to do that (41:22–23; 43:9; 44:7; 48:5).

The correspondence between the former and the new does not permit an understanding that is sheerly oppositional. The Hebrew envisions newness primarily in terms of the *renewing* cycles of nature and in the area of manual production and craftsmanship. "New" means "fresh," not "used up." Such is Yahweh's mercy every morning (Lam. 3:23) and Job's glory after what he had lost is restored to him (Job 29:20). "New" means "fresh," as this year's harvest (Lev. 23:16; 26:10; Num. 28:26; Song 7:14). "New" means "recently built, finished," such as a house, a wineskin, a rope, a wagon, a coat, a bowl, a threshing floor, a gate, a song. "To make new" means to "create," "to craft," to "renew what was destroyed" or used up.

The desire for the "new," for the restoration of what existed in former times of plenty or glory is, understandably, very strong during exilic and early postexilic times. The motto of the time was: "Renew our days as of old" (Lam. 5:21).

Levin argues that covenant theology is likewise concerned about the restoration of what has been lost – most especially Israel's intimacy with Yahweh.[163] Where the covenant is mentioned, it is the *new* covenant; it is new in that it is a reconstitution of that which had lost its natural self-evidence. The goal of covenant theology remains *restitutio ad integrum*. The new covenant in Jeremiah 31:31 is, therefore, not a qualitatively *new* covenant, but essentially a *renewed* covenant.

The Torah in the hearts. In his literary analysis of Jeremiah 31 Levin demonstrates that verse 33a belongs to a second supplementary layer in which the promised covenant is defined in conceptually new ways.[164] Through careful design, the Torah-logion stands out clearly from the rest of the covenant promise.[165]

Yahweh's Torah is presented in this verse as a written entity, probably as the Jewish law at an advanced stage. The focus is on the way in which it was recorded. The heart – the seat of the intellect, the memory and the will – metaphorically becomes the writing material onto which Yahweh promises to record the renewed Torah. God's law, until now something external for humanity, shall become internalized so that there is no gap or rift between God's will and human will.

---

[163] Levin, *Die Verheißung des neuen Bundes*, 140.
[164] Levin, *Die Verheißung des neuen Bundes*, 56–59.
[165] Cf. Levin, *Die Verheißung des neuen Bundes*, 258.

This promise must be interpreted in the context of the tradition of devotion to the Torah. Psalm 37:31 speaks of the righteous, who have the Torah of God in their hearts. The righteous, who can confess "your law is within my heart" (Ps. 40:8) and who "meditates day and night" on God's law (Ps. 1:2), receives the promise that Yahweh will one day write the Torah in his/her heart.

We find here the covenant promise in its legal and eschatological form, as it is characteristic of the late Old Testament period. The focus is the desire for a new indestructible relationship to God. The new covenant is now understood totally from the perspective of the Torah. Its promise is not to *restore* the broken relationship with God but to *complete* the relationship made possible by the Torah.

No new Torah is expected. That which will be new "after these days" is the nature of the Torah revelation. *Now*, the Torah is something external for Israel. *Then*, the Torah will become an inward reality written by God upon the hearts of Israel (Jer. 31). The disjunction – between God's commandment and what the human heart wills – will be healed by God himself.

The new covenant and the New Testament. Levin remarks (p. 265) that we find at the end of the biblical history of tradition the view that the promise of the new covenant has been fulfilled in the New Testament. This Christian interpretation (which superseded the Jewish interpretation) is no less valid than the interpretation that Jeremiah 31:31–34 received already within the boundaries of the Old Testament canon itself.[166] In the Christian reinterpretation however, the motif of *discontinuity* assumes a decisive prevalence. The events of Jesus' death and resurrection and the outpouring of the Spirit, which dominate the New Testament understanding of the new covenant, are not derived from Old Testament and Jewish presuppositions – they are the culmination of God's free and freeing action in salvation history.

Faith in the Jewish God and his Messiah stands fully in continuity with Old Testament theology and Jewish tradition, but we should not blind ourselves to the inherent tensions that exist. The Christian concept of the "new covenant" allowed the New Testament church to understand the Christ event as the establishment of a new relationship between God and the nations – one that related logically to God's pre-Christian saving relationship with Israel. In Christ, the promised new relationship with God is finally free of any ethnic

---

[166] Levin, *Die Verheißung des neuen Bundes*, 265. Levin quotes von Rad here, *Old Testament Theology*, II, 384: "The early Church's reinterpretation of Old Testament material to make the latter apply to itself is, therefore, even from the standpoint of the pre-Christian history of tradition, a perfectly legitimate procedure. Later Judaism itself carried this legacy of ancient Israel to the threshold of the New Testament period, and ... made the utmost effort to interpret it correctly and make it applicable to its own day."

restrictions. The covenant relationship with God is not limited to Israel, but is open to all.[167]

The uniqueness of the term "*new* covenant" in Jeremiah 31:31, and the fact that it does not appear in the intertestamental literature, focuses any analysis of the concept: wherever one finds New Testament references to "new covenant," "better covenant," "two covenants," or "first" or "old covenant," Jeremiah's text must be considered as the background.

Levin concludes with the important observation that Christian faith originates not only in the church's experience of the fulfillment brought through Christ, but also in the hope of the *future fulfillment* justified through Christ.[168] The Old Testament promises do not only stand behind the Christ event interpretively, they also lie before it in the form of Christian (and Jewish) eschatological expectation. At the end of the New Testament we are once again confronted with the promise of a new covenant – in a form that is at once very like that of the Old Testament, yet also fully christocentric:

> Then I saw a new heaven and a new earth, for the first heaven and the first earth had passed away, and there was no longer any sea. I saw the Holy City, the new Jerusalem, coming down out of heaven from God, prepared as a bride beautifully dressed for her husband. And I heard a loud voice from the throne saying, 'Now the dwelling of God is with men, and he will live with them. They will be his people, and God himself will be with them and be their God. He will wipe every tear from their eyes. There will be no more death or mourning or crying or pain, for the old order of things has passed away.' He who was seated on the throne said, 'I am making everything new!' (Rev. 21:1–5)

In summary, then: "The church lives from this promise of the new covenant until her Lord returns."[169]

4. A new covenant

In the book of Jeremiah, the covenant formula first appears in 7:23[170] and 11:4,[171] preceded by a reference to the exodus and the exhortation "Listen to my voice!" (NAB), "Obey me!" (NIV). God had made his relationship with

---

[167] Levin, *Die Verheißung des neuen Bundes*, 266.

[168] Levin, *Die Verheißung des neuen Bundes*, 278.

[169] Levin, *Die Verheißung des neuen Bundes*, 279.

[170] Jer. 7:23: "Obey me, and I will be your God and you will be my people. Walk in all the ways I command you, that it may go well with you."

[171] Jer. 11:4b: "I said, 'Obey me and do everything I command you, and you will be my people, and I will be your God.'"

Israel, as expressed by the covenant formula, conditional on keeping his commandments. This perspective drives the prophetic criticism of Israel (cf. Jer. 7:24; 11:8). The overriding question is whether Israel's faithlessness invalidates the pledge given in the covenant formula that Yahweh will be the God of Israel and Israel will be his people.[172]

The exile was a terrible and chaotic time. In the Deuteronomistic history, the catastrophes of 721 and 587 B.C. are interpreted as well-deserved judgments for the spiritual harlotry of Israel and Judah. The issue at hand for those in exile was this: Are these judgments final or only temporary?

In the context of the parable of the two fig baskets (Jer. 24), it says of the good figs (vv. 6–7):

> 'My eyes will watch over them for their good, and I will bring them back to this land. I will build them up and not tear them down; I will plant them and not uproot them. I will give them a heart to know me, that I am the LORD. They will be my people, and I will be their God, for they will return to me with all their heart.'

This passage would seem to answer the question posed above: Israel will remain God's people and he will remain their God. A new chapter in the history of this relationship begins after the Babylonian exile. Although part of Israel is "given up" by God, a new beginning is instituted with a remnant of the nation.

It is remarkable how the announcement of this new beginning is tied to the overall structure of the book of Jeremiah. God instructs Jeremiah in his "call vision" that his task will be "to uproot and tear down, to destroy and overthrow, to build and to plant" (Jer. 1:10). In Jeremiah 24:6, however, the destructive and reconstructive dimensions of Jeremiah's ministry are contrasted with each other: to build up – *not* tear down; to plant – *not* uproot. The destructive phase of God's action will be completed when those in exile return to the land. Their very return has a constructive gnosiological element: "so that they know that I am Yahweh." But the reconstruction that God has in mind is far more radical: he intends to give to those returning from the exile not only new knowledge, but also a new heart.[173]

In her disobedience, Israel had broken the covenant regulations (Ezek. 44:7). The prophets from the period leading up to the exile had increasingly reflected the notion that Israel was constitutionally unable to walk in the holiness required by the covenant obligations (cf. Jer. 13:23; Ezek. 2:3–4, 15). The larger question of the viability of the "covenant" model, therefore, emerges in the three greatest prophets ministering at the beginning and end of the exilic period (Jer. 31:31–34; cf. also 32:38–40; Ezek. 16:60, 62; 37:26; cf. 34:25; Isa.

---

[172] Rendtorff, *Bundesformel*, 71–2.
[173] Rendtorff, *Bundesformel*, 72–3.

54:10; 55:3). In particular, Jeremiah and Ezekiel clearly understand that if the covenant is to truly be an *everlasting* covenant (ברית עולם, Ezek. 16:60; 37:26), a different approach to dealing with the resilient disobedience of God's people must be found.[174]

Is this possible? In what may be high-water marks of Old Testament prophecy, the proclamations of Jeremiah, Ezekiel and Deutero-Isaiah announce that the answer is "Yes!" Their message is that the old has passed away, and that Yahweh will now create something totally new – a new exodus, a new covenant, a new Moses.[175]

Jeremiah 31:31–34 is certainly one of the most prominent passages of the Bible in this regard.[176] The new covenant (ברית חדשה; Jer. 38:31, LXX: διαθήκη καινή) it envisions is something unique and without direct parallels in the Old Testament.[177] It is echoed in the eucharistic passages of the New Testament and in passages such as 2 Corinthians 3:6, 14 and Hebrews 8:1–13; 9:15; 10:15–18. Jeremiah 31:31–34 also enjoys a unique status *within* the Old Testament.[178] It is sometimes seen as the "center of the Old Testament," but the Old Testament should not be understood to have a "center" in a way analogous to the center of a circle. One should, rather, perceive its center in terms of a painting in which the perspective point that allows the artist to render objects three dimensionally does not belong to the surface of the painting, but stands outside it in the deep background.[179] The eschatological perspectival "center" of the Old Testament lies in a future that, according to Levin, is inaugurated with the promise of the new covenant. This promise contains the goal toward which Old Testament salvation history, including covenant theology, moves.[180]

---

[174] Zimmerli, *Ezechiel,* II (Neukirchen-Vluyn: Neukirchener Verlag, 1979), 878.

[175] Cf. von Rad, *Old Testament Theology,* I, 127.

[176] Cf. Schenker, "Der nie aufgehobene Bund: Exegetische Beobachtungen zu Jer 31,31–34," in Zenger, *Der Neue Bund im Alten,* 85.

[177] Conceptually, the notion of an eschatological new covenant is present also in Ezekiel (Ezek. 16:60, 62; 37:23, 26) and in Deutero-Isaiah (Isa. 49:8 LXX: εἰς διαθήκην ἐθνῶν [covenant for the people]; cf. also 42:6; 55:3), where the Suffering Servant becomes the covenant (mediator) for the nations (cf. Klauck, *Herrenmahl und hellenistischer Kult: Eine religionsgeschichtliche Untersuchung zum ersten Korintherbrief* [Münster: Aschendorff, 1982], 313).

[178] Levin, *Die Verheißung des neuen Bundes,* 11–13.

[179] Zimmerli, "Zum Problem der 'Mitte des Alten Testaments,'" *EvT* 35 (1975), 103.

[180] In the same study Levin sets out to demonstrate how the promise of a new covenant, as seen from its history of effect, is one of the main sources for Old Testament salvation prophecy. This is true for the book of Jeremiah, where two of four sources for prophetic expectation of salvation in this book are recognizable in Jer. 31:31–34. The history of effect of Jer. 31:31–34 includes the salvation prophecies of Ezekiel and Hosea, as well as the covenant promise of the Priestly writing. Outside of its

Linguistic relations between Jeremiah 31:31–34 and Exodus 33 – 34[181] demonstrate that the gift of this new covenant should be understood within the theological framework of the Sinai covenant theology of Exodus 19 – 34. This covenant was not outdated, it was "broken" (v. 32: הפרו [פרר]). If it is to be reinstated, God must offer it anew. In this sense it would be a "new" covenant. Jeremiah 31:31–34 presents the new ברית ("covenant") *as* "new" because it is founded on Yahweh's willingness to forgive and to *renew* (Jer. 31:34; cf. also Exod. 34:9–10).[182] God's forgiveness of Israel is therefore an essential pre-requirement for the "new covenant." But this forgiveness must be safeguarded and maintained; therefore, the stability of the new covenant also requires the grafting of the Torah directly into the human heart, the seat of rebellion and sin. The incorporation of this dimension of experience into the Old Testament salvation logion is truly "new."[183] Unprecedented tracts of depth and immediacy in the divine-human encounter are now opened for God's people.[184]

Jeremiah's prophetic statement that God himself will prepare the hearts of the Israelites to be able to know him is followed immediately by the covenant formulation (v. 33).[185] In verse 34 the knowledge of God is connected in a long sentence with the covenant formula: "they will all know me, from the least of them to the greatest."[186]

Von Rad compares Deuteronomy and Jeremiah in this regard and concludes that there is only one real difference: Deuteronomy presents the old covenant, while Jeremiah speaks of a *new* covenant. In Jeremiah all confidence is placed upon the expectation of a new salvific act by Yahweh that will transcend the Sinai covenant. The distance between these two perspectives is significant. In Deuteronomy, Israel's ability to obey was not yet considered to be a problem. Jeremiah's and Ezekiel's pronouncements, however, have as their foundational context the realization that Israel is fundamentally incapable of obedience. The "newness" of the new covenant touches the dimension of anthropology: there will be a change in the nature of the human heart.[187]

The adjective "new" in Jeremiah 31:31 suggests a negative evaluation of the salvific orders upon which Israel had relied previously. Jeremiah, Ezekiel and

---

[180] (*Continued*) immediate area of influence one finds only Isaiah's salvation prophecy; it contains, however, a number of parallels in content.

[181] Cf. Exodus 33:13, 19; 34:9, 10, 28 with Jeremiah 31:33–34.

[182] Cf. Zenger, "Bundestheologie," 29; Lohfink, *Der niemals gekündigte Bund: Exegetische Gedanken zum christlich-jüdischen Dialog* (Freiburg: Herder, 1989), 63.

[183] Westermann, *Prophetische Heilsworte im Alten Testament* (Göttingen: Vandenhoeck & Ruprecht, 1987), 113.

[184] Schenker, "Der nie aufgehobene Bund," 112.

[185] See also Jer. 32:38.

[186] Rendtorff, *Bundesformel*, 74.

[187] Von Rad, *Old Testament Theology,* II, 270–71.

Deutero-Isaiah thus institute a fundamental shift in the orientation of faith: "The saving power of the old ordinances is abolished, and Israel can only find salvation in new, future saving actions on Yahweh's part."[188]

Jeremiah 31:31–34 presents a covenantal theology of relationality and obedience to God that rests on a *graced* inner motivation.[189] Within a Deuteronomistic frame of reference in which disobedience to the law was portrayed as the primary condition of the people this answer of obedience to God, prompted by a graced inner motivation, was so radical that it is not picked up at all in the Old Testament, and is almost absent from early Jewish literature. On the other hand, however, it served as a basic category of Christian self-understanding in its transforming reception in the New Testament.[190]

Ezekiel 36 characteristically rewords Jeremiah 31:31–34's pledge that Yahweh will write his law upon the hearts of his people. Eichrodt appropriately gives his explication of Ezekiel 36:24–28 the title: "The true re-creation of Israel."[191] This re-creation of the people takes place in three phases: first (v. 25) they are cleansed from the old ("I will cleanse you from all your impurities and from all your idols," v. 25b); second, immediately following, they are given the gift of a new heart and a new spirit (v. 26). This promise of renewal is also voiced in 11:19–20:

> 'I will give them an undivided heart and put a new spirit in them; I will remove from them their heart of stone and give them a heart of flesh. Then they will follow my decrees and be careful to keep my laws. They will be my people, and I will be their God.'

As we have noted, Jeremiah's description of the covenant as "new" (31:31) is here connected to the heart. Third and finally, Yahweh's Spirit is implanted into human hearts (v. 26); because the law is now written on our hearts and the Spirit has been bestowed, Yahweh's new creation can be fully realized. The

---

[188] Von Rad, *Old Testament Theology*, II, 284. Levin, *Die Verheißung des neuen Bundes*, 140, however, points out that God's covenant, where the notion appears, already is a *new* covenant, a conscious reenactment of that which has lost its natural self-evidence.

[189] See Groß, "Neuer Bund oder erneuerter Bund: Jeremiah 31:31–34 in der jüngsten Diskussion," in Hilberath and Saltler (eds.), *Vorgeschmack. Festschrift für Theodor Schneider* (Mainz: Matthias Grünewald, 1995), 110.

[190] Groß, *Zukunft für Israel*, 134. It must be pointed out that the promise of the Torah written into the hearts, according to Jer. 31:33a, does not primarily refer to the enablement for action but represents the eschatological fellowship with God per se in the sense of closeness to the God who reveals himself in the Torah (Levin, "Rezension: Groß, Walter: Zukunft für Israel," *ZABR* 5 [1999], 326).

[191] Eichrodt, *Der Prophet Hesekiel: Kapitel 19 – 48* (Göttingen: Vandenhoeck & Ruprecht, 1984), 347.

Old Testament action of the "Spirit" is not to facilitate abstract revelation, but to empower God's people for new undertakings (1 Sam. 10:6–7). In Ezekiel 36 (cf. also 11:20, where the Spirit of God is not mentioned explicitly), these "new undertakings" include obedience toward Yahweh's laws and a new quality of covenantal relationship. Whereas Jeremiah 31:31–34 spoke of implanting the law into human hearts, Ezekiel 36:27 emphasizes implanting the Spirit. Yahweh himself will join in helping his people keep his laws. This obedience is a prerequisite for staying in the land (v. 28). Here salvation history has moved one big step closer to the realization of that which Yahweh ultimately intended for his people in his initial covenant.[192]

The great promise of Ezekiel 36:25–28 – the inner renewal of the people – is also promised in 37:23. The removal of idolatry and its accompanying spiritual pollution is a key focus of Ezekiel 37:15–28, and a prerequisite for the reunification of Israel and Judah into one people. In verse 23 the covenant formula is linked with the announcement of this cleansing and serves as a concluding confirmation of the newly restored relationship between God and Israel. It also discloses the promise of a *new David*, who shall be king of this united kingdom (vv. 24–25). After verse 25b, the key word "everlasting" (עולם) dominates the tone of the passage. The fulfillments of God's promises last forever. Specifically, the promise is four-fold: (1) The people will receive a *durable dwelling* in the land and will live there forever (עד עולם). (2) *David's rule*[193] will extend forever (עד עולם). (3) God will make a *(new) covenant* with them, a "covenant of peace," an "everlasting covenant." While these terms are not further explained, this is the climax of the passage. The expression "covenant of peace" (ברית שלום) relates to protection against wild animals in Ezekiel 34:25 (cf. also Jer. 32:37) – a safeguard that makes it possible to live peacefully in the land. The expression "everlasting covenant" (ברית עולם) also, as in Jeremiah 32:40, relates to the overall biblical covenantal schema that begins with Noah and all creation (Gen. 9:16) and extends through the covenant with Abraham (Gen. 17:7) to the eschatological expectations of the prophets. Ezekiel 37 may be connected as well with God's words to Abraham in Genesis 17, because the "everlasting covenant" of Genesis 17:6–7 (as also in Ezek. 37:26b) addresses the increase of Israel. (4) Finally, we have the theme of the *dwelling of God among Israel* (vv. 26b, 27). Yahweh's sanctuary will remain in the midst of his people "forever" (לעולם). A note about the new sanctuary alludes to this important motif, which reappears in chapters 40 – 48. An expression unique to the book of Ezekiel, משכני ("my dwelling place"), underscores the fact that Yahweh will live "with" (על) his people. Through this intimate incorporation into the very house of God, Israel truly becomes the covenant people (cf. v. 27b; also Lev. 26:11).

---

192   Zimmerli, *Ezechiel*, 879–80.

193   We observe the covenant formula a second time in the context of the announcement of a new David in Ezek. 34:23–24 (Rendtorff, *Bundesformel*, 79).

Yahweh will be recognized among the nations by the fact that he has sanctified (that is, reserved for himself) Israel.[194] The covenant formula in verse 28b ("… you will be my people, and I will be your God") succinctly concludes this passage that began with verse 24b.

5. In conclusion: The Jewish perspective

Hermann Lichtenberger and Stefan Schreiner demonstrate in their article "Der neue Bund in jüdischer Überlieferung" ("The New Covenant in Jewish Tradition")[195] that, in spite of different accents in the respective Hebrew interpretive perspectives regarding Jeremiah 31:31–34, there has been a remarkable longstanding *opinio communis* (consensus) among Jewish exegetes on the following five points:

(1) The new covenant is not a new covenant in principle. There is no new Torah, but only a *renewal* of the first covenant.

(2) The renewal of the first covenant takes place on the basis of the Sinai Torah of Moses, which will remain operative even during the time of the Messiah.

(3) The "newness" of the new covenant consists exclusively in the giving of Moses' Sinai Torah (Jer. 31:33–34) in a fundamentally new way, as compared to its first giving.

(4) Because the giving of the new covenant is different, the results will also be different (v. 34). The new covenant cannot and will not be broken because the Torah will exist in *"their innermost."* The Torah will not be forgotten, nor will its laws be disregarded ever again.

(5) The new covenant is an event of the *messianic period*, which has not yet dawned.

The Jewish witness thus defers Jeremiah 31:33's promise regarding the implantation of the Torah into the hearts of the people until a future salvific period in history in which no one will need human teachers of the Torah because the presence of God will be ubiquitous. In contrast, the New Testament and early Christian tradition dissolve the Jewish marriage between covenant and Torah in favor of grounding the new covenant in the Christ event, which is considered to be universally valid, available to Jews and Gentiles alike, and capable of bestowing full reconciliation between God and humanity.[196]

---

[194] Rendtorff, *Bundesformel*, 78–79; Zimmerli, *Ezechiel*, 912–15.

[195] *Theologische Quartalschrift* 176.4 (1996), 272–90, p. 289.

[196] Cf. Groß and Theobald, "Wenn Christen vom neuen Bund reden: Eine riskante Denkfigur auf dem Prüfstand," *TQ* 176.4 (1996), 258.

2

The (New) Covenant in Early Judaism

1. The "new covenant in the land of Damascus"

The concept of a new covenant was not only an important part of the message of the eighth-century prophets – it also played a significant role in the Essene community at Qumran.

The surprising and somewhat mysterious term "new[1] covenant in the land of Damascus"[2] appears only in the Damascus scroll (VI, 19; VIII, 21 = XIX, 33/34 and XX, 12). In the context of this term, the Essene author looks to the past and describes the progenitors of the Essene fellowship. From that perspective, the "new covenant in the land of Damascus" is seen as older than their current "covenant of God."

Its characterization as a *"new"* covenant reveals that its development had a history. This history began with the "exodus" (departure) of a group of pious and righteous people from the "land of Judah" and their theological innovations in the "land of Damascus."[3] CD VI, 19,[4] for example, suggests that the calendrical liturgical regulations, especially those pertaining to the day of fasting, were a specific feature of the "new covenant" developed in the land of Damascus.

Correct Torah observation is the main obligation for this early group, and this activity is perhaps the raison d'être for the creation of the "new covenant in

---

[1] Or "renewed," cf. Talmon, "Eschatologie und Geschichte im biblischen Judentum," in Schnackenburg (ed.), *Zukunft: Zur Eschatologie bei Juden und Christen* (Düsseldorf: Patmos, 1980), 34–35.

[2] "Land of Damascus" is a cryptic name for the location of their exile in the desert of Qumran (cf. Lundbom, "New Covenant," in *ABD*, IV [New York: Doubleday, 1992], 1090).

[3] Lichtenberger and Lange, "Qumran," in *TRE* XXVIII (Berlin: Walter de Gruyter, 1997), 70–71.

[4] CD VI, 18b–19: "… to keep the Sabbath day according to the exact interpretation, and the festivals (19) and the day of fasting, according to what they had discovered, those who entered the new covenant in the land of Damascus." (All translations of texts from the Dead Sea scrolls are taken from Garcia Martinez, *The Dead Sea Scrolls Translated: The Qumran Texts in English* [Leiden: E. J. Brill, 1994].)

the land of Damascus." According to CD VIII, 21 and XIX, 33–XX, 1, after the death of the Teacher of Righteousness and before the final judgment, it is forbidden to accept those back into the community who fall away from the "new covenant in the land of Damascus."[5]

The "new covenant in the land of Damascus" was not used as a term of self-identification by the later Qumran community, only by its precursor group. There are, however, analogies between the two groups. In the later community we find the same *binding commitment to the Torah* and its commentaries as existed in the previous community.[6] Detailed study of the Mosaic law was normative for both groups. The new covenant, like the Mosaic law, had obligations that were attended and intensified through blessings and curses (cf. 1 QS II, 1–18).

The Qumran writings never contrast the "new" and the "old" covenant, as did the New Testament writers. "New" in the phrase "new covenant in the land of Damascus" does not mean that it was understood as oppositional to the Sinai covenant, but rather that the Qumran community understands *its* specific interpretation of the law as *the genuine re-installment of the Mosaic Torah, predicted by the prophets* (cf. the "fallen Sukkat of David," CD VII, 16–17). Hence, one can speak of Qumran as a community of the "renewed covenant."[7]

It must be stressed, however, that the concept of the "new covenant" was *not* understood by the Qumran community, as it was by the Christians, in terms of the all-important foundational text of Jeremiah 31:31–34.[8] The Qumranian "new covenant" stood:

- not for all of Israel, but for the faithful remnant who separated from the Israel that had broken the covenant;
- not for a Torah written upon the heart, but for a Torah knowledge gained by eager study; and
- not for direct intimate knowledge of Yahweh, which is mediated by the Spirit, but for a commitment to an authoritative interpretation of the Torah (especially pertaining to the cultic calendar).

Another significant difference is that the new covenant in the Qumran community is not depicted as established by God himself, but as an entity instituted by persons that people may choose to join. Hence, it must be underscored that

---

[5]   Lichtenberger and Lange, "Qumran," 60.

[6]   Lichtenberger and Stegemann, "Zur Theologie des Bundes in Qumran," 135–36.

[7]   Lichtenberger and Lange, "Qumran," 71.

[8]   Cf. Murphy-O'Connor, "The New Covenant in the Letters of Paul and the Essene Documents," in Horgan and Kobelski (eds.), *To Touch the Text: Biblical and Related Studies in Honor of Joseph A. Fitzmyer, S.J.* (New York: Crossroad, 1989), 200; cf. also Collins, "The Berith-Notion of the Cairo Damascus Document and Its Comparison with the New Testament," *ETL* 39 (1963), 556–65.

the "new covenant" in the Damascus scroll integrates none of the key demarcations of Jeremiah 31, apart from the feature of "newness" and a general link
to the Torah. For the Damascus scroll, the new covenant is essentially a recon-
stituted entity from the past. It differs from the new covenant in Jeremiah
31:31–34 in that, there, the new covenant:

- is founded upon Yahweh's renewing willingness to forgive, and
- receives its stability from the engraving of the Torah upon the hearts of
  the people (cf. 1.4, above).[9]

Until the destruction of Jerusalem in A.D. 70, the question of whether – and
how – Israel could fulfill her covenantal obligations was a matter of great controversy. The divergent views of Torah within Judaism, therefore, fuelled controversy. One of the fallouts was the emergence of exclusivist groups like the
one at Qumran that claimed to be the "real" Israel. The concept of the "new
covenant in the land of Damascus," and of a "covenant of conversion" (CD
XIX, 16 – XX,1) may be seen as distinctive manifestations of this controversy.

According to this view, although the covenant is a pre-existing entity and is
not *created* by joining a community,[10] practically speaking, one had to *commit*
oneself to correct understanding and practice of the Torah to fall into the circle
of the covenant.[11] For example, 1QS I, 16–17b states: "And all those who enter
in the Rule of the Community shall establish a covenant before God ..." The
intent of such a covenant is then interpreted: "in order to carry out all that he
commands."[12] In 18b–20, the ceremony of establishing a covenant is further
explained: When they enter a covenant, the priests and the Levites shall bless
the God of salvation and all the works of his faithfulness, and all those who
enter the covenant shall repeat after them: "Amen, amen."[13]

Entering a community, joining the covenant, keeping the commandments
of the Mosaic law and avoiding bad people, are all linked in the Dead Sea texts.
Other dimensions are evident as well. The covenant is called in 1QS I, 7 a *covenant of kindness (mercy)*. The Hymns underscore especially that God is the
author of the covenant – a covenant that those in danger can look to for refuge
and deliverance.

There remains, however, a clear distinction between those who belong to
the community of God's covenant and those who have not joined the covenant. The curse of the covenant is upon the latter (1QS II, 16; V, 12). But for

---

[9] Groß, *Zukunft für Israel*, 156–57.
[10] Lichtenberger and Stegemann, "Zur Theologie des Bundes in Qumran," 136.
[11] Maier, "Bund, IV: Im Judentum," in *LTK*, II (Freiburg/Basel/Wien: Herder,
     1994), 788–89.
[12] Cf. Garcia Martinez, *Dead Sea Scrolls*, Manual of Discipline, 2.
[13] Cf. also the following verses for a further explanation of the making of the covenant.

those who "walk according to these matters in perfect holiness, in accordance with his teaching," the covenant of God is a firm guarantee "that they shall live a thousand generations" (CD VII, 5–6).[14] The demand for total obedience is put in the framework of final election, a topic of particular import in the Hymnal scroll (cf. 1 QH XV, 13b–14, 18b, 19b–20a).

2. The covenant concept in Philo

2.1 Introduction

Although it is not our intention in this study to discuss extensively the concept of covenant in Philo, it is nevertheless important to observe how this great Greek-writing Jew of the first century used this concept.[15]

Philo, like the Septuagint, translated the OT ברית as διαθήκη.[16] In Philo's writings, διαθήκη appears 22 times with the meaning "covenant":[17]

Legum allegoriae (Leg.) 3.85.8 (twice)
De sacrificiis Abelis et Caini (Sacr.) 57.6 (twice)
Quod deterius potiori insidari soleat (Det.) 67.2; 68.2
Quis rerum divinarum heres sit (Her.) 313.4
De mutatione nominum (Mut.) 51.3;[18] 52.2; 52.3; 52.4; 53.3; 58.1; 58.2; 58.3; 58.5; 263.4
De somniis (Somn.) 2.223.4; 2.224.1; 2.224.2; 2.224.5; 2.237.3

Considering the extent of Philo's writings, "covenant" does not appear to be a key term for him.[19] But although he does not use this term

---

[14] Cf. Lichtenberger and Stegemann, "Zur Theologie des Bundes in Qumran," 137–38.

[15] Cf. Kutsch, "Bund," 404. Kutsch speaks of two "great Greek-writing Jews of the 1st century A.D.," namely, Philo and Josephus.

[16] Because Josephus wrote primarily for non-Jews, for Romans and Greeks (cf. Ant. XVI, 174), διαθήκη in his writing means only "legacy, will"; it is never used in the sense of "covenant" (Kutsch, "Bund," 404; cf. also Rengstorf (ed.), *A Complete Concordance to Flavius Josephus*, I [Leiden: E. J. Brill, 1983], 451). Συνθήκη is sometimes used in the sense of "covenant."

[17] διαθήκη in *Spec.* 2.16 means "legacy, last will."

[18] διαθήκας

[19] In 195, Baron, *A Social and Religious History of the Jews*, 389, n. 50 (quoted in Jaubert, *La notion d'alliance dans le Judaïsme aux abords de l'ère chrétienne* [Paris: Éditions du Seuil, 1963], 377, n. 8) maintained: "Curiously neither the idea of the covenant concluded by God with Israel, nor that of a 'new covenant' debated in

often,[20] it will become evident that an overview of his usage of this term is very important for this study.[21]

2.2 Διαθήκη in Philo: An overview[22]

Philo begins *Leg.* 3.85 by mentioning that "some even before their birth God endows with a goodly form and equipment, and has determined that they shall have a most excellent portion" (Ἐνίους δὲ ὁ θεὸς καὶ πρὸ τῆς γενέσεως καλῶς διαπλάττει καὶ διατίθεται καὶ κλῆρον ἔχειν ἄριστον προῄρηται).[23] He then mentions what Abram was told about Isaac (who is compared with hope) and quotes God's promise that God will make an *eternal covenant* with Abram.[24]

In *Sacr.* 57, Philo quotes from Deuteronomy 9:5[25] and comments significantly: "now the covenant of God is an allegory of *his gifts of grace*" (διαθήκη δ' ἐστὶ θεοῦ συμβολικῶς αἱ χάριτες αὐτοῦ)."[26] He concludes this passage with the

---

[19] (*Continued*) contemporary Palestinian circles, seems to play any role in Philo's thinking, despite his acceptance of the doctrine of the 'merits of the fathers.' Perhaps the fact that the Septuagint had watered (down) the biblical concept of *berit* to a mere contractual relationship *[sic!]* (διαθήκη) made Philo unaware of this pillar of Old Testament theology."

[20] One should not overlook the lost writing: Περὶ διαθηκῶν (Concerning Covenants).

[21] Jaubert, *La notion d'alliance*, 440, points out the significance of this term in Philo: "Philon n'abandonne aucune des lignes de force de La notion d'alliance: ni le culte du Dieu unique et personnel, ni l'élection d'Israël, ni la pratique de la Loi. Sa notion de *diathèkè*, dans son intuition fondamentale, est celle qu'attendaient les prophètes: l'alliance intérieure inscrite dans les cœurs, fondée sur la sainteté et sur la connaissance de Dieu." ["Philo does not abandon any of the important components of the idea of covenant: not the worship of God as unique and personal, not the election of Israel, not the practice of the law. His notion of *diatheke*, in the fundamental sense, is that which the prophets awaited: the covenant inscribed in their hearts, founded on holiness and on the knowledge (in the sense of 'recognition') of God."]

[22] See Schwemer, "Zum Verhältnis von Diatheke und Nomos in den Schriften der jüdischen Diaspora Ägyptens in hellenistisch-römischer Zeit," in Avemarie and Lichtenberger, *Bund und Tora*, 92–101, for an informative explanation of the term διαθήκη in Philo.

[23] All translations of Philo from Colson and Whitaker, *Philo*. The Loeb Classical Library (Cambridge, MA: Harvard University Press; London: William Heinemann, 1981). Here: I, 357.

[24] καὶ στήσω τὴν διαθήκην μου πρὸς αὐτὸν εἰς διαθήκην αἰώνιον ("and I will establish my covenant with him for an everlasting covenant").

[25] ἵνα στήσῃ τὴν διαθήκην, ἣν ὤμοσε τοῖς πατράσιν ἡμῶν ("that he might establish the covenant which he swears to our fathers").

[26] Vogel, *Das Heil des Bundes: Bundestheologie im frühen Christentum* (Tübingen/Basel: A. Francke Verlag, 1996), 210–21, characterizes his interpretation of the covenant concept in Philo as "God gives himself."

remark that, among the existing things, only the virtues and the virtuous activities are perfect.[27] It seems that Philo argues as follows: (a) The covenant (διαθήκη) is God's gift; (b) God's gifts are perfect; (c) virtue is perfect; hence, virtue is seen within a covenant context, it is God's gift and not the work of a human being.[28]

In *Det.* 67, Philo points to the blessing that Moses promised to Levi and quotes Deuteronomy 33:9, 10: "he watched over your word and guarded your covenant … he teaches your precepts to Jacob and your law to Israel (ἐφύλαξε τὰ λόγιά σου, καὶ τὴν διαθήκην σου διετήρησεν … δηλώσουσι τὰ δικαιώματά σου Ἰακὼβ καὶ τὸν νόμον σου Ἰσραήλ)." The "good person" (ἀστεῖος)[29] is the one who keeps the words and covenants of God (*Det.* 68). In *Her.* 313, Philo states that the wise person is heir to the knowledge of all revealed truth, and in that context quotes Genesis 15:18 where God makes a covenant with Abraham and promises him the land.

Mut. is an exposition of aspects of Genesis 17:1–5, 15–22. In *Mut.* 47, Philo explains the phrase "be blameless" (καὶ γίνου ἄμεμπτος, Gen. 17:1). He points out that the promise of a covenant is given to the righteous (blameless). In *Mut.* 52, he refers to Genesis 17:2: "I will confirm my covenant between me and you" (θήσω τὴν διαθήκην μου ἀνὰ μέσον ἐμοῦ καὶ ἀνὰ μέσον σοῦ). Covenants are established for the benefit of those who are worthy. The covenant, therefore, is a *symbol of grace*, which God has put between himself and the human, between the giver and receiver:

> Now covenants are drawn up for the benefit of those who are worthy of the gift, and thus a covenant is a symbol of the grace which God has set between Himself Who proffers it and man who receives.[30]

In *Mut.* 58, Philo quotes Genesis 17:4: "And I, I see my covenant with you" (κἀγώ, ἰδοὺ ἡ διαθήκη μου μετὰ σοῦ). He concludes that there are *many covenants* that mediate grace and gifts to the worthy. This statement is important in that it shows that Philo views "covenant" as covering a plethora of gifts, and therefore as essentially an expression of grace.[31] The highest form of covenant is God himself (τὸ δ᾽ ἀνώτατον γένος διαθηκῶν αὐτὸς ἐγώ εἰμι).

Διαθήκη appears again in *Mut.* 263, where Philo quotes Genesis 17:21: "But my covenant I will establish with Isaac (τὴν δὲ διαθήκην μου στήσω πρὸς Ἰσαάκ)." Virtue (ἀρετή [*Mut.* 261, 263]) plays a significant role in this context.

---

[27] ἐν τοῖς οὖσιν ἀρετὴ καὶ αἱ κατ᾽ ἀρετήν πράξεις ("is virtue and virtuous actions").

[28] Cf. Colson and Whitaker, *Philo*, II, LCL (Cambridge, MA: Harvard University Press, 1981), 491.

[29] Cf. Liddell and Scott, *Greek-English Lexicon*, 260.

[30] διαθῆκαι δὲ ἐπ᾽ ὠφελείᾳ γράφονται τῶν δωρεᾶς ἀξίων, ὥστε σύμβολον εἶναι διαθήκην χάριτος, ἣν μέσην ἔθηκεν ὁ θεὸς ἑαυτοῦ τε ὀρέγοντος καὶ ἀνθρώπου λαμβάνοντος.

[31] Schwemer, "Zum Verhältnis von Diatheke," 94.

Finally, διαθήκη also appears in Philo's writings in *Somn.* 2.223; 2.224 and 2.237, where he explains the two parallel dreams of Pharaoh, and especially the phrase "I thought that I stood." The ability to stand, according to Philo, belongs only to God. *In the covenant God gives this ability to the righteous and wise* (such as Noah and Abraham).

The covenant represents God's greatest *gifts* (τὴν πλήρη χαρίτων διαθήκην) and also his *highest law* and principle (νόμος δ᾽ ἐστὶ καὶ λόγος).[32] Philo points out that righteousness does not differ from (and is therefore identical with) the covenant of God[33] (τὸ δίκαιον ἀδιαφορεῖ διαθήκης θεοῦ).[34]

2.3 Components of meaning of διαθήκη in various contexts in Philo

	Ethical Dimension	Quote	Reference to Isaac	Close link with logos	Relation
Leg. 3.85	Ethical dimension obvious from the beginning of the passage 85	Gen. 17:19	x (eternal covenant)		x
Sacr. 57	Cf. ὁ δὲ ἀξιόχρεων, cf. also ἀρετή	Deut. 9:5			x
Det. 67–68	Cf. ἀστεῖος	Deut. 33:9–10		x	x
Her. 313	Cf. ὁ σοφός	Gen. 15:18			x
Mut. 52	Covenants are for the benefit of those who are worthy of the gift	Gen. 17:2			x
Mut. 58	Cf. τοῖς ἀξίοις	Gen. 17:4			x
Mut. 263	Cf. ἑκατέρας ἀρετῆς	Gen. 17:21	x		x
Somn. 2. 223–224	Cf. The reference to the righteous and wise, such as Noah and Abraham	Gen. 9:11		x	x
Somn. 2.237	Cf. ... περὶ τὸν σοφόν ...			x	x

[32] Cohn, Heinemann, Adler, *Die Werke Philos von Alexandria*, VI (Breslau: M. & H. Marcus/Jüdischer Buchverlag Münz, 1919), 263 (esp. n. 6) translate διαθήκη here in the sense of διάθεσις, which, according to Stoic terminology, describes the (intellectual) state of mind. Colson and Whitaker, *Philo*, V, 543, however, translate even here with "covenant." There are no compelling reasons to follow Cohn, et al., here.

[33] Colson and Whitaker, *Philo*, V, 553: "... justice and God's covenant are identical."

[34] The line of thought is not quite clear in 224 and 225. Colson and Whitaker, *Philo*, V, 545, believe that the argumentation can be understood as follows: "(1) the words 'I will make my covenant to stand to (or on) thee' give Noah the stability of the

"Grace" and "righteousness" are significant components of the meaning of covenant in the following passages. God himself functions prominently in *Mut.* 58:

	Grace/gift	God himself	Righteousness
Sacr. 57	God's covenant is a symbol of his gracious gifts (συμβολικῶς αἱ χάριτες αὐτοῦ)		
Mut. 52	The covenant is a symbol of grace (σύμβολον εἶναι διαθήκην χάριτος)		
58	Covenants mediate grace and gifts of grace to the worthy (χάριτας	The highest form of the covenant is God himself (τὸ δ' ἀνώτατον γένος διαθηκῶν	
Somn. 2.223	καὶ δωρεάς)	αὐτὸς ἐγώ εἰμι)	Righteousness and God's covenant are
2.224	His covenant filled with his gifts of grace (τὴν πλήρη χαρίτων διαθήκην ἑαυτοῦ)		Identical (τὸ δίκαιον ἀδιαφορεῖ διαθήκης θεοῦ)

2.3.1 Διαθήκη *in various contexts in Philo: Further comments*

Διαθήκη is a term that, first of all, implies *relationship*.[35] In this specific kind of relationship, the initiative comes from God and is received by human beings (cf. *Mut.* 52.4).[36]

---

[34] (*Continued*) covenant and make him part of it as the pedestal of the statue; (2) as Noah is pre-eminently ὁ δίκαιος, the covenant is also τὸ δίκαιον; (3) and as by the giving of the covenant τὸ δίκαιον is given to ὁ δίκαιος, Noah is given to himself."

In *Somn.* 2.237, Philo strongly links the *word* with the *covenant*: τὸν τοῦ ὄντος λόγον, ὃν διαθήκην ἐκάλεσε. In the next sentence, he focuses on the wise person (τὸν σοφόν).

[35] Louw and Nida, *Greek-English Lexicon*, 451, place διαθήκη in the semantic field "establish or confirm a relation."

[36] As in the Septuagint, Philo uses διαθήκη instead of συνθήκη so that it becomes clear that the initiative for establishing a covenantal relationship comes from God and is not the consequence of negotiations or a compromise (cf. Louw and Nida, *Greek-English Lexicon*, 452).

It is noteworthy that in each context where διαθήκη appears in Philo, an ethical dimension can be discerned. Also, Philo portrays the wise person (ὁ σοφός, cf. *Her.* 313) as heir to life-giving wisdom, which has clearly ethical undertones. The notions of "being worthy" and of "virtue" (ἀρετή) are expressions of this ethical factor.

In *Det.* 67 we find a close link between "covenant" and "word":[37]

> he watched over your *word*
> and guarded your *covenant*
> he teaches your *precepts* to Jacob
> and your *law* to Israel.[38]

In *Somn.* 2.223 Philo states, as we have said, that covenant is the highest law and principle (νόμος δ' ἐστὶ καὶ λόγος). "Covenant" and "word/law" seem to be synonyms in certain contexts in Philo (cf. *Somn.* 2.237: τὸν ... λόγον, ὃν διαθήκην ἐκάλεσε). Διαθήκη often appears in quotes from the Septuagint.[39]

Although covenant and word/law are almost synonyms, Philo underscores that "God's covenant is the special expression of the divine gifts and graces" (cf. *Sacr.* 57: διαθήκη δ' ἐστὶ θεοῦ συμβολικῶς αἱ χάριτες αὐτου; *Mut.* 52: σύμβολον εἶναι διαθήκην χάριτος; *Mut.* 58: εἴδη μὲν διαθήκης ἐστὶ πάμπολλα χάριτας καὶ δωρεὰς τοῖς ἀξίοις ἀπονέμοντα; *Somn.* 2.223: τὴν πλήρη χαρίτων διαθήκην). This phenomenon has been characterized by Sanders as a Jewish "covenantal nomism" through which "the gift and demand of God were kept in a healthy relationship with each other."[40]

Righteousness and divine covenant are, in fact, indistinguishable for Philo (*Somn.* 2.224: τὸ δίκαιον ἀδιαφορεῖ διαθήκης θεοῦ), and the highest expression of the covenant reality is the divine reality – God himself (*Mut.* 58: τὸ δ' ἀνώτατον γένος διαθηκῶν αὐτὸς ἐγώ εἰμι).[41]

2.4 Summary

Philo's theology primarily consisted of an exegesis of the Pentateuch. He therefore directs his main attention to the patriarchal covenants. By way of allegorical interpretation, this exegesis gains universal significance.[42] Philo's

---

[37] Cf. Jaubert, *La notion d'alliance*, 426–27.

[38] ἐφύλαξε τὰ λόγιά σου, καὶ τὴν διαθήκην σου διετήρησεν δηλώσουσι τὰ δικαιώματά σου Ἰακὼβ καὶ τὸν νόμον σου Ἰσραήλ.

　Note that after the chiastic structure (a, b, b, a) in the first two lines, a *parallelismus membrorum* follows in lines three and four.

[39] Twice (*Leg.* 3.85 and *Mut.* 263) there is a reference to Isaac.

[40] Sanders, *Paul and Palestinian Judaism: A Comparison of Patterns of Religion* (London: SCM Press, 1977), 427.

[41] Cf. Jaubert, *La notion d'alliance*, 431: "Dieu: fin suprême de la diathèkè."

[42] Cf. Schwemer, "Zum Verhältnis von Diatheke," 101.

explicative felicity in this regard may be traced to his familiarity with early middle Platonism.[43]

The purpose of διαθήκη is described in Philo as the unification of the soul with God (cf. *QG* 3, 42). Although God lives in the κόσμος νοητός, which is inaccessible to human beings (cf. *Post.* 16; *Mos.* 1, 158), souls who are divinely cleansed and enlightened have the opportunity to be united with God (cf. *Post.* 22–31; *Plant.* 58; *Conf.* 92–94, 146–49; *Migr.* 47; *Mut.* 51f.; *Abr.* 57, 98; *QG* 3, 15; *QE* 1, 10; 2, 47).[44] For these souls God is, himself, the "gift of the covenant" (cf. *Mut.* 58; *Somn.* 2,224).

Philo considers διαθήκη as the "symbol" of God's undeserved gift of grace. He emphasizes the steadfastness with which God grants this gift, which he also identifies with the logos, the law and wisdom. As a spiritual gift, διαθήκη is a mediator of perfect virtue. This gift of perfect virtue is actually the law written upon the heart.[45]

With his notion of intimacy with God by way of a divinely initiated soul cleansing, Philo essentially captures the ideal concept of the new covenant (compare how the promise of Jer. 31:31–34 is expressed in *Sacr.* 57; *Mut.* 51–53; and *Somn.* 2.223–224). However, Philo tends to overlook the dynamic historical perspective through which this covenant is realized. The notion that God is eternally unchangeable, which is very strong in Philo, excludes a full appreciation for the dynamic flow of salvation history (*Heilsgeschichte*), thus obscuring the distinction between the notions of "old" and "new" covenants. For Philo, what belongs to God's covenant (διαθήκη) is perfect and cannot be improved upon, replaced or superseded (cf. *Sacr.* 57). This notion of God's immutability secures the salvific foundation of the "soul's" stability in the midst of earthly mutability.[46]

---

[43] Siegert, "Philon v. Alexandrien," in *LTK*, VIII (Freiburg/Basel/Rom/Wien: Herder, 1999), 245. One must also point out Philo's eclecticism. He has integrated elements of the Middle Stoa with occasional influences from neo-Pythagoreanism (cf. Mach, "Philo von Alexandrien," in *TRE* XXVI (Berlin/New York: Walter de Gruyter, 1996), 525).

[44] Backhaus, *Der neue Bund und das Werden der Kirche: Die Diatheke-Deutung des Hebräerbriefs im Rahmen der frühchristlichen Theologiegeschichte*, NTA (Münster: Aschendorff, 1996), 288–89, who refers to Jaubert, *La notion d'alliance*, 431–37, here.

[45] This is how Schwemer, "Zum Verhältnis von Diatheke," 101, sees it.

[46] Backhaus, *Der neue Bund und das Werden der Kirche*, 288–90.

3

The (New) Covenant in the Jesus Tradition

1. Exegetical remarks on passages concerning the institution of the Lord's Supper

1.1 Introductory comments

In the Jesus tradition, the Lord's Supper explicitly portrays the concept of the covenant.[1] The institution of the Lord's Supper is narrated in Matthew 26:26–29, Mark 14:22–25, Luke 22:15–20 and 1 Corinthians 11:23–26. Analysis of the motifs that occur in these passages shows that some motifs appear in all four passages, while other elements occur in only one, two or three of these passages.

(a) Analysis of motifs

    (1) The covenant

        "Covenant" (διαθήκη) appears in all four passages:
        the new covenant (ἡ καινὴ διαθήκη, 1 Cor. 11:25)
        the new covenant (ἡ καινὴ διαθήκη, Luke 22:20)
        (the blood of) the covenant ([τὸ αἷμά μου] τῆς διαθήκης, Mark 14:24)
        (the blood of) the covenant ([τὸ αἷμά μου] τῆς διαθήκης, Matt. 26:28)

    (2) The kingdom of God

        This motif occurs in Matthew, Mark and Luke:
        in the kingdom of God (ἐν τῇ βασιλείᾳ τοῦ θεοῦ, Luke 22:16)
        the kingdom of God (ἡ βασιλεία τοῦ θεοῦ, Luke 22:18)
        in the kingdom of God (ἐν τῇ βασιλείᾳ τοῦ θεοῦ, Mark 14:25)
        in my Father's kingdom (ἐν τῇ βασιλείᾳ τοῦ πατρός μου, Matt. 26:29)
        1 Corinthians 11:26 uses the phrase "until he comes."

---

[1] Cf. Kirchschläger, "'Bund' in der Herrenmahltradition," in Frankemölle, *Der ungekündigte Bund?*, 117–34.

(3) Blood

The motif of blood appears in the following verses:
in my blood (ἐν τῷ ἐμῷ αἵματι, 1 Cor. 11:25)
in my blood (ἐν τῷ αἵματι μου, Luke 22:20)
my blood (τὸ αἷμά μου, Mark 14:24)
my blood (τὸ αἷμά μου, Matt. 26:28)

(4) Substitution

The motif of substitution (ὑπέρ) appears in the following passages:
for you (ὑπὲρ ὑμῶν, 1 Cor. 11:24; Luke 22:19–20)[2]
for many (ὑπὲρ πολλῶν, Mark 14:24)
for many (περὶ πολλῶν, Matt. 26:28)

(5) The motif of thanksgiving (εὐχαριστήσας) appears in: 1 Corinthians 11:24; Luke 22:17, 19; Mark 14:23; Matthew 26:27).[3]

(6) The following motifs are common to Luke 22:15–20, Mark 14:22–25 and Matthew 26:26–29:

Outpouring (ἐκχυννόμενον: Luke 22:20; Mark 14:24; Matt. 26:28)
Jesus' statement that he will not drink from the fruit of the vine until the kingdom of God comes appears in the Gospel of Luke before the words of institution (Luke 22:18) and in the Gospels of Mark and Matthew after the blessing of the cup (Mark 14:25; Matt. 26:29).[4]

(7) The following motifs are common to 1 Corinthians 11:23–26 and Luke 22:15–20:

The motif of the *new* covenant (ἡ καινὴ διαθήκη, 1 Cor. 11:25; Luke 22:20)
For *you* (ὑπὲρ (περὶ) ὑμῶν, 1 Cor. 11:24; Luke 22:19–20)[5]
The exhortation "do this in remembrance of me":
Do this in remembrance of me (τοῦτο ποιεῖτε εἰς τὴν ἐμὴν ἀνάμνησιν, 1 Cor. 11:24)

---

[2] In 1 Cor. 11, the notion of substitution appears only in the blessing of the bread. In Luke 22, however, it appears in the blessing of the bread and the cup.

[3] While Paul links the thanksgiving with the bread, Luke links it with the bread and the cup. Mark and Matthew, however, connect thanksgiving (εὐλογεῖν) with the bread and refer to the cup with a different verb for thanksgiving (εὐχαριστεῖν).

[4] Luke says: "… until the kingdom of God comes"; Mark: "… until that day when I drink it anew in the kingdom of God"; and Matthew: "… until that day when I drink it anew with you in my Father's kingdom."

[5] See text critical remarks.

Do this, whenever you drink it, in remembrance of me (τοῦτο ποιεῖτε, ὁσάκις ἐὰν πίνητε, εἰς τὴν ἐμὴν ἀνάμνησιν, 1 Cor. 11:25)[6]
Do this in remembrance of me (τοῦτο ποιεῖτε εἰς τὴν ἐμὴν ἀνάμνησιν, Luke 22:19)
The cup (τὸ ποτήριον, 1 Cor. 11:25,26; Luke 22:20 [twice])

(8) The following motifs are unique to 1 Corinthians 11:

"As often" plus conjunctive:
as often as you drink (ὁσάκις ἐὰν πίνητε, 1 Cor. 11:25)
as often as you eat (ὁσάκις γὰρ ἐὰν ἐσθίητε, 1 Cor. 11:26)
proclaiming the death of Jesus till he returns; you proclaim the Lord's death until he comes (τὸν θάνατον τοῦ κυρίου καταγγέλλετε ἄχρι οὗ ἔλθῃ, 1 Cor. 11:26)

(9) The following motifs are common to Mark 14:22–25 and Matthew 26:26–29:

the motif of "the blood of the covenant" (τὸ αἷμά ... τῆς διαθήκης, Mark 14:24; Matt. 26:28)
for + many (ὑπέρ + πολλῶν, Mark 14:24; Matt. 26:28)
the remark "until that day" (ἕως τῆς ἡμέρας ἐκείνης) (paralleling the motif of the kingdom of God [Mark 14:25; Matt. 26:29])

(10) The motif "for the forgiveness of sins" (εἰς ἄφεσιν ἁμαρτιῶν, Matt. 26:28) is unique to Matthew 26.

The analysis above demonstrates that motifs such as covenant, blood, substitution, praise/thanksgiving and the kingdom of God[7] are common elements of the Lord's Supper tradition in both Paul and the Synoptic Gospels. In addition, our analysis reveals that certain motifs connect *Luke* and *Paul*, while other motifs are common in *Mark* and *Matthew*. The tradition in Matthew is very close to that of Mark; it adds, however, the phrase "for the forgiveness of sins" (Matt. 26:28). The motif "to pour out," which links Mark and Matthew with Luke, does not occur in 1 Corinthians 11. The phrase "as often" plus conjunctive ("as often as you eat this bread and drink this cup") and the motif of the proclamation of Jesus' death until he returns appear only in the Pauline tradition of the Lord's Supper and can be viewed as early traces of a standing liturgical tradition.[8]

---

[6] This exhortation refers in Paul to bread and cup, but in Luke only to the bread.
[7] See, however, the remark in Paul "until he comes" (1 Cor. 11:26).
[8] The Pauline tradition also, however, contains elements that are very old.

1.2 Covenant and the Lord's Supper tradition in Paul (1 Cor. 11:23–26)[9]

Paul speaks about the Lord's Supper (κυριακὸν δεῖπνον) only in the first Epistle to the Corinthians (1 Cor. 10:1–4; 10:16–17; 11:17–34).[10] Paul links the Lord's Supper with the notion of the covenant in the section of 1 Corinthians dealing with worship problems in the Corinthian church (1 Cor. 11:2 – 14:40). The immediate context is abuse of the Lord's Supper celebration in the Corinthian community. The pericope 11:17–34 can be divided neatly into three subunits. Verses 17–22 discuss abuses in the Corinthian praxis of the Lord's Supper. Then in verses 23–26 Paul describes how the tradition was transmitted to him. He adds a warning in verses 27–32 against participating in the Lord's Supper in an unworthy manner and closes the passage (vv. 33–34) with a summation, referring to his instructions in verses 17–22.[11]

Paul's appeal to the Lord's Supper tradition in 1 Corinthians 11:23–26 has a regulatory function. He desires to preserve the unity of the Lord's Supper celebration, which is the essential import of *koinonia*. It was important that the elements of the Christian Eucharist were integrated with the secular dimensions of the community meal, for the celebration of the liturgy was also an occasion to satisfy hunger (cf. the phrase "after supper").[12]

In 1 Corinthians 11:23–26, Paul characterizes the Lord's Supper as a liturgical ceremony marking the time between Jesus' death and his return. This passage is introduced in verse 23 with a reference to the night in which the Lord Jesus (κύριος Ἰησοῦς) was betrayed. Paul then offers an interpretation of the ceremony's function that highlights its eschatological context. With the phrase "until he comes" Paul expresses the eschatological motif also present in the parallel versions of the liturgy in Mark 14:25, Matthew 26:29 and Luke 22:18.[13]

To add weight to his criticism of the Corinthian's cavalier behavior during the eucharistic celebration, Paul points out that the ritual was instituted by none other than Jesus himself. The solemnity of divine succession is reflected in terms inherent to the Lord's Supper tradition such as παραλαμβάνειν ("to take/to accept – often of a tradition") and παραδιδόναι ("to hand or give

---

[9] An extensive discussion of all exegetical problems found in the Lord's Supper texts lies beyond the limits of this study. The purpose of an exegetical analysis of these texts is to gain some clearer understanding of the covenant theme in these contexts.

[10] Hahn, "Das Herrenmahl bei Paulus," in Trowitzsch (ed.), *Paulus, Apostel Jesu Christi: Festschrift für Günter Klein zum 70. Geburtstag* (Tübingen: J. C. B. Mohr [Paul Siebeck], 1998), 23

[11] Hahn, "Herrenmahl bei Paulus," 23.

[12] Hahn, "Herrenmahl bei Paulus," 23–24.

[13] Hahn, "Herrenmahl bei Paulus," 24.

over/to entrust").[14] These are technical terms formally applied to the transmission of Jewish dogmatic tradition.[15] Paul reminds his reader that the historical Jesus, who is present himself in the sacrament as the exalted Lord, is the permanent guarantor of the validity of this tradition (vv. 23b–25[16]).[17]

In verse 23, the title "Lord," which Paul uses primarily to describe the risen Christ, is applied to the historical Jesus. This association has significant implications in terms of the authority carried by the tradition. Since the earthly Jesus who spoke the words instituting the Eucharist is now the risen one (cf. 1 Cor. 7:10, 12, 25; 9:14; also Rom. 14:14; 1 Thess. 4:15), his instructions carry divine authority. Paul's reference to "the night when he was betrayed" reinforces the historicity of the Christ event and roots its origins there rather than in myth or pagan cultic practice.[18]

Of course the verb παραδιδόναι (cf. Isa. 53:10, 12) does not refer to Judas' betrayal alone,[19] but also to Christ's sacrifice. Its primary referent is Jesus' self-giving "unto death." The blessing of the cup[20] speaks of a new covenant, established through the atoning and substitutionary death of Jesus. The proclamation of a new order of eschatological salvation (interpreted as a new covenant, cf. 2 Cor. 3:4–18) comprises the core of the blessing of the cup. This new eschatological order of salvation includes the forgiveness of previous sins (cf. Rom. 3:25). A new covenant had become necessary, because Israel had failed to keep the old covenant. Jeremiah's prophecy (Jer. 31:31–34 [LXX 38:31–34])

---

[14] Newman, *A Concise Greek-English Dictionary of the New Testament* (London: United Bible Societies, 1971).

[15] See Lang, *Die Briefe an die Korinther* (Göttingen: Vandenhoeck & Ruprecht, 1986), 150. Wolff, *Der erste Brief des Paulus an die Korinther, zweiter Teil: Auslegung der Kapitel 8–16* (Berlin: Evangelische Verlagsanstalt, 1982), 82, points out that the apostle falls back on a fully formed and standing tradition. This is demonstrated by the rabbinic terms that he uses: παραλαμβάνειν corresponds with the Hebrew קבל and παραδιδόναι with מסר. Since he used to be a Pharisee (cf. Phil. 3:5; Gal. 1:14), it is likely that Paul's thinking was based on his rabbinic background – rather than being influenced by the Greek scholarly tradition, mystery religions or Gnosticism.

[16] There is a clear change of persons in the interpretative v. 26 (Wolff, *Der erste Brief des Paulus an die Korinther*, 83).

[17] Klauck, *1. Korintherbrief* (Würzburg: Echter Verlag, 1992), 82.

[18] Wolff, *Der erste Brief des Paulus an die Korinther*, 83.

[19] Cf. v. 23, "on the night he was betrayed" (ἐν τῇ νυκτὶ ᾗ παρεδίδετο).

[20] Originally there was a meal between the bread and the cup ceremony in early Christian churches. The phrase "after the supper" (v. 25), which indicates that the cup was being passed around after some meal, supports this assumption. Because of the phrase "in the same way," the statement can also be understood to say that the wine, "like also" the bread, was served "after supper" (cf. Wolff, *Der erste Brief des Paulus an die Korinther*, 91).

about an eschatological new covenant has now been fulfilled through Jesus' death and resurrection.[21] The guests at the Lord 's Table partake, through the drinking of the cup, in the salvific effects of the blood shed by Jesus and are thus included in the new eschatological order – one intended by God to embrace all nations (cf. Isa. 25 and 53). The "blood" (αἷμα) here (cf. also v. 27; Rom. 3:25; 5:9) is "Jesus' atoning blood shed on the cross."[22]

Verse 26 reveals the theological meaning of the Lord's Supper. The celebration of the Lord's Supper proclaims the death of Jesus.[23] This proclamation is not a mournful lament, however, but a joyful witness to the victory through which God has set up his new eschatological order of salvation (cf. 1 Cor. 15:57).[24]

The statement "do this in remembrance of me" appears twice in the Pauline version of the institution of the Lord's Supper. This "remembering" takes place through both *word* and *deed*. Hahn points out that "remembrance" (ἀνάμνησις), like its OT equivalent זכרון, means memory as recalling or reimaging. "The remembering that actually makes the person of Jesus present is not possible except through remembering his death and the salvation it made possible."[25]

1.3 The Lord's Supper tradition in Luke[26]

The Lord's Supper tradition in Luke is found in the context of the passion (and Easter) narratives (Luke 22:1 – 24:53) and is preceded by the account of the plan of the Sanhedrin to kill Jesus (Luke 22:1–2) and the report of Judas' betrayal (Luke 22:3–6).[27] In Luke's Passion Narrative the Last Supper is discussed in considerable detail – including its preparation (Luke 22:7–13), its execution and the words that comprised it (Luke 22:14–20), as well as

---

[21] Fee, *The First Epistle to the Corinthians* (Grand Rapids: Eerdmans, 1987), 555; Lang, *Die Briefe an die Korinther*, 153.

[22] Hofius, "Herrenmahl und Herrenmahlsparadosis," in Hofius (ed.), *Paulusstudien* (Tübingen: J. C. B. Mohr [Paul Siebeck], 1989), 225.

[23] Καταγγέλλετε (proclaim) can be understood as carrying indicative or imperative force. Since the whole sentence (introduced with "for") creates a causative statement, the indicative should be preferred.

[24] Lang, *Die Briefe an die Korinther*, 153–54.

[25] Hahn, "Herrenmahl bei Paulus," 24.

[26] See Schürmann, *Der Einsetzungsbericht: Lk 22,19–20. II. Teil einer quellenkritischen Untersuchung des lukanischen Abendmahlberichtes Lk 22,7–38* (Münster: Aschendorffsche Verlagsbuchhandlung, 1955) for a detailed source-critical analysis of Luke's narrative of the Last Supper.

[27] The narrative about Jesus being anointed at Bethany is not part of the Lukan Passion Narrative (as is the case in Mark's Gospel), cf. Luke 7:36–50.

conversations, in the style of farewell speeches, that attended the meal (Luke 22:21–38).[28]

Excursus: Text critical analysis of Luke 22:19–20 and some theological consequences

Codex Bezae[29] contains the so-called short version of the Lukan text, which omits verses 19b and 20 (τὸ ὑπὲϱ ὑμῶν ... ἐκχυννόμενον), leaving a sequence in which the breaking of the bread follows the drinking from the cup, with no explanation offered for the taking of the cup. The short version reads as follows:

> Luke 22:15–20: And he said to them, 'I have eagerly desired to eat this Passover with you before I suffer. For I tell you, I will not eat it again until it finds fulfillment in the kingdom of God.' After taking the cup, he gave thanks and said, 'Take this and divide it among you. For I tell you I will not drink again of the fruit of the vine until the kingdom of God comes.' And he took bread, gave thanks and broke it, and gave it to them, saying, 'This is my body.' [The following words are then omitted: 'given for you; do this in remembrance of me.' In the same way, after the supper he took the cup, saying, 'This cup is the new covenant in my blood, which is poured out for you.']

B. F. Westcott and F. J. A. Hort used the short text in their version of the New Testament (1881), maintaining that verses 19b–20 are an example of what they called "Western Non-Interpolations." Although a large majority of manuscripts support the longer text, Westcott's and Hort's decision was very influential until the twenty-fifth version of the Nestle text.

The close relationship between Luke 22:19b–20 and 1 Corinthians 11:24b–25 seems to suggest a secondary adaptation from 1 Corinthians 11 on the part of Luke. The question arises why Luke, unlike Mark, would leave out an interpretation of the cup linking it with the sacrifice of the cross which was probably available to him (cf. Mark 14:24). Caird, who prefers the shorter reading, answers this question in the following way: "the explanation is ... to be sought in Luke's theology: for believing, as he did, that God's saving act was the whole of Jesus' life of service and self-giving, and that the cross was simply the preordained price of friendship with the outcast, he naturally felt little interest in sayings which appeared to concentrate the whole of God's redemption in the cross."[30]

New Testament scholars who prefer the short reading often point to Didache 9:1–3 as a witness to a Lukan Lord's Supper tradition where the taking of the bread follows the drinking from the cup. However, Niederwinner's

---

[28]   See Kremer, *Lukasevangelium* (Würzburg: Echter Verlag, 1988), 210.

[29]   As well as in the Latin manuscripts it[a,d,ff2,i,l].

[30]   Caird, *The Gospel of St. Luke* (New York: The Seabury Press, 1963), 238.

commentary on the Didache points out that 10:6 extends the invitation to the Lord's Supper, which follows immediately thereafter. Hence, the meal described in 10:1 cannot be a sacramental Eucharist, but was probably only a community meal.[31] According to the Didache, the liturgical order should be as follows: First, a community meal (possibly the "agape" feast) introduced with short benedictions on bread and wine (the wording clearly points to the pattern of Jewish wine and/or bread benedictions). This meal should be eaten in order to satisfy hunger. This meal (10:1) is followed by a thanksgiving prayer, which inaugurates the Lord's Supper (10:2–5). After the thanksgiving, the invitation to the sacramental Eucharist is extended (10:6) and prayers may be offered by the prophets (10:7). The Lord's Supper proper is then celebrated. It must be underscored that prayers during the meal in the Didache are in many instances modeled after Jewish prayers. The link between the church tradition and Judaism was still very strong at that time.[32]

New Testament scholars such as Pierre Benoit, E. Earle Ellis, Josef Ernst, Ferdinand Hahn, Joachim Jeremias (though he at first preferred the shorter reading), Werner Georg Kümmel and Heinz Schürmann eventually began to question Westcott's and Hort's predilection for the short version.[33] Schürmann, for example, pointed out that differences between Luke and Paul present a strong argument *against* a derivation of Luke 22:19b–20 from 1 Corinthians 11:24b–25.[34]

The following evidences suggest the originality of the longer version:

Manuscript evidence: the shorter reading is found only in one part of the western sources, namely in codex Bezae. The number of Latin manuscripts that reflect the longer version is roughly equal to the number that contain the shorter version.

---

[31] This is also supported by ἐμπλησθῆναι (to be satisfied or full). Ἐμπλησθῆναι can be understood metaphorically, as, e.g., in Rom. 15:24. The Didache, however, speaks here about the eating of bread and the drinking of wine – hence, ἐμπλησθῆναι describes the gratification of hunger and thirst (Niederwinner, *Die Didache* [Göttingen: Vandenhoeck & Ruprecht, 1989], 179, n. 49).

[32] See Niederwinner, *Die Didache*, 175–80; cf. also Wengst, *Didache (Apostellehre), Barnabasbrief, Zweiter Klemensbrief, Schrift an Diognet* (Darmstadt: Wissenschaftliche Buchgesellschaft, 1984), 47. Further critical comments on the notion that Didache 9:1–3 depicts an alternative Lord's Supper liturgy can be found in Fitzmyer, *The Gospel According to Luke (X–XXIV)* (New York: Doubleday, 1985), 1397–98.

[33] Cf. Fitzmyer, *The Gospel According to Luke*, 1388. Additional literature is also cited in Hahn, "Die alttestamentlichen Motive in der urchristlichen Abendmahls-überlieferung," *EvT* 27 (1967), 342, n. 24.

[34] For a detailed analysis of these differences see Schürmann, "Lk 22, 19b–20 als ursprüngliche Textüberlieferung," *Bib* 32 (1951), 382–85; Schürmann, *Der Einsetzungsbericht*, 49–56.

The fact that the valuable p[75] supports the longer reading enforces the argument for the longer version to the degree that Kurt Aland can remark that a text critical discussion about the primary character of the longer version has almost become superfluous.[35]

The rule of *lectio difficilior*[36] can be applied here: The longer version of the text that contains two references to the cup is the more complicated text. It is understandable that the second reference to the cup could have been omitted, which then leads to the sequence cup-bread (instead of cup-bread-cup).[37]

The development of the shorter version can be explained on the basis of the *disciplina arcana*.[38]

The immediate context for the Last Supper narrative is found in Luke 22:14–20, which is part of a larger section beginning in verse 7. The passages 7–13 and 14–20 are introduced in a parallel fashion:

> then *came* the *day of Unleavened Bread* … (Luke 22:7)

> and when the *hour came* … (Luke 22:14)

Note the intensification that occurs: "the day of the Unleavened Bread" in verse 7 becomes "the hour" in verse 14. The phrase "the hour," which is not chronologically further defined (as in Mark 14:17), characterizes an epoch-making event in salvation history (cf. Luke 22:53; John 12:23; 13:1, 17:1).[39]

---

[35] Aland, *Studien zur Überlieferung des Neuen Testaments und seines Textes* (Berlin: Walter de Gruyter, 1967), 165.

[36] The more difficult reading is normally to be preferred.

[37] Cf. Metzger, *A Textual Commentary on the Greek New Testament* (Stuttgart: Deutsche Bibelgesellschaft, 1994), 148: "It is easier to suppose that the Bezan editor, puzzled by the sequence of cup-bread-cup, eliminated the second mention of the cup without being concerned about the inverted order of institution thus produced, than that the editor of the longer version, to rectify the inverted order, brought in from Paul the second mention of the cup, while letting the first mention stand."

[38] Cf. Metzger, *A Textual Commentary*, 148, 150: "The rise of the shorter version can be accounted for in terms of the theory of *disciplina arcana*, i.e. in order to protect the Eucharist from profanation, one or more copies of the Gospel according to Luke, prepared for circulation among non-Christian readers, omitted the sacramental formula after the beginning words."

It is worth noting that while the level of possibility of the longer version was estimated in the third edition of the "United Bible Societies" Greek New Testament" with a "C," the fourth edition assigns a "B" to it. It seems that the decision for the longer version receives more plausibility.

For further discussion of this text critical problem, cf. Metzger, *A Textual Commentary*, 148–150; cf. also Schweizer, "Abendmahl I: Im NT," in *RGG* I (Tübingen: J. C. B. Mohr [Paul Siebeck], 1957), 14.

[39] Kremer, *Lukasevangelium*, 212.

In Luke 22:15, Jesus discloses to the apostles his great desire (ἐπιθυμίᾳ ἐπεθύμησα) to eat the paschal lamb with them before his sufferings.[40] He solemnly explains that he will not eat it any more until it is "fulfilled" in the kingdom of God (v. 16). Hence, this Passover points beyond itself toward the coming divine kingdom. The certainty of the coming of this kingdom is underlined in verse 18: "For I tell you I will not drink again of the fruit of the vine until the kingdom of God comes."

The kingdom of God was a key element in Jesus' preaching, and he often spoke of it using the metaphor of a feast or an eschatological meal (cf. Luke 14:15–24; 22:30; Isa. 25:6–8).[41] Through Jesus' reference to the kingdom of God, the Passion Narrative becomes eschatologically orientated. Jesus' words express the faith that his approaching death will not undermine his mission. Despite the somber context, the Lord's Supper is filled with eschatological hope.[42]

In Luke's narrative about the institution of the Lord's Supper, Jesus compares the giving up of his body to the eucharistic bread and the spilling of his blood to the wine. This sacrifice will take place on behalf of those who are present ("for you," ὑπὲρ ὑμῶν), rather than for the "many" (ὑπὲρ πολλῶν; see Mark 14:24).[43] The first traces of a liturgical context – the celebration of the Eucharist in the early church – are found in the words "do this in remembrance of me" (v. 19).

The blessing of the cup in Luke differs from that found in Mark in that the "this" (τοῦτό) in Mark 14:24 refers to the wine – the blood of sacrifice through which the new covenant is established. In Luke 22:20, however, the cup metaphorically *represents* the new covenant itself. The cup represents the

---

[40] The Synoptics describe Jesus' last meal with his disciples as a Passover (Matt. 26:26–29; Mark 14:22–25; Luke 22:15–20); in the Gospel of John Jesus dies in the afternoon of the day when the Passover would be enjoyed in the evening (John 18:28; 19:14) (cf. Lang, *Die Briefe an die Korinther*, 152). The question arises whether the approaching night was the night of the Pesach. There is an attempt to harmonize the differences between the Synoptics and the Fourth Gospel with the help of documents from Qumran. (The Qumran community used the sun calendar, while the temple in Jerusalem followed the moon calendar.) This attempt is not very persuasive. The Fourth Gospel does not attempt to create the impression that the meal that Jesus had with his disciples was a Passover meal.

[41] Cf. section 2 below.

[42] Cf. Kremer, *Lukasevangelium*, 212; Schweizer, *Das Evangelium nach Lukas* (Göttingen: Vandenhoeck & Ruprecht, 1982), 223.

[43] Hahn, *Christologische Hoheitstitel: Ihre Geschichte im frühen Christentum* (Göttingen: Vandenhoeck & Ruprecht, 1995), 61, points out that the motif of atonement in the Pauline/Lukan tradition does not show any dependency on Isa. 53, while in the tradition of Mark and Matthew the motif clearly alludes to the universal character of the promise in Isa. 53.

sacrificial death of Jesus through which the new covenant is established. "In my blood" (ἐν τῷ αἵματί μου) points to the death of Jesus – according to biblical understanding the blood was considered to contain life. The adjective "new" (καινός) appears in connection with the covenant in Jeremiah 38:31;[44] 1 Corinthians 11:25; 2 Corinthians 3:6; and Hebrews 8:8, 13; 9:15. "Newness" in these verses refers not to a new beginning in time, but to a new eschatological beginning.

Marshall[45] believes that because blood does not play a role in Jeremiah 31:31–34, Luke 22:20 is probably an allusion to Exodus 24:8 (see Mark 14:24). Wolff[46] also maintains that the Lukan passage is not a fulfillment of Jeremiah 31:31–34, since blood did not play a role in Jeremiah and because Jeremiah's prophecy had no significance in early Judaism. He is also of the opinion that Jeremiah 31:31–34 did not function prominently in early Christianity.[47] Schürmann,[48] on the other side, rightly affirms that the cup blessing of Paul and Luke speaks explicitly of the new, eschatological covenant of Jeremiah 31:31–34, which temporally and qualitatively fulfills all preceding covenants. I would argue that the notion of the eschatological covenant of Jeremiah 31:31–34 was as operative in Jesus' thinking as the notion of the imminent kingdom of God and the approaching outpouring of the Spirit. The Jeremiah promise creates the background to Jesus' words, for example in Matthew 5:12; 11:25, 30; 23:8, and has continuing repercussions in the apostolic churches (cf. Luke 1:77; Rom. 8:4; Heb. 8:8–12, 1 John 5:3; Rev. 21:7). The Lukan/Pauline covenant concepts are therefore quite in agreement with Jesus' own – a fact that bespeaks their authenticity.[49]

Karrer[50] is also of the opinion that the transmission of the Lord's Supper logia took place independently from Jeremiah 31:31–34. He lists two reasons for

---

[44] Jer. 38 in the Septuagint is the same as Jer. 31 in the Masoretic Text.

[45] Marshall, *The Gospel of Luke* (Exeter: Paternoster, 1978), 806–807.

[46] Wolff, *Der erste Brief des Paulus an die Korinther*, 86–87. Wolff, *Jeremia im Frühjudentum und Urchristentum* (Berlin: Akademie-Verlag, 1976), 134, underlines that the Lord's Supper tradition does not allude to Jer. 31 "because there are no conceptual parallels [!] to the prophecy in Jeremiah."

[47] However, as Jeremias, *Die Abendmahlsworte Jesu* (Göttingen: Vandenhoeck & Ruprecht, 1967), 188, points out, we know how alive the promise of the new covenant (Jer. 31:31–34) was in Jesus' time through the Essene writings, especially the Damascus scroll.

[48] Schürmann, *Der Paschamahlbericht, Lk 22, (7–14.) 15–18* (Münster: Aschendorffsche Buchdruckerei, 1968), 97.

[49] Hahn, "Die alttestamentlichen Motive," 371, also underlines the importance of Jer. 31:31: "From a conceptual perspective Jeremiah 31:31 has a distinct superiority."

[50] Karrer, "Der Kelch des neuen Bundes: Erwägungen zum Verständnis des Herrenmahls nach 1 Kor 11,23b–25," *BZ* 34 (1990), 219.

holding to this view. First, 1 Corinthians 11:25 does not conform to the Septuagint translation of the Jeremiah passage (38:31 in LXX) because, in the latter, "new" (καινός) *follows* the noun. Second, Jeremiah 31 does not define the covenant on the basis of a sacrifice; it must be understood as a promise for a life in the Torah. In response to Karrer's first argument, Greek grammar does not justify such conclusions based only on the position of an adjective. Regarding his second criticism, it must be pointed out that the New Testament appropriates and develops not only individual Old Testament texts and motifs, but also entire complexes of traditions, as demonstrated by Hahn.[51] Both Jeremiah 31:31–34 *and* Exodus 24:8 may be assumed as background for the Lord's Supper narrative (as well as Isa. 53:10–11, although to a lesser degree). Texts about the Sinai covenant (which was sealed with blood, see Exod. 24:8) and the promise of a "bloodless" new covenant (Jer. 31:31–34) supplement and condition each other in the Lord's Supper logia. Jeremiah 31:31 provides the salvation history framework, while Exodus 24:8 serves to illustrate the death of Jesus. The Markan tradition of the cup blessing has Exodus 24:8 in the foreground, while the Lukan/Pauline tradition refers primarily to Jeremiah 31:31.[52]

1.4 The Lord's Supper tradition in Mark[53]

Mark 14:22–25 illustrates how faithfully Mark preserved the historical references of the Lord's Supper tradition he received, and how he creatively made them relevant. Although the narrative elements of the text can be categorized as a "report," one must also attend to the "ritual character" of the text. Stylistically, Mark 14:22–25 can be classified as a liturgical text of the early church. However, the primary significance of the text lies not in its formal role as a liturgical reenactment of the Last Supper, but in its explication of the *meaning* of the Eucharist for the community of disciples.[54]

Mark includes the Lord's Supper tradition in the part of his Gospel that deals with Jesus' suffering and death, and the empty tomb (14:1 – 16:8).[55] The Lord's

---

[51] Hahn, "Die alttestamentlichen Motive," 373.

[52] Cf. Levin, *Die Verheißung des neuen Bundes*, 267.

[53] We shall not deal in detail with the institution of the Lord's Supper in Matthew (26:26–29) as there is a broad consensus among scholars that Matthew transmits an extended version of Mark 14:22–24. The Matthean account seems to be literarily dependent on Mark (cf. Schürmann, *Der Paschamahlbericht*, 153) – Matthew adds only one phrase to Mark's report: "for the forgiveness of sins" (Matt. 26:28) (see 3.1.1, above).

[54] See Kertelge, "Das Abendmahl Jesu im Markusevangelium," in Zmijewski and Nellessen (eds.), *Begegnung mit dem Wort: Festschrift für Heinrich Zimmermann* (Bonn: Peter Hanstein, 1980), 68, 70–71.

[55] Cf., e.g., Gnilka, *Das Evangelium nach Markus* (Zürich: Benziger Verlag, 1978), 216; Pesch, *Das Markusevangelium* (Freiburg: Herder, 1980), VIII.

Supper is preceded by the conspiracy of Jesus' enemies (14:1–2), the anointment of Jesus at Bethany (14:3–9), the betrayal by Judas (14:10–11), the preparation of the Passover (14:12–16) and the prediction that one of the disciples will deliver Jesus into the hand of his enemies (14:17–21).

A new unit starts in verse 22 with "and" (καί) and a genitive absolute "their eating" (ἐσθιόντων αὐτῶν). The breaking of the bread and its meaning are described in verse 22. The passing of the cup is depicted in verse 23. An additional verse (v. 24) explains the meaning of this act.

In verse 24, "covenant" and "blood" are closely connected by way of a genitive. An allusion is made to Exodus 24:8, where Moses interprets the blood he sprinkles on the people with the words: "This is the blood of the covenant that the Lord has made with you in accordance with all these words."[56] Thus Joachim Gnilka's heading for Mark 14:22–26, "The establishment of the covenant," is apt.[57] The covenant becomes valid on the basis of Jesus' death, and Jesus' blood stands in typological continuity with the blood of the previous covenant. Antitypically, the covenant instituted by Jesus becomes the "*new*" covenant, although it is here not explicitly characterized as such (cf., however, Luke 22:20 and 1 Cor. 11:25).[58]

Mark draws a closer parallel between the bread and the wine than Luke and Paul, and he presents the bread and the wine/blood as "elements" of the "covenant sacrifice." By interpreting the bread and the cup in this way, Mark portrays Jesus' death *as* the covenant sacrifice. The eucharistic meal thus mediates the redeeming power of Jesus' atoning death, and it also symbolizes participation in that death.

The blood ritual was an essential element of covenant institution in Exodus 24. The blood of the sacrifice was applied to both covenant partners (with the altar representing the divine partner – Exod. 24:6b), thereby connecting them with one another. The people were full partakers of the covenant agreement only after ratifying the covenant verbally when the written law was read to them. The covenant was then established by sprinkling the "blood of the covenant" on the people. Through this act they were dedicated as the holy people of Yahweh.[59]

The blood is not yet interpreted as atonement in Exodus 24:8. Targum Onkelos, however, alludes to atonement when it translates Exodus 24.8: "Moses took the blood and sprinkled (it) on the altar as an atonement for the people." It further reads, "This is the blood of the covenant which the Lord has

---

[56] Evans, "Jesus and Zechariah's Messianic Hope," in Chilton and Evans (eds.), *Authenticating the Activities of Jesus* (Leiden: E. J. Brill, 1999), 386, refers to Zech. 9:11 and especially to the eschatological perspective of Zechariah in this text.

[57] Gnilka, *Das Evangelium nach Markus*, 239.

[58] Kertelge, "Markusevangelium," 77.

[59] Noth, *Das zweite Buch Mose*, 160–61.

made with you concerning these things." Targum Jeruschalmi I has almost the same wording.[60]

The Markan phrase "which is being poured out for many" (τò ἐκχυννόμενον ὑπὲρ πολλῶν) explicitly refers to Isaiah 53:12,[61] where the death of Yahweh's Servant has an atoning dimension.[62] Mark 14:24 states that the blood of the covenant is poured out *for many* (ὑπὲρ πολλῶν). The Qumran community interpreted "the many" in a narrow sense, referring to their community. In the context of Isaiah's Servant songs, however, the term is not limited only to Israel – the Servant is called "the light for all nations" (cf. Isa. 42:6; 49:7–8). Atonement, therefore, carries a universal orientation in Mark;[63] the new covenant is of universal significance.[64]

If Gnilka's premise is correct,[65] the Last Supper is in a sense a conflation of the meals that Jesus had not only with his disciples, but also with sinners and various others during his earthly life. According to the synoptic tradition, one of Jesus' main rhetorical motifs is the eschatological meal of all nations at Zion (Isa. 25:6–8; cf. Luke 13:29/Matt. 8:11; Luke 14:15–24/Matt. 22:1–14). The farewell meal in Jerusalem is influenced by the image of this meal and differs from Jesus' previous table fellowships with tax collectors and sinners particularly in that it was a Passover meal to which Jesus invited only the Twelve.

---

[60] Strack and Billerbeck, *Das Evangelium nach Matthäus erläutert aus Talmud und Midrasch* (München: C. H. Beck'sche Verlagsbuchhandlung, 1926), 991.

[61] Cf. Hahn, *Christologische Hoheitstitel*, 61.

[62] Cf. McKenzie, *Second Isaiah* (New York: Doubleday, 1968), 136.

[63] Gnilka, *Das Evangelium nach Markus*, 246, is correct here, as opposed to Pesch, who limits this phrase (ὑπὲρ πολλῶν) to all of Israel (Pesch, *Das Markusevangelium*, 360).

[64] In his analysis of Old Testament motifs in the early church's transmission of the Lord's Supper, Ferdinand Hahn points out that we should use discretion when speaking about the "atoning sacrifice" of Jesus. The sacrificial character of Jesus' death is emphasized in only a few New Testament passages. Neither the "substitution" (ὑπέρ) phrases nor the logion in Mark 10:45 contain sacrificial language. Although it is impossible to deny the notion of an atoning covenant sacrifice in Mark 14:24, this does not apply to the Lord's Supper logia in general. The Pauline/Lukan version which links the atoning sacrifice with the bread, "this is my body (given) for you" (τοῦτό μού ἐστιν τὸ σῶμα τὸ ὑπὲρ ὑμῶν [διδόμενον]), contains no indication of the sacrificial character of Jesus' atonement. In Mark 14:24, the notion of sacrifice has developed through the combination of the atonement motif with the covenant concept. The idea of sacrifice is secondary. The basic motif of the cup logia in the Markan version is the substitutionary atonement for many. The blood of Christ was shed for this purpose.

[65] See Gnilka, *Das Evangelium nach Markus*, 244. Robbins, "Last Meal: Preparation, Betrayal, and Absence (Mark 14:12–15)," in Kelber (ed.), *The Passion in Mark* (Philadelphia: Fortress Press, 1976), 21–40, maintains: "My thesis is that his final meal completes the drama of the Feeding Stories (Mk. 6:30–44; 8:1–10)."

They represent, according to Luke 22:28–30/Matthew 19:28, the eschatological people of the twelve tribes.[66]

Verse 24 unfolds the meaning of the statement that Jesus is establishing the
new covenant through his blood in a twofold way. First, contextually speaking,
the circle of the Twelve can be seen as the "patriarchs of the new covenant"[67]
and thus representative of the new people of God. Second, the "for many"
mentioned here, as explained above, includes the unrighteous and the heathen
nations and is thus of universal significance. Christ, having died and been
raised, will appear victoriously as the regent of God's kingdom, revealing God's
kingship across the entire stage of creation history. In this sense God's universal
kingship and the new covenant are intimately related.[68]

Verse 25 relates that final meal to the eschatological meal that is to be held in
perfect fulfillment in heaven. Already in Isaiah 24 – 27 the meal at Sinai is
related to the eschatological meal with the nations at Zion. This scenario, as
described in Isaiah 24:6–8, is connected typologically in Isaiah 24:23 with
Exodus 24:9–11.[69] Jesus' words in Mark 14:25 are full of hope and foreshadow
a general resurrection. He will not drink wine again[70] until he drinks it anew in
the kingdom of God. Jesus looks forward to the imminent revelation of the
kingly rule of God that will not take place without him.

2. Jesus' proclamation of the kingdom of God in connection with the appointment of the Twelve

The motif of the "kingdom of God" (βασιλεία τοῦ θεοῦ), in conjunction with
the "appointment of the Twelve," plays a significant role in the Jesus tradition.[71] It is important that these motifs are also prominent in the Lord's Supper
tradition,[72] for they link the Lord's Supper tradition with the rest of the Jesus
tradition.[73]

---

[66] Cf. Stuhlmacher, *Biblische Theologie des Neuen Testaments. Band 1: Grundlegung von Jesus zu Paulus* (Göttingen: Vandenhoeck & Ruprecht, 1992), 133.

[67] Gnilka, *Das Evangelium nach Markus*, 249.

[68] Gnilka, *Das Evangelium nach Markus*, 246. Weinfeld, "ברית," in *ThWAT* (Stuttgart: W. Kohlhammer, 1973), 804–806, points out that new developments in covenant research prominently underline the notion of the kingly rule of God.

[69] See Stuhlmacher, *Biblische Theologie*, 140.

[70] "The fruit of the vine" is a Semitic idiom.

[71] Cf. Stanton, *The Gospels and Jesus* (Oxford/New York/Toronto: Oxford University Press, 1989), 187–203.

[72] Cf. 3.1, above.

[73] Ferdinand Hahn ("Die alttestamentlichen Motive," 367–68) made the following observations about the relationship between kingdom and covenant in the Lord's Supper tradition. He has pointed out that it is undisputed that the Lord's Supper

God's rule is profoundly reflected not only in Jesus' table fellowship with his disciples, but also in Jesus' meals with tax collectors and sinners.[74] Although God's rule in its fruition is envisioned by Jesus as a future reality, it is effectively realized for those participating in table fellowship with Jesus in the present as a prolepsis of that universal fulfillment.[75]

2.1 Jesus' proclamation of the kingdom of God

In Matthew (26:29) and Mark (14:25) Jesus states that he will not drink from the fruit of the vine again until the day he drinks it anew in the kingdom of God ("in the kingdom of my father," Matt. 26:29). "Jesus' Last Supper becomes, hence, the last expression of the proclamation of the coming basileia of God, which, after the foundational words in 1:15, dominates the entire gospel of Mark."[76] Interestingly, Jesus underscores this promise in Luke by repeating it twice (22:16, 18).[77]

---

[73] (*Continued*) tradition is very old and that the atonement notion is strongly embedded in this tradition. The question that arises, though, is how the covenant concept entered the Lord's Supper tradition. How did the connection develop between the idea of a new covenant and the death of Jesus? We must pay some attention to the logion in Luke 22:28–30 here. Matthew 19:28 is a somewhat easier parallel to this difficult piece of transmission. Probably two different logia were intermingled in Luke. When we set aside for a moment the motif of sitting on thrones and judging Israel (Luke 22:30b, which appears also in Matt. 19:28), as well as the later added introduction in v. 28, we receive the odd statement, found only in Luke: "And I confer on you a kingdom just as my Father conferred one on me, so that you may eat and drink at my table in my kingdom" (Luke 22:29, 30a). Although in this form it is not an authentic Jesus logion (against it point the "my Father" and especially "my kingdom" according to Hahn), the expression contains some ancient features. In the Septuagint, one finds "confer (decree) a covenant" (διατίθεσθαι διαθήκην) as the equivalent for "to make a covenant" (כרת ברית). The phrase "to confer a covenant" (διατίθεσθαι διαθήκην) is parallel to "restore a kingdom" (ἀποκαθιστάνειν βασιλείαν) (Acts 1:6). Hence, the covenant notion in its characteristic connection with the kingdom notion is, according to Hahn, indisputable for the logion in Luke 22:29, 30a. Probably, Luke 22:15–20 and vv. 28–30 were already combined in the special material that Luke included. This would then mean that the covenant concept was not only related to the death of Jesus, but that it also had found its place in the Lord's Supper tradition quite early.

[74] Cf. Lichtenberger, "'Bund' in der Abendmhalsüberlieferung," in Avemarie and Lichtenberger, *Bund und Tora*, 218.

[75] Kollmann, *Ursprung und Gestalten der frühchristlichen Mahlfeier* (Göttingen: Vandenhoeck & Ruprecht, 1990), 237.

[76] Kertelge, "Markusevangelium," 78.

[77] Paul's version does not have the term "kingdom of God"; one finds, however, the statement: "for as often as you eat the bread and drink the cup you proclaim the

The motif of the kingdom of God constitutes the center of Jesus' proclamation.[78] His mission to establish the rule of God is not only reflected in his preaching – it pervades all of his activities.[79]

Jesus spoke at the same time of a present and a future coming of the kingdom of God.[80] In Mark 14:25, Jesus relates the expression "that day" (ἡ ἡμέρα ἐκείνη) to the kingdom of God: "I tell you the truth, I will not drink again of the fruit of the vine until that day when I drink it anew in the kingdom of God." "That day" is, according to the Old Testament background of the term, the day when God will definitively encompass history (cf. Zech. 12:3; 13:1, 2; Joel 4:1). Jesus' announcements of the kingdom do not focus primarily upon an apocalyptic in-breaking of God, but point rather to God's presence and to the sense in which that presence is at once a participation in this future.[81]

Mark 14:25 includes a prophecy that both foretells Jesus' death and confirms the surety of his temporal return on the day that the kingdom is fully

---

[77] (Continued) Lord's death until he comes." Goppelt, Theologie des Neuen Testaments (Göttingen: Vandenhoeck & Ruprecht, 1985), 96, points out that the term "kingdom of God" was primarily personally oriented in Jesus' preaching and was therefore suppressed in the early church for theological reasons. Beside the request for the coming of the kingdom, there is the prayer: "Our Lord, come" (1 Cor. 16:22; Rev. 22:20). That is why Paul proclaims the "Lord" (κύριος) and almost never mentions the kingdom of God.

[78] Cf. Lindemann, "Herrschaft Gottes/Reich Gottes IV.2: Herrschaft Gottes bei Jesus und im Urchristentum," in TRE XV (Berlin/New York: Walter de Gruyter, 1986), 201; Gnilka, Jesus von Nazaret: Botschaft und Geschichte (Freiburg/Basel/Wien: Herder, 1990), 141; Goppelt, Theologie des Neuen Testaments, 95. Cf. also Chilton, "The Kingdom of God in Recent Discussion," in Chilton and Evans (eds.), Studying the Historical Jesus: Evaluations of the State of Current Research (Leiden: E. J. Brill, 1994), 255: "Consensus that the kingdom of God was the burden of Jesus' message ... provides our point of departure." Evans, "Authenticating the Activities of Jesus," in Chilton and Evans, Authenticating the Activities of Jesus, 6–25, lists ten activities of Jesus that he believes to be authentic. The second is: "Jesus was a Galilean who proclaimed the kingdom of God."

[79] See Gnilka, Jesus von Nazaret, 141.

[80] Chilton, "The Kingdom of God in Recent Discussion," 255, points out that since 1892, when Johannes Weiss published his Die Predigt Jesu vom Reich Gottes, the chronological aspect of Jesus' eschatology has been discussed: "Conventionally, scholars align themselves behind one of three options: a consistent eschatology, in which the kingdom is conceived of as wholly in the future; a realized eschatology, in which it is held to be available in the present (usually, within the ministry of Jesus himself); and an inaugurated or self-realizing eschatology, in which the kingdom is understood to have commenced, but also to await full disclosure."

[81] Cf. Goppelt, Theologie des Neuen Testaments, 105–106.

realized.[82] Here, as elsewhere, Jesus' preaching about the coming of God's rule is his *characteristic way of speaking about God.*[83]

The phrase "kingdom of God" in Jesus' message points to God's *merciful activity in salvation.* Jesus often depicted the salvific character of the kingdom figuratively using the image of a meal (cf. Matt. 8:11; Luke 14:15–24; also Mark 2:18–19).[84] While all of contemporary Judaism – including John the Baptist – strongly accentuated the eschatological dimension of judgment, Jesus does not put this emphasis at the forefront of his message. His vision of the kingdom of God is imbued with universal eschatological hope – a salvific circle that extends beyond Israel (cf. Matt. 8:11; Luke 13:28–29).[85] The kingdom and the covenant are coterminous with creation: "As 'king' [God] brings salvation to that to which he gave life."[86]

For contemporary Jewish apocalyptic, God was the hidden king who, in the imminent future, would be revealed to the whole world as the cosmic Judge. In light of this coming judgment, the observation of the Torah was seen to be of utmost importance in attaining salvation. The Torah was understood as God's eternal legal will – the normative standard for both Israel and the nations in the coming rule of God.[87]

The Jesus tradition, however, did not exclude from the kingdom of God those who did not observe the Torah. The Torah does not play a determinative role in the coming kingdom. In fact, Jesus' own message regarding the kingdom itself replaces the emphasis on Torah.[88] This message underscored the dynamic personal presence of God – a concept well understood in those

---

[82] Cf. Gnilka, *Jesus von Nazaret,* 284.

[83] Lindemann, "Herrschaft Gottes/Reich Gottes," 206.

[84] Cf. Schürmann, *Jesu ureigener Tod: Exegetische Besinnungen und Ausblick* (Freiburg/ Basel/Wien: Herder, 1975), 83.

[85] Matt. 8:11: "I say to you that many will come from the east and the west, and will take their places at the feast with Abraham, Isaac and Jacob in the kingdom of heaven."

Luke 13:28–29: "There will be weeping there, and gnashing of teeth, when you see Abraham, Isaac and Jacob and all the prophets in the kingdom of God, but you yourselves thrown out. People will come from east and west and north and south, and will take their places at the feast in the kingdom of God."

[86] Lindemann, "Herrschaft Gottes/Reich Gottes," 207, who quotes Schillebeeckx.

[87] Cf. 2 Baruch 77:15; 48:47; 2 Esdras 9:37. For rabbinic texts, see Billerbeck, *Die Briefe des Neuen Testaments und die Offenbarung Johannis: Erläutert aus Talmud und Midrasch,* I, 5th edn (München: C. H. Beck'sche Verlagsbuchhandlung, 1926), 245ff.

[88] See Lindemann, "Herrschaft Gottes/Reich Gottes," 207. Sanders, *Paul and Palestinian Judaism,* 422, points out that although Torah played a significant role in Palestinian Judaism (200 B.C. – A.D. 200), election and salvation in the end did not depend on human efforts but on God's grace.

times.[89] In this regard, research has shown links between Jesus' preaching and Sabbath hymns from Qumran, the Targumim and the book of Daniel.[90] For Jesus, the kingdom of God was a way of speaking about God's way of creating, rescuing and ruling – both in the present and the future – through power, justice and grace.

2.2 The circle of the Twelve

The best known of Jesus' disciples are simply called "the Twelve" in Mark (3:14; 6:7; 9:35; 10:32; 11:11; 14:17).[91] Matthew speaks of twelve disciples (10:1) and, once, of twelve apostles (10:2). In Luke's writings, the phrase "twelve apostles" is prominent (Luke 6:13; 9:10; 17:5; 22:14; 24:9–10). However, one must distinguish between the Twelve and the apostles. The apostles – as seen from a post-Easter perspective – comprise a larger group. The ancient creed in 1 Corinthians 15:3–7, for example, differentiates between the Twelve and "all the apostles" (v. 7).

The question has been raised concerning how and when the circle of the Twelve developed. Was the circle established only after Easter, or did Jesus himself create this group?

In light of the Judas tradition, it seems probable that Jesus himself collected the Twelve. It is unlikely that a group constructed after Easter could be so uniformly interpolated retrospectively into the life of the historical Jesus, or that Judas, who delivered Jesus into the hands of his enemies, would be repeatedly numbered as "one of the Twelve" (see, for example, Mark 14:10, 20, 43; Matt. 26:14). Also, the founding of such a group of twelve as a prophetic sign is highly consistent with Jesus' vision and activity.

It is therefore likely that the constitution of this group is one of the programmatic acts of Jesus. The number "twelve" is of great symbolic significance: the twelve messengers correspond to the twelve tribes of Israel (Matt.

---

[89] Cf. Chilton, *God in Strength: Jesus' Announcement of the Kingdom* (Freistadt: Verlag F. Plöchl, 1979), where he interprets Jesus' kingdom message in the light of the Targumim, especially the Targum of Isaiah.

[90] Cf. Chilton, "The Kingdom of God in Recent Discussion," 279–80: "The kingdom of God was a term of reference Jesus inherited from his milieu, instanced in the Songs and the Targumim, as well as in Daniel." In his research overview, Chilton points out the contribution of Schwemer (among others) and his study of God as King and his kingly rule in the Sabbath hymns of Qumran. He also underlines the various dimensions of the kingdom of God in the Psalms and in Daniel (cf., e.g., Dan. 2:44; 4:31c).

[91] Cf. Schmahl, "Die erste Bestimmung der Zwölf im Markusevangelium," in Kampling and Söding (eds.), *Ekklesiologie des Neuen Testaments: Für Karl Kertelge* (Freiburg/Basel/Wien: Herder, 1996), 133–38.

19:28 par.; Luke 22:29–30) and represent the eschatological community of the saved. At Jesus' time, only two-and-a-half tribes lived in Palestine – namely, Judah, Benjamin and half of the tribe of Levi. Since the fall of the northern kingdom, the other nine-and-a-half tribes had been considered lost. Only during the period of eschatological renewal would God restore the fullness of the twelve tribes. The fact that Jesus had "twelve" in his circle of disciples is therefore symbolic of the re-establishment of the eschatological people of God. "The Twelve as a body are the focal point of a renewed Israel."[92]

Jesus allows the Twelve to participate in his own authority. They partake in his activities of healing and preaching and are given the task of carrying the gospel to the nations. Like Jesus, they call for repentance (cf. Mark 6:12) and proclaim an ethic in keeping with the imminent advent of the "kingdom of God."[93]

Early Judaism maintained the hope that, during the messianic period, Israel would be restored to its fullness. One finds, for example, an eschatologically symbolic complement of twelve men (and three priests) representing Israel's laity in Qumran (1QS VIII, 1–2a: "in the Council of the Community there shall be twelve men and three priests, perfectly versed in all that is revealed of the Law"; cf. also 1QM II, 2). In the Pharisaic context, a complement of twelve was considered to be an "inner circle" of special significance. A "climate" had developed in Jewish thinking in which "Israel" – represented by the symbolic number "twelve" – held general eschatological significance.[94]

Flavius Josephus reports, in his idealizing way, that when the Israelites returned from the Babylonian exile and built a new temple, they sacrificed twelve rams in accordance with the number of the tribes (*Ant.* 11, 107). In the Letter of Aristeas (47–50) we read that the Jews sent representatives from each of the twelve tribes to participate in the translation of the Bible into Greek and to confirm the reliability of the law. The "Testaments of the Twelve Patriarchs" also underline the significance of the number "twelve."

Jesus' actions clearly harmonize with this context of eschatological expectation. A reference to the symbolism of the circle of the Twelve may be found already in the (pre-Markan[95]) statement of Mark 3:14: "he appointed twelve, *so that they might be with him*" (καὶ ἐποίησεν δώδεκα, ἵνα ὦσιν μετ' αὐτοῦ).[96] Jesus'

---

[92] Berger, "Kirche II: Neues Testament," in *TRE* XVIII (Berlin/New York: Walter de Gruyter, 1989), 210.

[93] Schmahl, *Die Zwölf im Markusevangelium: Eine redaktionsgeschichtliche Untersuchung* (Trier: Paulinus-Verlag, 1974), 143.

[94] Berger, "Kirche II: Neues Testament," 210; Schmahl, *Die Zwölf im Markusevangelium*, 40.

[95] See Gnilka, *Das Evangelium nach Markus*, I, 136–38.

[96] Cf. Stock, *Boten aus dem Mit-Ihm-Sein* (Rome: Biblical Institute Press, 1975), who takes the title of his book from this verse.

disciples – especially the Twelve – were appointed by Jesus to proclaim God's rule together with him.

The Twelve function as a visible sign of God's "new beginning" with Israel. It is therefore significant that the inauguration of the new covenant is announced during the Lord's Supper in the presence of the Twelve.[97] The Twelve signal not only God's new covenant beginning, but also its fulfillment in the New Jerusalem:

> It had a great, high wall with twelve gates, and with twelve angels at the gates. On the gates were written the names of the twelve tribes of Israel … The wall of the city had twelve foundations, and on them were the names of the twelve apostles of the Lamb. (Rev. 21:12, 14)

2.3 Preliminary conclusion

The message of the "kingdom of God" is the message of God's gracious salvation. In continuity with God's act of creation, one may also think of it as a proclamation of re-creation, a "making all things new" (Rev. 21:5; cf. 2 Cor. 5:17). It is the message of a king who brings salvation to those to whom he has given life. The last confirmation of Jesus' kingdom message occurs in the Lord's Supper tradition in the midst of the circle of the Twelve. The circle is a prophetic sign reflecting God's intention to eschatologically reconstitute Israel. Significantly, it is also in the presence of the Twelve that Jesus announces the inauguration of the new covenant.

3. Can the redemptive significance of Jesus' death be based on his own words?[98]

3.1 The problem

The redemptive death of Jesus, interpreted in the light of Easter, was definitively significant for the early church. The cross is the main lens through which

---

[97] Cf. Berger, "Kirche II: Neues Testament," 209–10; Collins, "The Twelve," in *ABD*, VI (New York: Doubleday, 1992), 670–71; Gnilka, *Jesus von Nazaret*, 187–89; Jeremias, *Neutestamentliche Theologie* (Gütersloh: Gütersloher Verlagshaus Gerd Mohn, 1971), 225–26; Klauck, "Die Auswahl der Zwölf (Mk 3,13–19)," in Klauck (ed.), *Gemeinde. Amt. Sakrament. Neutestamentliche Perspektive* (Würzburg: Echter Verlag, 1989), 135.

[98] This question needs to be asked in the light of the research on the "historical Jesus." In the framework of this study, the emphasis will be on the words spoken at the institution of the Lord's Supper.

Paul interprets the life of the earthly Jesus. Nevertheless, the question of Jesus' understanding of his death has taken center stage in many studies on the "historical" Jesus.[99] Many researchers are of the opinion that the greatest difficulty in attempting to reconstruct an image of the Jesus of history is ambiguity about *how he understood his own end; his death.*[100]

In his Heidelberg academic treatise of 1959, Rudolf Bultmann points out that we don't know if Jesus purposely engineered and embraced his suffering and death on the cross because, from the point of view of critical study, the New Testament predictions of his suffering and death must be understood as *vaticinia ex eventu* ("predictions originating out of a situation"). The fact that Roman soldiers crucified him cannot be perceived as an inevitable consequence of Jesus' mission; it eventuated from the mistaken assumption that his agenda was political. From a historical perspective, his death was a tragic mistake and without meaning. One should not, according to Bultmann, exclude the possibility that Jesus simply failed.

Bultmann's students, such as Ernst Fuchs and Günther Bornkamm, do not adopt their teacher's historical skepticism in quite the same way. They posit that, on his way to Jerusalem, Jesus reckoned with the possibility of his death. Still, they say, Jesus' death has no ultimate significance because (like Bultmann) Fuchs and Bornkamm see Jesus' predictions of his death, including the Lord's Supper accounts, as traditions created by the early church.[101]

The shift in the discussion of these issues, following scholarly attempts to move beyond the dominant influence of Bultmann, is noteworthy. For example, during the editors' conference of *Evangelische Theologie* (October 12–14, 1972), Hans-Georg Link voiced uneasiness about the priority given to the eschatological perspective at the cost of the historical perspective.[102] Wolfgang Schrage pointed out that Jesus' cross is interpreted in the Gospels *in the light of* the historical events in his life. Jesus' earthly life constitutes the grounds for theological reflection on his death on the cross. It was suggested at the conference that in the future it would no longer be possible to offer a persuasive interpretation of the cross apart from close attention to the historical activity of Jesus. The position of earlier liberal theology that Jesus had been surprised by his violent death does not give us a realistic understanding of Jesus' life.

---

[99] Cf. Gnilka, "Wie urteilte Jesus über seinen Tod?," in Kertelge (ed.), *Der Tod Jesu: Deutungen im Neuen Testament* (Freiburg/Basel/Wien: Herder, 1976), 13.

[100] Bultmann, "Das Verhältnis der urchristlichen Christusbotschaft zum historischen Jesus," in Dinkler (ed.), *Exegetica: Aufsätze zur Erforschung des Neuen Testaments* (Tübingen: J. C. B. Mohr [Paul Siebeck], 1967), 452.

[101] Cf. Stuhlmacher, *Biblische Theologie*, 127.

[102] Cf. Link, "Zur Kreuzestheologie: Gegenwärtige Probleme einer Kreuzestheologie. Ein Bericht über die Herausgebertagung der *EvTh* (12.–14. Oktober 1972)," *EvT* 33 (1973), 343.

The narratives regarding the institution of the Lord's Supper in the Gospels and in 1 Corinthians retrospectively reflect on the person and work of Jesus of Nazareth *from the Easter perspective.*[103] The all-important eucharistic life of the early church thus cannot be understood apart from the dimension of Easter. Although, as we have said, the last meal of Jesus should be considered in the context of the other eschatological table fellowships of Jesus during his earthly ministry, an interpretive approach that ignores Easter is insufficient to explain the Last Supper tradition. The certainty that the *exalted Lord is present* at the eucharistic celebration – which was decisively important for the early celebrants of the liturgy – is only explicable in light of the Easter experience.[104]

The eschatological table fellowship of Jesus points to the "already" salvific dimension of the in-breaking kingdom of God (cf. the motif of the wedding feast in Mark 2:18–19). Jesus sups even with the outcasts and the needy. Tax collectors and sinners are the special targets of this ministry (cf. Mark 2:17). Table fellowship was the primary expression of acceptance in Jesus' cultural milieu. Through Jesus' presence at such meals, God draws near to the lost and future salvation becomes a present reality. Jesus' statement at the end of the Lord's Supper logia in Mark 14:25 affirms that this form of fellowship will be continued and consummated in the eschaton:[105] "I tell you the truth, I will not drink again of the fruit of the vine until that day when I drink it anew in the kingdom of God."

---

[103] For the Lord's Supper texts, what Christina Hoegen-Rohls has demonstrated for John's Gospel holds true – a retrospective view from Easter had a profound effect on the interpretation of Jesus' life (cf. Hoegen-Rohls, *Der nachösterliche Johannes: Die Abschiedsreden als hermeneutischer Schlüssel zum vierten Evangelium* [Tübingen: J. C. B. Mohr (Paul Siebeck), 1996], 1–2).

[104] Cf. Hahn, "Zum Stand der Erforschung des urchristlichen Herrenmahls," *EvT* 35 (1975), 554. Hahn suggests a three-fold root of the Lord's Supper: the meal fellowships of Jesus during his earthly ministry; the last meal of Jesus with his disciples; and the "appearance meals," which were very important for the disciples to experience the presence of the Risen One during their meals together ("Thesen zur Frage einheitsstiftender Elemente in Lehre und Praxis des urchristlichen Herrenmahls," in Hahn [ed.], *Exegetische Beiträge zum ökumenischen Gespräch: Gesammelte Aufsätze* [Göttingen: Vandenhoeck & Ruprecht, 1986], 233).

[105] Cf. Hahn, "Die alttestamentlichen Motive," 345–46. Since Jesus held many different meal fellowships with his disciples, as well as with tax collectors and sinners, Lichtenberger ("'Bund' in der Abendmhalsüberlieferung," in Avemarie and Lichtenberger, *Bund und Tora*, 217) points to the wide consensus that the Lord's Supper has to be seen within this broad context. For a detailed discussion of Jesus' meal fellowships, see Bolyki, *Jesu Tischgemeinschaften* (Tübingen: Mohr Siebeck, 1998).

Hermann Patsch concluded his monograph on the Lord's Supper with these words of Albert Schweitzer: "The problem of the Lord's Supper is the problem of the historical Jesus."[106] Reflecting on the words of Jesus during his earthly ministry, Ferdinand Hahn breaks the problem down into three textual issues: (1) selection; (2) shaping or re-shaping; and (3) the reinterpretation of the Jesus tradition.[107] According to Hahn the words spoken at the institution of the Lord's Supper, like most of Jesus' words in the Gospels, consist of mixed forms. They were reshaped and reformed through retelling and have come to their current liturgical form in this way.[108]

Hahn's remarks remind us that the impact of the events of Good Friday and Easter on the New Testament writings must not be underestimated. The story of Jesus – including the institution of the Lord's Supper – is unquestionably presented retrospectively from the Easter perspective and reflects the conviction that the new covenant has become an eschatological reality with Jesus' resurrection.[109] The search for details about the historical Jesus, including his self-understanding, thus *need not be in contrast to the Jesus image that the Gospel writers have portrayed, but can be quite in agreement with it.*

For example, Hahn[110] points out that as Jesus proclaimed the in-breaking rule of God, he voiced sweeping criticisms of the law and culture both implicitly and explicitly. In the context of the religious and political totalitarianism in which he spoke, this led inevitably to his death. It would seem reasonable to assume that Jesus was aware of the implications of his challenge to these two powerful institutions.[111]

---

[106] H. Patsch, *Abendmahl und historischer Jesus,* Calwer Theologische Monographien 1 (Stuttgart: Calwer, 1972).

[107] Cf. Hahn, "Methodologische Überlegungen zur Rückfrage nach Jesus," in Kertelge (ed.), *Rückfrage nach Jesus* (Freiburg/Basel/Wien: Herder, 1974), 13–26.

[108] Gnilka, "Wie urteilte Jesus über seinen Tod?" 20, observes that the question that must be analyzed is this: in the transmission of Jesus' words, what is the relationship between authentic Jesus material and the new developments? The clarification of this question would reveal tendencies explaining the way original materials have developed.

[109] Cf. Hahn, *Christologische Hoheitstitel,* 451.

[110] Cf. Hahn, "Das Verständnis des Opfers im Neuen Testament," in Lehmann and Schlink (eds.), *Das Opfer Jesu Christi und seine Gegenwart in der Kirche: Klärungen zum Opfercharakter des Herrenmahles* (Freiburg: Herder; Göttingen: Vandenhoeck & Ruprecht, 1983), 66–9, which I largely follow here.

[111] Researchers who investigate the historical Jesus are of the opinion that it will not be possible methodologically to analyze Jesus' self-understanding in the texts, but scholars can attempt to search for his sense of call. It is asserted that one must be careful not to search for Jesus' self-understanding in heavily christological statements within the message of the early church. On the other hand, it is imperative to

Luke 13:33 is an important text to consider in this regard: "In any case, I must keep going today and tomorrow and the next day – for surely no prophet can die outside Jerusalem!" It is not likely that the early church would call Jesus a "prophet," so this logion may have come from Jesus himself. The passage contains material that can only be found in Luke's Gospel, and the way it has been formulated underscores its claim to authenticity. Luke 13:31–33 strongly suggests that Jesus did reckon with the possibility of death in Jerusalem, and that he conceived this death in terms of martyrdom. In the following Q logion (v. 34), Jesus cries out: "O Jerusalem, Jerusalem, you who kill the prophets and stone those sent to you, how often I have longed to gather your children together, as a hen gathers her chicks under her wings, but you were not willing!"

Luke 9:58 is another Q logion (also appearing in the gospel of Thomas) that demonstrates Jesus' awareness of the precariousness of his life: "Jesus replied, 'Foxes have holes and birds of the air have nests, but the Son of Man has no place to lay his head.'" Mark 10:45 states: "For even the Son of Man did not come to be served, but to serve, and to give his life as a ransom for many." The statement about the giving of his life "as a ransom for many" (λύτρον ἀντὶ πολλῶν) is often regarded as an interpretative exposition of the first part of the logion.[112] In Luke 22:7, Jesus affirms: "I am among you as one who serves."

---

[111] (*Continued*) analyze what issues have caused the emergence of a specific christological topic. These scholars allege that the explicit predictions of suffering in Mark 8:31, 9:31 and 10:32–33, and the short versions in Mark 14:21a, 41b, with their parallels, need to be disregarded for methodological reasons since early post-Easter Christology has already left its influence here.

For a discussion of fundamental questions about the understanding of Jesus' death as mediating salvation, see Vögtle, "Grundfragen der Diskussion um das heilsmittlerische Todesverständnis Jesu," in Vögtle (ed.), *Offenbarungsgeschehen und Wirkungsgeschichte: Neutestamentliche Beiträge* (Freiburg/Basel/Wien: Herder, 1985), 141–67.

[112] Cf. Kertelge, "Die soteriologischen Aussagen in der urchristlichen Abendmahlsüberlieferung und ihre Beziehung zum geschichtlichen Jesus," *TTZ* 81 (1972), 201. However, Roloff, "Anfänge der soteriologischen Deutung des Todes Jesu (Mk. X. 45 und Lk. XXII. 27)," *NTS* 19 (1972), 50–52, points out that the connection between the atonement motif and the motif of Jesus' "serving" (διακονεῖν) is very strong and quite old, and that it reflects an understanding of Jesus' death that was developed very early in the framework of the Lord's Supper celebration. He believes that v. 45b cannot be seen as a secondary (later) appendix by Mark, but that 45a and 45b together originate from the Lord's Supper tradition and go back to an Aramaic original. Wischmeyer, "Herrschen als Dienen – Mk 10,41–45," *ZNW* 90 (1999), 28–44 (here 28), agrees with this thesis: "Verses 42–45 can be understood as a string of verses already connected together in which Jesus

The motif of serving like a *slave* that characterized Jesus' earthly mission (cf. John 13:5–17) provided an interpretive key for the early church. In particular, they noticed the correspondence with the "service" of the Servant of Yahweh in Isaiah 53.[113] This key correspondence is only complete and unambiguous from a perspective in which Jesus, like the servant of Isaiah 53, also gives his life as a "ransom for many." And, indeed, this takes us very close to Jesus' own self-understanding.[114]

Jesus saw his entire work as commissioned by God. He perceived his ministry as the ultimate call to relational wholeness with God – an invitation to trust and obedience that brought forgiveness of sins, grace and salvation. It would seem fair to assume, then, that he viewed his possible fate in Jerusalem in the light of his own trust and obedience toward his Father. Jesus was willing to serve everyone whom God would send in his way[115] – and to serve them to the uttermost (John 15:13; cf. 1 John 3:16).

The logia referring to Jesus' call to discipleship deserve special attention.[116] Just as Jesus included the disciples in his own mission of proclamation and even in the performing of miracles (Matt. 10:7–8 par.; Luke 10:9), he expected them to share his attitude toward life and death. In this context, Mark 8:34–37 is especially significant:

---

[112] (*Continued*) understood his own person and his destiny (his death) as a model for service. The serving refers primarily to Jesus' service at the table during the final farewell meal."

[113] Mark 10:45 par. contains an allusion to Isa. 43:3–4 and 53:11–12. The early Jewish tradition about a "ransom" and about the suffering of the Lord's Servant, according to Isa. 53, dominates the soteriological dimension of this passage (Stuhlmacher, *Biblische Theologie*, 120–22). Cf., however, Hooker, *Jesus and the Servant: The Influence of the Servant Concept of Deutero-Isaiah in the New Testament* (London: SPCK, 1959), 74–79, who questions the allusion to Isa. 53. For a discussion of the problem, see Janowski, "Er trug unsere Sünden: Jes 53 und die Dramatik der Stellvertretung," in Janowski and Stuhlmacher (eds.), *Der leidende Gottesknecht: Jesaja 53 und seine Wirkungsgeschichte mit einer Bibliographie zu Jes 53* (Tübingen: J. C. B. Mohr [Paul Siebeck], 1996), 27–48; Stuhlmacher, "Jes 53 in den Evangelien und in der Apostelgeschichte," in Janowski and Stuhlmacher, *Der leidende Gottesknecht*, 93–104; and Bellinger and Farmer (eds.), *Jesus and the Suffering Servant: Isaiah 53 and Christian Origins* (Harrisburg, PA: Trinity Press, 1998).

[114] Schweizer, *Jesus, das Gleichnis Gottes: Was wissen wir wirklich vom Leben Jesu?* (Göttingen: Vandenhoeck & Ruprecht, 1995), 63, believes it is possible that the form of Mark 10:45 goes back to Jesus himself. Schweizer would, however, assume with even more certainty the same about Luke 22:27. Cf. also Kertelge, "Die soteriologischen Aussagen in der urchristlichen Abendmahlsüberlieferung," 201.

[115] Cf. Schweizer, *Jesus, das Gleichnis Gottes*, 59–63.

[116] See Hahn, "Das Verständnis des Opfers im Neuen Testament," 67.

Then he called the crowd to him along with his disciples and said: 'If anyone would come after me, he must deny himself and take up his cross and follow me. For whoever wants to save his life will lose it, but whoever loses his life for me and for the gospel will save it. What good is it for a man to gain the whole world, yet forfeit his soul? Or what can a man give in exchange for his soul?'

The following questions – which, according to our analyses, can all be answered in the affirmative – summarize our investigation so far: Did Jesus seriously reckon with the possibility of a violent death? Did Jesus evince a willingness to suffer martyrdom? Was Jesus able to integrate such martyrdom with his core mission?[117] Did the kingdom ethos that Jesus taught his disciples reflect this integration?

Schürmann points out that both Jesus' *eschatological* proclamations and his *theological* teachings need to be taken seriously and read together. In the context of our question, this translates into the supposition that Jesus' attitude of trust and subservience toward his Father makes it quite conceivable that he chose to proceed with his commission from God to proclaim the kingdom, while remaining open to the possibility that God might choose to act salvifically through the surrender of his own life. If Jesus knew that he was commissioned to establish the new order and that God wanted his death, then nothing was more natural than the assumption that, according to God's will, the death was to come for the purpose of the realization of the new order.[118]

We can now move a step further and ask whether Jesus understood his potential self-sacrifice as effecting salvation for others.[119] Although the limits of historical questioning obviously restrict our ability to formulate an answer,[120] Jesus' involvement with sinners, offering salvation even until his last hour, suggests that he understood his death as holding salvific significance.[121] In the context of the Lord's Supper tradition, Mark 14:25 and Luke 22:18 demonstrate that Jesus looked through the dark night of death toward a glorious dawn. His eschatological word about the coming kingdom of God is filled with trust. It is a confirmation that not only did he accept his imminent violent death, but he also fully maintained his

---

[117] Hahn, "Das Verständnis des Opfers im Neuen Testament," 67, n. 68; Schürmann, *Jesu ureigener Tod*, 16–65, here 44.

[118] Schürmann, *Jesu ureigener Tod*, 45–46.

[119] Cf. Schürmann, *Jesu ureigener Tod*, 46–53.

[120] Gnilka, "Wie urteilte Jesus über seinen Tod?" 41, points out that in the end, it is not that important whether one articulates Jesus' life-affirming attitude with the theological concept of substitution and/or atonement, or in whatever other way. Cf. also Hahn, "Zum Stand der Forschung," 554.

[121] Cf. Schürmann, *Jesu ureigener Tod*, 49–50.

expectation regarding the kingdom, which was the focal point of his proc-lamation.[122]

Continuing in this vein, it is clear that Jesus saw himself not only as messen-ger of the kingdom, but also as the *bringer* of the kingdom. Similarly, Jesus saw his martyrdom not just as a testimonial act of obedience to God that carried moral significance, but also as an act that precipitated the coming of the king-dom salvifically.[123] This attitude is evidenced in Jesus' speech in the Upper Room concerning his death. It is not necessary to determine the exact words he used to articulate the eschatological promise, or to determine to what extent it remained implicit, to make this claim.[124]

Jesus accepted his death as an expression of the perfect will of his Father. An exceptional feature of Jesus' interpretation of his death is the fact that he links it to the presentation of a *gift* – of bread and wine.[125] This linkage, and the expla-nation that followed, distinguish the Last Supper from meals that Jesus shared with others during his earthly ministry. On the evening before his death Jesus *explained the significance* of the bread and the cup. At the center of the cup logia is the interpretation that it represents his atoning death, which is at once the establishment of a *new covenant*.[126] The bread logia indicate that Jesus under-stood his own death as a necessary breaking of his body for the benefit of his

---

[122] See Gnilka, *Jesus von Nazaret*, 283.

[123] See Gnilka, *Jesus von Nazaret*, 284–85.

[124] Cf. Schürmann, *Jesu ureigener Tod*, 59.

[125] Gnilka, *Jesus von Nazaret*, 286. Crossan, *The Historical Jesus: The Life of a Mediterra-nean Jewish Peasant* (Edinburgh: T&T Clark, 1991), 360–67, denies a final meal in the life of Jesus and considers it to be the result of the creative imagination of the liturgic churches: "I do not presume any distinctive meal known beforehand, des-ignated specifically, or ritually programmed, as final and forever" (p. 361). Two of Schürmann's objections (Schürmann, *Jesu ureigener Tod*, 56–61) must be mentioned here: (1) He points out that the accentuated juxtaposition of the "breaking of the bread" at the beginning of the meal and the passing of the cup at the close of the same allow the inference that they have their origin in the last meal of Jesus, as these two acts were originally separated from each other by the course of a meal. The early church would have accentuated and eschatologically interpreted the meal itself rather than the two "gift gestures" of Jesus. (2) The disciples' behavior on Good Friday (cf. Mark 14:50) and afterwards (cf. Luke 24:21; John 20:19) demon-strates that before Easter they were not able to integrate into their thinking the notion that Jesus' death may have some salvific meaning. When searching for conti-nuity, one will find it in the life-affirming behavior of Jesus rather than in the disci-ples' faith. Evans, "Authenticating the Activities of Jesus," 20, lists Jesus' final meal as one of the authentic activities during his earthly ministry.

[126] Some scholars are of the opinion that this is an interpretation of the early church. Hahn, e.g., asserts that Mark 14:25 may have been the original cup logia.

disciples. Because Jesus breaks the bread himself, we can infer that he saw his death as a voluntary act. Jesus perceived his death as the ultimate giving of his very self for his own, in the context of the in-breaking rule of God, and from the perspective of its future fulfillment.[127]

---

[127]   Hahn, "Das Verständnis des Opfers im Neuen Testament," 69. The question of the most likely form in which the interpretation logia were historically transmitted has been discussed quite often. See, e.g., Lang, "Abendmahl und Bundesgedanke im Neuen Testament," *EvT* 35 (1975), 525–29; Merklein, "Erwägungen zur Überlieferungsgeschichte der neutestamentlichen Abendmahlstraditionen," *BZ* 21 (1977), 88–101, 235–44; Klauck, *Herrenmahl*, 297–32; Söding, "Das Mahl des Herrn: Zur Gestalt und Theologie der ältesten nachösterlichen Tradition," in Hilberath and Sattler, *Vorgeschmack*, 134–63; Feld, *Das Verständnis des Abendmahls* (Darmstadt: Wissenschaftliche Buchgesellschaft, 1976), 48–56; Hahn, "Die alttestamentlichen Motive," 340–42; also Backhaus, "Hat Jesus vom Gottesbund gesprochen?," *TGl* 86 (1996), 345.

Gnilka, *Jesus von Nazaret*, 287, and Kertelge, *Markusevangelium*, NEchtB, NT 2 (Würzburg: Echter Verlag, 1994), 142, believe that the older (and probably original) form of the cup logia possibly contained: "This cup is the new covenant in my blood." In Lang's (Lang, "Der Becher als Bundeszeichen: 'Bund' und 'neuer Bund' in den neutestamentlichen Abendmahlstexten," in Zenger, *Der Neue Bund im Alten*, 200, 205) opinion, however, the older version of the cup blessing, traceable to Jesus, only had: "This [the cup] is my blood." He points out that: (1) there is no reference to the covenant in the oldest accessible description of an early Christian Eucharist celebration in Justin Martyr around the middle of the second century, and (2) the tradition ascribes to Jesus a reference to the covenant only in the Lord's Supper context. Lang's reference to a Eucharist ceremony from the middle of the second century is not persuasive. For further critique on this contribution, see Backhaus, *Der neue Bund und das Werden der Kirche*, 296–97 and Lichtenberger, "'Bund' in der Abendmahlsüberlieferung," 220–21.

According to Merklein ("Erwägungen zur Überlieferungsgeschichte," 238), the Lord's Supper has been expanded from its original form – comprising the bread logia and Mark 14:23, 25 – to include a cup logion ("this is the cup of the new covenant in my blood" – τοῦτο τὸ ποτήριον ἡ καινὴ διαθήκη ἐν τῷ αἵματί μου). Klauck (*Herrenmah*, 314) also asks whether the bread logia and the eschatological perspective of Mark 14:25 would not already be sufficient to give meaning to the final meal. In this way one would also avoid a number of literary and tradition-historical annoyances.

Theißen and Merz (*Der historische Jesus: Ein Lehrbuch* [Göttingen: Vandenhoeck & Ruprecht, 1996], 373) point out that the historical Lord's Supper words behind the transmitted original form could have read: "This is my [or 'the'] body for you. This is the new covenant." The oldest tradition then additionally contains a reflection about the meaning of Jesus' death – about his blood.

3.2 The motif of the covenant

Our study is concerned primarily with the covenant motif in the Lord's Supper tradition. The New Testament covenant motif must be considered in the context of Old Testament and Jewish covenant concepts.[128] The term "covenant," when used theologically, points to an order of salvation granted and established by Yahweh, by which humans can orient their lives with the help of God.

Jeremiah 31:31–34 contains the promise of a "new covenant." The prophet recognizes the necessity of the new covenant, although he says little to define the sense in which it is new. No changes are projected regarding the content of Yahweh's self-revelation, but the relationship between God's will and human will is to undergo a dynamic alteration. The prophetic announcement also emphasizes that the saving power of the old ordinances have expired. Israel can find salvation only in Yahweh's new order of salvation.[129] The ineffectuality of the old covenant is announced in the Old Testament as well as in later Jewish writings. While the question of the exact nature of the new covenant remained unresolved,[130] expectations regarding its advent stayed alive.

Obviously the Christian new covenant tradition stems from from this expectation. It envisions Jesus' death as the trigger event through which the new redemptive order is established. In the Lord's Supper, persons may partake of the benefits of Jesus' atoning sacrifice in the power of the "new covenant."[131]

3.2.1 The authenticity of the covenant motif[132]

The term "covenant" (διαθήκη) occurs in Jesus' words in the Synoptic Gospels only in the Lord's Supper tradition.[133] While this is the case,[134] it must be noted that "covenant" does appear in *all* of the Lord's Supper traditions, despite the numerous differences between those varied traditions. The new covenant motif is integral to the Markan tradition (on which Matthew depends) and also

---

[128] Cf. Chapter 1, above; also Hahn, "Die alttestamentlichen Motive," 368–70.

[129] Cf. Hahn, "Die alttestamentlichen Motive," 369; von Rad, *Old Testament Theology*, II, 260–77.

[130] Hahn, "Die alttestamentlichen Motive," 369.

[131] Cf. Hahn, "Die alttestamentlichen Motive," 372.

[132] Cf. also the tradition-criticism questions about the "covenant" in Kirchschläger, "'Bund' in der Herrenmahltradition," 127–33.

[133] Cf. Lichtenberger, "'Bund' in der Abendmahlsüberlieferung," 217: "What tradition historical locus the formulations 'blood … of the covenant' … and 'new covenant in my blood' have and what meaning is given to them belong to the most controversial questions of New Testament exegetical and theological activity."

[134] Cf. Klauck, *Herrenmahl*, 314, n. 176.

to the Pauline/Lukan account. This fact argues for the authenticity of the motif.[135]

It must also be pointed out that the so-called "covenant silence" in the New Testament may, in fact, also argue for its authenticity.[136] Gerd Theißen and Annette Merz[137] point out that the making of a covenant is a unique act. When the "new covenant" was established by Jesus using the cup at the Last Supper, it was, at first, apparently valid only in that context and situation. To become a normative liturgical tradition, repetition was necessary – and Paul's command and instruction served this function. Because it was initially a unique event, it is no wonder that the "covenant" theme did not receive much attention in Jesus' proclamation. The observation that this term occurs only in isolated passages is, therefore, no argument against its authenticity.

Backhaus believes that the "covenant phrase" in the cup logia meets the criteria for historicity: namely, "repeated witness," "dissimilarity"[138] and "coherence":[139]

The criterion of repeated witness. The covenant motif is found in all the synoptic traditions, as well as in Paul.

The criterion of dissimilarity. This criterion appeals to a core corpus of Jesus sayings that cannot be explained either from the specific interests of early Christianity or from early Jewish precedents. With its eschatological claim to newness, the covenant motif in the interpretation of the cup fulfills this condition. The new covenant motif did not play an important role in the Judaism of Jesus' day or in other New Testament writings. A description of a new eschatological ברית/διαθήκη ("covenant") is rarely found in the writings of the

---

[135] Cf. Lichtenberger, "'Bund' in der Abendmhalsüberlieferung," 226. Evans, "Authenticating the Activities of Jesus," 22–23, underlines the likelihood of the authenticity of Jesus' statements about the covenant and God's rule. He relates these statements to Jesus' hope for a restoration of Israel. Although Sanders, *The Historical Figure of Jesus* (London: Allen Lane, 1993), 263, does not attempt to reconstruct the original words of Jesus at the last meal, he nevertheless affirms: "The passage in general has the strongest possible support ... there are two slightly different forms, which have reached us through two independent channels, the synoptic tradition and the letters of Paul."

[136] Cf. also Lichtenberger, "'Bund' in der Abendmhalsüberlieferung," 227, n. 59: "Does not the observation of Gräßer (*Bund*, 126) that Jesus' silence about the covenant continued into early Christianity speak specifically in favour of its authenticity?"

[137] *Der historische Jesus*, 373, cf. also n. 25.

[138] One can critically remark that the "covenant logion" of the interpretation of the bread differs also from all other Jesus traditions!

[139] Cf. Backhaus, "Hat Jesus vom Gottesbund gesprochen?" 352–56. I follow Backhaus in the following argument.

intertestamental period (for example, Philo, the Qumran or Essene literature, or rabbinic theology). Josephus completely avoids using this motif.[140] Erich Gräßer has summarized these findings by describing a "covenant silence" (*Bundesschweigen*).[141] The only exceptions are rare appearances of the term in Paul and in early Christian systematic treatises, such as the Epistle to the Hebrews, Barnabas and Justin.[142] It must be pointed out that the letters of Paul and the Epistle to the Hebrews function in the field of influence of the Lord's Supper tradition and cannot, therefore, be cited as independent traditions.

The criterion of coherence. Jesus and John the Baptist announced that Israel needed to repent. While John warned of the wrath to come, Jesus announced God's mercy and salvation in his proclamation of the advent of the kingdom of God (βασιλεία τοῦ θεοῦ). Jesus' proclamation was shaped by his unique *Abba*-relationship with God. It is within this context that Jesus' trust in the *renewal of the covenant* can be explained. During the Last Supper, a moment of intense existential significance, Jesus articulated, via word and the profound symbolism of the cup, the eschatological confidence and assurance that had undergirded his entire life and ministry. This is the core of the Lord's Supper tradition: that Jesus' message about God's kingdom finds its fulfillment in the promise of a new covenant.[143]

Theißen and Merz believe that the events of Jesus' final meal must be understood in the context of his conflict with the temple. *In the institution of the Lord's Supper he creates a new cultic activity* that supplants the sacrifices of the temple.[144] The Synoptics and Paul agree with the Gospel of John that Jesus' final meal was a symbolic act in which the core meaning was not verbal. Through Jesus' prophecy about, and his cleansing of, the temple, Jesus affirms that "this temple will be destroyed." In its place, God will build a *new* one. The criticism of the existing temple cult displays coherence with the symbolic implementation of a *new covenant* during Jesus' final meal with his disciples. The new cult and new covenant are free from the repeated sacrifices that marked the old cult and covenant. For – as Jeremiah 31:31–34 had prophesied – in the new dispensation God's will is engraved on his peoples' hearts and their sins are forgiven.[145]

---

[140]   Cf. 1.2.2.1, above; and Backhaus, "Hat Jesus vom Gottesbund gesprochen?" 353.

[141]   Gräßer, *Der Alte Bund im Neuen: Exegetische Studien zur Israelfrage im Neuen Testament*, WUNT 35 (Tübingen: J. C. B. Mohr [Paul Siebeck], 1985), 77.

[142]   Cf. Backhaus, *Der neue Bund und das Werden der Kirche*, 306–18.

[143]   See Backhaus, "Hat Jesus vom Gottesbund gesprochen?" 355.

[144]   Theißen and Merz, *Der historische Jesus*, 380–83. Cf. also Wright, *Jesus and the Victory of God: Christian Origins and the Question of God* (London: SPCK, 1996), 561: "Jesus' actions at the Last Supper are to be seen in close conjunction with his earlier actions in the Temple."

[145]   Theißen and Merz, *Der historische Jesus*, 382, point out that John's description of the final meal also contains traces of this detachment from the official cult: the washing

Jesus' final meal was marked by the anticipation of death and the expectation of the kingdom. It was partly a farewell meal and partly the celebration of a kingdom feast.[146] Neither John the Baptist nor Jesus consciously set out to establish a new cult or tradition. Both, however, expected the renewal of the world. According to Theißen and Merz, their symbolic cultic acts can be considered as eschatological sacraments. The final judgment was anticipated in baptism; the eschatological feast was anticipated in Jesus' ministry and death. Baptism for the forgiveness of sins is *de facto* a competing ritual to the temple cult; the Lord's Supper is a ritual substitution for the sacrificial cult.[147]

Lichtenberger mentions the possibility that, for Jesus, the institution of the new covenant may have offered a category through which to interpret the giving of his own life.[148] Backhaus, who assumes the covenant motif to be original in Jesus' proclamation, notes that from a history of religions perspective the promise of a new covenant with God does not put Jesus outside of the line of Israel's prophets. It actually completes the theocentric dynamic of prophetic eschatology in a radical way.[149] According to Backhaus, Jesus' originality lies in the fact that he connects the validity of the new covenant dynamic to his own message, ministry and death. The covenant that Jesus founded during the Lord's Supper is "the new order of salvation, that was prepared by God for his people already from time immemorial, that had become personified in Jesus' pre-existence and was now eschatologically finalized."[150]

---

[145] (*Continued*) of the feet, as a fully valid purification, takes the place of all official cleansing rituals of the temple that are outdated.

[146] Not only the post-Easter church, but also Jesus himself, understood his death as a sacrifice.

[147] Theißen and Merz have advanced the current discussion with their hypothesis. The characterization of the final meal as the foundation of a new cult and the interpretation of the Eucharist as a *substitutionary* ritual are, however, not very persuasive.

[148] Lichtenberger, "'Bund' in der Abendmhalsüberlieferung," 226–27. Lichtenberger adds: "Then Jesus would have broken his silence about the covenant in the end." Cf. also Wright, *Jesus and the Victory of God*, 561: "There is no reason to doubt that he intended, in speaking of the final cup of the meal in terms of his own death, to allude to this theme of covenant renewal. It fits precisely with all that we have seen of his agenda so far." Klauck, *Herrenmahl*, 314, points to the possibility that in the special situation of the final meal Jesus further developed his kingdom message through the announcement of a new covenant, which he grounded in his approaching death and secured for the future.

[149] Cf. also Stanton, *The Gospels and Jesus*, 179–83, who describes Jesus' self-understanding as prophet. Evans, "Authenticating the Activities of Jesus," 9, points out the importance of the theology of Deutero-Isaiah for the life of Jesus: "Influence of the theology of Second Isaiah is witnessed throughout Jesus' ministry."

[150] Backhaus, "Hat Jesus vom Gottesbund gesprochen?" 355–56. Cf. also Wright, *Jesus and the Victory of God*, 560: "The common meaning is that Jesus' coming death will

3.3 The meaning of the Easter event

In his paper entitled "Das Herrenmahl im Neuen Testament,"[151] Eduard Schweizer argues that Jesus explicated his role as servant-Messiah to his disciples during their final meal and promised to resume table fellowship with them in the coming kingdom of God. In one sense, the new covenant was already being realized, as the table fellowship that Jesus shared with tax collectors and sinners demonstrated. Jesus' own ministry was, in fact, nothing less than a manifestation of the new covenant kingdom. This ministry would be realized in its fullness in the coming three days. Jesus' interpretation of the bread and the cup was, therefore, the culminating teaching that summarized the meaning of all that had occurred and would occur. "*Easter* gave the early church the assurance that the *exalted Jesus continued to live among them*. The table fellowship with him, which signified so many essential dimensions of their faith, continued in a similar way."[152]

As previously noted, the final meal of Jesus is not an isolated symbol; it must be seen together with other instances of table fellowship that Jesus had with the disciples and with tax collectors, prostitutes and sinners. All of these were vehicles for demonstrating the *proximity of God's rule*. But while the meaning of the final meal is only fully visible from a post-Easter perspective, as Mark 14:25 makes clear,[153] the Lord's Supper is not merely the last of a series of symbolic meals. Its immediate reference to the death of Jesus gives it a unique quality. In Mark 14:25 the theology of the kingdom and the theology of the passion interpret each other mutually in profound ways.[154]

It need hardly be pointed out that the catastrophic impact of the crucifixion on Jesus' disciples left them with nothing to celebrate. It is rather astounding that Jesus taught them how to celebrate prior to this crushing event. The glorious reality of Jesus' resurrection enabled the disciples to overcome their despair in light of the apparent utter defeat at the cross. It was precisely in the context of the Lord's Supper liturgy that their joy could be voiced in all its profundity. The symbols given to the church in the Lord's Supper tradition gave eloquent voice to the inner meaning of Jesus' advent, teachings, suffering, death and resurrection. They disclosed new eschatological truths: that God and Jesus were mutually defining realities; that the death of Jesus has universal

---

[150] (*Continued*) effect the renewal of the covenant, that is, the great return from exile for which Israel had longed."

[151] In *Neotestamentica: Deutsche und englische Aufsätze 1951–1963* (Zürich/Stuttgart: Zwingli Verlag, 1963), 344–70.

[152] Schweizer, "Abendmahl I: Im NT," 17 (italics mine).

[153] Söding, "Das Mahl des Herrn," 157. Cf. 3.2.2, above.

[154] Söding, "Das Mahl des Herrn," 158.

salvific significance; and that Jesus' resurrection was a proclamation of salvation that the disciples must bear to all nations.[155]

Jesus' exact words during that final meal are unknown to us. It is clear that the disciples understood the eschatological and salvific significance of his death, as expressed in Jesus' explanations of the bread and the cup, only *after Easter*. But then, as now, the Jesus of the Lord's Supper is, for the church, not merely a historical figure, but the exalted Lord who will return at the end of time to complete the salvation he began by instituting the kingdom of God in his ministry (cf. Mark 14:25).[156]

Although textually the pre-Easter tradition has been combined with the post-Easter confession, this in no way means that the message of the pre-Easter Jesus is without significance. The core meaning and contours of the tradition were so clearly predetermined by Jesus himself that his proclamation remains determinative.[157]

3.4 Preliminary results

The central theme of Jesus' message was the "rule of God," or the "kingdom of God." In the context of Jesus' proclamation of God's rule, one finds an emphasis on discipleship and on the creation of a new people of God. This emphasis was expressed symbolically by Jesus through his appointment of the circle of the Twelve – an analogy to the twelve tribal heads of Israel.[158]

Jesus perceived that, through the breaking of his body, God would pour out blessing upon his disciples and the world. Mark 14:25 underscores Jesus' conviction that his work would only achieve fruition through this sacrifice. Although, as the Passion Narratives reveal, Jesus struggled to gird himself to face the darkness of that hour, he also maintained the trustful expectation regarding the coming kingdom of God that had been at the core of his proclamation.

The terms "kingdom of God" and "covenant" were naturally associated in Jewish thinking. Jesus envisioned his death as a self-giving that created a covenantal bridge for the in-breaking of the kingdom of God.[159] The motif of this *new* covenant was also rooted in the Jesus tradition, as in Mark 14:25, where Jesus announces that he will drink the fruit of the vine "anew" in the eschatological kingdom of God. In Mark 2:21–22 Jesus speaks about a new

---

[155] Hahn, "Die Verkündigung Jesu," in Hilberath and Sattler, *Vorgeschmack*, 125; Söding, "Das Mahl des Herrn," 158.

[156] Söding, "Das Mahl des Herrn," 159.

[157] Hahn, "Die Verkündigung Jesu," 126.

[158] Cf. 3.2, above; also Hahn, "Die Verkündigung Jesu," 127, 129.

[159] Hahn, "Das Verständnis des Opfers im Neuen Testament," 69.

cloth and new vine, and he gives his disciples a new commandment in the Johannine farewell discourse (John 13:34).[160]

In light of the Easter event, Jesus' death became the foundation of the Christian interpretation of the eschatological covenant prophesied by Jeremiah 31. The motif of the new covenant was woven into the motif of atonement (Isa. 53) – Jesus was, and is, seen as the servant of Yahweh who suffered vicariously for his people. The eschatological covenant ratified through the cross is realized in the community of Jesus' disciples.[161]

4. Summary and further perspectives

In the New Testament interpretation of Jesus' death, a litany of *Old Testament covenantal and sacrificial motifs*[162] are appropriated and modified (Exod. 24:8; Zech. 9:11; Jer. 31 [LXX 38]:31–34; cf. also the allusions to the Suffering Servant in Isa. 53:10–12). The early Christian notion of new covenant consists of an eschatological order of salvation in continuity with the Old Testament prophetic expectation of a new covenant. Through the death of Jesus, God establishes this new covenant. By means of the Lord's Supper, believers can participate in the benefits of the vicarious death of Jesus and the salvific power of the new covenant. The notion of "covenant," which had been progressively nuanced through the Old Testament literature, enabled early Christianity to articulate the numinous salvific reality they experienced in conjunction with the Christ event.

The biblical accounts of the institution of the Lord's Supper were conceived retrospectively from a post-Easter perspective and constructed so as to be summarily expressive of the significance of the person and work of Jesus of Nazareth. The early church formulated its Christology in light of the resurrection. However, the words of the Last Supper tradition were based on the words of the earthly Jesus himself. Motifs directly attributable to Jesus that formed the core of the tradition include especially Jesus' message of the *kingdom of God;* Jesus' self-interpretation according to the motif of *servanthood;* and the motif of *newness.*

The notion of the *new covenant* appears in the New Testament for the first time in the narratives about the Lord's Supper (Matt. 26:26–29; Mark 14:22–25; Luke 22:15–20; and 1 Cor. 11:23–26). These accounts can be grouped into *two tradition types.* Mark represents the first type, while Paul and Luke[163]

---

[160] Klauck, *Herrenmahl*, 314, 329–30.

[161] Cf. Hahn, "Abendmahl, I: Neues Testament," in *RGG* I (Tübingen: J. C. B. Mohr [Paul Siebeck], 4th rev. edn, 1998), 30.

[162] See Hahn, "Die alltestamentlichen Motive," 366, for a discussion of the juxtaposition of notions on atonement and covenant.

[163] Paul and Luke base their accounts on the same, or a closely related, tradition.

comprise the second. Both versions contain recognizably newer and older elements.[164]

The *differences* between the Lord's Supper narratives can be summarized as follows:

(i) Paul does not mention the Passover feast explicitly, while Mark 14:12–16, 26a and Matthew 26:17–19, 30a refer to it in the framing verses. The Passover is closely connected with the passing of bread and wine in Luke 22:15–18, 19–20.[165]

(ii) According to Luke/Paul there is a meal to satisfy hunger *between* the passing of the bread and the passing of the wine (μετὰ τὸ δειπνῆσαι). In Mark/Matthew this meal occurs *before* the passing of the bread and wine (ἐσθιόντων αὐτῶν). These differences may reflect different eucharistic praxes in early Christian churches.

(iii) The words spoken during the Lord's Supper celebration have different formulations in the two tradition types:

(a) In Luke/Paul, the atonement motif follows the interpretation of the bread, while the covenant notion is associated with the interpretation of the cup. In Mark/Matthew, both the atonement and the covenant motifs are integrated in the interpretation of the cup.
(b) In Mark/Matthew one finds an allusion to Exodus 24:8 ("the blood … of the covenant"; τὸ αἷμά … τῆς διαθήκης [Mark 14:24]). It is also stated that the blood of the covenant is poured out for "many," alluding to Isaiah 53:12. (Matthew adds the phrase "for the forgiveness of sins.") Luke/Paul speak about the atonement "for you" and about a "new covenant" in the sense of Jeremiah 31:31–34.
(c) Mark/Matthew speak of the blessing of the bread and thanksgiving for the cup, while Luke/Paul mention only thanksgiving.
(d) In the Lukan/Pauline version, "This is my body" and "This cup is" are juxtaposed:

And he took bread, gave thanks and broke it, and gave it to them, saying, '*This is my body* …'

In the same way, after the supper he took the cup, saying, '*This cup is* …' (Luke 22:19–20)

The Markan/Matthean version presents the phrases "This is my body/ This is my blood of the covenant" as parallel statements:[166]

[164] Hahn, "Abendmahl, I: Neues Testament," 11.
[165] See the *Excursus,* above, for a discussion of the text critical problems in vv. 19–20.
[166] 1 Cor. 10:16 demonstrates that Paul must also have known the other version when he speaks of the "body of Christ" and the "blood of Christ."

Jesus took bread, gave thanks and broke it, and gave it to his disciples, saying, 'Take it; *this is my body.*'

Then he took the cup, gave thanks and offered it to them, and they all drank from it.

'*This is my blood of the covenant* ...' (Mark 14:22–24)

(e) The command "Do this in remembrance of me" is missing in Mark/ Matthew. In Luke, it appears only after the interpretation of the bread, while in Paul it is found twice with the expansion "whenever you drink of it" after the interpretation of the cup.[167]

Despite these variations, there is full agreement among all four reports in their understanding of the *meaning* of the Lord's Supper.[168]

Paul and the Synoptics both underscore the role of the *historical Passover events* in the Last Supper narratives. The inauguration of the Lord's Supper is, therefore, clearly differentiated from the timeless cyclic myths and formulae of the mystery religions.[169] In 1 Corinthians 11, the Lord's Supper tradition is used by Paul to root Christian praxis in the action and authority of the historical Jesus, thus serving as a critical corrective to abuses in the church.

Both tradition types have an *eschatological orientation*. The narratives in Mark and Matthew conclude with an eschatological outlook by referring to the coming future table fellowship that shall occur in the kingdom (cf. Mark 14:25; Matt. 26:29). Luke's account (Luke 22:14–20) is likewise shaped eschatologically from its inception – in verse 16 Jesus speaks of the fulfillment of the Passover meal in the kingdom of God. Paul's reference to the Lord's Supper tradition in 1 Corinthians 11:23–26 concludes with the words "until he comes" (ἄχρι οὗ ἔλθῃ).

The sealing of the new covenant in the context of the Lord's Supper tradition has eminent *soteriological* significance (cf. "for you" in the Pauline/Lukan tradition; "for many" in Mark and Matthew). Participation in the eucharistic celebration is symbolic participation in the salvific reality of the Christ event. With the passing of the wine, a community of blessing is constituted – a blessing purchased through the atoning blood of Christ. The forgiveness mediated through that sacrifice creates fellowship with Christ and with God in the "new

---

[167] Hahn, "Abendmahl, I: Neues Testament," 11–12.

[168] See Lang, *Die Briefe an die Korinther*, 151. Wolff, *Der erste Brief des Paulus an die Korinther*, 88, also points out that with of all the differences that appear between the two main strands of the New Testament Lord's Supper tradition, their relatedness is very obvious. Cf. also Delling, "Abendmahl II: Urchristliches Mahl-Verständnis," in *TRE* I (Berlin/New York: Walter de Gruyter, 1977), 54.

[169] Cf. Klauck, *1. Korintherbrief*, 82.

covenant." Through Jesus' interpretation of the wine as representative of his blood, he presents himself as the mediator of salvation and of the (new) covenant established by God through his substitutionary death.[170] In the Lord's Supper tradition, the death of Jesus is set forth not as a theological theory, but as an efficacious salvific power.[171]

The sealing of the covenant during the Lord's Supper also carries an unmistakable *ecclesiological significance*. In Jewish thinking, a meal was not only an occasion for satisfying hunger – a meal also created and maintained community.[172] The old covenant was instituted by way of a blood ritual (Exod. 24:6–8) and a meal (Exod. 24:11). In the same way, the new covenant is inaugurated through the blood of Jesus and through the celebration of a eucharistic feast. The implicit fellowship with the crucified and risen Lord, that is at the heart of that celebration of table fellowship, creates the foundation for fellowship between the human celebrants of the feast.[173] In the celebration of the Lord's Supper, one enjoys fellowship not only with Christ, but also with one another.

Participation in the body of Christ is granted through the Eucharist; this is the essence of koinonia, or "communion": "Is not the bread that we break a participation in the body of Christ?" (1 Cor. 10:16). The "body of Christ" holds a double meaning here: it alludes both to the bread that represents the broken body of Jesus and his agape-motivated self-giving as well as to the eschatological shared fellowship with the crucified and risen Lord. It is that eschatological participation in Christ that, as the "body of Christ," constitutes the church ontologically.

We see both of these dimensions in 1 Corinthians 10. In verse 16, the bread is the eucharistic body of the Lord. In verse 17, the "body"[174] ("bread") points to the *church* – that is, according to Paul's ecclesiology, to the "body of Christ." The unity of the church is expressed through the one bread of the Eucharist. *Eschatologically*, a place is being prepared for the participants at the messianic table, where they will live in union with one another and peace with God. Together with their eucharistic table partners, all will sing the thanksgiving hymn of Isaiah 26:1–6.[175] The participants in this meal are the new people of God. They share in the atoning blood of Jesus – and in his mission – and

---

[170] Pesch, *Das Markusevangelium*, 360.

[171] Cf. Levin, *Die Verheißung des neuen Bundes*, 272.

[172] According to Exod. 12:3, Passover was supposed to be a family celebration; cf. Gnilka, *Jesus von Nazaret*, 282.

[173] Lang, "Abendmahl und Bundesgedanke," 532–33, 538. See also Levin, *Die Verheißung des neuen Bundes*, 272.

[174] Or "crucified body."

[175] Cf. Gnilka, *Theologie des Neuen Testaments* (Freiburg/Basel/Wien: Herder, 1994), 122; Stuhlmacher, *Biblische Theologie*, 140.

become messengers of the "new covenant," inviting Israel and all nations to participate in the great feast.[176]

The Last Supper differs from the meals Jesus shared with tax collectors and sinners in that it occurs within the circle of the *Twelve*. Although the notion of the circle of the Twelve is not explicitly mentioned in Paul's recollection of the institution of the Lord's Supper (cf., however, 1 Cor. 15:5),[177] it can be assumed that Paul still presupposes it. The election of the Twelve during the earthly ministry of Jesus has significant consequences for ecclesiology. By electing twelve disciples, Jesus recapitulates the expectation, rooted in prophetic and apocalyptic literature, that Israel will be restored during the messianic age as a people of twelve tribes.[178] The circle of the Twelve symbolizes Jesus' promise of eschatological salvation for Israel. The Twelve thus function as a visible sign of God's new beginning with Israel in the context of the (new) covenant promise. The twelve tribal heads of the new covenant[179] are representative of the totality of the new people of God.

The *sealing of the eschatological covenant through the death of Jesus* on the cross (cf. Mark 14:24: "This is my blood of the covenant"; Luke 22:20 and 1 Cor. 11:25: "This cup is the new covenant in my blood"[180]) appears in all of the Lord's Supper narratives. The interpretive nexus of the Lord's Supper in the New Testament is the concept of the creation of a new universal eschatological salvation order (a new covenant) through the death and resurrection of Jesus Christ.[181] Jesus' explanation of the meaning of the cup identifies the eucharistic meal as a *covenant meal*. This covenant, at heart, consists of a new life of fellowship with God based on the self-giving of Jesus.[182]

---

[176] Pesch, *Das Markusevangelium*, 360.

[177] In the synoptic Lord's Supper tradition the circle of the Twelve plays a prominent role.

[178] Cf. Isa. 11:11, 16; 27:12–13; 35:8–10; 49:22; 60:4, 9; 66:20; Mich. 7:12; Ezek. 39:27–28.; Pss. Sol. 11; 1 Hen. 57; 90, 32; 2 Bar. 4:36 – 5:9; Jos. Ant. 9, 133 (see Gnilka, *Das Evangelium nach Markus*, I, 139, following Schmahl, *Die Zwölf im Markusevangelium*, 36–39).

[179] Gnilka, *Das Evangelium nach Markus*, I, 249.

[180] The cup (or its content) is in the older Pauline/Lukan tradition not yet directly identified with the blood, as this can be observed in Mark (and Matthew) due to the growing tendency to harmonize the interpretation of the bread and the cup (Klauck, *1. Korintherbrief*, 83).

[181] See Lang, "Abendmahl und Bundesgedanke," 537.

[182] Kertelge, *Markusevangelium*, 142.

4

The New Covenant in Pauline Literature

1. Introduction

Outside of the "Lord's Supper tradition," the expression "new covenant" plays a significant role in the New Testament only in the Pauline literature (2 Cor. 3:6, 14; Gal. 4:24)[1] and the Epistle to the Hebrews (7:22; 8:6, 8, 9, 10; 9:4, 15, 16, 17, 20; 10:16, 29; 12:24; 13:20).[2] Nevertheless, διαθήκη[3] statements in the New Testament have significant weight and explosive force, especially in Paul and Hebrews.[4]

    N. T. Wright chose the title *The Climax of the Covenant* for his 1991 book about Christ and law in Pauline theology. He reasoned: "The overall title reflects my growing conviction that covenant theology is one of the main clues, usually neglected, for understanding Paul."[5] The significance of the covenant motif in Pauline theology has also been emphasized in works by B. W. Longenecker,[6] W. C. van Unnik,[7] T. J. Deidun[8] and Stanley

---

[1] Cf. also Eph. 2:12. Rom. 9:4 refers to the Old Testament instances of making a covenant, and Rom. 11:27 contains a quote from the Old Testament. Rom. 9 – 11, as well as Eph. 2:12, are mentioned in the discussion of Jewish-Christian dialogue (chapters 9.3.1 and 9.3.2, below). Cf. also Lichtenberger, "Alter und neuer Bund," *NTS* 41 (1995), 412–13.

[2] There are also some other instances where διαθήκη is found with the meaning "covenant": Luke 1:72; Acts 3:25; 7:8; Rom. 9:4; 11:27; Rev. 11:19.

[3] With the meaning "covenant."

[4] Lichtenberger, "Alter und neuer Bund," 413, rightly notices this.

[5] Wright, *The Climax of the Covenant: Christ and the Law in Pauline Theology* (Minneapolis: Fortress Press, 1993), xi.

[6] Longenecker, "Contours of Covenant Theology in the Post-Conversion Paul," in Longenecker (ed.), *The Road from Damascus: The Impact of Paul's Conversion on His Life, Thought, and Ministry* (Grand Rapids: Eerdmans, 1997), 125–46.

[7] Van Unnik, *La conception de la nouvelle alliance: Littérature et théologie pauliniennes* (Bruges: Desclée, 1960), 109–26.

[8] Deidun, *New Covenant Morality in Paul* (Rome: Biblical Institute Press, 1981).

Porter.[9] Papers by Helmut Merklein,[10] Jost Eckert[11] and Gerhard Sass[12] explore the framework of relations between the church and Israel and highlight the relevance of the covenant motif for Paul. Gerhard Dautzenberg examines the covenant motif in relation to questions on the beginnings of Christian anti-Judaism.[13]

We have alluded above to the fact that Gräßer speaks of a Pauline "covenant silence," postulating that Paul's emphasis on the principle of individual salvation dissolves the link between the nation and the covenant, making the concept theologically useless.[14] While it must be admitted that the eschatological new covenant shatters Old Testament covenant nationalism, there are numerous examples in the New Testament and early postbiblical literature of theological metaphors stressing collective unity, such as the body of Christ.[15] To become a Christian involves not only a personal appropriation of salvation, but also a corporate, ecclesiological dimension.[16]

The following paragraphs will focus on the Pauline passages in which the words καινὴ διαθήκη ("new covenant") occur, while taking into account the importance of considering words within the context of their respective semantic fields (cf. especially 4.2.3 and 4.2.4, below).[17]

---

[9] Porter, "The Concept of Covenant in Paul," in Porter and de Roo (eds.), *The Concept of the Covenant in the Second Temple Period*, Supplements to the Journal for the Study of Judaism 71 (Leiden/Boston: E. J. Brill, 2003), 269–85.

[10] Merklein, "Der (neue) Bund als Thema der paulinischen Theologie," *TQ* 176.4 (1996), 290–308.

[11] Eckert, "Gottes Bundesstiftungen und der neue Bund bei Paulus," in Frankemölle, *Der ungekündigte Bund?*, 135–56.

[12] Sass, "Der alte und der neue Bund bei Paulus," in Wengst and Sass (eds.), *Ja und nein: Christliche Theologie im Angesicht Israels. Festschrift zum 70. Geburtstag von Wolfgang Schrage* (Neukirchen-Vluyn: Neukirchener, 1998), 223–34.

[13] Dautzenberg, "Alter und neuer Bund nach 2 Kor 3," in Kampling (ed.), *"Nun steht aber diese Sache im Evangelium ..." Zur Frage nach den Anfängen des christlichen Antijudaismus* (Paderborn/München/Wien/Zürich: Ferdinand Schöning, 1999), 53–72.

[14] Gräßer, *Der Alte Bund im Neuen*, 77.

[15] Cf. Backhaus, *Der neue Bund und das Werden der Kirche*, 329–30.

[16] For an exposition of this dimension in Paul see Gräbe, "Καινὴ διαθήκη in der paulinischen Literatur: Ansätze zu einer paulinischen Ekklesiologie," in Kampling and Söding, *Ekklesiologie des Neuen Testaments*, 268.

[17] Cf. Louw and Nida, *Greek-English Lexicon*; Porter and de Roo, *The Concept of the Covenant*, 271–72.

2. The "new covenant" in 2 Corinthians 3

2.1 Exegetical comments

The concept of "new covenant" plays an important role in 2 Corinthians 3:4 – 4:6. This passage is part of a larger unit, 2 Corinthians 2:14 – 7:4,[18] which deals with Paul's apostolic ministry.

The pericope 2 Corinthians 3:4 – 4:6 can be subdivided as follows:[19]

2 Corinthians 3:4 – 4:6: Servants of a new covenant of glory

> A (3:4–6): God has enabled us to be servants of a new covenant of the Spirit;
>
> B (3:7–11): The all-surpassing glory of the ministry of the Spirit;
>
> C (3:12–18): "With an unveiled face": glory and freedom through the Spirit;
>
> D (4:1–6): We do not grow weary because there is trust in God's enlightenment.

Paul uses several antithetic pairs of contrasts in his arguments in these passages. The "old covenant" (παλαιὰ διαθήκη) is contrasted with the "new covenant" (καινὴ διαθήκη).[20] This "new covenant" (καινὴ διαθήκη) is "not of the letter but of the spirit" (οὐ γράμματος ἀλλὰ πνεύματος). The following phrases are used synonymously with, or point to, the "ministry of the new covenant": "ministry of the Spirit (διακονία τοῦ πνεύματος, 3:8); "ministry of righteousness" (διακονία τῆς δικαιοσύνης, 3:9); "that which lasts" (τὸ μένον, 3:11); and "this ministry" (ἡ διακονία αὐτη, 4:1).

---

[18] 2 Cor. 2:14 – 7:4 is found between the autobiographical units 1:8 – 2:13 and 7:5–16 and is a relatively independent part of this epistle (Lambrecht, *Second Corinthians*, SP 8 [Collegeville, MN: The Liturgical Press, 1999], 43). See also Bornkamm, *Die Vorgeschichte des sogenannten Zweiten Korintherbriefes* (Heidelberg: Carl Winter Universitätsverlag, 1965), 21: "Between [the units] one finds the first great *apologia* (defense) of the apostolic ministry, starting abruptly (without transition) in 2:14 and ending very clearly in 7:4; theologically this is, without doubt, the most important piece of the epistle."

[19] Cf. Gräbe, "Δύναμις in the Sense of Power in the Main Pauline Letters" (D.D. Thesis, University of Pretoria, 1990), 137–39.

[20] Hofius, "Gesetz und Evangelium nach 2. Korinther 3," in Hofius, *Paulusstudien*, 75, rightly points out that already in v. 6 it is objectively assumed that καινὴ διαθήκη (new covenant, v. 6a) relates antithetically to the παλαιὰ διαθήκη (old covenant), although the term appears only in v. 14b.

This ministry (of the new covenant) is then contrasted with: "the ministry of death" (διακονία τοῦ θανάτου, 3:7); "the ministry that condemns people" (διακονία τῆς κατακρίσεως 3:9); and "what was fading away" (τὸ καταργούμενον, 3:11).

From this pattern of contrasts a threefold conclusion is drawn, moving from the lesser to the greater: "how much more" (εἰ … πῶς … μᾶλλον, 3:7–8; εἰ … πολλῷ μᾶλλον, 3:9, 11). This intensification is closely linked with the use of the term "glory" (δόξα), which, as noun and verb, appears in this passage fourteen times (3:7 [twice], 8, 9 [twice], 10 [3 times], 11 [twice], 18 [twice]; 4:4, 6). The Septuagint renders the Hebrew כבד as δόξα (glory). The concept of glory (כבד) makes significant theological statements about God's nature, about his position as ruler and about the powerful radiance of his majesty.[21] In this light, 2 Corinthians 3:7–18 may be seen as a Christian midrash[22] on Exodus 34:29–35.

2.2 The meaning of "new covenant" in the context of 2 Corinthians 3:4 – 4:6

The comparison of the new and old covenants, which begins in subunit A (3:4–6), continues in B (3:7–11). The new covenant is considered to be greater; the old covenant lesser. The old covenant is referred to in the context of phrases such as "ministry of death" (v. 7), "ministry of condemnation" (v. 9) and "what fades away" (v. 11). In comparison,[23] the new covenant is described as: "the ministry of the Spirit" (v. 8), "the ministry of righteousness" (v. 9) and "that which lasts" (v. 11).

In interpreting "new covenant" here, it is helpful to know: (i) that Paul links the term "servant" (διάκονος) with the "new covenant" (see below); (ii) that he interprets the new covenant pneumatologically (cf. "not of the letter but of the Spirit," 3:6b; "ministry of the Spirit," 3:8); and (iii) that he perceives his ministry of the new covenant to be a "ministry that brings righteousness" (3:9).

---

[21] Klauck, *2. Korintherbrief*, NEchtB, NT 8, 3rd edn (Würzburg: Echter Verlag, 1994), 37–38.

[22] The *Oxford Dictionary of the Jewish Religion* (Oxford: Oxford University press, 1997), 463, defines midrash as "the discovering of meanings other than literal in the Bible." It was widely used in early Judaism and "denotes the literature that interprets scripture in order to extract its full implications and meaning … midrash made possible a vivid application of the scriptural word to a later situation."

[23] It must be noted that the motif of "glory" (δόξα) plays an important role in this context; cf. also De Oliveira, *Die Diakonie der Gerechtigkeit und der Versöhnung in der Apologie des 2. Korintherbriefes. Analyse und Auslegung von 2 Kor 2,14–4,6; 5,11–6,10* (Münster: Aschendorff, 1990), 69.

Paul calls himself a "servant" (διάκονος) of the "*new covenant*" in 2 Corinthians 3:6. Parallel statements in other Pauline Epistles include his self-designation as a "servant" of the *gospel*.[24] In Romans 1:1, 9 Paul speaks of "having been set apart for the gospel" (ἀφωρισμένος εἰς εὐαγγέλιον θεοῦ); he "serves" God "in the gospel of his son"; he is "a minister (λειτουργός) of Christ Jesus to the Gentiles" while he proclaims "with the priestly duty ... the gospel of God" (Rom. 15:16); together with Timothy he "serves" (ἐδούλευσεν) "in the work of the gospel" (Phil. 2:22). In Colossians 1:23 and Ephesians 3:6–7 Paul is called a "servant" of the gospel.

In 2 Corinthians 3:6, Paul states[25] that it is God who enables the apostles to be servants of the new covenant.[26] Paul depicts the new covenant as God's new eschatological initiative enacted in Christ.[27] The new covenant is then immediately interpreted *pneumatologically*: it is "not of the letter but of the Spirit."[28] The specifically Pauline feature is the antithetical addition "not of the letter but of the Spirit."[29]

Paul uses this rhetorical turn to attack his enemies,[30] whom he accuses of serving "the letter." In verse 3 he noted that, contrariwise, he has worked in

---

[24] As Hofius, "Gesetz und Evangelium," 77, rightly states.

[25] Kertelge, "Buchstabe und Geist nach 2 Kor 3," in Dunn (ed.), *Paul and the Mosaic Law: The Third Durham-Tübingen Research Symposium on Earliest Christianity and Judaism* (Tübingen: J. C. B. Mohr [Paul Siebeck], 1996), 118–30, perceives 2 Cor. 3:6 to be the topic statement which is then exegetically developed in 2 Cor. 3:7–11.

[26] The significance of the new covenant for the way in which Paul understands his own ministry is discussed by Lane, "Covenant: The Key to Paul's Conflict with Corinth," *TynBul* 33 (1982), 3–29.

[27] This is how Lambrecht, *Second Corinthians*, 43, sees it.

[28] Although some New Testament scholars believe that these words are linked to the "servants" (cf. Meyer, *Critical and Exegetical Handbook to the Epistles to the Corinthians* [New York: Funk & Wagnalls, 1890], 465; Plummer, *A Critical and Exegetical Commentary on the Second Epistle of St. Paul to the Corinthians* [Edinburgh: T&T Clark, 1915], 88), we observe here a qualitative genitive that describes the new covenant (cf. Furnish, *II Corinthians* [New York: Doubleday, 1984], 199; Horn, *Das Angeld des Geistes: Studien zur paulinischen Pneumatologie* [Göttingen: Vandenhoeck & Ruprecht, 1992], 316).

[29] Cf. Kertelge, "Buchstabe und Geist," 122. Kremer, "'Denn der Buchstabe tötet, der Geist aber macht lebendig': Methodologische und hermeneutische Erwägungen zu 2 Kor 3,6b," in Zmijewski and Nellessen, *Begegnung mit dem Wort*, 228, emphasizes that Paul uses πνεῦμα (Spirit) here to characterize the new covenant (v. 6a) and the New Testament ministry (v. 8a), or even the Christian existence (v. 17) as such. Cf. also Hafemann, *Paul, Moses, and the History of Israel: The Letter/Spirit Contrast and the Argument from Scripture in 2 Corinthians 3* (Tübingen: J. C. B. Mohr [Paul Siebeck], 1995), 145–48.

[30] For an overview of research on the question of Paul's opponents in 2 Corinthians see Bieringer, "Die Gegner des Paulus im 2. Korintherbrief," in Bieringer and

the Corinthian church in the "spirit of the living God" (πνεύματι θεοῦ ζῶντος). Paul criticizes the "recommendation praxis" of his opponents (v. 1), paralleling it with the "tablets of stone,"[31] and, in developing that comparison, notes that the community of the Corinthian church – a reality written "on tablets of human hearts" (v. 3) – is all the recommendation that he needs.[32] This is a clear reference to the key new covenant passage, Jeremiah 31:33.

The motif of the Spirit dominates 2 Corinthians 3 (cf. 3:6 [twice], 8, 17 [twice], 18). The new covenant context for these passages includes not only Jeremiah 31 (LXX 38):31–34, but also Ezekiel 36:26–27, which designates the Spirit of God as the eschatological purveyor of the new covenant reality and as the divine agent of cleansing and sanctification. In 2 Corinthians 3:6–18 Paul describes the "new covenant" as mediated through the dynamic presence of the Spirit.[33] The new covenant is an eschatological phenomenon brought about by the Spirit that fulfills the promises of the prophets.[34] Through Christ the old covenant[35] – that is, the law understood as a soteriological means – has come to an end, and a new power and promise for life are instituted. The new covenant is written into human hearts by the Spirit.[36] Thus the new covenant creates an eschatological people of God in whom God's Spirit is unleashed with life-creating force. The church that arises through Paul's apostolic ministry is the realization of the eschatological renewal that the prophets had predicted.[37]

---

[30] (*Continued*) Lambrecht (eds.), *Studies on 2 Corinthians*, BETL CXII (Leuven: University Press; Uitgeverij Peeters, 1994), 181–221. He concludes (p. 221) that the textual evidence that would provide information on the enemies is very limited. So we know very little about them.

[31] Kertelge, "Buchstabe und Geist," 122.

[32] Gräßer, "Paulus, der Apostel des neuen Bundes (2 Kor 2:14 – 4:6)," in De Lorenzi (ed.), *Paolo-Ministro del Nuovo Testamento (2 Co 2:14 – 4:16)* (Roma: Benedictina Editrice, 1987), 15.

[33] Schnackenburg, *Die Kirche im Neuen Testament: Ihre Wirklichkeit und theologische Deutung. Ihr Wesen und Geheimnis* (Freiburg/Basel/Wien: Herder, 1961), 140–41.

[34] Klauck, *2. Korintherbrief*, 37.

[35] Paul, to a high degree, identifies the old covenant with its written document, the Torah (Klauck, *2. Korintherbrief*, 40).

[36] Furnish, *II Corinthians*, 201. Lambrecht, *Second Corinthians*, 43, points out that the subject of this passage's discussion is between "the written, not executed, hence powerless Law and God's new covenant wherein the Spirit (cf. Ezekiel 11 and/or 36) is active. The contrast is salvation-historical, not hermeneutical."

[37] See Lambrecht, *Second Corinthians*, 46. Lambrecht, p. 47, notes concerning the passage 2:14 – 3:6: "A most impressive factor in this pericope is Paul's conviction regarding God's work in Christ, his own ministry, and the identity of Christian life: all of it is the fulfillment of the spiritual newness of the covenant prophesied by Jeremiah and Ezekiel."

A new covenant implies a new eschatological order of salvation.[38] The Mosaic law could not, in itself, provide life-giving *pneuma*. The law (νόμος), which according to Romans 7:14 *is* "spiritual" (πνευματικός), is lacking in this sense.[39] From the perspective of salvation history a new entity, a "new covenant," is needed – one that will overcome the powerlessness of the old letter-law through the power of the Spirit.[40]

Paul concludes his discussion on the servants of the new covenant with the statement: "for the letter kills, but the Spirit gives life" (τὸ γὰρ γράμμα ἀποκτέννει, τὸ δὲ πνεῦμα ζῳοποιεῖ, 2 Cor. 3:6). In Bultmann's words: "The new covenant is a covenant of life."[41] Paul's doctrine of justification sets death and life as the opposite outcomes of the law and the gospel, respectively (cf. Rom. 8:2): "because through Jesus Christ the law of the Spirit of life set me free from the law of sin and death."[42] This rationalization stands behind Paul's argument in 2 Corinthians 3:6 as well; his apostolic ministry is fundamentally different than that of his opponents because the gospel that he serves is fundamentally superior to that of his opponents.[43]

Paul's concept of a "new covenant" differs significantly from the understanding of new covenant held by the Essene community of Qumran. While they, too, understood themselves to be a community empowered by God's eschatological Spirit, obedience to the regulations of the Torah was of utmost importance for the Essenes. They saw no incompatibility between "life in the

---

[38] See Käsemann, *Paulinische Perspektiven,* 2nd rev. edn (Tübingen: J. C. B. Mohr [Paul Siebeck], 1972), 258.

[39] Why is the law lacking in this sense? The answer is provided by Rom. 8:3: "For what the law was powerless to do in that it was weakened by the sinful nature, God did by sending his own Son in the likeness of sinful man to be a sin offering."

[40] Kertelge, "Buchstabe und Geist," 124. Dautzenberg, "Alter und neuer Bund nach 2 Kor 3," 247, critically questions Paul's antithetic argumentation in this context. He believes that Paul accepts as his starting point contemporary Christian thinking on salvation and negates Jewish positions through his antithetic form of thinking. When characterizing the law as a "letter that kills" (2 Cor. 3:6) and positioning it against the "spirit that gives life," Paul offends, according to Dautzenberg, not only Jewish piety, focused in the Torah, but also Christian, Jewish and Hellenistic respect for the Torah and the commandments as regulations following from the covenant. This critique seems unjustified, in my opinion, against the background of Paul's line of argument, as described above.

[41] "Der neue Bund ist ein Bund des Lebens." Bultmann, *Der zweite Brief an die Korinther* (Göttingen: Vandenhoeck & Ruprecht, 1976), 81. He points out that because for Paul the "new covenant" by definition has the meaning of a covenant that leads to life, it must, therefore, be a "covenant of the Spirit."

[42] Rom. 8:2: ὁ γὰρ νόμος τοῦ πνεύματος τῆς ζωῆς ἐν Χριστῷ ᾿Ιησοῦ ἠλευθέρωσέν σε ἀπὸ τοῦ νόμου τῆς ἁμαρτίας καὶ τοῦ θανάτου.

[43] Kertelge, "Buchstabe und Geist," 123.

spirit" and "life under the law." For Paul, however, these were two opposite and mutually exclusive ways of existence.[44]

2.3 Covenant (διαθήκη) and righteousness (δικαιοσύνη)

Louw and Nida point out in their *Greek-English Lexicon Based on Semantic Domains* that διαθήκη ("covenant") and δικαιοσύνη ("righteousness") belong to the same semantic field: "establish or confirm a relation."[45] Our study of 2 Corinthians 3 affirms this relationship.

It is remarkable that Paul interprets his ministry of the new covenant in 3:9 as a "ministry of *righteousness*" (διακονία τῆς δικαιοσύνης). Kertelge has pointed out the Old Testament background of Paul's concept of justification, and especially the role of the covenant, in this regard: "The 'righteousness' of Yahweh describes in Old Testament writings his *covenantal behavior*. In the covenant Israel experiences Yahweh's righteousness as the reason (condition) for its existence."[46]

The "righteousness of God" in the Old Testament is a *relational concept* that signifies his *covenantal conduct* towards his people. In affirming Yahweh's righteousness, the Old Testament presents the ground for the covenantal relationship between God and his people: through the covenant God blesses his covenantal partner and offers them life.[47] Israel can rely on the righteousness of the Lord to defend them from their enemies (cf. Judg. 5:11[48]). The poor and the oppressed especially reckon on the "righteousness of God" as a concrete help in time of need (cf. Ps. 35:23–24[49]). Isaiah and Jeremiah see God's righteousness expressed especially in the coming Messiah:

---

[44] Furnish, *II Corinthians*, 199; Sekki, *The Meaning of Ruah at Qumran*, SBLDS 110 (Atlanta: Scholars Press, 1989), 223. Cf. also Hafemann, "The Spirit of the New Covenant, the Law and the Temple of God's Presence: Five Theses on Qumran Self-Understanding and the Contours of Paul's Thought," in Adna, Hafemann and Hofius (eds.), *Evangelium, Schriftauslegung, Kirche: Festschrift für Peter Stuhlmacher zum 65. Geburtstag* (Göttingen: Vandenhoeck & Ruprecht, 1997), 172–89.

[45] Louw and Nida, *Greek-English Lexicon*, 451–53. The significance of this observation has recently been stressed by Porter, *Concept of Covenant*, 274–75.

[46] Kertelge, "δικαιοσύνη," in Balz and Schneider (eds.), *EWNT* (Stuttgart: Kohlhammer, 1980), 790; cf. also Kertelge, *"Rechtfertigung" bei Paulus: Studien zur Struktur und zum Bedeutungsgehalt des paulinischen Rechtfertigungsbegriffs* (Münster: Aschendorff, 1967), 15–24. In the Septuagint, δικαιοσύνη is the consistent translation of the Hebrew צדקה (Kertelge, *Rechtfertigung*, 24).

[47] Kertelge, *Rechtfertigung*, 23.

[48] "They recite the righteous acts of the Lord."

[49] Ps. 35:23–24: "Awake, and rise to my defense! Contend for me, my God and Lord. Vindicate me in your righteousness, O LORD my God."

He will reign on David's throne and over his kingdom, establishing and upholding it with *justice and righteousness* from that time on and forever. (Isa. 9:7)

In his days Judah will be saved and Israel will live in safety. This is the name by which he will be called: The LORD Our *Righteousness*. (Jer. 23:6)

During the exile, Israel experiences God's righteousness as his liberating action (Isa. 45:21–22). God will lead them home (43:16–21), save them (43:1) and eventually *establish an everlasting covenant for them*.[50] Isaiah underscores the eschatological character of the "righteousness of God" and of the salvation that Yahweh will soon bring for his people (Isa. 46:13; 51:5, 8).[51]

By taking the semantic field in which the covenant concept occurs seriously, we are driven to recognize the centrality of the parallel themes of "covenant" and "justification"/"the righteousness of God" (δικαιόω; δικαιώσις; δικαιοσύνη) in Pauline theology. Justification by faith is intimately linked to Paul's "understanding of the 'story' of God's promises and covenant-faithfulness."[52]

At the center of the concept of the new covenant in the New Testament, and of Paul's concept of justification, one finds the substitutionary, atoning death of Jesus. Kertelge has summarized the meaning of Jesus' death for the early Christian proclamation of justification as follows: "God communicates to humanity his *righteousness*, that forgives sins and *renews the covenant*; this salvific devotion and care and, with it, the 'proof of his righteousness' has become possible through the substitutionary atoning death of Jesus."[53]

2.4 New covenant and new creation

Paul concludes his argument in 2 Corinthians 5:17–19 by describing his "ministry of reconciliation" (διακονία τῆς καταλλαγῆς). He does not use the

---

[50] Isa. 54:10: "'Though the mountains be shaken and the hills be removed, yet my unfailing love for you will not be shaken nor my covenant of peace be removed,' says the LORD, who has compassion on you."

Isa. 55:3: "Give ear and come to me; hear me, that your soul may live. I will make an everlasting covenant with you, my faithful love promised to David."

[51] Isa. 46:13: "I am bringing my righteousness near, it is not far away; and my salvation will not be delayed."

Isa. 51:5,8: "My righteousness draws near speedily, my salvation is on the way, and my arm will bring justice to the nations … But my righteousness will last forever, my salvation through all generations."

[52] Seifrid, *Justification by Faith: The Origin and Development of a Central Pauline Theme*, NovTSup LXVIII (Leiden: E. J. Brill; New York: Köln, 1992), 270.

[53] Kertelge, "δικαιοσύνη," 791 (translation and italics mine).

expression "new covenant" as a descriptor here, but rather "new creation," in order to describe the nature of the salvation wrought through Christ.[54]

For Paul, God has acted in such a way that he has made new life possible for believers (cf. Rom. 7:6).[55] In his death Christ has broken through the history of "un-redemption" (*Unheilgeschichte*) and created a new beginning for humanity.[56] Through this sacrifice, a *new covenant is instituted that is at once a "new creation"* (2 Cor. 5:17).[57]

3. Two covenants in Galatians 4:21 – 5:1

The theme of Galatians 3:1 – 5:12 can be summarized as "The call of freedom: dying and living with Christ"; 4:21 – 5:1 provides the hermeneutical reason for this call: the achievement of eschatological freedom.[58]

The topic as well as the argumentative function of Galatians 4:21 – 5:1 is quite different from Galatians 3:6–29. In the latter passage Paul provides a fundamental exposition of the Christian reception of Israel's tradition, but in the former he attempts to motivate *his listeners* to make a certain *decision* (4:31 – 5:1). He argues that his hearers are, through their faith, sons of the promise, as Isaac was (Gal. 4:28–30) – and not essentially children of Hagar, "according to the flesh," as their attempts to achieve righteousness through circumcision might suggest (Gal. 4:21; 5:2–12).[59]

Hans Dieter Betz[60] has characterized this passage as the sixth argument of the *probatio* of the Epistle to the Galatians. It contains the concluding scriptural proof of the *propositio* of Galatians 2:15–21, namely, that Gentile Christians, such as the Galatians, are descendants of Abraham's free wife Sarah and not children of the slave woman Hagar. Paul characterizes his method of

---

[54] Hahn, "Zum Stand der Erforschung," 553–63, rightly points out that although there is no direct reference to the Lord's Supper, the usage of the motif "new covenant" is very important for Paul's understanding of the Eucharist words. It is remarkable that 2 Cor. 5:18–21 also has a link to the atonement concept.

[55] This semantic circle also includes Rom. 2:27–29, where Paul contrasts the circumcision of the heart through the Spirit with the letter of the law.

[56] Kertelge, "Das Verständnis des Todes Jesu bei Paulus," in Kertelge (ed.), *Grundthemen paulinischer Theologie* (Freiburg/Basel/Wien: Herder, 1991), 69.

[57] Cf. Hafemann, *Paul, Moses, and the History of Israel*, 429–36, who in concluding remarks to his exposition of 2 Cor. 3:12–18 points to "The New Covenant as the Inauguration of the New Creation."

[58] Cf. Vouga, *An die Galater* (Tübingen: Mohr Siebeck, 1998), vii.

[59] Cf. Vouga, *An die Galater*, 114.

[60] Betz, *Der Galaterbrief: Ein Kommentar zum Brief des Apostels Paulus an die Gemeinden in Galatien* (München: Chr. Kaiser Verlag, 1988), 410–11.

interpretation in verse 24a as "allegorical" (ἅτινά ἐστιν ἀλληγορούμενα). What he calls allegorical is actually a mixture of – as we would call it – allegory and typology.[61]

Galatians 4:21 – 5:1 fulfills an important function in the overall epistle: with the term "freedom" (v. 1), the passage directly defines the last section of the third main part (5:2–12) and also provides a transition to the section of Galatians dealing with ethical instruction. The abrupt movement from 4:20 to 4:21[62] can be explained in light of the apostle's indignation about the church's behavior. The problem situation, as described in 1:6–9, forces Paul to start a new argument,[63] which is born out of the "being perplexed" (ἀπορούμαι; cf. 4:20). Out of this "distress" Paul feels compelled to return to the topic of law and promise.[64] The address in verse 21 stylistically follows the usual patterns in Hellenistic diatribes.[65]

It is obvious that Paul takes for granted that his readers are familiar with certain exegetical and theological insights. The comparison of the two covenants in Galatians 4:21 – 5:1 is, for Paul, not really the main topic, but a *supporting idea* used to underscore a different point – namely, that it is impossible to envision the law as a legitimate way of salvation in addition to the gospel.[66]

It is interesting that Paul uses the term "covenant" here. Dunn believes that Paul employs this term because it presents a significant category of Jewish self-understanding: "Israel as the elect people of God, the nation with whom among all the nations he had chosen to make his covenant, and to whom he had given his law."[67]

The contrasting natures of the covenants in Galatians 4:21 – 5:1[68] are Paul's rhetorical touchstone. The contrast consists in one being a covenant of promise

---

[61] Or, to put it more precisely, he considers that which he wants to interpret to be "allegorical."

[62] Gal. 4:20–21: "How I wish I could be with you now and change my tone, because I am perplexed about you! Tell me, you who want to be under the law, are you not aware of what the law says?"

[63] Becker, "Der Brief an die Galater," in Becker, Conzelmann and Friedrich, *Die Briefe an die Galater, Epheser, Philipper, Kolosser, Thessalonicher und Philemon* (Göttingen: Vandenhoeck & Ruprecht, 1976), 55.

[64] Mußner, *Der Galaterbrief* (Freiburg/Basel/Wien: Herder, 1988), 316–17.

[65] Betz, *Der Galaterbrief*, 414.

[66] Luz, "Der alte Bund und der neue Bund bei Paulus und im Hebräerbrief," *EvT* 27 (1967), 319. Cf. also Gräßer, *Der Alte Bund im Neuen*, 76.

[67] Dunn, *The Epistle to the Galatians*, BNTC (Peabody, MA: Hendrickson, 1993), 249.

[68] Betz, *Der Galaterbrief*, 419, notes that διαθήκη ("covenant") points to a world order. Created by divine will and decision, it contains God's definition of the foundation and purpose of human life.

and the other being a covenant of law.[69] The underlying premise for this argument is the christologically conceived notion of "new covenant" (καινὴ διαθήκη) found in 1 Corinthians 11:23–25 (cf. also 2 Cor. 3:6).[70]

Martyn stresses that what Paul describes here as *two* covenants, is actually two ways in which the *one* covenant with Abraham and his descendants can be understood (there was no covenant with Ishmael, cf. Gen. 17:18–21):[71] The Abraham covenant viewed in terms of freedom and promise is the valid expression of God's electing grace – contrary to a covenant portrayed in terms of law and flesh.

The starting point in Paul's exposition is the contrast between the slave Hagar and the free Sarah. Paul emphasizes not only that the two mothers each had a different social status, but also the contrast between their two sons. The slave woman's son is born "according to the flesh" (κατὰ σάρκα "in the ordinary way"), while the free woman's son is conceived "as the result of a promise" (δι' ἐπαγγελίας).[72] The comparison of the two women is then allegorically applied to the typological contrast between the two covenants, with which Paul assumes his audience to be familiar.[73] The covenant made at Sinai is symbolically represented by Hagar and her slavery (which she passes on to her descendants).[74] Verses 25 and 26 expand the interpretation with the help of a newly introduced, albeit traditional, contrast: that of the earthly and the heavenly Jerusalem. The earthly, present Jerusalem, as the "classical" locus of the law, belongs to the Sinai = Hagar side of the equation. Thus Hagar (and her son

---

[69] In Gal. 3:15, 17 Paul speaks only of one covenant, after he has separated promise and law. The term "covenant" is linked only to "promise" – so he can differentiate between "covenant" and "law." Cf. Martyn, *Galatians* (New York: Doubleday, 1997), 455.

[70] Vouga, *An die Galater*, 117–18. Dunn, *The Epistle to the Galatians*, 249–50, believes that Paul avoided using the covenant concept too often because he feared causing confusion. Although the concept of the new covenant appears in 1 Cor. 11:25 and in 2 Cor. 3:6, Paul prefers in the Epistle to the Romans (when he returns to the same topic) to contrast "promise" and "law" (see Rom. 4:13–22; 9:7–9; 15:8; however, cf. "covenant" in 9:4 and 11:27).

[71] Cf. also Martyn, *Galatians*, 436: "Paul does not draw the thought of two covenants from a literal reading of Genesis 16 – 21. Nothing is clearer in those stories than the singularity of the covenant God made with Abraham and the passing down of that covenant through Isaac and not through Ishmael. There is, thus, no Hagar covenant."

[72] Cf. Betz, *Der Galaterbrief*, 416–17.

[73] Luz, "Der alte Bund und der neue Bund," 320.

[74] Becker, "Der Brief an die Galater," 57. The transmission of the text in v. 25a is not very clear. For a discussion of text critical problems see Mußner, *Galaterbrief*, 322f.

"according to the flesh") → slavery → Sinai covenant → earthly Jerusalem. They are all of a kind.[75]

Verse 26 turns attention to the other side of the equation (although we must note that the parallel structure is not maintained with complete consistency – we are missing the part that reflects Sinai). Paul begins by pointing to a Jerusalem that stands in opposition to the earthly Jerusalem, one that is "above" (ἄνω) with God in heaven.[76] Hence, the following concepts are linked: the Free (Sarah) and her son "as a result of a promise" → the "new" covenant → the Jerusalem from above.

It is important to see that the "heavenly Jerusalem" is not a cipher of future salvation but of an already present entity. It is one which is "our mother" and the mother of all believers in Christ. The "mother" carries over from the allegories of Sarah and Hagar and is also inherent in the general understanding that Jerusalem, or Zion, was the "mother" of Israel.

In a parallel fashion, the heavenly Jerusalem is the mother of believers born for freedom, and not of Judaizers clinging to the law.[77] So the decisive conclusion is that the community of believers does not belong under the law but is associated instead with Sarah, the free woman. Through the church the "new" covenant, the heavenly Jerusalem, has become a present eschatological reality.[78]

The notion of Jerusalem as a holy city that does not belong to this world goes back to the model of the Old Testament temple (for example, Pss. 2:6; 48:2; 50:2; 78:68; Isa. 18:7; Mich. 4:1–2). This literary notion was superseded in the Hebrew imagination by the real temple and city, and by the drama of its political and geographic reality and fortunes. Stereological and eschatological hopes were woven about the concrete city of Jerusalem, as with Mount Zion

---

[75] Becker, "Der Brief an die Galater," 57.

[76] Paul borrows the differentiation between an earthly and a transcendent Jerusalem from Jewish thinking. Cf. Billerbeck, *Briefe des Neuen Testaments*, 573; Mußner, *Der Galaterbrief*, 325–27.

[77] Mußner, *Der Galaterbrief*, 326–27.

[78] Becker, "Der Brief an die Galater," 57–58. Vouga, *An die Galater*, 118, points out that Paul somewhat modifies the traditional concept of the "heavenly Jerusalem," as the contrasts above/below and new/old do not imply any idea of succession: the "present" and the "heavenly" Jerusalem exist in parallel. They represent existential attitudes "under the law" and "free" through faith. Parallels in Gal. 4:21–5:1 and 2 Cor. 3 cannot be overlooked, although the opponents in Galatians have a much stronger nomistic orientation. The freedom (ἐλευθερία) of the church is defined here more concretely as freedom from the law, but, just as in 2 Cor. 3, it is rooted in the gift and rule of the Spirit (Gal. 4:29; 5:5, 16–18; Klaiber, *Rechtfertigung und Gemeinde: Eine Untersuchung zum paulinischen Kirchenverständnis* [Göttingen: Vandenhoeck & Ruprecht, 1982], 163).

(cf., for example, Joel 3:5; 4:16–21). In this way, Jerusalem becomes a metaphor for a transcendent city and a stereological reality.[79]

Paul, then, is claiming that a new era has dawned in salvation history. Believers are not to live out of the old salvation order of Sinai anymore, but in a new redemptive "setting" – that of a new covenant established by the death of Jesus. It is possible to speak of a "Jerusalem from above" in 4:26 because God, in sending his Son to make believers free, co-heirs with Christ (cf. 4:4–5), has created a new divine household (cf. Eph. 2:19). They have their home in heaven, whence the Savior, the Lord Jesus Christ, is expected to come (Phil. 3:20). In this sense the "heavenly Jerusalem is ... our mother."[80]

Important motifs from Galatians 4 also appear in Hebrews 12.[81] Hebrews 12:22a sets up "Mount Zion" as a prominent symbol and contrasts it to the earthly Sinai, along with the covenant enacted there. Mount Zion and the "heavenly Jerusalem" are more than mere earthly places; they become symbols of a transcendent eschatological reality: the locus of divine presence, the "city of the living God." The "you have come" (προσεληλύθατε) that appears as the first word in the sentence of Hebrews 12:22 points clearly to the fact that the motif of the heavenly Jerusalem is interpreted here as "fulfilled eschatology." The church has already come to Zion, to the heavenly Jerusalem; Christians are already, in Paul's words, children and inhabitants of the "Jerusalem from above." This heavenly Jerusalem is the true salvific reality. In contrast, all

---

[79] Elliot, "Jerusalem II: Neues Testament," in *TRE* XVI (Berlin/New York: Walter de Gruyter, 1987), 611. See also Longenecker, *Galatians,* WBC (Dallas: Word, 1990), 214, for references to the concept of the "heavenly Jerusalem" in Jewish wisdom and rabbinic literature.

[80] Borse, *Der Brief an die Galater* (Regensburg: Verlag Friedrich Pustet, 1984), 172, believes that one must avoid further differentiations of the term "heavenly Jerusalem" because the explanations otherwise would transgress the limits set for it by Paul's framework of figurative equivalency. In his extensive interpretation of Galatians 4:21 – 5:1 Martyn, *Galatians,* 457, emphasizes: "In the preceding comment we have seen that virtually all of the elements in Paul's exegesis of Genesis 16 – 21 are pairs of opposites specifically focused on the *two Gentile missions,* the one pursued by him and the one conducted by the Teachers" (italics mine). From this background he interprets the "present Jerusalem" and the "Jerusalem from above" as "a tale of two churches." "The present Jerusalem, that is to say, the Jerusalem church insofar as it allows the False Brothers to sponsor the Law-observant mission to the Gentiles, while blocking support for the circumcision-free Gentile mission ... The Jerusalem Above, that is to say, the mother of the churches born in the circumcision-free mission to Gentiles ... lacking official support from the Jerusalem church" (p. 466).

[81] Cf. also Rev. 3:12; 21:2–4 (the statement of the covenant in v. 3 is remarkable: "and they will be his people, and God himself will ... be their God").

earthly things (Heb. 12:18–21) are but reflections and "shadows" of that truer reality (Heb. 8:5; 10:1). In Hebrews 12:24 the author concludes his description of the believers' new position by asserting that those who have come to Jesus, the "mediator of a new covenant," have become members of a new salvation order. The legal foundation for this eschatological transition is laid by the "sprinkled blood," that is, by the sacrificial death of Jesus, through which a new covenant was established.[82]

4. Summary

In his theology of the (new) covenant, Paul proclaims that a new period of salvation history has dawned. The Christ event has introduced an eschatologically new era in God's history with humanity. Paul stresses that the redemptive significance of the law has dramatically changed. The law as "letter" in 2 Corinthians 3 corresponds to the Sinai of slavery in Galatians 4 and to the law as the partner of sin in Romans 5. In each instance, Paul portrays the negative side of the law's role during the period from Moses until Christ and concludes that this era is now completed.[83]

Paul links motifs such as freedom, promise and the Jerusalem from above (Gal. 4) with the new salvation period of the (new) covenant. In 2 Corinthians 3 this new covenant is interpreted pneumatologically as an eschatological phenomenon brought about by the Spirit in accordance with the prophets' predictions.[84] In this chapter Paul characterizes the ministry of the new covenant by references to the Spirit and to the term "righteousness." The significance of the fact that "covenant" and "righteousness" belong to the same semantic field has been discussed in 4.2.3, above.

The presence and the effectiveness of the Spirit establish the eschatological character of the church and in this way mark the contrast between the new and the old covenants. Spirit and righteousness are not only the *gifts* of the new

---

[82] Cf. Weiß, *Der Brief an die Hebräer* (Göttingen: Vandenhoeck & Ruprecht, 1991), 676, 681–82; Lohse, "Zion-Jerusalem im nachbiblischen Judentum," in *TWNT* VII (1964), 337.

[83] Cf. Dunn, *The Theology of Paul the Apostle* (Grand Rapids/Cambridge: Eerdmans, 1998), 149–50; also Martyn, "Apocalyptic Antinomies in Paul's Letter to the Galatians," *NTS* 31 (1985), 418–24.

[84] Sass, "Der alte und der neue Bund bei Paulus," 232, draws attention to the "prophetic perspective" in Paul. Paul understands the various covenant traditions of the Tanak from the perspective of the prophets' promises. The decisive centre of the new covenant concept is, for him, the forgiveness of sins, which alone makes it possible for the covenant to endure eternally. The already available deposit (pledge) of the new covenant event is the experience of the Spirit's activity.

covenant for the church, but also the *powers* that define the nature and ministry of the church.[85] The new covenant, established by the substitutionary atoning death of Jesus, is effective through the power of the Holy Spirit in the post-Easter period. This is the reason why the expression "new creation" (2 Cor. 5:17–19) can take the place of the motif of the "new covenant." The church is a fellowship of "new creations" – that is, of those who have experienced, through the renewing power of the Holy Spirit, that "if anyone is in Christ, there is a new creation. The old has gone, the new[86] has come!" (TNIV).[87]

Paul's statements about a new covenant are part of his message that *God has acted in an eschatologically new way.* He has made a new life possible for believers – in contrast to the old way of living: "But now, by dying to what once bound us, we have been released from the law so that we serve in the new way of the Spirit, and not in the old way of the written code" (Rom. 7:6). To this message also belongs Romans 2:27–29, where Paul contrasts the circumcision of the heart by the Spirit with the written code of the law.[88]

The question that arises as a result of Paul's proclamation of the new covenant is this: How is the continuity of God's activity between the old and the

---

[85] Klaiber, *Rechtfertigung und Gemeinde*, 161–62.

[86] Martin, *2 Corinthians* (Waco, TX: Word Books, 1986), 54, underlines the significance of the adjective "new" in Paul's message of the new covenant. Eckert, "Gottes Bundesstiftungen und der neue Bund bei Paulus," 156, also stresses the dimension of the eschatologically new in Paul's understanding of the new covenant: "Christian identity results from its eschatology, from its belief that in Christ 'the fullness of time' and salvation have come (Gal. 4:4) and that 'in Christ' 'the new creation' has been given (2 Cor. 5:17) ... As much as Paul accentuates, especially when addressing Hellenistic Christians, God's faithfulness to Israel in his covenants with them, as seriously would he and his multifarious covenant concept be misunderstood if his emphasis on the unbroken covenant would not bring out the eschatologically new and the new covenant sufficiently clearly as the gospel."

[87] Sanders, *Paul and Palestinian Judaism*, 514, points out that Paul goes beyond categories of covenant when he compares Christ, not with Moses, but with Adam. He continues: "But the primary reason for which it is inadequate to depict Paul's religion as a new covenantal nomism is that that term does not take account of his participationist transfer terms, which are the most significant terms for understanding his soteriology. The covenantal conception could readily encompass the discussion of Christ's dying for past transgression, but it is not adequate to take into account the believer's dying with Christ."

[88] Rom. 2:27–29: "The one who is not circumcised physically and yet obeys the law will condemn you who, even though you have the written code and circumcision, are a lawbreaker. A man is not a Jew if he is only one outwardly, nor is circumcision merely outward and physical. No, a man is a Jew if he is one inwardly; and circumcision is circumcision of the heart, by the Spirit, not by the written code. Such a man's praise is not from men, but from God."

new covenant to be understood? How is the relationship between the church and Israel to be defined? Can Paul be used as the one principal witness *against* the attempt to speak of a new covenant, established by Jesus of Nazareth, which encompasses Israel and the nations? Is Paul against the confirmation of the one undissolved (unbroken) covenant of God with his people?

The weight and the scope of validity of Paul's antithetic comparisons of the "old" and "new" covenant are driven by pragmatic concerns and concrete historical situations. Approaching the issue from a broad perspective, it would be an exaggeration not to see any continuity between the covenants at all. This would then also mean that, in the end, there can be no continuity (or bridge) between God's activity in the old and new covenants, which Paul vehemently contests and disproves in Romans 9 – 11.[89] While affirming the eschatological newness of the new covenant, Paul has left no doubt that the election of Israel has lasting character.[90]

---

[89] Sass, "Der alte und der neue Bund bei Paulus," 233.

[90] See Merklein, "Der (neue) Bund als Thema der paulinischen Theologie," 307.
    See Chapter 9.3.1, below, for an explanation of Rom. 9 – 11 and the consequences of these passages for Jewish-Christian dialogue.

5

The New Covenant in the Epistle to the Hebrews

1. Introduction

> The main theme of Hebrews is the theological expansion of reflection about the passion to the realm of the mystery of the heavenly cult, with the atonement at its center. The author of Hebrews achieves, with the question of the Old Testament cult, that which Paul accomplished with regard to the Old Testament law … The high priest Christ, who has sacrificed himself "once for all" and has entered the Holy of Holies, is the *end of the cult as a way to salvation.*[1]

The Christology of the Epistle to the Hebrews is of great importance because of the clarity of its witness regarding Jesus Christ. This Christology also has a clearly *pastoral* purpose: "The writer's pastoral task was to help the community realize the reality of God's decisive action in Christ and of Christ's present ability to intervene on their behalf."[2] Paul Ellingworth believes that the majority of those to whom the Epistle to the Hebrews[3] was addressed had come to faith in

---

[1] Gräßer, *An die Hebräer*, I (Zürich: Benziger Verlag, 1993), 25–26. For an exposition of the background of the Epistle to the Hebrews see Hurst, *The Epistle to the Hebrews: Its Background and Thought* (Cambridge: Cambridge University Press, 1990).

[2] Cf. Lane, *Hebrews 1 – 8*, WBC (Dallas: Word Books, 1991), cxxxviii.

[3] Buchanan, *To the Hebrews* (New York: Doubleday, 1972), 246, treats Hebrews 1 – 12 and 13 separately and characterizes the first 12 chapters of the epistle as a homiletic midrash. There is broad consensus that the Epistle to the Hebrews is a "sermon or homily" (cf. Lane, *Hebrews 1 – 8*, lxxiv). Gräßer, *An die Hebräer*, 15 (pointing to Dibelius), however, rightly emphasizes the thoroughly literary form of Hebrews and believes that it is more of a "book … in fact, the only book in the New Testament, 'that has only one theme: Christ is the true high priest'." In his monograph *Covenant and Sacrifice in the Letter to the Hebrews*, Dunnill, 261, points out that the "inner genre" of the Epistle to the Hebrews is "a covenant-renewal rite" (SNTSMS 75 [Cambridge: Cambridge University Press, 1992]). See McCullough, "Hebrews in Recent Scholarship (Parts 1 & 2)," *IBS* 16.2 (1994), esp. 110–17, for an overview of the history of research.

Christ from Judaism[4] and lived in cities such as Rome where Judaism (but not Christianity) enjoyed official recognition. In such circumstances there was a tendency to play down, or even betray, the unique and specifically Christian dimension of faith. Against this background, the author of Hebrews places his main emphasis on "Christ as the essential and inseparable culmination of God's purposes for his own people, under old and new dispensations alike. The writer's distinctive teaching about the high priesthood of Christ is the central focus of this positive appeal."[5]

In Hebrews 4:14–16 the author speaks of "holding firmly to the faith we profess" and "approaching the throne of grace with confidence." He summarizes the parenetic purpose of the Epistle to the Hebrews as follows. On one hand, readers are encouraged to hold fast to the word that they have heard (2:1), to the confession (4:14; 10:23), to the trust/confidence (παρρησία, 3:6; 10:19, 35) and hope (ἐλπίς, 3:6; 6:11) that is a part of this confidence (παρρησία). They are also encouraged to have patience (ὑπομονή 10:36; 12:2, 7), a virtue that they had displayed during previous times of persecution (10:32–34).

On the other hand, readers are encouraged to exhibit "dynamic" virtues (drawn, perhaps, from the cultic arena) of approaching the throne of grace (προσερχώμεθα; 4:16; cf. 10:22)[6] and making every effort to enter God's rest (σπουδάσωμεν … εἰσελθεῖν, 4:11). In addition, readers are exhorted to persevere in the race (δι᾽ ὑπομονῆς τρέχωμεν … ἀγῶνα, 12:1).[7] The church proved itself in persecutions (cf. 10:32–34; also 6:10; 13:7) but has used up in the meantime all of the energies of their good beginning.[8]

Intensification is one of the important rhetorical devices used by the author of Hebrews. The comparative adjectives κρείσσων/κρείττων and the comparative adverb κρεῖττον, meaning "of higher quality," or "better," appear twelve times in the epistle and are of decisive significance in its argument. This

---

[4]　The important role that Jewish cultic traditions play in the text does not necessarily point to Jewish Christians as addressees, cf. Attridge, *The Epistle to the Hebrews* (Philadelphia: Fortress Press, 1989), 12. Theobald, "Zwei Bünde und ein Gottesvolk: Die Bundestheologie des Hebräerbriefs im Horizont des christlich-jüdischen Gesprächs," *TQ* 176.4 (1996), 311–13, also believes that it is not yet satisfactorily proven that the addressees of the epistle were primarily *Jewish Christians*. One cannot read Hebrews as a *Tractatus contra Judaeos* ("tract against Jews").

[5]　Ellingworth, *The Epistle to the Hebrews: A Commentary on the Greek Text* (Grand Rapids: Eerdmans, 1993), 80.

[6]　See Thüsing, "'Laßt uns hinzutreten …' (Hebr 10,22): Zur Frage nach dem Sinn der Kulttheologie im Hebräerbrief," in Söding (ed.), *Studien zur neutestamentlichen Theologie* (Tübingen: J. C. B. Mohr [Paul Siebeck], 1995), 184–200.

[7]　Attridge, *The Epistle to the Hebrews*, 22.

[8]　Backhaus, *Der neue Bund und das Werden der Kirche*, 71–72.

intensification is observed primarily in relation to the new priesthood (cf. 7:1), the new covenant (cf., for example, 8:6–13) and the new sacrifice (cf. 10:5–10).[9]

1.1 Hebrews and Judaism

One question that arises is whether we can observe sentiments of anti-Judaism in Hebrews. The early Christians perceived themselves very much *part of Judaism*. "For that reason NT statements critical of Judaism have to be interpreted within the context of intramural conflicts among Jews in the first century."[10] Hebrews is a Jewish-Christian document that is strongly influenced by Hellenistic Judaism. Despite a significant discontinuity, constant meditation about the Scriptures presupposes, however, a continuity with the "old Israel." Even when discontinuity is emphasized, as in Hebrews 8:13, it is made clear that God himself has annulled the validity of the first covenant. The principle that a new activity of God results in the previous one being made obsolete (Heb. 7:11–12) is a Jewish-Christian perspective. The idea that Mosaic and Levitical regulations have been fulfilled through the priestly mediation of Christ is a typical characteristic of the Jewish Christianity of the Epistle to the Hebrews. Lane believes:

> the comparison of the old and new covenants, not only here but elsewhere in the homily (for example, 12:18–29), is not an indication of the polemical anti-Judaic character of Hebrews. For the writer this represents simply an application of a hermeneutical method by which he sought to make clear to his audience the irrevocable guarantee of the divine promise that had been subjected to questioning. It is an expression of pastoral strategy.[11]

2. Jesus as guarantee of a better covenant (Heb. 7:20–22)

> And it was not without an oath! Others became priests without any oath, but he became a priest with an oath when God said to him: 'The Lord has sworn and will not change his mind: "You are a priest forever."' Because of this oath, Jesus has become the guarantee of a better covenant. (Heb. 7:20–22)

The term "covenant" (διαθήκη) appears in the Epistle to the Hebrews for the first time in 7:20–22 – quite abruptly without any preparation or further explanation. It is a characteristic of this letter's composition that

---

[9] See Lane, *Hebrews 1 – 8*, cxxix–cxxxv.
[10] Lane, *Hebrews 1 – 8*, cxxvi.
[11] Lane, *Hebrews 1 – 8*, cxxxiii.

important themes are mentioned first and are then, only later, systematically developed.[12]

Hebrews 7:1–28 is formally, as well as conceptually, an independent unit: 7:1 begins a new topic, while 7:28 summarizes the main points of the passage.

Formally, Hebrews 7:20–22 is a self-contained complete sentence. Its main focus is not the covenant as such, but a covenant that is "better" by virtue of its christological significance. Jesus is the guarantor of this better covenant.[13] He is juxtaposed with the Levitical priests by way of an antithetical parallelism. The old salvation order they represent is not discarded or condemned but considered temporary, or provisional.[14] The point of reference for this comparison, which is at first structurally oriented, finally becomes *the person of Jesus as the new high priest*.[15] The proper name "Jesus" is further highlighted by its placement at the end of the sentence. From its first appearance, "covenant" (διαθήκη) presents itself as the function of the cultic and priesthood theology of Hebrews.[16] The "better covenant" is the covenant of the forgiveness of sins because God's salvation has finally been realized. Therefore, the first covenant is "old" because it failed in exactly this decisive point (8:13).[17]

The qualification of this covenant (διαθήκη) as "better" (κρείττων) is illustrated by the association of Jesus as high priest with the order of Melchizedek's priesthood. This priesthood, and the covenant it represents, is better because it is heavenly rather than temporal. To this covenant belong such eschatological gifts as rest (4:11), an eternal homeland (11:14), an enduring city (13:14) and a heavenly cult established and guaranteed by the blood of the eternally living priest (cf. 8:6; 9:14–15; 12:24; 7:25).[18]

The covenant guaranteed in Christ is, in contrast to the Levitical covenant, irrevocable and eschatologically valid, because it is founded on the "son, who has been made perfect forever" (7:28; cf. 5:9). Only this "better covenant" exhibits the perfection (τελείωσις) that allows participation in eschatological salvation and the Shabbat celebration of the people of God (4:9). The law (νόμος), that functions as the contrasting term in 7:18–19, could not achieve this. The covenant guaranteed in Christ has the power to mediate a "drawing near" to God (7:19) and entry into eternal salvation (7:25; cf. 5:9). The

---

[12] See Backhaus, *Der neue Bund und das Werden der Kirche*, 74.

[13] Backhaus, *Der neue Bund und das Werden der Kirche*, 75, 80–82.

[14] Backhaus, *Der neue Bund und das Werden der Kirche*, 93.

[15] Backhaus, *Der neue Bund und das Werden der Kirche*, 99.

[16] Backhaus, *Der neue Bund und das Werden der Kirche*, 111.

[17] Gräßer, *An die Hebräer*, II, 56.

[18] See Gräßer, *An die Hebräer*, II, 57. He points out (n. 38) that the closeness to the cult is determined by the Old Testament ברית ("covenant"): the priestly privileges (Num. 25:13), the atonement cover (Exod. 31:7), the curtain (Exod. 27:21) and the blood of the sacrifice (Exod. 24:8) are all linked with God's covenant.

superiority of the better covenant rests in its effectiveness to work out salvation.[19]

3. Christ as the high priest and mediator of a better covenant based on better promises (Heb. 8:6)

> But the ministry Jesus has received is as superior to theirs as the covenant of which he is mediator is superior to the old one, and it is founded on better promises.

Hebrews 8:6 functions as a bridge between Hebrews 7 and 8:1 – 10:18. This verse further develops the theme of Jesus as heavenly high priest introduced in 7:20–22 and emphasizes the superiority of Jesus' ministry (λειτουργία). Hebrews 8:6 forms a bridge to a quotation from Jeremiah (8:8–12). All of this sets the stage for the central soteriological exposition of 8:1 – 10:18.[20]

The contrast in Hebrews 8:1–6 between the heavenly and the earthly cult order parallels the contrast in chapter 7 between the eternal validity of the one cult order and the transitory validity of the other, and between the one eternal priest and the many mortal priests (7:12, 16, 23–25). On the basis of these comparisons, 8:6 concludes that the ministry Christ has received is ontologically superior (διαφορώτερον) to that of lesser priests, and that the covenant (διαθήκη) of which he is mediator is founded on better promises (ἐπαγγελίαι)[21] than the old one and is thus superior to it.

The three comparative expressions in 8:6 are worth noting: superior ministry (διαφορώτερα λειτουργία), superior covenant (κρείττων διαθήκη) and better promises (κρείττονες ἐπαγγελίαι). "Better promises"[22] is emphasized by its position at the end of the construction of 8:6. This emphasis underscores that the comparison of the two sanctuaries in 8:1 – 10:18 shows the priesthood and sacrifice of Christ conveying a salvific import of better hope (κρείττων ἐλπίς, 7:19). The goal of this better hope is described in terms of being "made perfect" (τελείωσις, 11:40), entering into rest (κατάπαυσις, 4:11), approaching a heavenly city (πόλις, 11:10, 16; 12:22; 13:14), an unshakeable kingdom (βασιλεία, 12:28), the heavenly sanctuary (τὰ ἅγια, 10:19) or simply the presence of God (7:19; cf. 4:16). The verb "to give the law" (νομοθετέω, see also 7:11) relates the gift of the better promises (ἐπαγγελίαι) antithetically to the gift

---

[19] See Frey, "Die alte und die neue διαθήκη nach dem Hebräerbrief," in Avemarie and Lichtenberger, *Bund und Tora*, 274.

[20] See Backhaus, *Der neue Bund und das Werden der Kirche*, 126.

[21] See Frey, "Die alte und die neue διαθήκη," 275.

[22] See Backhaus, *Der neue Bund und das Werden der Kirche*, 151, on the relationship between ἐπαγγελία (promise) and διαθήκη ("covenant").

of the law (νόμος).[23] The point here is that the "better promises" are unalterably valid and legally binding.[24]

The two qualities that constitute the superiority of the covenant of "better promises" are: (1) it is heavenly in rank, because it is based on the ministry (λειτουργία) of the heavenly high priest; (2) unlike the Levitical cult, it is able (through Christ) to accomplish the ministry (λειτουργία) of forgiveness of sins. The superior quality of the new covenant flows from the soteriological effectiveness of Christ's atoning death (cf. 9:15).[25] Jesus is thus the mediator of the new covenant. This characterization of "covenant mediator" (διαθήκης μεσίτης) is of great significance for covenant Christology (cf. 8:6; 9:15; 12:24). Jesus establishes a new relationship between God and his people in that his atoning death makes possible new soteriological provisions from God. In this, Christ parallels Moses as the "mediator of the first covenant."[26]

4. Jeremiah 31 (LXX 38): 31–34: The new covenant and the forgiveness of sins; annulment of the first covenant (Heb. 8:1–7 and 10:15–18)

The topic of Hebrews 8:7–13 is God's annulment of the Sinaitic cult order. This passage, together with 10:15–17 as an *inclusion,* consolidates the central soteriological thrust of Hebrews under the rubric of the covenant. The author of the Letter to the Hebrews places the central statements about the covenant (see also 10:1–10) in the context of the history of a promise. The first covenant is "not without fault" because it is rooted in the sphere of human and earthly imperfection.[27]

In 8:8–12, the author of Hebrews sets forth the fundamental promise from Jeremiah 31 (LXX 38):31–34, without additional explanations and without significant changes to the Septuagint text available to him. Only in the framing of verses 7–8a and 13 does the author show what role this quote plays in the flow of his argumentation.[28]

---

[23] See Backhaus, *Der neue Bund und das Werden der Kirche,* 146 on νόμος (law) and διαθήκη ("covenant") in Hebrews.

[24] See Frey, "Die alte und die neue διαθήκη," 276.

[25] See Frey, "Die alte und die neue διαθήκη," 227.

[26] See Backhaus, *Der neue Bund und das Werden der Kirche,* 156. Cf. also Attridge, *The Epistle to the Hebrews,* 221: "In Judaism various mediators were envisioned including intercessor angels and the spirit. The primary mediator was, of course, Moses in his role as agent of the Sinai covenant."

[27] Backhaus, *Der neue Bund und das Werden der Kirche,* 179–80.

[28] Frey, "Die alte und die neue διαθήκη," 277–78.

The first-order heuristic value of the Jeremiah passage is not the author's concern.[29] His focus is not the promise of the new covenant, but rather to critique the old covenant. In verses 7–13 the author underscores the reasons for the need for a change from the first to the "second" and from the old to the "new" salvation provisions. The framing verses 8:7 and 8:13 contain, primarily, statements about the new covenant. Forgiveness of sins, the subject upon which the author wishes to focus, appears in 10:16–17. The central part of the Jeremiah quote receives no emphasis or attention. The author does not touch on the Torah being written in the heart, knowledge of God, or the covenant formula. In contrast to the Epistle of Barnabas, the motif of breaking the covenant does not take center stage.[30]

The focus of the author of Hebrews is the "new" that characterizes the new covenant, and that newness is the reality of the forgiveness of sins. The promise "for I will forgive their wickedness and will remember their sins no more"[31] comprises the final lines of the quote in Hebrews 8:12 and is reemphasized in 10:16–17.[32]

It is remarkable to note the modifications of the Jeremiah quote in 10:15–18, as compared to 8:8–12. In 8:8–12 the quote is introduced as a direct address of God and is understood as a verdict against the "old" covenant. Now (in 10:15–18), it appears as a current testimony of the Holy Spirit spoken to the Christian church (cf. v. 15: "testifies to us" – μαρτυρεῖ δὲ ἡμῖν). The "house of Israel" and the "house of Judah" (8:10) are substituted in 10:16 with the more general "with them" (πρὸς αὐτούς). The promise about the Torah is, as in 8:10, included without any special emphasis. The covenant formula and the promise of the knowledge of God are left out completely. The expression "and their lawless acts" (καὶ τῶν ἀνομιῶν αὐτῶν) in verse 17, that expands beyond Jeremiah 31[38]:34 and Hebrews 8:12b, points to the significance of the promise of the forgiveness of sins, which then is also confirmed by the conclusion in verse 18.

In short, a new provision for forgiveness of sins came into being when Christ entered the heavenly sanctuary as the high priest and once and for all offered his own blood as an atoning sacrifice (cf. Heb. 1:3; 2:17; 9:11–12; 10:12–14). "In the reality of the forgiveness of sins and in free access to God

---

[29] Cf. Backhaus, *Der neue Bund und das Werden der Kirche*, 180.

[30] This motif is linked in the textual tradition of the Septuagint (in contrast to the Masoretic text) with an explicit statement of rejection: "They did not remain faithful to my covenant (διαθήκη), and I turned away from them (καὶ ἐγὼ ἠμέλησα αὐτῶν)." Heb. 8:9 cites this version. (Frey, "Die alte und die neue διαθήκη," 278–79.)

[31] ὅτι ἵλεως ἔσομαι ταῖς ἀδικίαις αὐτῶν καὶ τῶν ἁμαρτιῶν αὐτῶν οὐ μὴ μνησθῶ ἔτι; Jer. 31 [38]: 34b.

[32] Frey, "Die alte und die neue διαθήκη," 279.

himself (7:19) lies the 'better' (κρεῖττον), the superiority of the new covenant in comparison with the Levitical cult, stated as thesis in 7:22 and 8:6."[33]

5. The soteriological foundation of the new covenant (Heb. 9:15–22)

> For this reason Christ is the mediator of a new covenant, that those who are called may receive the promised eternal inheritance – now that he has died as a ransom to set them free from the sins committed under the first covenant. (Heb. 9:15)

> The passage 9:11–22 represents a soteriological ... explication of the διαθήκη [covenant] motif which elaborates the basic thesis of 9:15a from a legal metaphorical as well as cult typological perspective: God constitutes in Christ's atoning death the 'legal status' of the new covenant as an anti-type to the Sinai covenant ... While further covenant statements simply vary the thesis of 9:15 (cf. 10:15–18, 29; 12:22–24; 13:20), this verse [9:15] represents not only the climax, but also the sum of the whole covenant theology of Hebrews.[34]

The author of the Epistle to the Hebrews describes in impressive ways the sanctuary, worship and soteriological effectiveness of the first covenant and the new covenant:

The first covenant	The new covenant
The earthly, "man-made," "imitation" sanctuary (9:24)	The true, original, heavenly sanctuary (9:24)
The "tabernacle" of the wilderness period with its furniture (9:1–5; cf. 8:5)	The "greater and more perfect tabernacle" (9:11), that is not made with hands and does not belong to this creation (9:11)
The worship of Levite priests and the yearly sacrifice of the high priest on the Day of Atonement (9:6–7)	The "better" (9:23) sacrifice of the high priest Christ, made once and for all in the heavenly sanctuary (9:11–12, 24–25)
Sacrifices made with the "foreign" blood of animals that, according to the author of Hebrews, can never really take away sin (9:25; 10:2)	Christ enters the heavenly sanctuary by virtue of his own blood and is sacrificed, effecting eternal salvation (9:12; cf. 9:15), forgiveness (9:22; 10:18) and true separation from sin (9:26)
Earthly external regulations of the "flesh" (9:10), such as food regulations and ceremonial washings, causing only external purity of the flesh (9:13)	Purity of conscience (9:14) and forgiveness of sins; the perfection (τελείωσις; cf. 9:9; 10:14) wrought by the blood of Christ, which provides access to the heavenly sanctuary and the presence of God

---

[33] Cf. Frey, "Die alte und die neue διαθήκη," 279–80, here 280.
[34] Backhaus, *Der neue Bund und das Werden der Kirche*, 185–86.

The relationship between the old and new salvation order is not a merely temporal one of succession and of replacement of the old by the new (8:7, 13; 10:9). This relationship has metaphysical and qualitative aspects as well. Specifically, the two stand in relationship to each other as copy (*Abbild*) to original (*Urbild*) (8:5; 10:1). The former is earthly, fleshly and temporary, the latter is heavenly and eternal. The new covenant is incomparably superior to the old due to its heavenly origin, the range of salvific revelation it mediates (9:8) and especially in its salvific efficiency.[35]

In 9:11–20, as in 7:22 and 8:6, the author of Hebrews links high priest Christology with covenant terminology. Jörg Frey points out that the two soteriological statements found in 9:11–12 and 9:15 summarize the theology of the whole epistle: (1) Christ, as high priest, has once for all entered the heavenly sanctuary by virtue of his blood and, through his sacrifice, achieved an everlasting salvation (αἰωνία λύτρωσις); (2) as a result, he has become the "mediator" (cf. 7:22) of the new covenant so that through the absolution (ἀπολύτρωσις) of sins achieved by his death, the elect (κεκλημένοι) can receive the promised eternal inheritance.[36] It is noteworthy that these key statements appear at the compositional center of Hebrews (8:1 – 10:18).

Christ's cross and exaltation are interpreted here cult typologically, according to the model of the Day of Atonement (Lev. 16). The author of Hebrews, however, underscores that the atonement wrought by Christ's sacrifice (9:7, 26, 28) is unique in that its effect is forever valid (10:12, 14; "once for all," ἐφάπαξ, 7:27; 9:12; 10:10).

Hebrews emphasizes Christ's entering the Most Holy place (cf. 6:20; 9:11–12, 24).[37] This entry into the true sanctuary characterizes his ascent into the heavenly world. From a more particularly Hebrew perspective, it signifies that Christ, in his role as high priest, has penetrated through the heavenly היכל ("temple") behind the sacred curtain (6:19–20; 10:19) and into the Most Holy place of the heavenly sanctuary. The corollary of Jesus' earthly death on the cross is that he brings his blood before God as an atoning sacrifice as a high priest in the heavenly sanctuary. This heavenly enactment of the ritual of atonement represents a better (κρείττων) and more efficacious covenant (cf. Heb. 9:11–12 and 9:24–26). As Moses (cf. 9:18–22) was the *mediator*[38] of the old covenant, Christ is the mediator of the new covenant (9:15; cf. 8:6; 12:24). The term "mediator" (μεσίτης) is closely related with "guarantee" (ἔγγυος, 7:22) and introduces a strong legal component to the context of 9:15. The

---

[35] Frey, "Die alte und die neue διαθήκη," 281.
[36] Frey, "Die alte und die neue διαθήκη," 282–83.
[37] Frey, "Die alte und die neue διαθήκη," 283.
[38] See Gräßer, *An die Hebräer*, II, 168–69, for a discussion of the appropriation and influence of the term "mediator."

implications of Jesus' function as mediator are alluded to in 9:15. Christ's death on the cross is the blood sacrifice through which the absolution (ἀπολύτρωσις) of sins is achieved in finality. The new relationship with God made possible by this sacrifice is negatively characterized as freedom from sins and positively characterized as the assurance of eschatological salvation.[39]

The fundamental significance of Jesus' death is elaborated in 9:16–17 and 9:18–22. The author of Hebrews uses διαθήκη in verse 16 to mean "last will." Although Christ has before been called the mediator and guarantee of God's covenant, he is here shown to be its testator as well. Verse 18 transitions from a legal to a cult typology, because a διαθήκη (will) becomes effective only in case of death; "not even the first covenant was inaugurated without blood" (οὐδὲ ἡ πρώτη χωρὶς αἵματος ἐγκεκαίνισται). In verses 18–21, the author's main purpose is to explicate the fundamental meaning of Jesus' death according to the blood ritual recorded in Exodus 24. The discussion is framed by "blood" (αἷμα, v. 18) and "blood shedding" (αἱματεκχυσία, v. 22), indicating the theme of the passage.

At the center of the passage are the "words of institution" from Exodus 24:8: "this is the blood of the covenant, which God has commanded you to keep" (τοῦτο τὸ αἷμα τῆς διαθήκης ἧς ἐνετείλατο πρὸς ὑμᾶς ὁ θεός).[40] This phrase differs from the actual wording of the Septuagint: "behold, the blood of the covenant, which the Lord made with you concerning all these words" (ἰδοὺ τὸ αἷμα τῆς διαθήκης ἧς διέθετο κύριος πρὸς ὑμᾶς περὶ πάντων τῶν λόγων τούτων). Frey makes four observations concerning the differences between the passages:[41]

> (1) The dissolution of the *figura etymologica* through the substitution of διέθετο by ἐνετείλατο probably follows only stylistic motives.
>
> (2) The substitution of "God" (θεός) for "Lord" (κύριος), placed pointedly at the end of the phrase, has theological significance and accentuates the divine initiative of salvation.
>
> (3) The specification "concerning all these words" (περὶ πάντων τῶν λόγων τούτων) can be neglected because the author of Hebrews does not perceive the covenant to be an obligation involving some kind of law (νόμος) or book (βιβλίον).
>
> (4) The change from "this is the blood" (τοῦτο τὸ αἷμα) to "behold, the blood" (ἰδοὺ τὸ αἷμα) can be explained through the assumption that the author knew this formulation from the Lord's Supper tradition (Mark 14:24: "this is my blood of the covenant" [τοῦτό ἐστιν τὸ αἷμά μου τῆς διαθήκης]; cf. Matt. 26:28) and adapted the text of the quote from Exodus 24:8 to a word-

---

[39] Frey, "Die alte und die neue διαθήκη," 286–88.
[40] Frey, "Die alte und die neue διαθήκη," 289.
[41] Frey, "Die alte und die neue διαθήκη," 290.

ing also familiar to his addressees (cf. the use of the formula τὸ αἷμά τῆς διαθήκης in 10:29 and 13:20). The expression "blood of Christ," referring to his death, as well as the covenant motif — which is so important in this context — have their origin in the eucharistic tradition.[42]

6. Stereotypical phrases with covenant in the *peroratio* (Heb. 10:29; 12:24; 13:20)

The *peroratio*,[43] according to ancient rhetorical theory, had two primary tasks: to remind the listeners of the basic thesis of the argumentation *and* to stir their emotions.

Backhaus points out that the language of Hebrews complies with these rules exactly in places where the covenant theme is discussed in stereotypical expressions in the *peroratio* (10:19 – 13:21). Three aspects of the specific meaning of "covenant" in the *peroratio* may be observed (from a compositional, conceptual and rhetorical perspective):

> (1) *Compositionally,* the covenant formulae are placed at the beginning (10:29), climax (12:24) and end (13:20) of the *peroratio.*

> (2) *Conceptually,* all three covenant statements use stereotypical language and reflect the central covenant passage 9:11–20 and especially 9:15, 20. The verses 7:20–22; 8:6, 7–13 and 10:15–18 are also rehearsed (epitomized).

> (3) *Rhetorically,* the covenant formulae belong to passages of the *peroratio* that are explicitly emotionally loaded.[44]

The *peroratio* picks up the expression about Christ being the "mediator of the new covenant" (12:24; cf. 8:6; 9:15) and discusses the "blood of the covenant" (10:29; 13:20) twice. The rhetorical significance of these latter two statements is expanded by readers' familiarity with the church's communal meal tradition.[45]

The covenant term (διαθήκη) appears for the first time in the *peroratio* in the framework of a "threat speech" (10:26–31). The author develops the significance of the Christ covenant in 8:1 – 10:18. He then underscores the seriousness of falling away from the faith. He concludes with an *a minori ad maius*

---

[42] Hegermann, "διαθήκη," in Balz and Schneider, *EWNT*, 185. Frey, "Die alte und die neue διαθήκη," 291, points out (following Backhaus) that, even though the author of Hebrews does not attribute to the Christian Eucharist special theological significance of its own, he nevertheless alludes to the liturgical blessing of the cup and in this way draws from the early Christian reservoir of meaning.

[43] Concluding or summarizing part of a speech.

[44] See Backhaus, *Der neue Bund und das Werden der Kirche,* 213–14.

[45] Frey, "Die alte und die neue διαθήκη," 292.

("from the lesser to the greater") argument. In Deuteronomy 17:6, the one who breaks the law must die. The punishment for rejecting the great salvation gained through baptism can only consist in something most severe: the "eternal judgment" (6:2; cf. 10:30).[46]

Three criteria that mutually interpret each other identify those upon whom such judgment will fall: "who has trampled the Son of God under foot" (ὁ τὸν υἱὸν τοῦ θεοῦ καταπατήσας); "who has treated as an unholy thing the blood of the covenant" [(ὁ) τὸ αἷμα τῆς διαθήκης κοινὸν ἡγησάμενος]; "who has insulted the Spirit of grace" [(ὁ) τὸ πνεῦμα τῆς χάριτος ἐνυβρίσας]. One and the same sin is portrayed with three different participles: (1) as trampling (καταπατεῖν) the *bringer* of salvation, the Son of God (υἱὸς τοῦ θεοῦ); (2) as treating as unholy (κοινὸν ἡγεῖσθαι) the salvation *sacrifice*, the blood of the covenant (αἷμα τῆς διαθήκης); and (3) as insulting (ἐνυβρίζειν) the gift of salvation, the Spirit of grace (πνεῦμα τῆς χάριτος). Gräßer points out that the number "three" is not accidental – it is a convention that characterizes the falling away as final.[47]

The author picks up the blood of the covenant (αἷμα τῆς διαθήκης) – the "blood of institution" of Exodus 24:8, quoted already in 9:20 – and points to the all-surpassing blood of Golgotha (cf. also 9:12, 14; 10:19). The postscript "by which he was sanctified" (ἐν ᾧ ἡγιάσθη, 10:29) is especially significant. Hebrews here establishes a correlation of cult typologies between old and new covenants, Yom Kippur and Good Friday (cf. 9:7, 12, 14, 19, 21–22, 25; 10:19; cf. 13:12, 20). The "ritual of sprinkling" of the old covenant (Exod. 24:3–8; Heb. 9:19–21) is made to correspond to baptism (9:13; 10:22). This correlation is confirmed by the aorist ἡγιάσθη ("was sanctified"). In baptism, the new covenant "blood of institution" offers access to the church.[48]

In 13:20–21, the formula "blood of the covenant" occurs in *a positive* way. In 13:20–21 we find the only clear statement on Jesus' resurrection in the Epistle to the Hebrews. It is linked to the covenant motif: "who through the blood of the eternal covenant brought back from the dead our Lord Jesus, that great Shepherd of the sheep."[49] This statement is crafted in close dependence on Isaiah 63:11–14 (LXX)[50] and Zechariah 9:11 (LXX).[51] Only the phraseology

---

[46] Gräßer, *An die Hebräer*, III, 43; Frey, "Die alte und die neue διαθήκη," 292.

[47] Gräßer, *An die Hebräer,* III, 44–5.

[48] Gräßer, *An die Hebräer*, III, 46.

[49] ὁ ἀναγαγὼν ἐκ νεκρῶν τὸν ποιμένα τῶν προβάτων τὸν μέγαν ἐν αἵματι διαθήκης αἰωνίου, τὸν κύριον ἡμῶν Ἰησοῦν.

[50] ὁ ἀναβιβάσας ἐκ τῆς γῆς τὸν ποιμένα τῶν προβάτων ... ὁ ἀγαγὼν (v. l. LXX Symmachus: ἀναγαγὼν) ... Μωϋσῆν... ([who] brought up from the sea the shepherd of the sheep... who led [v. 1. Symm. "raised"] Moses...).

[51] καὶ σὺ ἐν αἵματι διαθήκης ἐξαπέστειλας δεσμίους σου ἐκ λάκκου (and thou by the blood of thy covenant has sent forth thy prisoners out of the pit).

"from the dead" (ἐκ νεκρῶν) instead of "out of the pit" (ἐκ λάκκου) and "eternal" (αἰώνιος) are original to the author. The reason for Jesus' resurrection from the dead and his inauguration as shepherd and high priest lies in his atoning death that has established the new salvation order. The addition of "eternal" (αἰώνιος) underscores the final and superior character of that order.[52]

By reminding readers of the soteriological reality of the new covenant established by Christ, this letter as a whole conveys a comforting assurance in the face of threatening faith weariness.[53] At the climax of the *peroratio* the author of Hebrews provides an elevated restatement of the salvific position of the church. In contrast to the people of God at Sinai, the church approaches Mount Zion, the *heavenly* Jerusalem (12:18–21). It is again emphasized that Jesus is the mediator of a "new covenant" (νέα διαθήκη) through the "sprinkled blood that speaks a better (κρεῖττον) word than Abel."[54] Abel, together with the "cloud of witnesses," could testify only as someone who is hoping for eschatological salvation. The blood of Jesus, however, speaks a better[55] word (cf. 11:40) insofar as it announces an ontologically *completed* salvation. In the blood of Christ's sacrifice and in the new covenant, access to the invisible heavenly reality has been mediated and guaranteed.[56]

7. Summary

The author of Hebrews has the remarkable ability to keep various perspectives in balance. He manages to maintain the tension between realized and future eschatology. He characterizes the Christ event from the perspective of both continuity and discontinuity with its Jewish origins.

The notion of a "new covenant" plays a key role in building this conceptual bridge in two ways. (1) Through a creative reinterpretation of the covenant term from a *cultic* perspective, the author succeeds in describing the *continuity* of the Christ event with the cultic background of Israel. The Christ event is the final fulfillment of the cultic heritage of Israel. (2) The *discontinuity* of the *newness of the covenant* lies in the final, lasting and superior status of the

---

[52] Frey, "Die alte und die neue διαθήκη," 293.
[53] Frey, "Die alte und die neue διαθήκη," 293.
[54] According to the best manuscripts, v. 24 does not speak of the "blood of Abel" but of Abel himself, who "speaks" and whose speaking is contrasted with the "sprinkled blood" (cf. Frey, "Die alte und die neue διαθήκη," 294, esp. n. 133).
[55] Backhaus, *Der neue Bund und das Werden der Kirche*, 220, points out that κρεῖττον (better) should be understood as an adjective rather than adverbially.
[56] Frey, "Die alte und die neue διαθήκη," 294. For further explanations on this passage in relation to Gal. 4, see 4.3, above.

salvation established by Christ as the summation of the soteriological heritage of Israel.[57]

The author of Hebrews attributes special significance to Scripture verses such as Jeremiah 31 (38 LXX):31–34 and Exodus 24:8 (LXX). In spite of the important role that these verses play, the author emphasizes the texts selectively. The continuous point of reference and structural center of his covenantal exegesis is the *confession of Christ*.[58]

The covenant motif is also central in the *soteriology* of the Epistle to the Hebrews. The reality of the forgiveness of sins is granted to those who participate in the new covenant. On the basis of eschatological purity, they are assured at the same time of eschatological salvation, entrance to the heavenly city and heavenly sanctuary and participation in the everlasting Shabbat celebration of the people of God.[59] It is likely that the author adopted his soteriological perspective on the function of covenant from the Christ confession, possibly in connection with the Lord's Supper tradition. However, he has developed the covenant motif far beyond the traditional linguistic usage to usage as a soteriological core term.

The author of Hebrews explicates the essence of the salvation order inaugurated through the atoning death of Christ in *antitypical contrast to the covenant of Sinai*. The relationship between the two covenants can be described with three key terms: *difference, correspondence* and *superiority*.

Because of its heavenly and eternal essence and its salvific efficacy, the Christ covenant, when contrasted with the Sinaitic covenant, is radically *different*. Through the introduction of the new covenant (7:11, 19; 8:13; 10:9), the old becomes outdated (8:13) and its validity expires (7:18; 10:9) – it becomes obsolete (10:18) and has to die (8:13). The author of Hebrews underlines the *cancellation* of the old earthly order and its *replacement* by a new eschatological salvation founded upon Christ's death. One can, therefore, not speak of a restitution or fulfillment of the first covenant.

With the *cancellation of the first covenant,* Hebrews proclaims a "change of the law" (νόμου μετάθεσις, 7:12); a "setting aside" (ἀθέτησις) of the previously valid Levitical regulations (7:18). In the same way as the Sinai covenant (διαθήκη), this "law" (νόμος) was God's ordinance. But, like the Sinai covenant, it is temporary, not eternal. Christ, however, is never characterized as "law giver" for those who receive his covenant. It is remarkable that, when

---

[57] See Lehne, *The New Covenant in Hebrews* (Sheffield: Sheffield Academic Press, 1990), 119.

[58] Cf. Backhaus, *Der neue Bund und das Werden der Kirche*, 355: "From a New Testament perspective … a Christian covenant theology seems untenable without a recourse to the constitutive significance of the Christ event."

[59] Frey, "Die alte und die neue διαθήκη," 296. I am mainly following Frey, 297–305, in this context.

Moses appears in parallel to Jesus in 9:18–22 as a "mediator of the covenant," there is no reference to the giving of the law. The author does not present his exhortations in Hebrews by referring to a new law. Instead, he refers to the "wandering people of God" and uses the motivating examples of the "cloud of witnesses" and Jesus' way of suffering (12:1–2).

The author of Hebrews bases his reproach of the sufficiency of the Sinai covenant on *Scripture*. However, he does not cite reasons such as the sin of the wilderness generation to argue that the covenant was broken (cf. Jer. 38:32 [LXX]; Heb. 8:9). He argues exclusively on the basis of the message that "in these last days he (God) has spoken to us by his Son" (1:1–2).[60]

Although the author is very keen to depict for his church the incomparability of salvation in Christ,[61] it must be stressed that in no instance does Hebrews create a polemical opposition of fronts[62] that denies the correspondence of the two covenants. The intention of the author is to exhort and comfort. However, it must also be pointed out that Hebrews provides no support for the "one covenant" model proposed in contemporary Jewish-Christian dialogue.[63]

The author of Hebrews has chosen the term "new covenant" in order to confirm the self-understanding of the church he addresses. This identity indeed has roots in the cultic heritage of Israel. Hebrews, however, gives primacy to the fact that the church participates in a new, qualitatively *superior*, worship and identity rooted in a heavenly reality.

---

[60] Frey, "Die alte und die neue διαθήκη," 304.

[61] Cf. Weiß, *Der Brief an die Hebräer*, 415: "The eternal and final character of the 'better salvation order' is depicted even more clearly when the readers of Hebrews realize – with the help of their Bible, which the author is teaching them to read correctly – the temporary and transitory character of the 'old' salvation order."

[62] Lohfink, *Der niemals gekündigte Bund*, 25–8, rejects the opinion that the new covenant was essentially a combat term of the early church. He believes that the discussion of the "new covenant" is older than the bitter fight between Jewish and Christian brothers and sisters: "Even if the historical Jesus should not have introduced in the Upper Room the 'new covenant' as a category of interpretation – does not this word already belong prior to anti-Jewish polemics and, independently from it, to the Lord's Supper tradition of the early Christian churches? Is this not even typical *Jewish* Christian language?" (p. 26).

[63] Nevertheless Backhaus, *Der neue Bund und das Werden der Kirche*, 362, concludes: "God unites Judaism and Christianity under the one and only covenant with God. The covenant is neither a covenant of Judaism nor one of Christianity but the eternal covenant of God for Judaism and Christianity. Both religions interpret their participation in the covenant in their own different ways. For Christianity the fundamental ground of the covenant relationship is God's eschatological salvific act in Jesus Christ. The tension that develops this way to the Jewish covenant understanding must be maintained in the mutual hope toward the coming of the Messiah and the fulfillment of God's covenant."

Everywhere in the New Testament one observes traces of Jewish-Christian debate, although the final separation between the two traditions did not occur in the New Testament period. "Paradoxically enough, it is the writer of Hebrews who – while passionately arguing along Jewish lines – moves furthest in the direction of the breach with Judaism that was later to take place."[64] Backhaus has, however, developed four thesis statements setting forth how Hebrews can provide impulses for Jewish-Christian dialogue:[65]

> *Thesis I:* The normative self-definition of Christianity by the covenant concept in Hebrews inspires the specific Christian contribution to a Jewish-Christian covenant theology.
>
> *Thesis II:* The covenant concept of Hebrews must be interpreted in light of its special situation in the history of theology and in the light of what this text aimed to accomplish (its text pragmatic function). In the current conditions in which the dialogue between Christians and Jews take place, the uniting dimensions of the Hebrew text need to be emphasized.
>
> *Thesis III:* A theology of religions will, beside the covenant concept of Hebrews, also consider the self-definition of Judaism through the covenant motif.
>
> *Thesis IV:* The remaining irreducible tensions between the contrasting Jewish and Christian theologies of covenant can only be resolved eschatologically.

The book of Hebrews was not framed with the issues of contemporary Jewish-Christian dialogue in mind. The author uses the Levitical salvation order as an example for any earthly worship. Its regulations are a symbol for the operation of the current time period, the old eon (cf. 9:9). Since the new covenant has been established, the old is disappearing. "However, it continues functioning as the space where the people of God are on their way and in which they, assured by the promise of their salvation anchored in heaven (cf. 6:19), strive toward the final transformation (μετάθεσις) of creation (12:27) and the receiving of the promised goods of the 'unshakeable kingdom' (12:28)."[66]

The Letter to the Hebrews does not only emphasize the discontinuity between old and new covenants. Elements of *continuity* that can be noted in Hebrews include: the "unchangeable heavenly reality"; the self-revelation of God and his eternal promises;[67] and the image of the people of God. It is worth

---

[64] Lehne, *The New Covenant in Hebrews*, 124.

[65] Only four thesis statements are quoted here that are discussed in Backhaus, *Der neue Bund und das Werden der Kirche*, 355–63.

[66] Frey, "Die alte und die neue διαθήκη," 302.

[67] Theobald, "Zwei Bünde und ein Gottesvolk," 323, emphasizes in the context of the problem of relations between church and Israel the contribution of the ἐπαγγελία (promise) motif. He points out that, in spite of the anti-typical discussion of the two covenants, "the structural term of Hebrews that encompasses all salvation history

noting once more that the author of Hebrews does not echo negative prophetic motifs regarding Israel's breaking the covenant. He does not teach, as
does Barnabas 4:6–8, that Israel is rejected, blinded (as in John 12:40) or hard-
ened (as does Paul in Rom. 11:25). "Moreover, he depicts before the eyes of
his addressees a 'cloud of witnesses' from pre-Christian salvation history who
together with the Christian church are as believers on their way toward final
completion and will there be united to one *ecclesia* before God's throne (cf.
12:23)."[68]

"Law" and "covenant" were closely connected linguistically in the Jewish
theological lexicon. Hebrews was revolutionary in that it suggested an essential
transformation of this rubric. The transformation consists primarily in the fact
that the determining semantic center has been reorganized: The Torah as
foundation has now been replaced by the atoning death and heavenly exaltation of Jesus Christ.[69] Like Paul and John, the author of Hebrews thus sets forth
in his own way the principle of *"solus Christus"* (Christ alone).[70]

---

[67] (*Continued*) from Abraham to Christ," the ἐπαγγελία (promise), cannot be overlooked. God's promise unites all those in Israel and the church who find themselves
on the faith journey under the mutual goal of entering into the one kingdom of God
(12:28). However, when one attempts to correlate this approach with the model of
one covenant overarching the church and Israel, one must take into account the
christological foundation of this promise: the condition for the possibility as well as for
the realization of the promise is the *one* way to salvation, which the high priest Jesus
has walked once for all into the heavenly Most Holy place as our forerunner (precursor) (6:20). Hebrews does not know of any other way to unbar access to the
divine *sanctissimum* (Holy of Holies).

[68] Frey, "Die alte und die neue διαθήκη," 305–306. Hofius, "Biblische Theologie im
Lichte des Hebräerbriefes," in Pedersen (ed.), *New Directions in Biblical Theology:
Papers of the Aarhus Conference, 16–19 September 1992*, NovTSup 76 (Leiden: E. J.
Brill, 1994), 124–25, points out, from the perspective of the Epistle to the Hebrews,
that a biblical theology must be critical to the extent that it does not consider the
relationship between the Old Testament and the New Testament principally and
exclusively under the premises of continuity, but also expects some quite weighty
discontinuity. On the other side, it should not *a priori* simply declare discontinuity to
its premise. "If biblical theology – following the hermeneutical canon of Hebr 1.1 +
2a – maintains in principle the *sameness* of God in the Old and the New Testaments,
it will on the basis of the New Testament witness about Christ also search specifically for the continuity in God's speaking, and here especially in the context of *promise and fulfillment*, and this way emphasize God's faithfulness to his word."

[69] Backhaus, *Der neue Bund und das Werden der Kirche*, 328.

[70] Frey, "Die alte und die neue διαθήκη," 306; cf. also Weiß, *Der Brief an die Hebräer*,
786, who points out that the comfort and exhortation speech of Hebrews is in no
way interested in an abstract discussion, "but before all else and very purposefully [it
intends to relate] the transmitted teaching on Christ closer to life and existence."

6

The Reflection of the Concept of the New Covenant in the Johannine Literature

1. "A new commandment I give unto you"

In the long history of the study of the concept of the covenant, the terms "covenant" and "law" have often been used almost synonymously. In the Old Testament, the "law" as a component of meaning of the covenant concept is very important across a broad spectrum of contexts, especially in the Deuteronomic/Deuteronomistic literature and theology.

In the writings of the apostolic fathers and the apologists, the terms "new law" and "new covenant" are closely related. For example, in his *Dialogue with Trypho* 11:4, Justin describes the new law and the new covenant (ὁ καινὸς νόμος καὶ ἡ καινὴ διαθήκη) as belonging to those from all nations who await divine salvation (cf. also 34:1).

In the New Testament, John 13:34 portrays Jesus proclaiming: "a new commandment I give unto you" ('Εντολὴν[1] καινὴν δίδωμι ὑμῖν). Schnackenburg points out that Jesus entrusts his disciples with the "new commandment" of mutual love as his *last will*.[2] In verse 33, Jesus tells his disciples that he will only remain with them for a short time. After his departure, his disciples are to maintain their relationship with him by demonstrating love and concern to those around them.[3]

---

[1] 'Εντολή ("command") and νόμος ("law") are synonyms. Louw and Nida, *Greek-English Lexicon,* I, 426, describe the difference between these two terms in the following way: "The difference between a 'law' (νόμος) and 'a command' (ἐντολή) is that a law is enforced by sanctions from a society, while a command carries only the sanctions of the individual who commands. When, however, the people of Israel accepted the commands of God as the rules which they would follow and enforce, these became their laws." The New Testament also speaks of the one νόμος (law) that contains a multitude of ἐντολαί (commandments) (cf., e.g., Eph. 2:15).

[2] Schnackenburg, *Das Johannesevangelium,* III: *Teil* (Freiburg/Basel/Wien: Herder, 1975), 59.

[3] See Schnackenburg, *Das Johannesevangelium,* 59.

The meaning of the "new commandment" should be understood especially in light of John 13:14–15; 15:12–15 and 1 John. John sees the locus of the "newness" of the new commandant as residing in the person and work of Jesus. Through Jesus, God's unparalleled love for his cosmos has been definitively revealed (John 3:16, cf. 1 John 4:9). In Augustine's words: "This love renews us so that we become new persons, heirs of the new covenant, singers of the new song."[4] Thomas Aquinas (Cai nr. 1835) lists three reasons for this newness: its renewing power (according to Col. 3:9); its source in the Spirit, who arouses love; and the creation of a new covenant.[5] Cognates of "newness" are found throughout a rich field of biblical references to eschatological salvation: for example, new covenant (1 Cor. 11:25; cf. Jer. 38:31 LXX); new creation (2 Cor. 5:17; Gal. 6:15); new personhood (Eph. 2:15); and a new heaven and new earth (Rev. 21:1; cf. Isa. 66:22).[6]

It is remarkable that love is referred to as a "commandment." In the Old Testament, the Ten Commandments are set in the framework of the covenant between God and Israel at Sinai. These commandments were covenant guidelines dictating Israel's comportment as God's chosen people. When Jesus declares that love is the new commandment that he imposes upon those whom he calls his own (cf. John 13:1; 15:16) as a sign intended to distinguish them from others (v. 35), one can detect an allusion to the covenant concept of the Lord's Supper tradition (cf. Luke 22:20: "the *new* covenant in my blood"; also 1 Cor. 11:25).[7] Brown observes:

> The newness of the commandment of love is really related to the theme of covenant at the Last Supper – the 'new commandment' of John xiii 34 is the basic stipulation of the 'new covenant' of Luke xxii 20. Both expressions reflect the early Christian understanding that in Jesus and his followers was fulfilled the dream of Jeremiah (xxxi 31–34).[8]

---

[4] Augustine, In Jo. tr. LXV, 1 (CC 36, 491), quoted by Schnackenburg, *Das Johannesevangelium*, 60.

[5] Quoted by Schnackenburg, *Das Johannesevangelium*, 60, n. 16.

[6] Cf. Klauck, *Der erste Johannesbrief* (Zürich: Benziger, 1991), 122.

[7] Cf. Brown, *The Gospel According to John* (New York: Doubleday, 1970), 612: "the evangelist shows implicitly that he is thinking of this Last Supper scene in covenant terms." Cf. also Harrisville, "The Concept of Newness in the New Testament," *JBL* 74 (1955), 79.

[8] Brown, *The Gospel According to John*, 614. It must be pointed out that John speaks of the new commandment in the same place and framework of Jesus' ministry, where the Synoptic Gospels speak of the new covenant in the context of the Lord's Supper. (Cf., e.g., Judas mentioned in the immediately preceding verses: John 13:31, Matt. 26:25 and Mark 14:17–21, while Luke has it in the following verses: 22:21–23.)

The new covenant is, by definition, an internalized covenant. Its distinguishing mark is an intimate knowledge of God that facilitates a new level of closeness between God and his people. The themes of intimacy, of "indwelling" and of a mutual knowledge recur in the farewell discourse (cf. 6.2).[9]

1 John 2:8 reveals the person of Jesus as a new and all-encompassing manifestation of the will of God. The Johannine key word "truth" (ἀλήθεια) appears in this verse, along with "truthful" (ἀληθής) and "true" (ἀληθινός): "Yet, I am writing you a new command; its truth is seen in him and in you, because the darkness is passing and the true light is already shining."[10] Klauck comments: "That which is true inwardly interrelates with God's self-revelation, whose truth encounters humanity in Jesus Christ as revealed reality. With this the new eon dawns, and believers live in this new reality as new persons, they are inwardly stirred and changed by it."[11] The opposition of darkness and light[12] is a motif familiar from Jewish apocalypticism and early Christian baptismal teaching (1 Thess. 5:4–5; Eph. 5:8).[13]

2. Internalization as a dimension of the new covenant

In his 1978 paper *Interiority and Covenant: A Study of εἶναι ἐν and μένειν ἐν in the First Letter of Saint John*, Edward Malatesta points out how important the motif of the internalization of the new covenant is in 1 John.[14] The writing of the law upon the heart, the new heart and the indwelling presence of God's Spirit (cf. Jer. 31 and Ezek. 36) make the new covenant qualitatively different from previous covenants. These new gifts facilitate a new kind of fellowship with God and a new level of intimacy of faith and of love in their recipients.

For John, this new fellowship is made real in and through Jesus Christ, the mediator of the new covenant. The new law put into one's heart is the new commandment of love (1 John 2:7–8). The gift of the Spirit, which is available

---

[9] Brown, *The Gospel According to John*, 614.

[10] πάλιν ἐντολὴν καινὴν γράφω ὑμῖν, ὅ ἐστιν ἀληθὲς ἐν αὐτῷ καὶ ἐν ὑμῖν, ὅτι ἡ σκοτία παράγεται καὶ τὸ φῶς τὸ ἀληθινὸν ἤδη φαίνει.

[11] See Klauck, *Der erste Johannesbrief*, 122.

[12] Cf. Melito, ΠΕΡΙ ΠΑΣΧΑ, 68.

[13] Klauck, *Der erste Johannesbrief*, 123.

[14] AB 69 (Rome: Biblical Institute Press, 1978). Already in 1917, Kennedy, "The Covenant-Conception in the First Epistle of John," *EvT* XXVIII (1916–17), 23–26, drew attention to the covenant concept in 1 John. Klauck, *Der erste Johannesbrief*, 266, however, warns against the attempt to derive the theology of 1 John from the Old Testament covenant concept and points in this regard to Kennedy, Boismard, Malatesta and Edanad.

to all believers, makes the reception of Christ's revelation possible and protects against the danger of heresy (cf. 2:20, 27; 3:24; 4:13).[15]

In his monograph *Habt keine Angst: Die erste johanneische Abschiedsrede*, Johannes Beutler applies Malatesta's insights to the analysis of the first farewell discourse in John's Gospel. He begins by pointing out the degree to which the themes of loving and keeping his commandments/words predominate in the Old Testament, from its earliest textual layers until even long after the exilic times. The connection between "the love for God" (or "fear of God") and the "keeping of the commandments" is most distinctly developed in Deuteronomy. In almost all references where "love for God" is mentioned, the "keeping" of his commandments is listed as one of the evidences of this love. The various layers of Deuteronomy are not simply exhortations about the law, but rather primarily expositions of the "greatest commandment" (cf. Deut. 6:6–13). The greatest commandment, then, is *foundational to the definition of the new covenant* that Yahweh makes with Israel (cf. 1.2.2.2, above).

Beutler's analyses of Deuteronomic texts, Old Testament wisdom literature and apocryphal writings, Qumranian Essene texts and the Synoptic Gospels lead him to conclude that the Jesus of the Johannine farewell discourse (cf. 14:15, 21a, 23b, 24a) is speaking squarely from a tradition with its earliest roots in ancient Near Eastern treaty language. The Decalogue, Deuteronomy and the other biblical, Jewish and Christian sources we have mentioned share a common heritage. This heritage is recognizable by its emphasis on the "greatest commandment" of Deuteronomy 6:4–13, which is echoed in the New Testament literature. Texts such as John 5:42 and 8:42 clearly parallel the "greatest commandment" of Deuteronomy 6:4–13 and resonate soundly with Deuteronomic monotheism and covenant theology.[16]

2.1 *"Remain in me and I will remain in you" (John 15:4): The Johannine formula of the new covenant*

Malatesta proposes an ingenious interpretive rubric regarding the expressions "to be in" (εἶναι ἐν) and "to remain in" (μένειν ἐν) in 1 John:

> Our study attempts to show how in his Letter, John uses the interiority expressions as an especially apt manner of describing the interior nature of New Covenant communion. Indeed we believe that these expressions when in personal, reciprocal form, serve as the Johannine equivalent of the Covenant formula: 'I will be your God, and you shall be my people' has become 'God is

---

[15] Cf. also Klauck, *Der erste Johannesbrief*, 166.

[16] Beutler, *Habt keine Angst: Die erste johanneische Abschiedsrede (Joh 14)* (Stuttgart: Verlag Katholisches Bibelwerk, 1984), 55–62.

Love, and he who remains in love remains in God, and God remains in him' (4:16; see 3:24; 4:13, 15).[17]

Although the motif of "internalized law" is not as prominent in John's Gospel as it is in 1 John,[18] John 15:7 certainly emphasizes that obedience toward Jesus is the consequence of the indwelling of the Spirit, who helps the disciples internalize the witness and truth of Jesus (14:26; 16:12–13).

The expression "if you remain in me" (John 15:7) picks up verse 4a and offers the disciples the conditional promise of answered prayer. In 15:7, we find a variation of the indwelling formula, or immanence formula: "you in me and *my words in you.*" This variation echoes 14:10: "I am in the Father, and the Father is in Me." Whoever receives Jesus' words within receives Jesus himself internally and commits him or herself to preserve his words and to translate them into action (cf. 12:47–48; 17:8). What follows from this union with Christ is the assurance of answered prayer.[19]

Here John defines the new covenant as essentially a *relational concept*. The promise of Jeremiah 31:31–34, of course, focused on just such an internalization of the covenant relationship. The law was not to become irrelevant, but internalized. It is therefore significant that the motif of internalization – found also in the discourse on the vine and his branches, "If you remain in me and I in you, you will bear much fruit" (John 15:5, TNIV) – becomes a concrete element of the eucharistic covenant meal in the life of the Johannine community: "Whoever eats my flesh and drinks my blood remains in me, and I in them" (John 6:56, TNIV).[20]

Wilckens rightly concludes[21] that what Jesus says in John 14:1 onwards is a summary of everything he taught and did during his earthly mission. After his death, Jesus' teaching mission will continue through the Paraclete. The Spirit provides a link between the period of Jesus' historical activity and the present

---

[17] Malatesta, *Interiority and Covenant*, 23–24. Cf. Scholtissek, *In ihm sein und bleiben: Die Sprache der Immanenz in den johanneischen Schriften* (Freiburg: Herder, 2000), B. IX for further literature about the relationship between John's immanency statements and covenant theology.

[18] Pryor, *John: Evangelist of the Covenant People: The Narrative and Themes of the Fourth Gospel* (Downers Grove, IL: InterVarsity Press, 1992), 159–60, believes that "while John is aware of and presumes the new covenant theology of Jeremiah (as 1 John also strongly supports), in the presentation of his christology and ecclesiology he goes back more readily and consciously to the covenantal themes of Exodus and Deuteronomy."

[19] Schnackenburg, *Das Johannesevangelium*, 115.

[20] Cf. Wilckens, *Das Evangelium nach Johannes* (Göttingen: Vandenhoeck & Ruprecht, 1998), 242–43.

[21] Wilckens, *Das Evangelium nach Johannes*, 232.

situation of the Gospel author. John 14:26 states that the Paraclete will teach the disciples everything. In Judaism, receiving authoritative teaching is the precursor to having the ability to authentically interpret Scripture. In Qumran, it is the "teacher of righteousness" – a Torah exegete that elucidates the will of God – who becomes the prophet capable of interpreting the present and future. John also calls the revelatory activity of the earthly Jesus "teaching" (John 7:16–17; 7:28; 8:28). The Paraclete continues this revelatory teaching of Jesus. He does not introduce new teaching, however, but deepens and elucidates what Jesus himself has taught (cf. also 16:13).[22]

The Gospel writer's emphasis parallels, for the post-Easter church, an important lesson that Israel had to learn. For Israel, God showed himself historically to be the God of the covenant through his mighty acts of salvation. It was of utmost importance for the ongoing spiritual life of Israel, however, that these miracles not become mere reminiscences. Israel therefore learned to *remember* them in the context of Scripture and liturgy so that all generations could continue to participate in their reality. Shabbat and the other annual feasts were established as time of collective "remembering" (cf. Deut. 5:15; Exod. 12:14; 13:3; Deut. 16:3, 12). In times of trouble, the individual righteous man or woman would recollect the mighty acts of God as a way of gaining assurance and sustaining faith (cf., for example, Pss. 48:9–11; 105:5–6; 106:7; 111:4; 143:5).

Each interpretation of the Torah is considered in Judaism to be a *teaching,* in the sense that it is an assertion and commitment to the covenantal will of God. In a similar but more elevated way, Jesus' interpretations carry the authority of God's teaching (7:16–17; 8:28), as does the Paraclete's reconstruction of Jesus' teaching after Easter.[23] John's thinking, which is Trinitarian in its orientation, envisions the Father vouchsafing the word to the Son, which the Son embodies and reveals. The Spirit acts as the messenger of the Father and the Son and implements the word in the heart of the hearer.

For the Johannine community, the future was already present. The promises of Jesus that were encountered on the textual level of the Gospel were taken to be spiritually realized actualities. Through the dimension of the Spirit, John reveals the interrelatedness of realities that are usually perceived to be separate and opposed: heaven and earth, space and time, history and the eschaton, God's will and human action. Most especially, the believer is revealed to be in union with the divine reality of the Father and the Son, through the Spirit – a unity of spirit and love.[24] The two central motifs of the covenant – *Yahweh's*

---

[22] Schnackenburg, *Das Johannesevangelium,* 94–5; Schnelle, *Das Evangelium nach Johannes* (Leipzig: Evangelische Verlagsanstalt, 1998), 235.

[23] Wilckens, *Das Evangelium nach Johannes,* 232.

[24] Schnelle, *Das Evangelium nach Johannes,* 248–49. Cf. Scholtissek, *In ihm sein und bleiben,* F II.4: "The *condition to make* [unity] *possible* and the *medium* of this post-

close relationship with his people and the *obedience* of his people toward the covenantal will of Yahweh – are preserved and reconceived in light of John's Christology and pneumatology.

1 John 3:23–24 declares that the commandments that must be kept (v. 22c) are reducible to one, which is formulated with a double emphasis: to believe in the name of Jesus Christ and to love one another. Keeping this commandment enables believers to experience an abiding close fellowship with God that is imbued with the rich resources of faith and love. In 1 John 4:13 this fellowship is interpreted pneumatologically: "We know that we live in him and he in us, because he has given us of his Spirit ... And so we know and rely on the love God has for[25] us" (1 John 4:13, 16). At the center of this exposition about love is the statement "God is love,"[26] which, together with the statements "God is light" (1 John 1:5) and "God is spirit" (John 4:24), comprise John's topology of divine reality. All three of these statements encourage specific motivations for action. Because God is Spirit, it is necessary to worship him in spirit and truth; because he is light, we must walk in the light (1 John 1:7); because God is love, we must show love to the community of believers. The close relationship that exists between the theme of love and the language of immanence/indwelling becomes clear in the statement "whoever lives in love lives in God, and God in him" (v. 16).[27]

In both John's Gospel and in the Epistle, an important emphasis that follows upon the theme of immanence and indwelling is reciprocity. The covenant formula has a reciprocal structure: "I will be your God, and you will be my people" (Jer. 7:23). This relationship between covenant and God "living among his people" is repeated in Exodus 29:5–46, Leviticus 26:11–12 and especially in Ezekiel 37:26–28: "it will be an everlasting *covenant* ... I will put my sanctuary *among them* forever ... *and I will be their God and they will be my people* ... when my sanctuary is *among them* forever." This motif is picked up again in Revelation 21:3.[28]

On one hand we find, in John, a "silence about the covenant" (*Bundesschweigen*) because the word "διαθήκη" (covenant) does not appear either in the Gospel or in John's Epistles. However, two of the most important themes of Old Testament covenant theology are taken up and interpreted anew in the Gospel and the Epistle. We find an ethical expression of the

---

[24] (*Continued*) Easter presence of Christ in the believers is the mission and the activity of the *Paraclete*, the Easter gift of the Dying and Risen per se."

[25] The "in" (ἐν) of the Koine Greek can also be translated with the meaning "into" (εἰς): the love that God awakens in our innermost (Klauck, *Der erste Johannesbrief*, 261).

[26] Cf. also 1 John 4:8.

[27] Klauck, *Der erste Johannesbrief*, 224–25, 256–68.

[28] Cf. Klauck, *Der erste Johannesbrief*, 266.

covenant motif, which is emphasized in the Deuteronomistic tradition.[29] As we have seen, this tradition is connected in John with the priestly motif of Yahweh's presence in his community (cf. 1.3.6.1, above).

3. Summary

The Johannine perspective is important for our study of the new covenant and its relationship to Old Testament covenant theology. It is clear that the two central themes of Old Testament covenant theology – relationship to Yahweh, as expressed in the reciprocal covenant formula, and the ethical consequences of this relationship[30] – are also central to the promise of the new covenant. However, they are interpreted differently in light of the characteristic eschatology of the new covenant. "God's law, for humanity so far an external notion, shall become for them the most intimate, their very own, a second nature."[31] The Torah will then be the innermost reality for Israel, written by God into their hearts.[32]

Although one cannot detect a covenant theology in the Johannine literature in the narrow sense of the word since the term does not appear in John, one can still speak of a *reflection of the new covenant notion*. John's statements are important because they provide a framework in which the two key Old Testament covenant themes we have delineated are interpreted by the early church christologically and pneumatologically in ways that shape all of Christian theology.[33]

---

[29] It is remarkable that Clement of Alexandria interprets the new covenant in *Quis dives salvetur* 37, 4 with the statement: "My love I give unto you" (an allusion to John 13:34 and 14:27). Cf. 7.4.2, below.

[30] Cf. especially the Deuteronomic/deuteronomistic theology.

[31] Levin, *Die Verheißung des neuen Bundes*, 260.

[32] Cf. Levin, *Die Verheißung des neuen Bundes*, 264.

[33] The question is valid: why does John not use the term διαθήκη ("covenant")? Vogel, *Das Heil des Bundes*, 352–53, points out that a reference to the covenant concept was often guided in New Testament times by the desire to emphasize something *essentially* Jewish (Judaism fencing itself off from Gentiles) or something Jewish that was seen as *exclusively valid* (competing group identities inside of non-Christian Judaism or in contrast between non-Christian Jewish and Christian groups) in order to support the legitimacy of one's own religious views. Against this background, it then seems plausible that the Gospel of John in its concentration on Christology avoids the covenant term. Gräßer, *Der Alte Bund im Neuen*, 24 (see also p. 77), points out that the covenant term is very closely connected with the national identity (that is, with Israel). When promises of salvation crossed national boundaries and the

---

(*Continued*) principle of individual salvation was established, the covenant concept became theologically useless. John especially underlines the *personal* structure of faith (cf. the dimension of personal indwelling that is emphasized by Scholtissek, *In ihm sein und bleiben*, F. II.3). Smith, *The Theology of the Gospel of John* (Cambridge: Cambridge University Press, 1995), 135–39, mentions that although ecclesiology does not receive prominent treatment in John (Christology does), the church still constitutes the presupposition of John's theology. When coming from the perspective of God's election, discipleship and church seem to be the necessary consequence. "On the other hand, if one focuses on faith and obedience, everything seems to depend on the individual's decision and behaviour" (p. 138).

7

The New Covenant in the Second Century[1]

1. The covenant[2] in the Epistle of Barnabas

1.1 Introduction[3]

As Barnabas 16:3–4 assumes the destruction of Herod's temple, the Epistle of Barnabas must be dated after the year A.D. 70. It must also be dated before A.D. 190, as Clement of Alexandria quotes the letter in his writings.[4] In the light of his interpretation of Barnabas 4:3–5 and 16:3–4, Ferdinand Prostmeier concludes that the letter was written between the spring of A.D. 130 and February or March A.D.

---

[1] The notion of covenant plays a significant role in the second century in the Epistle of Barnabas (which can be characterized as a "treatise on early Christian covenant theology," cf. Backhaus, *Der neue Bund und das Werden der Kirche*, 306), in Justin, Irenaeus and Clement of Alexandria. Although Melito speaks of the books of the old covenant (τῆς παλαιᾶς διαθήκης βιβλία), he does not mention the term "new covenant." In a short *excursus* we shall analyze the question of a theology of a new covenant in Melito at the conclusion of this chapter.

[2] For an exposition of the meaning of διαθήκη ("covenant"), cf. Prostmeier, *Barnabasbrief* (Göttingen: Vandenhoeck & Ruprecht, 1999), 208–11. Cf. also Chapter 1.2, above. Prostmeier points out that in the Epistle of Barnabas, as is common in the writings of the Apostolic Fathers, Scripture quotes often present the basis for the meaning of διαθήκη ("covenant").

As we have seen, διαθήκη in the New Testament has two possibilities of meaning, namely "covenant" and "last will/testament." "Last will" has the significant component of meaning that the initiative originates from only one party. (Cf. Louw and Nida, *Greek-English Lexicon*, I, 452, for the translation of ברית with διαθήκη.) Sometimes it seems that Barnabas alludes to both of these components of meaning – agreement/contract ("covenant") and last will (testament) – and it is not always easy to decide which of them is in the foreground and which is only secondary.

Prostmeier translates διαθήκη with "assurance of salvation" (*Heilszusicherung*), cf., e.g., p. 189 (Barn. 4:6). "Assurance of salvation" is in some contexts an (important) component of meaning of διαθήκη.

[3] Because this chapter deals with the reception of the early Christian covenant tradition, some introductory questions (such as time of writing, etc.) need to be briefly discussed for the reader's orientation.

[4] See Prostmeier, *Barnabasbrief*, 111, for the specific passages in Clement of Alexandria.

132,[5] probably in Alexandria.[6] The author of the epistle is unknown. Since the author understands himself to be a carrier of tradition and agent of the transmitted teaching (cf. Barn. 1:5, 8; 4:9a; 17:1; 21:7, 9) – whose apostolic legitimacy is inherent (cf. Barn. 5:9; 8:3a) – this anonymity seems programmatic.[7]

1.2 The covenant concept in Barnabas: A table

The following motifs play an important role in the covenant theology of Barnabas:

- The Jews have *lost* their covenant – their covenant *was broken*.
- Barnabas places Jews and Christians *over against* one another in his covenant theology.
- The *document of the covenant* that Moses received is mentioned twice.
- *Jesus* is closely connected to the covenant of the Christians.

Lost/broken	Over against one another: Jews–Christians	Covenant document of Moses	Jesus
4:8: "but when they turned back to idols they lost it"[8] 4:1–3	4:6–7[9] 4:8 13:1[10] 14:5[11]	4:7 14:2	4:8[12] 14:5 14:7

---

[5] Cf. Prostmeier, *Barnabasbrief*, 118. Carleton Paget, *The Epistle of Barnabas: Outlook and Background* (Tübingen: J. C. B. Mohr [Paul Siebeck], 1994), 28, is, however, of the opinion that this epistle was written during the time of Nerva (A.D. 96–98).

[6] Prostmeier, *Barnabasbrief*, 130; Carleton Paget, *The Epistle of Barnabas*, 42. Prostmeier, however, points out the programmatic anonymity of the place of writing and the location of the addressees.

[7] According to Prostmeier, *Barnabasbrief*, 130.

[8] English translations from *The Apostolic Fathers, Epistle of Barnabas, Papias and Quadratus, Epistle to Diognetus, The Shephard of Hermas*, ed. and trans. Ehrman, LCL (Cambridge, MA/London: Harvard University Press, 2003).

[9] "Watch yourselves now and do not become like some people by piling up your sins, saying that the covenant is both theirs and ours. For it is ours."

[10] "But let us see if this people is the heir, or the former, and if the covenant belongs to us or to them." Wengst, *Didache*, 177, n. 207, points out that this sentence is the heading for chapters 13–14: "Whether the Jews or the Christians are the people of God, is for the author from the outset mutually exclusive."

[11] "So that *those people* might be completely filled with sins, and that *we* might receive the covenant through the Lord Jesus, who inherited it."

[12] "Their covenant was smashed – that the covenant of his beloved, Jesus, might be sealed in our hearts, in the hope brought by faith in him."

Note also the following:[13]

Barnabas 6:19 underscores that Christians are heirs (κληρονόμοι) of the covenant of the Lord Jesus. Διαθήκη ("covenant") must be understood here in an eschatological sense, because the content of the covenant is linked to the end times and to the final peace of creation (cf. 6:17–18).

In 9:6 the author of the Epistle of Barnabas attempts to disprove the assumption that Israel's covenant relationship was based on circumcision. He argues that circumcision is not a matter of the flesh, but the heart.

Barnabas 13:2–7 demonstrates through the examples of the patriarchs Isaac, Jacob and Abraham that Christians are prophetically intended to inherit the covenant.

1.3 Further explanations: One and only covenant

"The peculiarity of the epistle of Barnabas consists in the notion that Scripture offers *only* future revelation oriented toward the coming time of fulfillment in Christ."[14] Although the covenant theology of Barnabas differs from conventional covenant theology, his scriptural orientation allows him to maintain the traditional semantic field of the term. The motifs of circumcision (9:6–9), the patriarchs (14:1) and the divine oath (14:1) remain central. The term νόμος (law),[15] which is closely related to the covenant concept, plays such a significant role in the Epistle of Barnabas (10:2) that one can actually characterize his covenant theology as a "new covenantal nomism" (cf. 2:6).[16]

In 4:6b Barnabas writes against those who believe that "the covenant is both theirs and ours" (ἡ διαθήκη ἐκείνων καὶ ἡμῶν). It seems as if Barnabas' opponents desired rapprochement with the Jews, who were accepted as the people of God. From this perspective there was little difference between the Jewish and the Christian covenants. Barnabas, however, was of the opinion that Christian identity was endangered by this view.[17] From his perspective, a battle regarding the meaning of Scripture was underway – one in which the Jews were seen as an inner threat.[18]

The Epistle of Barnabas is a treatise on early Christian covenant theology that is developed along the lines of a "covenant doublet" (4:6b–8 and

---

[13] Cf. Backhaus, *Der neue Bund und das Werden der Kirche*, 310.

[14] Wengst, *Didache*, 131.

[15] Cf. also δικαιώματα (commandments, regulations) in Barnabas.

[16] See Backhaus, *Der neue Bund und das Werden der Kirche*, 312.

[17] See Carleton Paget, *The Epistle of Barnabas*, 59. Backhaus, *Der neue Bund und das Werden der Kirche*, 307.

[18] Backhaus, "Das Bundesmotiv in der frühchristlichen Schwellenzeit: Hebräerbrief, Barnabasbrief, Dialogus cum Tryphone," in Frankemölle, *Der ungekündigte Bund?*, 222.

14:1–4).[19] Barnabas defines the Christian covenant in terms of an assumed *covenant breach at Sinai*. Moses received the covenant (in the form of stone tablets[20]) from God. But because the Israelites turned to idols they voided this covenant. "And their covenant was smashed – that the covenant of his beloved, Jesus, might be sealed in our hearts, in the hope brought by faith in him" (4:8b). Barnabas insists that the covenant belongs to the Christians. The covenant of Sinai, along with its intended relational dimensions with God, never materialized for Israel. However, Israel's loss is Christianity's gain: "that the covenant of his beloved, Jesus, might be sealed in our hearts" (ἵνα ἡ τοῦ ἠγαπημένου Ἰσοῦ ἐγκατασφραγισθῇ εἰς τὴν καρδίαν ἡμῶν).

Backhaus points out that the "Jesus covenant" can be considered as a "document" analogous to the tablets given to Moses. It is a "new law of our Lord Jesus Christ" (καινὸς νόμος τοῦ κυρίου ἡμῶν Ἰησοῦ Χριστοῦ) (2:6; cf. 3:6); one that does not rest upon ceremonial regulations that effect salvation (cf. 4:1). While Barnabas insists that there is only one covenant – that of the Christians[21] – it must be understood that this single covenant (or "document") has never changed. Its recipients, however, have changed. Instead of belonging to the people of Israel, the covenant now belongs, through Jesus' suffering and teaching, to the "new people" (5:7) of God – the Christians (4:8; 14:4–5). Because Barnabas unambiguously relates the covenant (and the Scriptures) to the Christians, there can be no continuity between the Jewish and Christian economies of salvation; no common salvation history.[22]

It is remarkable that Barnabas speaks of a covenant of *Jesus* (4:8; 6:19: κληρονόμοι τῆς διαθήκης κυρίου [heirs of the covenant of the Lord]).[23] Although not as prominently as, for example, in the Epistle to the Hebrews, the Epistle of Barnabas emphasizes that the covenant was established through the death of Jesus.[24] The Epistle of Barnabas refers to Isaiah 42:6–7 and links the covenant of Jesus with the notions of "a light for the Gentiles," "the opening of eyes" and "the

---

[19]　Cf. Backhaus, *Der neue Bund und das Werden der Kirche*, 306, and Carleton Paget, *The Epistle of Barnabas*, 114.

[20]　The covenant is understood to be a "*covenant document.*" The motif "last will, testament" is an important component of the meaning of covenant here (cf. Backhaus, *Der neue Bund und das Werden der Kirche*, 309).

[21]　Backhaus, *Der neue Bund und das Werden der Kirche*, 309–10.

[22]　Backhaus, "Bundesmotiv in der frühkirchlichen Schwellenzeit," 224.

[23]　According to Backhaus, *Der neue Bund und das Werden der Kirche*, 312, the author probably believes that Jesus is the actual heir of the covenant and forwards this privilege to his own, either through his suffering (14:4) or through his word (14:5). This language proves Barnabas' distance to the theocentric orientation of the covenant, evident in Old Testament-early Jewish, as well as early Christian, theology.

[24]　Cf. 14:5; also 5:7 and 7:5, for the notion that a new people has originated through the death of Jesus (Carleton Paget, *The Epistle of Barnabas*, 220).

freeing of captives from prison." Alluding to Isaiah 61, he also underlines the activity of the Holy Spirit.

1.4 Theological evaluation

Barnabas reserves the covenant only for the Christians and speaks exclusively of the "covenant of the beloved Jesus" (διαθήκη ... τοῦ ἠγαπημένου Ἰησοῦ). But a more systematic understanding of the covenant concept is not present in Barnabas' theology. In this respect, he differs from Paul and the Lord's Supper tradition found in the Synoptics. On one hand, the covenant received by "us" (14:5) is identical with the covenant of Sinai. Yet the concept that the new covenant replaces or renews the Old Testament covenant does not exist in Barnabas. While the covenant is of pivotal importance for Barnabas, the concept is not filled with content derived from Christ's message.[25] Therefore, there is no "new covenant" per se – only new recipients of the old Mosaic covenant.

We find in Barnabas a strange mixture of conservatism and radicalism. Because he rejects all of the Jewish institutions, he is more radical than the New Testament writings. On the other hand, he is atypically conservative because he insists that the whole Old Testament, including the Pentateuch, remain the authoritative teaching guide for the church.[26]

Barnabas polemicizes in 4:6 against the notion that Jews as well as Christians have any part in the covenant.[27] The coherence of his position rests upon the premise that the essence of the Christ event and the essence of the covenant are one and the same.[28] In his opinion, the exclusivity of the salvific significance of the Christ event is threatened if any covenant apart from that event is given any credence. The aim of his treatise is therefore to prove that there is no positive relationship between the "Scriptures" and Israel.

Whether the author of Barnabas was historically isolated in some sense, and whether this isolation influenced his theological perspective, is sheer conjecture.[29] It is, however, clear that this piece of literature was not motivated by any

---

[25] Vogel, *Das Heil des Bundes*, 335–36.

[26] Windisch, *Der Barnabasbrief* (Tübingen: J. C. B. Mohr [Paul Siebeck], 1920), 395. Cf. also Carleton Paget, *The Epistle of Barnabas*, 263: "those who were converts to Christianity from Judaism may have liked B.'s solution because, in an admittedly radical way, it was conservative. It imputed the highest value to the Jewish law (and Jewish scripture) without claiming that in some way that revelation was flawed." In this way he has rescued the Jewish Scriptures for the church.

[27] Vogel, *Das Heil des Bundes*, 336.

[28] Vogel, *Das Heil des Bundes*, 336–37.

[29] Carleton Paget, *The Epistle of Barnabas*, 263–64, points out that Barnabas' attempt at solving the problematic relationship between Christian revelation and its Old Testament and Jewish predecessors did not gain support in the end. We don't know the

external threat or historical danger in the church of which we are aware. In all probability, the author was wrestling with his own theological issues.[30]

2. The new covenant in Justin (the Martyr)

2.1 Introduction

Justin was born in Flavia Neapolis (the contemporary Nablus), in Samaria. His father had a Latin name (Priscus), and his grandfather's name was Bacchios (a Greek name). It is possible that his family were Latin or Greek colonists.[31] Justin was well versed in the philosophy of middle Platonism. His encounter with Christianity was unexpected and unplanned (cf. *Dial.* 3). When an old man pointed him to the books of the prophets he realized that the prophets, "and those men who are friends of Christ," had the truth (*Dial.* 8:1). Believing that he had found the "true" philosophy, Justin "from then on carries a philosopher's robe in his function as a Christian wandering preacher."[32] During the last years of his life Justin lived in Rome. The majority of his writings probably originated there. A severe clash with the cynic Crescens took place there, leading Justin to predict his own death (*2 Apol.* 3:1). He died as a martyr around the year A.D. 165.[33]

It is not clear whether Justin's *Dialogue with Trypho* was based on a real conversation. It is possible that Justin designed his dialogue to imitate a Platonic dialogue. It may be assumed that such dialogues were commonly understood to be free reconstructions of real conversations, and that Justin intended his book to be understood in the same way.[34] Eusebius did not consider the book to be literary fiction. The transmitted text does not mention the scene of the *Dialogue.* Eusebius points to Ephesus; Hyldahl[35] (based on *Dial.* 1:3) argues for Corinth. Trypho was a refugee from the Bar Kochba war.

---

[29] (*Continued*) reasons for it. In many regards it was just a wrong presentation of biblical history. His writing, however, was popular and respected – at least in Egypt. The Epistle of Barnabas serves as an important reminder that our knowledge of early Christianity is still very fragmentary.

[30] Vielhauer, *Geschichte der urchristlichen Literatur: Einleitung in das Neue Testament, die Apokryphen und die Apostolischen Väter* (Berlin/New York: Walter de Gruyter, 1975), 606–607.

[31] He was not circumcised (cf. *Dial.* 28:2).

[32] Skarsaune, "Justin der Märtyrer," in *TRE* XVII (Berlin: Walter de Gruyter, 1988), 471.

[33] Skarsaune, "Justin der Märtyrer," 472, points out that the year of his death, which is transmitted in the *Chronicon Paschale* as A.D. 165, can be considered as quite correct.

[34] Cf. Skarsaune, "Justin der Märtyrer," 472.

[35] Hyldahl, *Philosophie und Christentum: Eine Interpretation der Einleitung zum Dialog Justins,* ATDan 9 (Kopenhagen: Prostant Apud Munksgaard, 1966), 97.

2.2 New covenant in Justin: A table

The concept of a new covenant plays a significant role in the argument in the *Dialogue with Trypho*.[36] The following motifs are connected to the new covenant concept:

	Jesus Christ, God	**Jer. 38 (LXX)**	**Universal expansion**	**New law**	**New – Old**
11:3–5	God has announced the making of a new covenant through the name of the crucified Jesus	x[37]	For the enlightenment of Gentiles … all nations	x	x[38]
34:1	"The law of the Lord is perfect." Justin affirms that this quote from the Psalms refers to Christ, to the "new law" and "new covenant."	x	Eternal kingdom	x	x[39]
43:1	Christ, as eternal law and new covenant … according to the will of the father	x[40]	For the whole world	Eternal law … new covenant	x[41]
51:3	The new covenant … announced by God is Christ himself				x

---

[36] Cf. also Kinzig, *Novitas Christiana: Die Idee des Fortschritts in der alten Kirche* (Göttingen: Vandenhoeck & Ruprecht, 1994), 128–32.

[37] "And by Jeremiah, concerning this same new covenant."

[38] Justin speaks of the making of a new covenant for the enlightenment of Gentiles and underlines that those who are led to God through the crucified Christ are the true spiritual Israel.

[39] He contrasts the Mosaic law with a new law and a new covenant.

[40] Justin points to the prophecies mentioned above.

[41] "End in Christ."

	Jesus Christ, God	Jer. 38 (LXX	Universal expansion	New law	New – Old
67:9–10	God's declaration ... he will make a new [covenant]	x	... for each people	Covenant of Horeb – new covenant. This covenant (of a new kind) shows what command-ments have eternal value	x[42]
122:3, 5–6	God has predicted he will send a new covenant ... Christ ... God's covenant	x[43]	– New covenant as *eternal* law – Christ covenant for *Gentiles* – Limits of the earth	New covenant, eternal *law*	x[44]

2.3 New covenant: Explanations and summary

The new over against the old. In the context of the dialogue, Justin purposefully juxtaposes the new and the old. The true spiritual Israelites are those who are led to God through the crucified Christ (11:3–4). The new law and new cove-nant transcend and supersede the old Mosaic law (34:1). The old covenant finds itself in conflict with a new covenant of a different kind (67:9). The old covenant (characterized by circumcision, Shabbat, sacrifices, gifts and feasts) finds its end and goal in Christ, the Son of God, according to the Father's will (43:1). Justin asks: "If the law were able to enlighten the nations and those who possess it, what need is there of a new covenant?" (122:5).

---

[42] Over against the old covenant, that was made with fear and trembling, is set a differ-ent covenant of a new kind that was made without fear and trembling, without thunder and lightning.

[43] Cf. also the allusion to Isa. 42:6–7; 49:8.

[44] Justin puts the law, as Trypho understands it, over against the new covenant: "If the law were able to enlighten the nations ... what need is there of a new covenant?" However, he calls the new covenant an eternal law – over against the old law is Christ.

A new law. Justin uses the term "new law" synonymously with "new covenant." In 11:4 he states that "He is the new law, and the new covenant, and the expectation of those who out of every people wait for the good things of God" (cf. also 34:1). In 43:1 he speaks of the promise of an *eternal* law[45] and a new covenant for the whole world. He poses the rhetorical question whether the Scriptures contain God's promise that he will make a new covenant besides the one made at Horeb.[46] The new covenant reveals which commandments and activities have eternal value and are fit for every nation. God's intent in universal revelation is to set forth a "new covenant and an eternal law" (καινὴν διαθήκην καὶ νόμον αἰώνιον) (122:5).

The parallelism between the new and eternal *covenant* and the new and eternal *law* points to the "new covenantal nomism" of Justin. Justin emphasizes that the noetic ethical dimension of the new covenant is based on the revelation of Christ as "the new lawgiver" (ὁ καινὸς νομοθέτης, 18:3; cf. 12:2; 14:3–4).[47]

Universal expansion. When Justin speaks of a new covenant in his discussion with Trypho, he underscores that the new covenant is a universal expansion and expression of the covenant. The new covenant is given for the enlightenment of Gentiles and belongs to those among *all peoples* who await divine salvation (11:4). The eternal law and the new covenant are for the *whole world* (43:1), for *every people* (67:10).[48]

Justin emphasizes an important new sociological dimension of the new covenant concept, namely that the covenant does not have meaning only for those who belong to a specific ethnic group. With the establishment of the new covenant, old ethnic and political demarcations are exploded and replaced by a broader and more inclusive view of humanity.[49]

---

[45] Cf. Isa. 2:3; 51:4; Mich. 4:2.

[46] Justin notes that Trypho answered the question positively.

[47] Backhaus, "Bundesmotiv in der frühkirchlichen Schwellenzeit," 227.

[48] Christ as the covenant of God receives the nations as his inheritance and *the uttermost parts of the earth* for his possession (122:5).

[49] Cf. Mendenhall and Herion, "Covenant," 1201: "At precisely the same time that rabbinic Judaism was 'building a fence around the Torah' (and rationalizing such by a general appeal to the OT covenant tradition), apostolic Christianity was expanding. In early rabbinic Judaism, 'covenant' was largely a formal or symbolic dogmatic concept that gave meaning mainly to those already within a group whose base of solidarity and cohesion was primarily ethnic. In early apostolic Christianity, on the other hand, 'covenant' was largely a socially enacted historical reality that accompanied sufficient functional changes in old patterns of behavior so as to rupture old ethnic and political bases of social solidarity and cohesion and to replace these with a larger vision of the human community. Certainly the tenor here was initially set by Jesus himself, who not only sought relationships with people who were outside the 'proper' cultural boundaries ... but also challenged the legitimacy of those boundaries."

Theocentric dimension. Although Jesus Christ is the *new* in Justin's message of a new covenant, Justin emphasizes that the initiative expressed in the new covenant is God's. God promised to establish a new covenant (11:4; 51:3; 67:10); he proclaimed that he would found a new covenant (34:1; 122:5). *In accordance with the will of the Father* the traditions of the old covenant found their end and purpose in Christ. Thus, the theocentricity of biblical covenant theology is retained in Justin's writing. The Father promised a new covenant, sovereignly abolished the old and established a new covenant in Christ.[50]

Christocentric dimension. Alluding to Jeremiah 38:31–33 (LXX), Justin emphasizes that the new covenant came into being "through the name of him who was crucified, Jesus Christ" (11:3–4).[51] Through Jesus Christ, "the eternal law and new covenant came for the whole world" (Χριστόν, ὅστις καὶ αἰώνιος νόμος καὶ καινὴ διαθήκη τῷ παντὶ κόσμῳ;[52] 43:1). The new covenant promised by God is Christ himself (51:3).[53] In light of Isaiah 42:6–7 and 49:8, Justin says in 122:3, 5 that God made Christ to be the *covenant of the people* (Θήσω σε εἰς διαθήκην γένους, 3), *the covenant of the heathen* (εἰς διαθήκην ἐθνῶν, 5).

3. The new covenant in Irenaeus

3.1 Introduction

Irenaeus was probably born around A.D. 140 and lived as a child in Smyrna on the west coast of Asia Minor. The experience of emigrating from Asia Minor to South Gaul impressed upon him the universality of Christianity. Irenaeus henceforth thought in terms of a universal church encompassing the known world – much of which he saw in crossing to South Gaul. Irenaeus became bishop of Lyon in A.D. 177. His greatest works can probably be dated between 180 and 185. He died around 200.

During the time of Irenaeus, the ideological clash between Christianity and Gnosticism escalated to a fever pitch. Irenaeus' preaching and writing were,

---

[50] Backhaus, "Bundesmotiv in der frühkirchlichen Schwellenzeit," 227.

[51] In 11:3 he explicitly lists Jeremiah: "and by Jeremiah, concerning this same new covenant" (διὰ Ἰερεμίου περὶ ταύτης αὐτῆς τῆς καινῆς διαθήκης). The allusion to Jer. 31 in other places is also clear, although Justin only refers to the prophets, or simply points out that God has promised a new covenant.

[52] Greek text from Goodspeed, *Die ältesten Apologeten: Texte mit kurzen Einleitungen* (Göttingen: Vandenhoeck & Ruprecht, 1984), 139; ΒΙΒΛΙΟΘΗΚΗ ΕΛΛΗΝΩΝ 3 (1955), 245–46.

[53] Cf. Skarsaune, *The Proof from Prophecy: A Study in Justin Martyr's Proof-Text Tradition: Text-Type, Provenance, Theological Profile* (Leiden: E. J. Brill, 1987), 175: "Justin cannot finish his discussion on the law without bringing in Christ the New Law."

therefore, not exercises in abstract supposition but "hasty and engaged clarification" prompted by the presence of "acute and concrete danger."[54] What he produced is, therefore, polemic in style.

3.2 The new covenant: An overview[55]

Irenaeus interprets the new covenant exclusively in terms of Jeremiah 31. In *Epideixis tou apostolikou kērygmatos* 90 he says that "our" calling consists in a renewal in the Spirit, and not in the old way of the written code (cf. Rom. 7:6). He then quotes Jeremiah 31:31–34.[56]

Irenaeus contrasts the grace of the new covenant with the Mosaic law. He underlines, however, that both are grounded in the will of one and the same God for the benefit of humanity (*Haer.* 3, 12,11; cf. also 4, 9,3: "For there is one salvation and one God"). Interestingly, Irenaeus interprets the Jerusalem council's list of moral injunctions for Gentile converts in Acts 15:23–29 as a *new covenant of freedom/liberty* that those who believe in God through the Holy Spirit receive (*Haer.* 3, 12,14).[57]

Irenaeus interprets Matthew 13:52 allegorically (*Haer.* 4, 9,1) and points out that in the phrase "treasures new and old" Jesus refers to the two covenants.

> Now, without contradiction, He means by those things which are brought forth from the treasure new and old, the two covenants; the old, that giving of the law which took place formerly; and He points out as the new, that manner of life required by the Gospel, of which David says, 'Sing unto the Lord a new song;' and Esaias, 'Sing unto the Lord a new hymn' and Jeremiah says: 'Behold, I will make a new covenant, not as I made with your fathers' in Mount Horeb. But one and the same householder produced both covenants, the Word of God, our Lord Jesus Christ … who has restored us anew to liberty, and has multiplied that grace which is from Himself.

---

[54] Brox, *Irenäus von Lyon*, I (Freiburg: Herder, 1993), 12.

[55] See Bacq, *De l'ancienne à la nouvelle Alliance selon S. Irénée* (Paris: Namur, 1978) for an extensive description of the new covenant notion in Irenaeus.

[56] As other apologists, Irenaeus occasionally explicitly mentions Jeremiah. Sometimes he only refers to the "prophets," cf. *Haer.* 4, 9,3: "For the new covenant having been known and preached by the prophets" (translation here and elsewhere from Roberts and Donaldson (eds.), *Ante-Nicene Fathers*, I)

[57] The new covenant of freedom is contrasted here (*Haer.* 3, 12,15) with the *first covenant*. The group of apostles around James had such a respect for the first covenant that they would not eat together with the Gentiles. These were those who, due to their upbringing in Palestinian Judaism, were not able to separate easily from the first covenant with its venerable keeping of the law (see Brox, *Irenäus*, III, 161, n. 88).

Irenaeus also characterizes the two covenants allegorically in *Haer.* 4, 25,1. Abraham, the model of faith, is seen as having received the *covenant of circumcision* according to justification by faith *even before his physical circumcision*, "so that in him both covenants might be prefigured, that he might be the father of all."

Although God has replaced the commandments of slavery (given through Moses) with a new covenant of freedom, Irenaeus underscores the *higher ethical claims* of the new covenant. Those who belong to the new covenant should not only abstain from evil deeds, but also from evil desires. According to Irenaeus (*Haer.* 4, 16, 5), sons should fear their fathers more than slaves and should have greater love for them as well. Irenaeus quotes Jesus' words from Matthew 12:36; 5:28 and 5:22 and concludes that we will be held accountable to God not only for that which we do – as is the case with slaves – but also for what we say and think.

In *Haer.* 3, 17,2 Irenaeus links the new covenant with the *Spirit*. Irenaeus quotes Luke to the effect that the Holy Spirit was poured out on the disciples after the ascension at Pentecost, empowering them "to admit all nations to the entrance of life, and to the opening of the new covenant." In *Haer.* 4, 33,14 Irenaeus emphasizes that the new covenant God will make with the people will not be like the one he made with the forefathers at Horeb. It will be instituted by God, giving them a new heart and a new Spirit (cf. Ezek. 36:26). He then quotes Isaiah 43:18–21: "Forget the former things … see, I am doing a new thing." He concludes that the prophet was clearly announcing the new covenant, and that the new wine of the covenant will flow forth from the Spirit; "[that is] the faith which is in Christ, by which He has proclaimed the way of righteousness sprung up in the desert, and the streams of the Holy Spirit in a dry land … that they might show forth his praise."

Irenaeus (*Haer.* 3, 11,8) differentiates *four covenants*, with the number four having special significance. He points out that "the living creatures are quadriform, and the Gospel is quadriform, as is also the course [the order of salvation] followed by the Lord." Hence, humanity was given four encompassing covenants: one at the time of Adam before the flood; a second at the time of Noah after the flood; the third with the giving of the law under Moses; and the fourth as the new covenant that renews humans "and sums up all things in itself by means of the Gospel," lifting up humanity and bearing them "upon its wings into the heavenly kingdom."[58]

In *Haer.* 4, 4,2 Irenaeus speaks further about the order of salvation:

---

[58] τετάρτη δὲ ἡ τοῦ εὐαγγελίου διὰ τοῦ Κυρίου ἡμῶν Ἰησοῦ Χριστοῦ ("the fourth is the gospel through our Lord Jesus Christ"). Brox, *Irenäus*, III, 115, nn. 59–60, notes that Aphrahat, the Syrian, is also familiar with the notion of several covenants between God and humanity. For him, however, the number "four" does not play such a role as for Irenaeus. He lists five covenants: with Adam, Noah, Abraham, Moses and

Since, then, the law originated with Moses, it terminated with John as a necessary consequence. Christ had come to fulfil it: wherefore 'the law and the prophets were' with them 'until John.' And therefore Jerusalem, taking its commencement from David, and fulfilling its own times, must have an end of legislation *when the new covenant was revealed.* For God does all things by measure and in order.

Haer. 3, 12,5 demonstrates the extent to which Irenaeus considered the notion of a new covenant as central to the *self-understanding* of the Christian church. Having quoted extensively from Acts 4:24–28, Irenaeus notes: "These [are the] voices of the Church from which every Church had its origin; these are the voices of the *metropolis of the citizens of the new covenant*; these are the voices of the apostles; of the disciples of the Lord, the truly perfect, who, after the assumption of the Lord, were perfected by the Spirit."

Irenaeus' expression *"citizens of a new covenant"* leads us to texts such as Galatians 4:21–31; Hebrews 12:22–24 and Philippians 3:20. In Galatians 4 and Hebrews 12, the *new covenant* and the *heavenly Jerusalem* are closely linked.[59] As partakers of the new covenant, believers become fellow-citizens with the saints (Eph. 2:19) who have their homeland in heaven (Phil. 3:20).[60]

In refuting the Marcionites' claim that the God of the Old Testament differs from the God revealed in the Gospels, Irenaeus (*Haer.* 4, 34,3) asks how the prophets could predict everything that Christ preached, suffered and accomplished – and how they could *announce a new covenant* – if their prophetic inspiration had come from an alien God. For example, the prophetic predictions concerning the Lord's passion are unique in terms of the nature of the prophesies made and the manner of their fulfillment:

> For neither did it happen at the death of any man among the ancients that the sun set at mid-day, nor was the veil of the temple rent ... nor was any one of these men raised up on the third day, nor received into heaven ... nor did the nations believe in the name of any other, nor did any from among them, having been dead and rising again, lay open *the new covenant of liberty.*

In *Haer.* 3, 34,4 Irenaeus declares that the Jews must recognize the significant differences that differentiate the old from the new covenant. If someone should

---

[58] (*Continued*) "in the last generation" an everlasting covenant (Aphrahat, *Demonstrationes*, 11,11) (cf. 8.2, below).

A somewhat different version of the sequence of covenants is found in Anastasius Sinaita (fragment 11): "One (after) the flood with Noah, under the rainbow ... a second with Abraham under the sign of circumcision ... a third in the lawgiving of Moses ... a fourth is the Gospel of our Lord Jesus Christ."

[59] Cf. also Gal. 4:26: "the Jerusalem that is above is free, and she is our mother" (ἡ δὲ ἄνω Ἰερουσαλὴμ ἐλευθέρα ἐστίν, ἥτις ἐστὶν μήτηρ ἡῶμν.

[60] Cf. 4.3, above.

claim that the new covenant was realized with the rebuilding of the temple after the Babylonian exile under Serubbabel or through the return of the Judeans from Babylon after seventy years, he should consider that at that time only the temple of stone was re-erected, because the law was still kept on stone tablets. No new covenant was given. The Jews continued to follow the Mosaic law. Since the Lord's advent, however, the new covenant, *a peace-making and life-giving law*, "has gone forth over the whole earth."

3.3 The new covenant: A schematic presentation

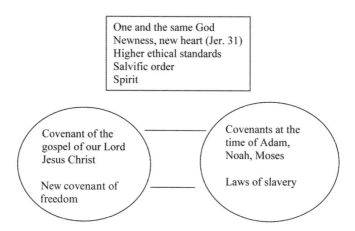

3.3.1 Explanation of schematic presentation

In the light of our investigation of the new covenant motif in 7.3.2 above, the following contours can be delineated:

- Both the law of Moses and the grace of the new covenant were established *by one and the same God*;
- Irenaeus emphasizes the *newness* of the new covenant (the new heart; cf. Jer. 31[61]);
- Although the new covenant is a covenant of freedom, Irenaeus highlights the *higher ethical standards* of the new covenant;
- The dimension of a new *order of salvation* is an important component of the meaning of "new covenant" in Irenaeus' writings;
- The function of the *Spirit* is emphasized;
- The concept of a new covenant was integral to the way the early church defined itself.

---

[61] Jer. 38 in the Septuagint.

Irenaeus contrasts the *covenant of the gospel of the Lord Jesus Christ* with the covenants given to Adam, Noah and Moses and juxtaposes the *new covenant of freedom with* the enslaving commandments of the Mosaic law and covenant.

3.4 Summary

Although Irenaeus affirms that the same God founded both the old and the new covenants, he draws attention to the *eschatological newness* of the new covenant. No new covenant was established through the restoration of the temple, or after the return of the Jewish people from seventy years of Babylonian exile. But a universal new covenant, a peace-making and life-giving law, has been extended to all humanity since the advent of Christ. This new covenant of freedom is experienced by those who trust in God through the Holy Spirit. Irenaeus emphasizes the *new* in the new covenant. To this newness belongs life according to the gospel. It is the singing of a new song, the re-creation of the inner person, as described in Jeremiah 31:31–33. Through this newness the Father returns true freedom to his creatures and multiplies his grace.

The "order of salvation" is an important component of Irenaeus' covenant theology. Humanity has been entrusted with four covenants, the first three being the Adamic, the Noahic and the Mosaic covenants. Fourth and finally came the covenant of the gospel of the Lord Jesus Christ, which renews people, lifts them up and gives them wings to ascend to the kingdom of heaven.

The new covenant is substantially different from the covenant given to Moses at Horeb. Through the new covenant of freedom, God abolished the enslaving commandments of that covenant. Irenaeus emphasizes, however, that even higher ethical standards attend the new covenant and are required of those who have received "the power of freedom." He describes the new covenant as a life-giving law.

The *Spirit* plays an integral role in the reception and living out of the new covenant. The Spirit descended on the disciples after the ascension of Jesus and empowered them to lead all nations into life. Alluding to Ezekiel 36:26, Irenaeus affirms that through the new covenant God gives people a new heart and a new Spirit.

The Christian community views its *own identity* in terms of the new covenant. Irenaeus interprets the outcome of the Jerusalem council in Acts 15 as an expression of the freedom of the new covenant. The liberated, Spirit-filled congregation is the new covenant congregation. Through his death and resurrection the Lord inaugurated the new covenant of freedom – it is remarkable how often Irenaeus portrays the new covenant as a new covenant of freedom.

Eusebius mentions that Irenaeus was praised in a letter to the bishop in Rome as "a zealot of the *covenant of Christ*" (ζηλωτὴν ὄντα τῆς διαθήκης Χριστοῦ).[62] Van Unnik correctly points out that this way of introducing Irenaeus to the bishop in Rome would only have made sense if the concept of the covenant of Christ[63] had been widely accepted and held in high esteem.[64]

4. The new covenant in Clement of Alexandria

4.1 Introduction

Clement of Alexandria was born towards the middle of the second century (around A.D. 140–150) in Athens (or perhaps Alexandria). He was probably educated in Athens and received instruction in Christian beliefs there. His main work was done in Alexandria, the center of Jewish-Hellenistic education. Eusebius of Caesarea dates Clement's most important writings between A.D. 193 and 203.[65] Eusebius also reports that Clement left Alexandria during the persecution against Christians undertaken by Septimus Severus in the years 202 and 203.[66] He later became the theologian and confidant of Alexander, bishop of Jerusalem.[67] Alexander's letter, mourning the death of Clement, should be dated A.D. 221, according to Méhat.[68]

---

[62] *Historia Ecclesiastica* V.iv.2 (Lake, *Eusebius: The Ecclesiastical History*, LCL [London: William Heinemann; Cambridge, MA: Harvard University Press, 1965], 444).

[63] Nowhere else do we find a link between "zealot" (ζηλωτήν) and "covenant of Christ" (διαθήκη Χριστοῦ). Cf. Van Unnik, " Ἡ καινὴ διαθήκη – A Problem in the Early History of the Canon," in Cross (ed.), *Studia Patristica,* IV (Berlin: Akademie-Verlag, 1961), 213: "It is not merely said that he was zealous for God's or Christ's sake, for the benefit of the church, though that seems more or less implied; it is expressed in this way 'for the covenant of Christ.'"

[64] Van Unnik, " Ἡ καινὴ διαθήκη," 213: "If he is highly praised for his zeal for the 'covenant of Christ' and recommended for that reason, this could only be suitably and sensibly done on condition that this quality was generally accepted, in other words that it was generally accepted as a good of the highest value and that it had some relation to the subject-matter or to what is called by Eusebius 'the peace of the church.'"

[65] Cf. Méhat, "Clemens von Alexandrien," in *TRE* VIII (Berlin: Walter de Gruyter, 1981), 101.

[66] This conclusion can be reached, according to Stählin, *Clemens Alexandrinus,* I (Leipzig: J. C. Hinrichs'sche Buchhandlung, 1936), 20, n. 1, when considering Eusebius' *Hist. eccl.* VI, 6 together with VI 3, 1.

[67] Eusebius, *Hist. eccl.* VI, 11 (Méhat, "Clemens von Alexandrien," 102.).

[68] Méhat, "Clemens von Alexandrien," 102.

4.2 A new order of salvation: καινὴ διαθήκη in the sense of a new covenant

Clement instituted significant developments in the use and understanding of the phrase καινὴ διαθήκη ("new covenant"). Its pre-Clementine usage was, as we have seen, primarily to suggest a new order of salvation. Clement helped pioneer the use of καινὴ διαθήκη to refer, as well, to the books of the New Testament.

The salvation historical dimension is evident in the following passages in the *Paedagogus*:

In *Paedagogus* I, V 20,2 Clement points out that the νήπιαι[69] are the new minds which have sprung into being *according to the new covenant* (αἱ κατὰ τὴν διαθήκην τὴν καινὴν ἀνατείλασαι).

Although *Paedagogus* I, VI 33,4 does not speak of a new covenant, the salvation history dimension of its covenant theology comes to the fore when Clement mentions that Jews are heirs of the previous covenant (κατὰ τὴν προτέραν[70] διαθήκην) while Christians are heirs *according to the promise*.[71]

Paedagogus I, VII 59,1 describes the old people with an old covenant (τῷ πρεσβυτέρῳ λαῷ πρεσβυτέρα διαθήκη) in contradistinction to the young people and their "young covenant" (καινῷ δὲ καὶ νέῳ λαῷ καινὴ καὶ νέα διαθήκη).[72]

A salvation history perspective also surfaces in the *Stromateis*.[73] Commenting on Ephesians 2:5, "For those who were dead in their sins, are made alive with Christ," Clement adds: "by the covenant made with us (διὰ τῆς ἡμετέρας διαθήκης)" (*Stromateis* II, XX 47,3).

The beginning of the fifth chapter of *Stromateis* VI alludes to Peter's preaching.[74] Clement observes that the Greeks had some knowledge of the true God, but he adds that it is now possible to worship God in a new way through Christ, citing Jeremiah 38:31 (LXX): "Behold, I make with you a new covenant, not as I made with your fathers in Mount Horeb." The concept of "newness" is then further explained: "He made a *new covenant* with us; for what belonged to the Greeks and Jews is old. But we, who worship Him in a new way, in the third

---

[69] Stählin does not translate νήπιαι in this instance.

[70] προτέραν (previous) underlines this salvation history dimension.

[71] Cf. Gal. 4:1–5.

[72] Cf. also 59,2: "This is my new covenant written in the old letter" (ἡ νέα διαθήκη παλαιῷ κεχαραγμένη γράμματι).

[73] *Stromateis* are words that present, without a strict outline, a great deal of varied content in a free structure. This kind of title and informal presentation of different material in one piece of literature was quite popular during the time of Clement.

[74] From the *Kerygma Petri*, cf. Stählin, *Clemens*, IV, 264, n. 2 (see also 9.1, below).

form, are Christians. For clearly, as I think, he showed that the one and only God was known by the Greeks in a Gentile way, by the Jews Judaically, and in a *new and spiritual way* by us."

Clement continues by noting that God is the giver of all these covenants. He even speaks of *different* covenants (διαφόροις … διαθήκαις) of the one Lord: "For that, as God wished to save the Jews by giving to them prophets, so also by raising up prophets of their own tongue … he distinguished the most excellent of the Greeks." The dynamic of different orders of salvation is clearly emphasized here. Because Clement speaks of different covenants, it seems as if he perceives an order of salvation for the "most excellent of the Greeks." It is obvious that Clement interprets the covenant concept from the perspective of his own philosophical horizon.

Quis dives salvetur is a Clementine homily on Mark 10:17–31. In *Stromateis* VI, V Clement tries to make a way for the educated Greek to embrace Christianity by showing its continuity with Greek philosophy. In reference to the Markan passage, he opposes the literal interpretation that riches make it impossible to obtain salvation. Clement emphasizes that dispassion concerning the things of this world and love and service of one's neighbor embody the true sense of the gospel.[75] No owner of earthly possessions who is acquainted with the greatness of God's love should consider himself excluded from the blessings of the Lord (*Quis dives salvetur* 3,5–6). With joy he should submit to the *Logos* and to Christ: "Let his appointed food and drink be *the Lord's new covenant* (ἡ καινὴ διαθήκη τοῦ κυρίου), his exercise the commandments, his grace and adornment the fair virtues of love, faith, hope, knowledge of the truth, goodness, gentleness, compassion, gravity; in order that … he may with a good conscience stand before the judge a victor, admitted to be worthy of the fatherland above" (*Quis dives salvetur* 3,5–6).[76]

This passage is of great importance, as the *new covenant* appears here in the context of the *Lord's Supper*. It is noteworthy, however, that the new covenant is here related to both food *and* drink, while it is only linked to the cup in the synoptic tradition and in Paul. The question arises whether a tradition lies in the background of the text that parallels the Gospel of John (cf. τροφή ["food," Clement] / τρώγων ["whoever eats," John 6:56] // ποτόν ["drink," Clement] / πόσις ["drink," John 6:55])?[77]

It is also interesting to note how Clement connects the concept of new covenant with the commandments and then with love, faith, hope, knowledge of

---

[75] Cf. Stählin, *Clemens*, I, 37–8.

[76] Butterworth, *Clement of Alexandria*, LCL (Cambridge, MA: Harvard University Press, 1979).

[77] John 6:55–56: "For my flesh is real food and my blood is real drink. Whoever eats my flesh and drinks my blood remains in me, and I in him."

truth, goodness and so on.[78] The new covenant is also related to the thought of heavenly citizenship (cf. Gal. 4:26; Phil. 3:20; Heb. 12:18–21)![79]

A very important statement is found in *Quis dives salvetur* 37,4: "And when He is about to be offered[80] and is giving Himself up as a ransom (λύτρον), *he leaves us a new covenant*[81] (καινὴν ἡμῖν διαθήκην καταλιμπάνει)*.*" Clement then links this new covenant with Jesus' statement: "I give you my *love*" (alluding to John 13:34 and 14:27).

At the end of *Stromateis* I (XXIX 182,2) Clement interprets the Moses story and comments that Moses calls the Lord a "covenant" when he says: "Behold I am my covenant with thee." *"Covenant,"* says Clement, *is God himself,* the author of all, who creates the world order, because θεός (God) has his name from θέσις (statutes) and from "order" or "arrangement." Covenant theology becomes here the climax of all of Clement's theology.

The notion of "oneness/unity" is also of key importance to Clement. In *Stromateis* VI (XXIII 106,3) he affirms that there is *only one covenant leading to salvation,* reaching us from the creation of the world (μία ... διαθήκη ἡ σωτήριος ἀπὸ καταβολῆς κόσμου). Parallel to this one and only covenant he writes (in 106,4) about the one and only unchangeable gift of salvation, from the one and only God, through the only Savior – and refers to the one people that is coming into being in the context of the church consisting of both Greeks and Jews: "And so both reach the 'oneness of faith'" (107,1).

In *Stromateis* VII, XVII 107,5 he underlines the unity, or oneness, of the church – his argument again goes back to the notion of a new covenant:

> Therefore in substance and idea, in origin, in pre-eminence, we say that the ancient and catholic church is alone, collecting as it does into the unity of the one faith – which results from the peculiar covenants,[82] or rather *the one covenant in different times*[83] by the will of the one God, through one Lord.

4.3 Title for the books of the New Testament

In certain contexts Clement uses the word διαθήκη to refer to the books of the New Testament (or of the Old Testament or of both Testaments). Following are a few examples:

---

[78] The fruits of the Spirit in the New Testament.

[79] Cf. 4.3, above.

[80] The expression σπένδεσθαι (being poured like a drink offering) is taken from 2 Tim. 4:6 (Stählin, *Clemens*, II, 269, n. 3).

[81] Or "testament."

[82] It seems better to translate here with "covenant" instead of "testament" (against the translation in the *Ante-Nicene Fathers,* II, 555).

[83] τῆς κατὰ τὰς οἰκείας διαθήκας, μᾶλλον δὲ κατὰ τὴν διαθήκην τὴν μίαν διαφόροις τοῖς χρόνοις.

Stromateis I, IX 44,3

Stromateis III, XI 71,3 (νέα διαθήκη)

Stromateis III, XVIII 108,2 (κατὰ τὴν διαθήκην τὴν καινήν)

Stromateis V, I 3,3 (αἱ ἐντολαὶ αἵ τε κατὰ τὴν παλαιὰν αἵ τε κατὰ τὴν νέαν διαθήκην)

Stromateis V, Cap. XIII 85,1 (διά τε τῆς παλαιᾶς διά τε τῆς νέας διαθήκης)

Stromateis VII, Cap. VI 34,2[84]

4.4 Conclusion

With the writings of Clement of Alexandria we have reached the end of the second century. The dimension of salvation history (i.e., καινὴ διαθήκη in the sense of a new *covenant*) continued to play an important role in the development of new covenant theology during this period. In certain passages καινὴ διαθήκη is, however, also used as the title for the books of the *New Testament*. There are also a number of passages in which it is not clear whether new covenant refers to God's order of salvation, or whether the reference is to the New Testament writings. Clement talks of *both* testaments, *different* covenants, but also about the *one and only* covenant (cf. Barn. 7:1). As does Philo the Jew, so Clement also affirms that "the covenant" is God himself. Clement's covenant theology – especially the way he relates the orders of salvation to the "most excellent of the Greeks" – is a clear example of how a concept is interpreted within an existing philosophical horizon. The way in which Clement connects Johannine motifs to the covenant concept is also noteworthy.

---

[84] There are also instances where the reference to the Scriptures of the Old and New Testaments is at the centre – but a salvation history dimension may also be possible. Cf., e.g., *Stromateis* I, V 28,2; II, VI 28,6–29,2; VI, V 42,1–2, and especially the following two instances:

In *Stromateis* IV, XXI 134,2 Clement writes that the letters of Paul "depend on the Old Testament (ἐκ τῆς παλαιᾶς ... διαθήκης)." Διαθήκη, meaning Old Testament, refers here to the writings of the Old Testament.

Stromateis VII, XVI 100,5 speaks of the "connection of the testaments (τῶν διαθηκῶν)." Here διαθῆκαι also refers to the collection of writings comprising the Old and New Testaments.

Excursus: (New) covenant in Melito

Although Melito referred to the "books of the old covenant" (τῆς παλαιᾶς διαθήκης βιβλία),[85] the notion of a new covenant does not occur in his writings. Other concepts closely related to the covenant theme in early Christian literature do, however, play an important part in Melito's ΠΕΡΙ ΠΑΣΧΑ – for example, the contrasts between old and new,[86] temporal and eternal, earthly and heavenly.[87]

The Passover, seen from the perspective of two orders of salvation. Melito points out that the mystery of the Passover consists in the fact that it is new (καινόν) and old (παλαιόν), eternal and temporary – old because of the law and new because of the Word (παλαιὸν ... κατὰ τὸν νόμον, καινὸν δὲ [κατὰ τὸν] λόγον); temporary because of its type and eternal because of grace.[88] In ΠΕΡΙ ΠΑΣΧΑ 4 he notes that the law is old, while the Word is new – the lamb is transitory (φθαρτόν), but the Lord is ἄφθαρτος (imperishable).

In the new salvation period, says Melito (ΠΕΡΙ ΠΑΣΧΑ 42), the law has been fulfilled and its power has been given to the gospel (παραδοὺς τῷ εὐαγγελίῳ τὴν δύναμιν). At one time the slaughtering of sheep had significant meaning, but now it is worthless because of the Lord's life; the death of sheep was valuable, but now it is meaningless because of the Lord's salvation; the blood of sheep was valuable, but now it is worthless because of the Lord's Spirit; the earthly Jerusalem (ἡ κάτω Ἰερουσαλήμ) was valuable, but now it is meaningless because of the Jerusalem from above (ἄνω Ἰερουσαλήμ).[89] The mystery of the Passover has been fulfilled in the body of the Lord (τετέλεσται ἐν τῷ τοῦ κυρίου σώματι).[90]

Christ has freed us and led us from slavery to freedom, from darkness to light, from death to life. He has made us into a new priesthood and an eternally

---

[85] Fragment 3.1.16, cf. Hall, "Melito in the Light of Passover Haggadah," *JTS* 22 (1971), 66. However, Melito's statement has already been preceded and prepared by καινὴ διαθήκη being used as a title for the books of the *New Testament*. Kinzig, "καινὴ διαθήκη: The Title of the New Testament in the Second and Third Centuries," *JTS* 45 (1994), notes that this statement by Melito can have several meanings and one can, therefore, not decide whether he was already familiar with a collection of writings called the New Testament.

[86] Cf. Kinzig, *Novitas Christiana*, 132–36.

[87] Melito's ΠΕΡΙ ΠΑΣΧΑ is an early example of Christian *artistic fiction*. Cf. Hall, "Melito," xxiii: "There is no question that *PP* is a work of Greek rhetoric." Cf. also Halton, "Stylistic Device in Melito, ΠΕΡΙ ΠΑΣΧΑ," in Granfield and Jungmann (eds.), *Kyriakon: Festschrift Johannes Quasten*, I (Münster: Aschendorff, 1970), 249–55.

[88] ΠΕΡΙ ΠΑΣΧΑ, 3.

[89] ΠΕΡΙ ΠΑΣΧΑ, 44, 45.

[90] ΠΕΡΙ ΠΑΣΧΑ, 56.

chosen people (καὶ λαὸν περιούσιον αἰώνιον). "New" and "eternal" are attributes often associated with the new covenant.[91]

5. The development of the covenant motif in early Christian literature: Conclusion and theological evaluation

The concept of covenant belongs, in its origin, to the *Jewish* tradition. It is, therefore, understandable that the process through which the new covenant concept became part of a specifically *Christian* identity was marked by certain tensions.[92]

The interpreter experiences tension between the importance of the new covenant (for example, in the Eucharist tradition) and the fact that, apart from the Epistle to the Hebrews, the concept occurs infrequently in the New Testament.[93] However, as we have seen, the concept of a new covenant has had an important history of effect (*Wirkungsgeschichte*) in early Christian literature. The period in which the Epistle to the Hebrews, the Epistle of Barnabas and the writings of Justin were created was the high tide of early Christian covenant theology (cf. Backhaus: *frühkirchliche Schwellenzeit*). The covenant concept also played an important role in the writings of Irenaeus and Clement of Alexandria, as well as the early third-century Syrian church father Aphrahat.[94]

From the middle of the second century, the notion that God made two covenants with his people gained acceptance. The new covenant of God with the church – which opened salvation to all, regardless of ethnicity – was seen as overshadowing the old covenant with Israel. This theology of replacement, however, never eclipsed the vision of God's unitary action in salvation history. The historically new was seen as being in continuity with what had preceded it. In this way, the earliest intimations of a theology of salvation history began to emerge. Ecclesiologically, the writings of the early Christian authors show how the application of new covenant theology served an important role in the church's evolving process of self-definition as a sociological entity. The church used covenant language to define itself in relation to both Jews and non-Jews.[95]

---

[91] Hall, "Melito," 31–2, underlines the close links between this passage (ΠΕΡΙ ΠΑΣΧΑ 68) and Mishnah *Pesahim* x. 5 as well as *Exodus Rabbah* 12.2.

[92] Backhaus, "Das Bundesmotiv in der frühchristlichen Schwellenzeit,", 212.

[93] Cf. März, "Bund III: Im Neuen Testament," in *LTK* (Herder: Freiburg/Basel/Wien, 1994), 786: "… statistical findings are remarkable and seem to indicate, at least for some parts of the NT, a certain hesitance toward a formal reception of covenant theology."

[94] See Chapter 8, below.

[95] Kinzig, *Novitas Christiana*, 199.

Clement used the concept καινὴ διαθήκη ("new covenant") both to speak of the theology of salvation history and to designate the writings of the New Testament.[96] In a similar way, Tertullian uses *testamentum* in certain contexts to refer to the biblical books and uses it elsewhere in a theological context to refer to "last will/covenant." Although in Origen's commentaries καινὴ διαθήκη refers primarily to the New Testament, the theological meaning also occurs.[97]

How can this development be explained? Five phases can be identified. It is important to point out that although these phases can be distinguished, they cannot be isolated from one another as overlapping did occur.

Phase 1. In this early phase the covenant concept occurs, but only seldom. The reinterpretation of the covenant concept in light of the Christ event was just beginning (cf. the Gospels and the Pauline letters). The early church is familiar with the new covenant concept but does not utilize it widely.

Phase 2. During this phase an active *christological integration* takes place, as authors relate the covenant concept to Christology. The author of the Epistle to the Hebrews depicts Christ as the "guarantor" and "mediator" of a better covenant (cf. Heb. 7:22; 8:6). In his own way, Barnabas also strives to link covenant theology with Christology.[98]

Phase 3. Two aspects characterize this phase:

As a result of the development of the covenant concept christologically, further innovations in new covenant theology became workable *possibilities*.

As Christianity loosened its organic tie to its mother religion, it became easier to speak of the new covenant within the specific framework of Christian theology.[99] Justin,[100] Irenaeus and Clement of Alexandria belong to this phase.

---

[96] Kinzig, "καινὴ διαθήκη," 528–29, also draws attention to the fact that καινὴ διαθήκη in Justin and Irenaeus is never used as a book title: "The first unequivocal testimonies are found around the year 200 in the writings of Clement of Alexandria … Even though the boundaries between διαθήκη as a theological term and as a book title are blurred, in a significant number of cases (5) διαθήκη does appear to have the technical meaning in which we are interested here." Kinzig points out the following instances: *Str.* I,44,3; III,71,3; IV,134,4; V,85,1; VII,100,5. Kinzig, "καινὴ διαθήκη," 520–23, provides an overview of the history of research on the question of the development of the New Testament canon.

[97] See Kinzig, "καινὴ διαθήκη," 529–32, for an analysis of instances in Tertullian and Origen.

[98] Vogel, *Das Heil des Bundes*, 318–38, characterizes the "'covenant' as an articulation of Jewish – Jewish Christian identity rivalry" in the Epistle to the Hebrews and the Epistle of Barnabas. Cf. also p. 353.

[99] Cf. Backhaus, "Das Bundesmotiv in der frühchristlichen Schwellenzeit," 217.

[100] Backhaus, "Das Bundesmotiv in der frühchristlichen Schwellenzeit," 217, emphasizes that Justin presupposes the christological integration of covenant theology and in this way represents the history of effect (*Wirkungsgeschichte*) of the Epistle to the Hebrews.

In the writings of these authors the notion of the new covenant became an essential part of Christian identity.

Phase 4. Since Christianity did not consider itself any longer as part of the Jewish religion, it became an embarrassment to describe its own salvation history simply in terms of the holy writings of another religion.[101] During this period, Origen made significant strides in interpreting the Old Testament from the perspective of Christian self-understanding. The Old Testament was clearly a self-revelation of God; the difficulty was to see how God's revelation to Israel could be interpreted in such a way as to address the issues and identity of the church. To establish itself in its discussions with the Jews, the early church had to show that Jesus as the Christ fulfilled the promises of the Old Testament. At the same time, it had to persuasively present itself to the Hellenistic world as an old religion that embodied the dynamic of promise and fulfillment that Judaism had incorporated.[102] In this period, καινὴ διαθήκη became increasingly synonymous with the *New Testament writings.*[103]

Phase 5. The reflection of the notion of a new covenant. This last phase is somewhat different than the preceding phases in that it describes a line of development in which essential elements of the Old Testament covenant concept were assimilated and reinterpreted in light of the Christ event and the outpouring of the Holy Spirit – apart from the explicit use of *the word "covenant"* (διαθήκη). In the Johannine writings, for example, the two elements that characterize the heart of Deuteronomic covenant theology – the relation between God and his people and the emphasis on obedience to God's Torah – are interpreted in a new way. Although the word "covenant" (διαθήκη) does not occur here, we find in John a nuanced reflection of what the new covenant had come to mean within the circle of Christian theology (as we saw in Chapter 6, above).

---

[101] Backhaus, "Das Bundesmotiv in der frühchristlichen Schwellenzeit," 216.

[102] So Osb, *Origenes Commentarii in Epistulam ad Romanos: Liber Primus, Liber Secundus* (Freiburg: Herder, 1990), 7–9.

[103] This development explains the transition from a theological usage of καινὴ διαθήκη (in the sense of a new covenant) to a "technical" usage (as a reference to the books of the New Testament) and also explains why this "technical" meaning does not appear in Justin or Irenaeus. Kinzig, "καινὴ διαθήκη," 543, explains the reason for this phenomenon with his thesis that the early church did not accept Marcion's canon, but nevertheless continued to use *his expression for it: καινὴ διαθήκη:* "Owing to Marcion's influence, the term had probably become popular in the church at large, before the 'orthodox' canon took its final shape. The Église savante initially tried to fend off this new designation. *This explains why it is found neither in Justin nor in Irenaeus*" (italics mine). This assumption, however, does not seem necessary.

8

The New Covenant in the Syrian Tradition: Aphrahat

1. Introduction

Aphrahat, the "Persian sage" (approximately A.D. 300–350)[1] is the oldest witness to the independence and originality of the Syrian theological tradition.[2] He provides insights into a developing form of Christianity with which churches to the west of the Euphrates were largely unfamiliar. His was a form of Christianity that was very close to early Palestinian Christianity.[3]

Aphrahat was a monastic bishop in Mar Mattai, close to what is today Mossul, in Iraq. He wrote twenty-three exhortations in elegant, classical Syriac. The first ten of these compositions were systematic presentations of Christianity written in A.D. 337[4] for his pastorate of monastics. The additional thirteen (written in A.D. 344) deal with urgent issues relevant to the church in Iran. This church was suffering persecution because it refused to pay taxes to Shapur II, who sought funds to finance his war against Christian Rome.

Because there were many believing Jews in the Iranian church, the contemporary Jewish-Christian debates were of special significance to Aphrahat.[5] It is remarkable that there is no hint of anti-Semitism in his writings. Jacob Neusner notes: "On the contrary, Aphrahat conducts the debate through penetrating criticism, never vilification. Though hard-pressed, he throughout maintains an attitude of respect."[6]

---

[1] See Neusner, *Aphrahat and Judaism: The Christian-Jewish Argument in Fourth-Century Iran* (Leiden: E. J. Brill, 1971), xi.

[2] Cf. Bruns, *Aphrahat: Unterweisungen* (Freiburg: Herder, 1991), 5.

[3] See Neusner, *Aphrahat and Judaism*, xii, who confirms the earlier opinion of F. C. Burkitt.

[4] See Neusner, *Aphrahat and Judaism*, 4.

[5] Although the Jews comprised a minority in Aphrahat's world, "Aphrahat had to strengthen the wavering faith of the flock against the attraction of Judaism and the destructive influence of the Jews' critique" (Neusner, *Aphrahat and Judaism*, 125).

[6] Neusner, *Aphrahat and Judaism*, 5.

2. The notion of a new covenant: An overview

The concept of a (new) covenant played an important role in the Syrian church. On the basis of such a covenant, a new community was established that viewed itself as the true Israel in contrast to the Jews. Vööbus observes:

> We are first impressed with the covenant-consciousness in the primitive Syrian Christianity. The Christian faith is perceived as a new covenant and this is the decisive factor determining all others in the understanding of the new religion, even to the shaping of its implications. The covenant (*qeiāmā*) assumes the structural position of moulding all its theology, ethics and organizations.[7]

Aphrahat speaks about the covenant primarily in *Demonstrationes* 2 ("About Love"); 11 ("About Circumcision"); 12 ("About the Passover"); 16 ("About the Nations Instead of One People"); 18 ("About Virginity and Holiness"); and 23. *Dem.* 6 deals with the "sons of the covenant" (*bnay qyāmâ*).[8]

In *Dem.* 2,3 Aphrahat discusses the covenant of promise (Gen. 18:18; 22:18; 26:4; Gal. 3:8). God stopped sending seers and prophets to the Israelites because they did not listen to the great prophets.[9] For this reason, the old covenant had to be fulfilled in the new: "Obsolete and out-dated are the works (contained) in the law … For from the point when the new is given, the old is abolished" (*Dem.* 2,6).

The most extensive presentation of Aphrahat's covenant theology can be found in *Dem.* 11 ("About Circumcision"), as circumcision was a key topic in the debates with Jews. Aphrahat holds that circumcision without faith has no value (11,2). Therefore, as long as the law is not followed, circumcision is meaningless. God made various covenants throughout history – with Adam, Enoch,[10] Noah and Abraham. Each of these patriarchs kept the covenant during his time and believed that the one God[11] made covenants with each generation as he pleased (11,3). In each such instance, the relationship between law and covenant changed.[12] When the Mosaic covenant was not kept, however, God established a new covenant with the last generation – an unchanging

---

[7]　Vööbus, *History of Ascetism in the Syrian Orient: A Contribution to the History of Culture in the Near East*, I (Louvain: Secrétariat du CorpusSCO, 1958), 12.

[8]　For translations of Aphrahat, see Bruns, Peter, *Aphrahat: Unterweisungen,* 2 volumes, Fontes Christiani 5 (Freiburg: Herder, 1991).

[9]　See *Dem.* 4,6; 14,33 and 17,11 for the term "great prophet" as christological title (Bruns, *Aphrahat,* 103).

[10]　Although the word "covenant" is not used here.

[11]　Literally, "that it is one," cf. Bruns, *Aphrahat,* 285.

[12]　See also Jacob of Sarug, *adv Iud.* 4,105f. and Ephraem, *diat.* 5, 13f. (Bruns, *Aphrahat,* 294, n. 5.).

covenant. The circumcision connected with that covenant is the one of which Jeremiah spoke: "Circumcise your hearts!" (Jer. 4:4).

God's covenant with Moses included the law and commandments. When the Israelites failed to keep these, God abolished their covenants and the law as well, promising to establish a new covenant that would be unlike the old covenant. Aphrahat quotes from Jeremiah 31:34 ("They will all know me, from the least of them to the greatest") and notes that in this covenant no circumcision of the flesh and no exclusive people of God prevails. Aphrahat concludes in 11,11: "Those who have been circumcised in their hearts live and will be circumcised a second time at the true Jordan, [the] baptism for the forgiveness of sins."[13] "As soon as he (the sinful person) has circumcised his heart from the evil works,[14] he approaches baptism, the fulfillment of the true circumcision, joins the people of God and participates in the body and blood of Christ" (*Dem.* 12,9). Through baptism, believers participate in the new covenant and are connected with the people of God.[15]

Aphrahat notes that "our" Savior ate the Passover together with his disciples during the appropriate night of the fourteenth (of Nisan) and truly performed the sign of the Passover for his disciples. After Judas had left them, he took the bread, spoke the blessing and gave it to his disciples with the words (Aphrahat then quotes Jesus' words): "This is my body. Take, eat it, all of you!" In the same way, he spoke a blessing on the wine and said to his disciples: "This is my blood – the new covenant[16] – which is poured out for many for the forgiveness of sins. This you should do in remembrance of me as often as you gather!"

In *Dem.* 16,7, Aphrahat quotes Isaiah regarding Jesus: "I have made you a covenant for the people and a light for the Gentiles" (Isa. 42:6). Christ has become light and life for us (cf. John 8:12; 12:35, 36). It is interesting how Aphrahat references the covenant concept in 18:1: "I want to instruct you, my beloved, about that which also distresses myself, namely about this holy covenant and the holy virginity in which we stand." "Covenant" here becomes an *all-encompassing term for the Christian message.*

Speaking typologically, Aphrahat contrasts Moses and Jesus in *Dem.* 23,12.

> Through *Moses* the covenant was promised to the people of Israel, that he would give them the land of the Canaanites as inheritance. Through *Jesus* the covenant

---

[13] Cf. Duncan, *Baptism in the Demonstrationes of Aphraates the Persian Sage* (Washington, DC: The Catholic University of America Press, 1945), 32–36, for an exposition of the topic baptism-circumcision-covenant in the early church.

[14] This circumcision happens when a sinful person repents and is redeemed through the blood of Christ (*Dem.* 12,9).

[15] Cf. Duncan, *Baptism in the Demonstrationes of Aphraates*, 89.

[16] Bruns, *Aphrahat*, 303, n. 5, points out that although Bert, following Wright, assumes in his translation a haplographic *d* ("This is my blood of the New Testament"), this change does not seem necessary – either from the *Diatessaron* 45 or from the Armenian text.

was promised that he would give the land to the peoples. *Moses* died on the other side of the Jordan and the covenant he had promised the people became effective. *Jesus* died in the land of our death, and the covenant he had promised the peoples became effective, because he had promised to give them the land of life. The Lord showed *Moses* the land of the promise, when Israel had not yet inherited it. *Jesus*, our Savior, rose from the dead and proceeded to prepare for us the land he had promised, as he told his apostles: 'I am going there to prepare a place for you. I will then come back and take you to be with me that you may also be where I am' (John 14:2–3).

Aphrahat addresses the "sons of the covenant" (*bnay qyāmâ*) in the sixth chapter of his instructions. From 6,1.7.20 on it becomes clear that all who have, by a vow, decided to live a life of renunciation and asceticism are included in this group. Married persons may also be included (cf. 6,7; 7,18). The sons of the covenant are therefore not identical either with the clergy or with the entire church. Rather, they represent an elite group that plays an important role in the life of the church.[17]

3. "Sons (or daughters) of the covenant" in the early Syrian church

In his book *Symbols of Church and Kingdom: A Study in Early Syriac Tradition*, Robert Murray[18] points to the significance of the meaning of the word *îḥîḏāyâ* (Syriac for μονογενής and μοναχός) for understanding the covenant concept in the writings of the Syrian church. The following three aspects of the meaning of *îḥîḏāyûtâ* are noteworthy:

- singleness (leaving one's family and abiding in an unmarried state);
- integrity ("single-mindedness"); and
- having a special relationship with the *îḥîḏāyâ*, Christ, with whom dedicated ascetics relate in a special and intimate way.

Those who live in this way create some kind of "church inside the church," called the *Qyāmâ* ("covenant").[19] During the fourth century, the *Bnay (bnāt) Qyāmâ* was a visible group in the church. Some lived in private homes and some in small communities, but they were not separated from the laity and were not called monks or nuns.

[17] Cf. Bruns, *Aphrahat*, 180.

[18] Murray, *Symbols of Church and Kingdom: A Study in Early Syriac Tradition* (Cambridge: Cambridge University Press, 1975), 13.

[19] See Murray, *Symbols*, 13, n. 5, for a discussion of the meaning and translation of this word. He concludes on p. 14: "However, the meaning 'covenant' or 'pact' being a normal sense of the word … I will retain the conventional rendering, 'sons (or daughters) of the covenant' for *Bnay (bnāt) Qyāmâ*."

Clearly, the covenant concept in Syrian literature has specific *ecclesiological connotations*. The question arises whether the church in Syria, like the Qumran community, characterized itself with the term "covenant." Some early witnesses indicate that *qyāmâ* was used of the Syrian Christian church as such.[20] However, there is not enough evidence to fully substantiate this assumption. There is some indication that there was a time when only those who committed themselves to celibacy received baptism, and that only those who had taken their stand for Christ (*qāmw*) in this way were eligible to participate in the *qyāmâ* (covenant).[21] Further, in the ceremony of initiation into the covenant, the motif of the "holy war" was used to emphasize the commitment to celibacy.[22] Aphrahat, however, allows for the possibility of marriage before baptism (*Dem.* vii, 345.12–13).

Excursus: Covenant in the pseudo-Clementine literature?

In his essay "Problems of the Clementine Literature," Birdsall points to the many questions that have not yet been answered in pseudo-Clementine research.[23] It can, however, be affirmed that: (1) the literature is of Jewish-Christian, or Ebionite, origin;[24] and (2) it belongs to "the class of fictitious writing 'with a purpose.'" Research has shown that these documents have a very

---

[20] Murray, *Symbols*, 14, mentions a passage in the *Doctrina Addai,* as well as in *Od. Sol.* 9,11 and in the *Apology* of pseudo-Melito, that seem to have such meaning. In Aphrahat's writings, the term qyāmâ may point to the church in *Dem.* v, 232.6–8 and also perhaps in *Dem.* xiii, 105.25.

[21] Cf. Murray, *Symbols*, 15.

[22] Murray, *Symbols*, 17. Drijvers, "Syrian Christianity and Judaism," in Lieu, North and Rajak (eds.), *The Jews among Pagans and Christians in the Roman Empire* (London/ New York: Routledge, 1992), 129, underlines the decisive role which ideas of Tatian, the Assyrian, have played in Syrian Christianity. Tatian was a student of Justin Martyr in Rome and returned to his homeland in A.D. 177. He taught that sexual abstinence (*enkrateia*) was the only path for a human being to achieve salvation and to regain immortality.

[23] Cf. Birdsall, "Problems of the Clementine Literature," in Dunn (ed.), *Jews and Christians: The Parting of the Ways A.D. 70 to 135* (Tübingen: J. C. B. Mohr [Paul Siebeck], 1992), 347. Cf. also the research review of Jones, "The Pseudo-Clementines: A History of Research, Parts I and II," *SecCen* 2, 1–33; 63–96.

[24] Cf. Strecker, *Das Judenchristentum in den Pseudoklementinen* (Berlin: Akademie Verlag, 1981). Simon, *Verus Israel: A Study of the Relations between Christians and Jews in the Roman Empire (135–425)* (Oxford: Oxford University Press, 1986), 36–37, notes the Jewish influence upon these documents and notes that a "basically Jewish structure is clearly discernible under their Christian varnish."

complicated history of development.[25] In the forms in which we currently have them, they may date from the first half of the third century.[26]

The covenant motif. The covenant concept does not appear in the pseudo-Clementine literature.[27] Although obedience to the will of the Creator is emphasized, it is not connected with a covenant: "But his friendship is secured by living well, and by obeying his will; which will is the law of all that live."[28]

Teachings about the nature and work of the true prophet are prominent in these writings. The true prophet has been manifested in a number of different forms from Abraham to the Lord Jesus. Additional details about these prophetic manifestations and their relationship to one another remain unclear.[29] However, it may be said that the pseudo-Clementine literature portrays Jesus as the true prophet, but not as the mediator of a new covenant.

The pseudo-Clementine writings also mention the importance of baptism, but the covenant idea does not play a role in this context. Baptism takes the place of the Mosaic *sacrifice*.[30] Baptism is seen in a dualistic context. The current era finds itself under the rule of the female principle. In order to receive the teaching of the true prophet and inherit the kingdom of heaven, baptism is necessary.[31]

Jesus' teachings play an important role in the pseudo-Clementine literature, but there is little emphasis on the historical foundations of the Christ event. There is no mention of Jesus' birth. His death receives attention in the homilies, only in the phrase *idiou aimatos ēmelei* (3.19.1), in a passage that is considered to be the work of an editor.[32]

Although the term "covenant" as such does not appear in the pseudo-Clementine literature, one can detect what Stephen Wilson calls the "two-covenant notion of the Pseudo-Clementines":[33]

---

[25] Cf. Waitz, *Die Pseudoklementinen, Homilien und Rekognitionen: Eine quellenkritische Untersuchung*, published already in 1904 (Leipzig: J. C. Hinrichs'sche Buchhandlung, 1904). There is a widespread assumption that the *Kerygmata Petrou*, for example, could have been a source for the pseudo-Clementine homilies (cf. Robinson and Koester, *Trajectories through Early Christianity* [Philadelphia: Fortress Press, 1971], 125).

[26] See Riddle, "Introductory Notice to the Pseudo-Clementine Literature," in Roberts and Donaldson, *The Ante-Nicene Fathers*, VIII, 70.

[27] A covenant relationship between God and his people is not mentioned, although the covenant is referred to in a different sense in *Recognitiones IV, X*: "every creature kept an inviolable covenant with the human race."

[28] *Recognitiones*, I, XXVI (translation from *Ante-Nicene Fathers*, 73–346).

[29] See Birdsall, "Problems of the Clementine Literature," 352.

[30] *Recognitiones*, I, XXXIX.

[31] Cf. Birdsall, "Problems of the Clementine Literature," 354.

[32] See Birdsall, "Problems of the Clementine Literature," 355.

[33] See Wilson, *Related Strangers: Jews and Christians 70–170 C.E.*, (Minneapolis: Fortress Press, 1995), 161.

It is therefore the peculiar gift bestowed by God upon the Hebrews, that they believe Moses; and the peculiar gift bestowed upon the Gentiles is that they love Jesus … But he who is of the Gentiles, and who has it of God to believe Moses, ought also to have it of his own purpose to love Jesus also. And again, the Hebrew, who has it of God to believe Moses, ought to have it also of his own purpose to believe in Jesus; so that each of them, having in himself something of the divine gift, and something of his own exertion, may be perfect by both. (*Recognitiones*, IV, V)[34]

Despite the fact that the covenant is not explicitly mentioned, traces of a covenantal substructure can, nevertheless, be realized.

---

[34] Translation *Ante-Nicene Fathers*, VIII, 136.

9

The New Covenant: Christian Identity and the Dialogue with the Jews

1. The new covenant and Christian identity

> Learn then, ye also, holy and righteously what we deliver to you and keep it, worshipping God through Christ in a new way. For we have found in the Scriptures, how the LORD says: 'Behold, I make with you a new covenant, not as I made (one) with your fathers on the Mount of Horeb.'[1] A new one he has made with us. For what has reference to the Greeks and Jews is old. But we are Christians, who as a third race *worship him in a new way.*[2]

This passage points to the clear and distinct self-understanding of the early church as rooted in the concept of the new covenant.[3] In explicating the text above, which Clement of Alexandria quotes from the *Kerygma Petri*, he explains that the one God is recognized by the Greeks in a Gentile way, by the Jews in a Jewish way and by Christians in a new and spiritual way.[4]

In the Epistle of Barnabas, the author maintains that there is only *one* covenant and that it now legitimately belongs not to the Jews, but to the Christians. Justin Martyr, however, continues a tradition which had already begun in the New Testament. According to this view, one now must speak of "two" covenants. The "new covenant" promised by Jeremiah has been realized through Christ. The concept of the "new covenant" is integral to differentiating Christianity from Judaism, offering at once a disassociation from Judaism ("old-new" terminology) *and* a link with it (covenant theology).[5]

---

[1] Cf. Jer. 31(38):31–32; Deut. 29:1; Heb. 8:8–9.

[2] *Kerygma Petri*, fragment 2d (Hennecke-Schneemelcher, *New Testament Apokrypha*, II [Philadelphia: Westminster Press, 1964], 100). Cf. Clement of Alexandria, *Stromateis* VI, V 39–41 (see 7.4.2, above).

[3] Cf. Wilson, *Related Strangers*, 93: "it contains one of the clearest assertions of a Christian sense of self-identity."

[4] *Stromateis*, VI, V 41,7.

[5] Kinzig, *Novitas Christiana*, 125, 131–32.

The degree to which the notion of the new covenant defined the self-understanding of the early Christians may be seen in Irenaeus' designation in a letter to the bishop of Rome as a "zealot for the covenant of Christ" (ζηλωτὴς … τῆς διαθήκης Χριστοῦ). Irenaeus interprets the conclusions of the apostolic council in Acts 15 as expressions of the *new covenant of freedom* (*Haer.* 3, 12,14). In *Haer.* 3, 12,5 he speaks of the *citizens of the new covenant*. Irenaeus explicitly mentions that the Lord died, rose from the dead and established a "new covenant of freedom" (*Haer.* 4, 34,3). Within the Syrian church we encounter the *Bnay Qyāmâ*, the "sons of the covenant," describing a specific group of believers. But, of course, we must not forget that the concept of the new covenant (by which early Christians defined their identity) carried connotations beyond that of Jewish Christian self-assertion against non-Christian Judaism.[6] Even for Christians who were not Jews the term had a rich independent dignity. "It is undisputed … that the shapers of the early Christian tradition (Paul, Hebrews and Barnabas, followed by Justin, Irenaeus, Tertullian) defined and reflected on (pagan) ecclesiological identity from the perspective of covenant theology."[7]

2. The new covenant and the early Christian dialogue with the Jews

In this section we will discuss the ways in which the notion of the new covenant functioned in debates between Christians and (especially) Jews. In addition, we will consider whether the idea of a new covenant necessarily lead to anti-Semitism.

The development of an early Christian covenant theology became a *possibility* when Christianity dissolved its organic connection to its Jewish mother religion. It became an *obvious (natural) possibility* as the urgent question arose: How would the young church legitimate itself from a biblical and salvation history perspective? It also became a *theologically attractive possibility* when early Christian authors discovered the value of new covenant theology to enrich their Christology.[8]

All of the early Christian theologians were unanimous in their appreciation of the *newness* of the new covenant. With the Christ event, a new soteriological schema had been introduced.[9] For Justin, this new schema is synonymous with a new eternal *law*. Since the Lord's arrival, the new covenant, *a law that makes*

---

[6] Against Vogel, *Das Heil des Bundes*, 356.
[7] Cf. Backhaus, "Rezension," 151.
[8] Backhaus, "Das Bundesmotiv in der frühchristlichen Schwellenzeit," 217.
[9] Cf. the various covenants that Irenaeus (*Haer.* 3, 11,8) and Aphrahat (*Dem.* 11,11) differentiate.

peace and brings life, has spread across all the earth (Irenaeus, *Haer.* 3, 34,4). Irenaeus emphasizes that the new covenant carries an even higher ethical demand than the old covenant (*Haer.* 4, 16,5). However, he also declares that the new covenant is a covenant of *freedom* (*Haer.* 4, 34,3 and elsewhere). The new covenant is an eschatological entity (Irenaeus *Haer.* 3, 12,5; cf. how Clement of Alexandria [*Quis dives salvetur* 3,6] interlinks the new covenant [καινὴ διαθήκη] with the notion of a heavenly homeland).

The "new covenant" also carries *new sociological connotations. Covenantal salvation is expanded to include all,* not just those who belong to a certain ethnic group. The new covenant includes Gentiles, and indeed those among *all nations* who desire salvation (Justin's *Dial.* 11,4; cf. also the *whole world,* 43,1 and *each people,* 67,10).

In his article on "Jewish-Christian Relations in Barnabas and Justin Martyr," William Horbury notes that the early church faced the real danger of Gentile Christians migrating toward Judaism.[10] To counteract this drift, the early Christian apologists constantly emphasized the *incomparability* of salvation in Christ.

Different early writers express varying attitudes toward *Jewish-Christian relations. Barnabas* is basically "a work of defence."[11] In Justin, on the other hand, one can talk of a "Jewish-Christian missionary rival"[12] – his apologetic work is less defensive.[13] "Justin is a significant witness to the possibility of civilized dialogue based on mutual knowledge and respect."[14]

For Irenaeus, who understood himself to be a Gentile Christian, the debate between Jews and Gentiles seems to be settled. In case it became necessary to maintain conscious disassociation from them, it was enough to repeat the conventional arguments. The debate with Gnosticism, however, was raging in full force during Irenaeus' lifetime. The Christian objections to and refutations of Gnosticism still, to a large degree, needed to be systematized.[15]

---

[10] Cf. Horbury, "Jewish-Christian Relations in Barnabas and Justin Martyr," in Dunn, *Jews and Christians,* 318: "In the Epistle of Barnabas ... the writer thinks that Christians are in danger of going over to the Jewish community, and for Justin too this is a live possibility."

[11] See Backhaus, "Gottes nicht bereuter Bund: Alter und neuer Bund in der Sicht des Frühchristentums," in Kampling and Söding, *Ekklesiologie des Neuen Testaments,* 50.

[12] Horbury, "Jewish-Christian Relations," 336.

[13] Horbury, "Jewish-Christian Relations," 345.

[14] Wilson, *Related Strangers,* 290. Backhaus, "Gottes nicht bereuter Bund," 51, however, points out that in Justin's writings the old and the new people of God, the old and the new covenant, the old and the new law contrast each other in an ethical dualism of "bad" and "good." According to Backhaus, the model of the "old covenant" has, in Irenaeus and Tertullian, negative polemical connotations.

[15] See Brox, *Irenäus,* 7, 13. See also Brox, "Juden und Heiden bei Irenäus," *MTZ* 16 (1965), 90: "The question of the Jews is, therefore, not the theme of Irenaean

Aphrahat, the most ancient Christian witness from the Syrian tradition, was heavily involved in Jewish-Christian debate. However, there is no anti-Semitism in his writings, and they speak of appreciation of and respect for Judaism. His covenant theology developed especially in the context of discussions regarding the custom of circumcision. He argues forcefully that true circumcision is circumcision of the *heart*. Beside the circumcision of the heart there is a second circumcision: the circumcision at the "true Jordan," which is baptism for the forgiveness of sins (*Dem.* 11,11). For Aphrahat, the *holy* (new) covenant is the *whole* Christian message. As mentioned above, the "sons of the covenant" (*Bnay Qyāmâ*) were an important group in Aphrahat's church.[16]

In early Jewish-Christian debates, the notion of a new covenant was, of course, a key motif.[17] Justin, Irenaeus, Clement of Alexandria and Aphrahat[18] emphasized the difference, the incomparability, the unsurpassable and eschatological character of the new covenant.[19] The notion of the covenant was also of great importance in the theology of the Syrian church.[20] In general, early Christian authors developed the notion of a new covenant in various ways[21] depending on their differing historical situations and relationships with the Jews. The notion of a new covenant, however, never became a "combat term of the early church."[22]

---

[15] (*Continued*) apologetics, because Jewish nomism was – compared to the situation of the first Christian churches – not anymore the urgent, relevant danger for the church." Still, Irenaeus' attacks on the Jews are not without passion – he considers them to be hopelessly bypassed by God's advancing plan of salvation.

[16] See 8.3, above.

[17] It must be pointed out, however, that in writings where the salvation history perspective does not appear, the covenant concept plays no role either – as, for example, in the pseudo-Clementine literature and also in the Gospel of Thomas.

[18] Barnabas finds himself on a different level here because he accepts only one covenant. See 7.1, above.

[19] See Luz, "Der alte Bund und der neue Bund," 335.

[20] Cf. Vööbus, *History of Ascetism in the Syrian Orient*, 12; cf. 8.2, above. Berger, *Theologiegeschichte des Urchristentums: Theologie des Neuen Testaments* (Tübingen/ Basel: Francke Verlag, 1995), 321, however, believes that "the general termination of the covenant idea in the writings of the Apostolic Fathers" points to the fact that in the end this instrument was considered to be difficult and probably unsuitable for the debates with Judaism. In light of the function of the covenant idea in the second century, as demonstrated above, this opinion of Berger seems questionable. Hughes, "Hebrews," 92, rightly notes: "The covenant theme ... seems to have had a more widespread influence in the theology of the early church than perhaps has heretofore been recognized."

[21] See Chapter 7, above. What this may mean for contemporary theology will be discussed in Chapter 11, below.

[22] Cf. Lohfink, *Der niemals gekündigte Bund*, 25–28.

Although debates with the Jews essentially subsided during the time of Irenaeus, the "new covenant" was still important from the perspective of the theology of salvation history. During the second century, the faction of Christians who were swayed by Judaizing ideas decreased. *Within* the church, a different set of questions gained ascendancy, namely, the "resolution of the inner-Christian problem of the harmony of the testaments."[23] It is remarkable that, already in Clement, "new covenant" can denote both God's new eschatological order of salvation and, in some contexts, the writings of the "New Testament" in contrast to the Scriptures of the "Old Testament." When we reach Origen's commentaries, the term καινὴ διαθήκη (new covenant) is in most instances a description of the writings of the New Testament.

3. Approaches to Christian-Jewish dialogue today

What is the significance of new covenant theology for the Jewish-Christian dialogue today?[24] Or is there any significance? Is the first covenant "obsolete, outlived and nearing its end" (cf. Heb. 8:13)?

The overriding concern in early New Testament thinking about the new covenant was to solve the religious and sociological issues surrounding the question of Christian identity.[25] While Paul stresses the tension between the natures of the two covenants in his debates with opponents within the Christian community in Galatians and 2 Corinthians, in Romans 9 – 11 he tackles the question of the status of Israel in salvation history more sympathetically. In fact, he struggles[26] with the issue personally, for it concerns the matter of his own Jewish identity.[27] But his primary focus is the relationship of Israel and church.[28]

---

[23] Horbury, "Jewish-Christian Relations," 330.

[24] The fourth issue of the *Theologische Quartalschrift* 176 (1996) attempts to answer this question from various perspectives (e.g., from the perspective of Pauline theology [Helmut Merklein] and of the Epistle to the Hebrews [Michael Theobald]).

[25] Backhaus, "Gottes nicht bereuter Bund," 53.

[26] Cf. Räisänen, "Römer 9–11: Analyse eines geistigen Ringens," in *ANRW* II, 25.4 (Berlin: Walter de Gruyter, 1987), 2891–939.

[27] Cf. Backhaus, "Gottes nicht bereuter Bund," 48. In regard to Jewish-Christian dialogue Merklein, "Der (neue) Bund als Thema der paulinischen Theologie," 291, underlines the following points. 1) It must be taken seriously that Paul was a *Jew* and did theology with his Jewish conceptual presuppositions. "It should come as no surprise that the 'messianic' Jew, Paul, arrives at different results than rabbinic Judaism, as the Judaism of the first century was far from being homogenous at all." 2) The *distance in time* must receive proper attention. The eschatological situation of that time, which we today are not able to reconstruct fully, and the situation of the twentieth century, shaped by Auschwitz, have profound consequences for this debate.

[28] Merklein, "Der (neue) Bund als Thema der paulinischen Theologie," 307.

Romans 11 should be seen as offering a corrective to strains of anti-Judaism in Christian theology. In his paper "What is New in the New Covenant," delivered during the Jerusalem symposium "People and Covenant" (1988), Rendtorff proposes that an important task of current theology is "to formulate a new understanding of the Christian notion of the 'new covenant' which is free from any anti-Jewish implication."[29] It is remarkable that Romans 9 – 11 played a very important role during Vatican II in the exposition on the Jews:

> As this Sacred Synod searches into the mystery of the Church it recalls the spiritual bond linking the people of the New Covenant with Abraham's stock …

> The Church, therefore, cannot forget that she received the revelation of the Old Testament through the people with whom God in his inexpressible mercy deigned to establish the Ancient Covenant. Nor can she forget that she draws sustenance from the root of that good olive tree onto which have been grafted the wild olive branches of the Gentiles (cf. Rom. 11:17–24). Indeed, the Church believes that by His cross Christ, our Peace, reconciled Jew and Gentile, making them both one in Himself (cf. Eph. 2:14–16).

> Also, the Church ever keeps in mind the words of the Apostle about his kinsmen, "who have the adoption as sons and the glory and the covenant …" (Rom 9:4–5) …

> Although the Church is the new people of God, the Jews should not be presented as repudiated or cursed by God, as if such views followed from the holy Scriptures …

> Besides, as the Church has always held and continues to hold, Christ in his boundless love freely underwent his passion and death because of the sins of all men, so that all might attain salvation. It is, therefore, the duty of the Church's preaching to proclaim the cross of Christ as the sign of God's all-embracing love and as the fountain from which every grace flows.[30]

3.1 Romans 9 – 11

The most useful New Testament perspective on the Jewish-Christian dialogue is found in Romans 9 – 11.[31] Paul mentions the covenant at the beginning (9:4)[32] and end (11:27)[33] of the passage.

---

[29] Rendtorff, *Canon and Theology* (Edinburgh: T&T Clark, 1994), 196.

[30] Abbot (ed.), *The Documents of Vatican II* (New York: Guild Press; America Press; Association Press, 1966), 663–67.

[31] Merklein, "Der (neue) Bund als Thema der paulinischen Theologie," 307.

[32] Rom. 9:3–4: "For I could wish that I myself were cursed and cut off from Christ for the sake of my brothers, those of my own race, the people of Israel. Theirs is the adoption as sons; theirs the divine glory, *the covenants*, the receiving of the law, the temple worship and the promises."

[33] Rom: 11:27: "And this is my covenant with them when I take away their sins."

He begins his discussion by signaling his deep distress (cf. 9:2). One may thus assume that the occasion for Paul's meditation was probably not an external attack of some kind, but rather questions that concerned himself as Jew. Although the precise conundrum is not stated, it can be inferred indirectly from the tension arising in verses 3, 4 and 5a. Verse 3 indicates that Paul's previous discourse on justification is the background against which he is speaking. The point of tension is that his closest relatives, his "race," reject (*in majorem*) the gospel and remain "cut off from Christ." At the decisive moment when God's eschatological activity is poised to achieve its consummation, the resistance of the people of God threatens to exclude them.[34]

Paul holds that his people have dignity as a nation. The adoption (υἱοθεσία), the glory (δόξα) and the covenants (διαθῆκαι) belong to them. In Romans 9:4 Paul extols their election by God and describes the salvific ordinances implied by the honorary name "people of Israel." They are, legally speaking, sons of God.[35] Theirs is the glory of God, the radiating atmosphere and the power of his immediate presence. This glory accompanied the fathers in the desert (cf. Exod. 16:10); Moses received the Torah in God's glorious presence (Exod. 24:16); the glory of God's presence had its place first in a tent (Exod. 40:34–35) and then in the Jerusalem temple (Isa. 6:3; Heb. 9:5). Paul also lists other things that accrue to Israel and swell her greatness: the various covenants, following one after another;[36] the giving of the law; the cult and the promises.[37]

Paul presents his vision of the noble olive tree: Jewish Christians are branches that naturally belong to the olive tree, Gentile Christians have been grafted in. Both live from the same root: the forefathers of the people of Israel (11:13–24). There is no reason for Gentile Christians to boast about their new

---

[34] Merklein, "Der (neue) Bund als Thema der paulinischen Theologie," 304.

[35] Cf. Exod. 4:22; Hos. 11:1; Jub. 2:20.

[36] The question remains, though, what Paul means with διαθῆκαι (covenants) in the plural. In his letters he only speaks of the old and the new covenant (cf. Gal. 4:24). It is possible that he refers to the covenants that God made with Israel in the past (with Abraham, at Sinai, with David), or that he simply points to the covenant that was made with the patriarchs and has been renewed. Dunn, *Romans 9 – 16* (Dallas: Word Books, 1988), 534, however, believes that "covenants" here also refer to the old and the new covenant: "If so, the tension between his natural loyalty as an Israelite and his convictions regarding the gospel is maintained. Israel has first 'claim' on the new covenant as well as the old. However much more widely the new has been extended, it was still primarily Israel and Judah who were in view when it was first announced (Jer 31,31–34)."

One can find terminological and conceptual parallels in early Judaism for the "covenants," in the plural, cf. 2 Macc. 8:15; Wis. 18:22; 4 Ezra 3:32; 5:29 (Merklein, "Der (neue) Bund als Thema der paulinischen Theologie," 304, n. 30).

[37] Wilckens, *Der Brief an die Römer,* II (Zürich: Benziger Verlag, 1993), 187–88.

position (cf. 11:18). The overriding question that remains to be answered is this: What will happen to members of Israel who will not believe the gospel (the natural branches who remain cut off from the olive tree)? In 9:6–33 Paul had lauded the sovereign freedom of God, who has started a new soteriological initiative in Christ. How is this sovereignty to be reconciled with God's covenantal promise to Israel?

The answer comes in the form of revelation. Paul has a mystery (μυστήριον) to tell: the hardening that has come upon Israel in part will continue until the full number of Gentiles has achieved salvation, and so all Israel will be saved (καὶ οὕτως πᾶς Ἰσραὴλ σωθήσεται; 11:26). This statement is followed by fragments of several texts from Isaiah (cf. Isa. 59:20–21; 27:9): "The deliverer will come from Zion; he will turn godlessness away from Jacob. And this is my covenant with them when I take away their sins" (11:26b–27). This covenant belongs to the end times. Romans 11:27 points to the eschatological moment of election. *As God has turned to the Gentiles in his sovereign mercy, in the same way will he remember in divine freedom his covenantal faithfulness to Israel.* This hope, however, is based on Christ, because the deliverer from Zion is, according to Paul, Christ himself.[38] Paul is able to solve the problem of Israel by using Scripture to see all within the context of the faithfulness of God in the covenant. The final resolution of the continuity and discontinuity between God's covenant with Israel and the gospel of Christ will be revealed only in the *eschaton.*[39]

What is the "covenant" to which Paul refers in Romans 11:27?[40] The covenant that God made with Abraham and his son Isaac in Genesis 17 is three times specified as an "everlasting covenant." Romans 11:29 emphasizes that God's "call" to Abraham is "irrevocable." This indicates that the "covenant" discussed in Romans 11:27 is the same "old covenant" that God made with

---

[38] See Backhaus, "Gottes nicht bereuter Bund," 49. Hofius, "Das Evangelium und Israel: Erwägungen zu Römer 9–11," *ZTK* 83 (1986), 319, also underlines that Paul in no way attempts to establish a special way around the gospel. Israel will hear and receive the gospel from the lips of the returning Christ. Räisänen, "Römer 9–11," 2918–919, however, is somewhat critical of the idea of a "parousia Christ" who will come from Zion in order to turn Israel's fate, and he asks whether Paul hopes for a miracle from God, who is able to do everything (cf. Rom. 11:23b), in connection with apostolic proclamation.

[39] Kertelge, "Biblische Theologie im Römerbrief," in Pedersen (ed.), *New Directions in Biblical Theology: Papers of the Aarhus Conference, 16–19 September 1992*, NovTSup 76 (Leiden: E. J. Brill, 1994), 56. Cf. also Dunn, *Romans*, 691: "The climax will be the fulfillment of his heart's prayer (10:1) – Israel's salvation, Israel's restoration to full communion with its God. Whatever is happening to Israel now, Paul has been given the divinely revealed assurance that … God's faithfulness to his first love will be demonstrated for all to see."

[40] Rom. 11:27: "And this is my covenant with them when I take away their sins."

Abraham and his son Isaac. This covenant is, however, viewed from the perspective of the promise of the forgiveness of sins by Ezekiel and Jeremiah, a
perspective clearly reflected in the words accompanying the eucharistic cup.[41]
Romans 11 also has pivotal significance for the hope of Christians, as it speaks
about the covenant with Israel which has never been terminated.[42]

The *newness* of the new covenant consists in God's initiative in the life,
death and resurrection of Jesus Christ. According to Romans 11, the *old* of the
old covenant is the call and election of Israel. "Old" does not mean "obsolete"
here; that covenant retains *lasting validity*. Here one finds the enduring theological dignity of Judaism for Christian theology. It is obvious that a certain tension remains, but the resolution of that tension is a mystery that can be solved
only eschatologically.[43] With the salvation of Israel the old and the new covenants are again united – the old covenant is confirmed and Israel is integrated
into the new covenant.[44]

3.2 Ephesians 2:12

The author of the Epistle to the Ephesians characterizes the Gentile situation
before and after Christ as being close to and being far from Israel:[45]

> Therefore, remember that formerly you who are Gentiles by birth and called
> 'uncircumcised' by those who call themselves 'the circumcision' (that done in the
> body by the hands of men) – remember that at that time you were separate from
> Christ, excluded from citizenship in Israel and foreigners to the covenants of the
> promise, without hope and without God in the world. But now in Christ Jesus you
> who once were far away have been brought near through the blood of Christ. (Eph.
> 2:11–13)

---

[41] Cf., e.g., Matt. 26:28: "This is my blood of the covenant, which is poured out for
many for the forgiveness of sins."

[42] Backhaus, "Gottes nicht bereuter Bund," 50. Mußner, "Gottes 'Bund' mit Israel
nach Röm 11,27," in Frankemölle, *Der ungekündigte Bund?* 168, also notes that this
way one can legitimately speak of a covenant with Jews that was never annulled by
God, as the Pope did on November 17, 1980 in front of representatives of German
Jews. Mußner offers a helpful overview of results of recent exegesis on Rom. 11:27
in the German language (pp. 157 – 62) as well as a syntactical semantic analysis of this
text (pp. 163–68).

[43] Cf. Backhaus, "Gottes nicht bereuter Bund," 54–5.

[44] Ferdinand Hahn (in a personal conversation).

[45] In contrast to Rom. 9 – 11, the problem discussed here is not that Israel refuses to
believe in Christ, but unity between Jewish and Gentile Christians in the church, or
the understanding that Gentile Christians should develop for their Jewish brothers
and sisters (cf. Schnackenburg, *Der Brief an die Epheser* [Zürich: Benziger Verlag,
1982], 108–109).

Fundamental to this text is the pattern "formerly – now" (in conscious allusion to Isa. 57:19).[46] The author unfolds his explication through the contrasting statements "separated from Christ" (v. 12a) and "in Christ Jesus' (v. 13a). The former status of the recipients of this epistle (before they came to faith) is described by the apposition "separated from Christ":

> 12 separated from Christ,
>
> 12bα alienated from the community of Israel
>
> 12bβ cut off from the covenants of the promise
>
> 12cα having no hope
>
> 12cβ godless in the world.[47]

Verse 13 underscores that Christ Jesus became the turning point in changing their status ("Christ Jesus" is stressed grammatically in that it appears at the beginning of the sentence construction). The alienation of the Gentiles has been overcome in "Christ Jesus."[48] The Gentiles now have a share in Israel's covenants and promises through the blood of Christ.[49] The difference between those who were once far away and those who are close is eliminated. This transformation has also changed the status of Israel; the people once close to God have now received new access to God in Christ.[50]

It is interesting that the Epistle to the Ephesians considers God's covenant (or, covenants[51]) with Israel as an essential part of God's salvific activity. Through the blood of Christ, the Gentiles now *also* participate in these "covenants of the promise" (v. 12).[52]

---

[46] Cf. Pfammater, *Epheserbrief* (Würzburg: Echter Verlag, 1987), 22.

[47] Schnackenburg, *Der Brief an die Epheser*, 105.

[48] Cf. Gnilka, *Der Epheserbrief* (Freiburg/Basel/Wien: Herder, 1977), 137; Schnackenburg, *Der Brief an die Epheser*, 111.

[49] Pokorný, *Der Brief des Paulus an die Epheser* (Leipzig: Evangelische Verlagsanstalt, 1992), 114.

[50] Schnackenburg, *Der Brief an die Epheser*, 111.

[51] Cf. Rom. 9:4.

[52] Gnilka, *Der Epheserbrief*, 135, believes that the promise intends to direct attention to the life principle of Israel. However, Schnackenburg, *Der Brief an die Epheser*, 110, and Pokorný, *Der Brief des Paulus an die Epheser*, 115, underline that the singular points to the promise fulfilled in Jesus Christ. The more general meaning (hope as life principle of Israel) seems to be preferable in this context, listing the salvific privileges of Israel.

Excursus: Quotes from liturgical prayers

The following quotations reflect the anti-Jewish character of some older liturgical prayers. The revisions following introduce changes that reflect the theology of Romans 9 – 11, namely, that Israel's covenant was never annulled.

Anglican Book of Common Prayer (1662 edition)

Good Friday

O merciful God, who hast made all men, and hatest nothing that thou hast made, nor wouldest the death of a sinner, but rather that he should be converted and live: *Have mercy upon all Jews, Turks, Infidels, and Heretics,*[53] and take from them all ignorance, hardness of heart, and contempt of thy Word; and so fetch them home, blessed Lord, to thy flock, that they may be saved among the remnant of the true Israelites, and be made one fold under one shepherd, Jesus Christ our Lord, who liveth and reigneth with thee and the Holy Spirit, one God, world without end. *Amen.*

Revision (1928)

O merciful God, who hast made all men, and hatest nothing that thou hast made, nor wouldest the death of a sinner, but rather that he should be converted and live: *Have mercy upon thine ancient people the Jews,* and upon all that have not known thee, or who deny the faith of Christ crucified; take from them all ignorance, hardness of heart, and contempt of thy Word; and so fetch them home, blessed Lord, to thy flock, that they may be saved among the remnant of the true Israelites, and be made one fold under one shepherd, Jesus Christ our Lord, who liveth and reigneth with thee and the Holy Spirit, one God, world without end. *Amen.*

Catholic Sunday Missal: Intercessions for Good Friday

VI. For the Jewish people

Let us pray
for the Jewish people,
the first to hear the word of God,
that they may continue to grow in the love of his name
and in *faithfulness to his covenant.*
Silent prayer.
Then the priest says:
Almighty and eternal God,
long ago you gave your promise to Abraham and his posterity.
Listen to your church as we pray

---

[53] Italics mine.

that the people you first made your own
may arrive at the fullness of redemption.
We ask this through Christ our Lord.
Amen.

"Lent, Holy Week and Easter," Supplement to ASB.[54] Intercessions for Good Friday

Let us pray for God's ancient people, the Jews,
the first to hear his word –
for greater understanding between Christians
and Jew
for the removal of our blindness and bitterness
of heart
that God will grant us grace to be faithful to his
covenant and to grow in the love of his name,

Silence

Lord, hear us.
Lord, graciously hear us

Lord God of Abraham,
bless the children of your covenant, both Jew
and Christian;
take from us all blindness and bitterness of heart,
and hasten the coming of your kingdom,
when Israel shall be saved,
the Gentiles gathered in,
and we shall dwell together in mutual love and
peace under the one God and Father of our Lord
Jesus Christ.

Amen.

4. The relationship between the old (first) and new covenant

The relationship between the two parts of the Christian Bible and the question
of the relationship between the covenants is not primarily a historical problem
"but a theological issue, which must be discussed anew in each new era because
theology is reflection on faith under the 'signs of the times.'"[55] Anti-Judaism, which

---

[54] *Alternative Service Book*, 1980.
[55] Zenger, "Thesen zu einer Hermeneutik," 143 (italics mine); cf. also Zenger, "Zum
Versuch einer neuen jüdisch-christlichen Bibelhermeneutik: Kleine Antwort auf
Horst Seebass," *TRev* 90.4 (1994), 275.

has left its traces even in liturgical prayers, is such a sign of the times today. "Theology after Auschwitz" has emphasized the importance of incorporating relevant context and history in theological reflection.[56]

The question of the relationship between the old and new covenants cannot be solved through a historical-critical analysis, although one cannot bypass historical-critical exegesis of the texts. For in addition to textual questions, one must consider reader-oriented questions: How is the text received by contemporary readers? In what situations and with what expectations do they hear the texts? How do they read their existence in and through the texts? Even as a static written entity, the text has the ability to continue speaking. A "reception hermeneutic" frees the text to speak from multiple perspectives.[57] This is essential, since each generation must deal anew with fundamental theological questions, such as the one discussed here.

To turn from hermeneutical issues to the questions at hand: it must first be emphasized that the question of the relationship between the old (first) and new (second) covenants is not the equivalent of the question of the relationship between the Old and New Testaments. The theme of a *new covenant* is *already* an intrinsically important theme of the *Old* Testament.[58]

The new covenant of Jeremiah 31:31–34 is quite different from the first covenant, made with the fathers. Still, this first covenant is not called "old covenant," as for example in Hebrews 8:13, a text that was written under new, *different conditions.* "This old is a *continuum* … The covenant is not revoked, or cancelled (*aufgehoben*), except perhaps in the positive sense that it is elevated (*auf=emporgehoben); lifted up to its true level."[59] The prophetic text does not say that the covenant has been broken by the people and therefore has been abolished by Yahweh. On the contrary, the Torah, as described by Jeremiah, is to be written into the innermost being of the people; into their hearts. In the second covenant, God takes his people by their hands and teaches them in a new, more intensive way. With the implantation of the Torah into the hearts of his people, God himself inaugurates the salvation era. In this way the covenant made with the fathers reaches its final fulfillment.[60]

Karl Barth speaks of the new covenant in terms of an *intensive amplification* of the Old Testament covenant concept. According to the prophetic promises in

---

[56] See Metz, quoted in Zenger, "Zum Versuch einer neuen jüdisch-christlichen Bibelhermeneutik," 275.

[57] See Zenger, "Thesen zu einer Hermeneutik," 145.

[58] Cf. 1.4, above.

[59] Miskotte, "Meditationen zur Jer 31,31–34," in Eichholz (ed.), *Herr, tue meine Lippen auf,* V, quoted by Kraus, "Der Erste und der Neue Bund: Biblisch-theologische Studie zu Jer 31,31–34: Manfred Josuttis zum 60. Geburtstag," in Dohmen and Söding, *Eine Bibel,* 65.

[60] See Kraus, "Der Erste und der Neue Bund," 67.

Jeremiah 31:31–34 and 32:38–41, the covenant with Israel will experience a radical structural change in the end times. However, one could only speak of this intensification or restructuring as a "replacement" covenant in a positive sense.[61] Jeremiah 31:35–37 unambiguously maintains the lasting validity of the covenant with Israel. There can be no thought of terminating this covenant as such. The character of the "new" covenant is not *cancellation*, but *revelation*. *Inherent in the revelation* of the "new" and "eternal" eschatological covenant is an affirmation of the meaning and validity of the first covenant.[62]

> The relationship of God with Israel, which is the substance of the covenant, is not held up, that is to say, arrested, and set aside and destroyed, even on the New Testament understanding of the passage. What is done away … is only its 'economy,' the form in which it is revealed and active in the events of the Old Testament … In accordance with the completely changed conditions of the last time this form will certainly be altered, and so radically that it will no longer be recognizable in that form, and to that extent a new covenant will actually have been concluded.[63]

In the end time covenant, God himself will write his law into the hearts of his people (Jer. 31:33). He will put a new Spirit in their innermost being. He will take away their heart of stone and replace it with a heart of flesh, so that they may walk according to God's laws (Ezek. 36:26–27). In this way the circumcision of the heart (Deut. 30:6) will be accomplished by God himself.[64] The continuity of the new covenant[65] with the covenant made with the patriarchs is predicated from first to last upon *God's faithfulness*. Despite the terrible period of exile, Yahweh will create something completely new!

Early Christian theology maintained that God acted in a completely new way in Jesus Christ. Already in the Lord's Supper tradition, Jesus' death was interpreted as the establishment of an *eschatological new* covenant. In early theology, the old and new covenants were generally seen as existing in tension with each other.[66] This dualism was a by-product of the church's quest to establish a separate and distinct identity theologically, sociologically and liturgically. This quest was essential if the church was to counter the danger of Christians converting to Judaism. Because individual communities encountered this threat

---

[61] That is, as a *renewal*.

[62] Barth, *Church Dogmatics*, IV, 1, 32.

[63] Barth, *Church Dogmatics*, IV, 1, 32. Note: There is a play here on the German word "*aufheben*," which positively means to "raise up," but negatively means to "repeal" or "set aside."

[64] Barth, *Church Dogmatics*, IV, 1, 32–33.

[65] Here we refer specifically to the new covenant as presented in the Old Testament.

[66] Cf. Barnabas, who is an extreme example of this – he does not accept an old covenant but only the one (new) covenant.

differently according to their situations, one can observe different strands of early Christian covenant theology.

In summary, we must reiterate that, in light of biblical exegesis, and in light of the tragic anti-Jewish history of the church, it must be robustly maintained that God's covenant with the forefathers has never been annulled. Romans 9 – 11 points to the continuing (lasting) bond of the church to Judaism.[67] "This 'bond' must be characterized as a 'holy' bond because it originates in the mysterious will of God."[68]

At the same time, Christian theology must also, together with all of early Christian literature, proclaim the "new" that has come in Christ. *"The 'new covenant' is God's covenant in the imminent kingdom. It is the salvation that God had prepared for his people from time immemoria ... that is eschatologically valid."*[69]

At the time of Jeremiah, "Israel" had failed. Without God's forgiveness there was no future. The promise of God to write the Torah into their hearts was of greatest importance. Is this not achieved when Christians are baptized into the death of Christ Jesus so that they can live a new life (Rom. 6)?[70]

Excursus: Two twentieth-century voices

A Jewish voice. An initial historical experiment in what is today called Jewish-Christian dialogue was attempted in January 1933 when Karl Ludwig Schmidt and Martin Buber met in Stuttgart. Martin Buber remembers that, in its loftiness, the cathedral in Worms (Wormser Dom) was for him a symbol of Christianity; the faith experience of his own people, though, was impressed on him at the Jewish cemetery in Worms:[71]

---

[67] Seebass, "Hat das Alte Testament," 274 (referring to Körtner and Dunn), points to the possibility of "commonality" that would emphasize *Israel as the name of continuity*. Cf. Dunn, "Who Did Paul Think He Was? A Study of Jewish Christian Identity," *NTS* 45 (1999), 192–93: "So, who did Paul think he was? ... An Israelite? Yes; ... As a term which identified by (historic) relation to God and not by relation to other peoples, and which, by doing so, could transcend (or embrace) the differences between nations, it best expressed Paul's new perception of his own identity and the identity he wanted to promote among his converts."

Zenger, "Zum Versuch einer neuen jüdisch-christlichen Bibelhermeneutik," 276–77, however, points out that the way that Seebass and Körtner dispute the title "Israel" for Judaism cannot be justified in the New Testament with Romans 9 – 11 (cf., however, Gal. 6:16).

[68] The declaration *Nostra aetate* of Vatican II, quoted by Zenger, "Zum Versuch einer neuen jüdisch-christlichen Bibelhermeneutik," 275.

[69] Backhaus, "Gottes nicht bereuter Bund," 41–2.

[70] Seebass, "Hat das Alte Testament," 273.

[71] Cf. Backhaus, "Gottes nicht bereuter Bund," 33.

I stood there and experienced everything all over again, I died all those deaths again: all those ashes ... all the silent misery is mine; *but the covenant has not been revoked for me.* I am lying on the ground, dashed down as these stones. *But God has not terminated my covenant.*

The cathedral is how it is. The cemetery is how it is. *But God has not terminated our covenant.*

Buber points to the pain and the shame/disgrace of the Jews, but still he concludes: "However, there is a divine sense that tells us that *God, as he promised (Isa. 54:10), will never let us fall out of his hand.*"[72]

A contemporary "Messianic-Jewish" voice. Believers in Christ from Jewish backgrounds have always been part of churches all over the world. Today, however, we see the development of Messianic Jewish communities that hold on to Jesus as Messiah, but at the same time maintain many aspects of their Jewish tradition and culture. John Fieldsend, an Anglican priest and leader of a Messianic community in England, explains:

The importance of a right understanding of the *irrevocable nature of God's covenant with the Jews* is not in any way to exalt Jewishness or Israel. Far from it, we would plead guilty to our own Scriptures' assessment of us as a stiff-necked people. We would stress, however, that a right understanding of the nature of the covenant is vital for our understanding of God. If it is possible that God could change his mind about the Jewish people and Israel, then no Christian can be secure about God's faithfulness to his promise about salvation through faith in Jesus.

God's faithfulness to the Jewish People and the Christian doctrine of assurance of salvation hang on the same line, that God cannot lie.[73]

---

[72] Buber, quoted in Schmidt, "Kirche, Staat, Volk, Judentum: Zweigespräch im jüdischen Lehrhaus in Stuttgart am 14. Januar 1933," in *Neues Testament – Judentum – Kirche: Kleine Schriften* (München: Chr. Kaiser Verlag, 1981), 165 (italics mine).

[73] Fieldsend, *Messianic Jews: Challenging Church and Synagogue* (Kent: Marc Olive Press [Monarch Publications], 1993), 47–8 (italics mine). The title of this chapter in Fieldsend's book is called "Our Covenant Keeping God."

10

The Reception of the New Covenant in the History of Theology: Two Perspectives

1. Introduction

The theme of the covenant has played an important role in the history of theology.[1] In the preface to his well-researched study of the origins of federal theology in sixteenth-century Reformed thinking, David Weir notes: "[This] is the first of what is hoped will be a series on the importance of the theme of covenant in early modern European and colonial American history. As such it represents a specific study of a broader theme of human and divine commitment in the Judaeo-Christian tradition."[2] From this we can infer how profoundly the theme of human and divine commitment – which, of course, is the heart of covenant theology – remains a central and not yet fully resolved issue in theological discourse.

2. The new covenant in early federal theology

The sixteenth and seventeenth centuries saw significant changes in the way Reformed theology subdivided the schema of salvation history. Calvin (1509–

---

[1] Vorgrimler, *Der ungekündigte Bund: Systematische Aspekte*, 232, however, points out that the term "covenant" as a technical term is not (yet) integrated into dogmatics and fundamental theology. As an example he draws attention to the fact that in the new *Lexikon für Theologie und Kirche*, II (1994), 789, there are only two references for the entry "covenant, systematic theological": Communio and Federal theology. These two articles contain nothing that would hint at including the term "covenant" in the systematic nomenclature. However, as Vorgrimler notes, Karl Barth seems to be an exception here.

This chapter will therefore analyze the reception of the new covenant concept from the perspective of *early federal theology* as well as from the perspective of *Karl Barth*. In Chapter 11 we will suggest some approaches to a theology of the new covenant.

[2] Weir, *The Origins of the Federal Theology in Sixteenth-Century Reformation Thought* (Oxford: Clarendon Press, 1990), vii.

64) spoke in his *Institutiones* about an old covenant (which extended from the fall to Christ) and a new covenant (extending from Christ to the day of judgment).[3] However, the Westminster Confession of Faith, written about eighty years later, spoke of a covenant of works and a covenant of grace.[4] Weir analyzed this shift from old and new covenant language to a covenant of works and a covenant of grace, searching for the origins of the "covenant of works" and federal theology.[5] He concluded that the guiding concern of federal theology was to provide an answer to the question of the relationship between God's sovereignty and Adam's fall, as explicated through the doctrine of predestination.

To illustrate: Ursinus suggested in 1562 that an Edenic pre-fall covenant existed between God and Adam. According to Weir, "our conclusion is that the federal theology's distinguishing characteristic – the prelapsarian covenant with Adam – had its origins in the predestinarian discussions which took place during the sixteenth century."[6]

The notion of a pre-fall covenant has significant consequences for sacramental theology, for the relationship between church and state and for many other areas.[7] A pre-fall covenant of works binds all humanity together, both pre-fall and post-fall. All must obey this covenant. The role of the state in enforcing such a covenant may be seen to be significant, as it can serve to enforce God's law. In the framework of a covenant of works, human beings are essentially defined in terms of obeying the law – since the beginning of creation. God's law has been written on the hearts of humans since the beginning, and was not given only at Sinai.

In a certain sense, the covenant of works is the primary covenant that God has made with humanity: Weir comments: "The Adamic relationship of perfection in Eden takes on greater weight than the Abrahamic relationship of grace … The federal theologian thus interpreted Jer 31:31–34 as, in some sense, a return to the covenantal state of Eden, when the law of God will be written on the hearts of the redeemed elect."[8]

It is remarkable that none of the commentaries on Genesis 1–3 from the sixteenth century (before 1590) mentions a pre-fall covenant. The rise of federal theology, according to Weir, "seems to stem from systematic, dogmatic thinking, not from exegetical study of Scripture."[9]

---

[3] *Institutes,* ii, 10–11, *CO* ii, 313–40, quoted by Weir, *Origins*, 1.

[4] Westminster Confession of Faith, Points 7 and 9, cf. Weir, Origins, 1.

[5] Federal theology came into full power with the magnificent work by Coccejus (1603–69), *Summa Doctrinae de Foedere et Testamento Dei* (Heron, "Bund 3: Dogmatisch," in *EKL*, I [Göttingen: Vandenhoeck & Ruprecht, 1986], 571).

[6] Weir, *Origins*, 158.

[7] Cf. Weir, *Origins*, 158.

[8] Weir, *Origins*, 6–7.

[9] Weir, *Origins*, 158.

2.1 Emphasis on unity/continuity of God's covenant – baptism

Federal theology "[uses] the biblical term of the covenant ... in order to grasp and present *the unity* of God's salvific activity in the Old and New Testament."[10] As far as can be traced historically, the beginnings of federal theology go back to the Reformation in Zürich and the discussions with the rising Anabaptists. In conversations of 1524/25 and in his baptismal paper (*Taufschrift*) of 1525, Zwingli argued for the validity of infant baptism from the Old Testament. As in the Old Testament, the children of Christians are no less God's children than the adults. He put the sacrament as a symbol fully on the same level in the Old and New Testaments. Baptism has taken the place of circumcision. In his *In catabaptistarum strophas elenchus* (1527), under the subtitle *De foedere sive testamento* (SW VI/1,155–172), he decisively opposes the Anabaptist position (that in questions of baptism one can only use arguments from the New Testament) – covenant and Testament are seen as the same. "As the covenant, so also faith and the people of God are the same in the Old and New Testament ... This unity of the covenant, the people of God with its descendants, establishes for Zwingli the right to baptize children of Christian parents."[11]

In Heinrich Bullinger's theology the covenant concept also plays a central role. He accepts Zwingli's use of the covenant concept to defend infant baptism, but he expands it to a much broader idea. He employs the covenant notion for a unified perspective on history: "history, for Bullinger, is not marked by radical discontinuity between the Old and New Testaments, *but by unity and continuity.*"[12]

The framework of federal theology is problematic in various regards. Two of the most important of these are (1) the conditional character of the covenant of grace; and (2) the separation between a covenant of works and a covenant of grace (or, between nature and grace in general). The implications of such assumptions create significant theological and pastoral difficulties.[13]

---

[10] Goeters, "Föderaltheologie," 246 (italics mine).

[11] Goeters, "Föderaltheologie," 246–47.

[12] Weir, *Origins*, 10 (italics mine). Weir, 9, also points out that both Testaments comprise a unity for Calvin: they are identical in (1) *substantia* and (2) reality (*re ipsa*); they differ, however, in *administratio*.

[13] Cf. Heron, "Bund," 571.

3. A christocentric perspective on the new covenant: Karl Barth

The motifs "covenant" and "creation" are brilliantly discussed in the theology of Karl Barth (1886–1968). In his magisterial works, Barth engages the intentions of earlier federal theology and attempts to correct them.[14]

We have already mentioned Karl Barth's understanding of the relationship between the old and the new covenants (see 9.4, above). His concept of a new covenant, however, requires further attention. Echoing his exposition of *Jer. 31:31–34* (CD IV/1, 32–33), we will analyze Barth's foundational understanding of "covenant" and why this term gained such central significance for him.

As we have noted, Barth considered the new covenant to be an *"intensive amplification"* of the existing covenant concept. Specifically, following Jeremiah 31, Barth sees this intensification as having a three-fold configuration:

The covenant will be *new and different,* not the way "I made [it] with their forefathers …, [which] they broke" (Jer. 31:32). God will write his law into their hearts, so that he can more truly be their God and they can more truly be his people (v. 33). Barth interprets this statement in Jeremiah thusly: Because the first covenant was broken, in the new covenant "the circle of the covenant which in its earlier form is *open* on man's side *will … be closed.*" The covenant will be kept *mutually,* that is on both sides: "not because men will be better, but because God will deal with the same men in a completely different way, laying His hand, as it were, upon them from behind, because He Himself will turn them to Himself. To His faithfulness – He Himself will see to it – there will then correspond the complementary faithfulness of His people" (CD IV/1, 32–33).

The fact that *all* will know God in the new covenant (Jer. 31:34), Barth explains this way:

But if the new and eternal form of the covenant means the ending of the fatal controversy between God and man it also means the ending of the corresponding necessity (the redemptive necessity) for that human antithesis or opposition between wise and foolish, prophets and people, teachers and scholars, the *ecclesia docens* and the *ecclesia audiens,*[15] which even at its very best indicates a lack and encloses a judgment. It is at this point that Paul comes in (2 Cor. 3:6–7) with his doctrine of the old and the new διαθήκη, the one of the prescriptive letter, the

---

[14] Cf. Heron, "Bund," 571. Busch, "Der eine Gnadenbund Gottes: Karl Barths neue Föderaltheologie," *TQ* 176.4 (1996), 341, even speaks of *Karl Barth's new federal theology.*

[15] "The church teaching and the church listening."

other of the liberating spirit which leads to obedience. (CD IV/1, 33; cf. also IV/3, 34)

The newness of the new covenant also consists in the fact that God will *forgive* sin (Jer. 31:34). This results in the removal of the covenant breach and the opening of the way for God to implant the Spirit in the innermost part of his people. In both of these senses the new covenant does not replace the old covenant but completes it. New covenant forgiveness means that "God himself negates, according to his prophecy, Israel's unfaithfulness, but not his own faithfulness … toward this people."[16]

The emphasis and the problem of predestination, which led in federal theology to the idea of a pre-fall covenant of works, is solved by Karl Barth in a *christocentric* way: Jesus Christ is both electing God and elected human, prefigured by the eternal "logos" of John 1:1–18.[17] Karl Barth's universalist concept of the doctrine of predestination results in the preference of the election of the community before the election of the individual.[18] The doctrine of creation is conceptualized analogically and christologically from the perspective of the universal salvific will of God. The world is the arena of God's revelation, because the covenant fulfilled in Christ is the "inner foundation" of creation and creation is the "external manifestation" of the covenant. Barth underlines that the covenant is the goal of creation and that creation is the way in which the covenant is realized.

> The inner basis of the covenant is simply the free love of God, or more precisely the eternal covenant which God has decreed in Himself as the covenant of the Father with His Son as the Lord and Bearer of human nature, and to that extent the Representative of all creation.[19]

In his theology of reconciliation, Barth echoes the core idea of the Epistle to the Hebrews that Jesus Christ is the *mediator and guarantee* of the new covenant (cf. Heb. 9:15).[20] He underscores that Christ, as reconciler and reconciliation, is the fulfillment of the covenant: "But that one thing in the middle is one person, Jesus Christ. *He is the atonement as the fulfillment of the covenant.*"[21] Because the reconciliation of humans with God, that is the return of humans through God and to God, happened in Jesus Christ, "he himself [is] the *Mediator and pledge of the covenant. He is the Mediator* of it in that he fulfills it – from God to man and

---

[16] Busch, "Der eine Gnadenbund Gottes," 342.
[17] Cf. Barth, *Church Dogmatics*, II/2, 96; cf. also IV/2, 32.
[18] Jüngel, "Barth, Karl," in *TRE* V (Berlin: Walter de Gruyter, 1980), 263.
[19] Barth, *Church Dogmatics*, III/1, 97.
[20] Cf. Gräßer, *An die Hebräer*, II, 168–69.
[21] Barth, *Church Dogmatics* IV,1, 122 (italics mine).

from man to God. He is the *pledge* of it in that in His existence He confirms and maintains and reveals it as an authentic witness – attesting Himself!, in that its fulfillment is present and shines out and avails and is effective in Him."[22]

3.1 A christological perspective: Emphasizing the discontinuity between circumcision and baptism

Karl Barth also reflects from a christological perspective on baptism and underlines that the goal of baptism is God's reconciliation in Jesus Christ through the Holy Spirit. Baptism is an expression of God's activity in judgment, mercy, salvation and revelation.

> Baptism is for those who newly join the community the first concrete step of faith, love and hope and service. It is the first step by which they publicly and bindingly confess and commit themselves to their recognized and acknowledged Lord as *Mediator of the covenant*, and also to the mutual fellowship of Christians.[23]

Barth also underlines the form of Christian baptism as a request, or petition "that the outpouring of the Spirit might take place again, and especially on these newcomers to faith."[24] The meaning of baptism "is man's conversion – the conversion of all who have part in it. It is the conversion which takes place in the knowledge of the work and word of God. It is the common forsaking of an old way of life and the common following of a new way of life."[25] Barth once more points to Jesus Christ as the origin and meaning of the baptismal ceremony and connects it with the idea of the covenant:

> Baptism takes place both in the power of His appointment and also towards (εἰς) His name, i.e., in orientation to the reality which is revealed in His name, which is also the name of His Father and His Holy Spirit. It takes place in orientation toward the reality of the *covenant between Him and man* which is established, fulfilled and faithfully kept by God.[26]

From this christological perspective the continuity between circumcision and baptism is severed; therefore, Barth rejects infant baptism.[27]

---

[22] Barth, *Church Dogmatics* IV,1, 136 (italics mine).
[23] Barth, *Church Dogmatics* IV,4, 72 (italics mine).
[24] Barth, *Church Dogmatics* IV,4, 77; cf. also 210.
[25] Barth, *Church Dogmatics* IV,4, 139.
[26] Barth, *Church Dogmatics* IV,4, 195.
[27] Cf. Barth, *Church Dogmatics* IV,4, 165ff.

11

Transmission and Reinterpretation: Interpretive Trajectories for a "Theology of a New Covenant"

1. Transmission and reinterpretation

By describing the relationship between God and humankind in terms of a covenant, the Old Testament authors emphasize that this relationship is not grounded in the natural order, but upon *God's activity in history.*[1] In Genesis 17:7, at the beginning of the history of Abraham and of Israel's history, God states that he will establish "an everlasting covenant between me and you and your descendants after you for the generations to come, to be your God and the God of your descendants after you."[2] Israel's history has, from the beginning, been shaped by God's covenantal intent.[3] This truth serves as a central Old Testament touch point for reflecting on the relationship between God and his people. The theologically weighty term "covenant" is an "interpretative pattern for the unifying momentum of Old Testament religious history; and for the notion – self evident at first and later elaborated in times of crisis – that the national God Yahweh and Israel belong together, as expressed in the covenant formula: 'Yahweh, the God of Israel; Israel, the people of Yahweh.'"[4]

Von Rad points out that the history of the community that trusted in Yahweh was characterized by ongoing divine acts of intervention and renewal that marked new periods in tradition history. The Old Testament reflects a growing prophetic anticipation:[5] Yahweh's covenant with the forefathers, the revelation of his name, the Passover event, the covenant at Sinai, the foundation of Zion, the covenant with David, God's inhabiting the temple in the ark

---

[1] Vriezen, *An Outline of Old Testament Theology* (Oxford: Basil Blackwell, 1958), 140.
[2] Cf. 1.3.6.2, above.
[3] Although the actual covenant *theology* was developed only in the Deuteronomic era.
[4] Gertz, "Bund, II: Altes Testament,", 1863.
[5] Von Rad, *Old Testament Theology,* II, 321.

of the covenant – all of these developments are both fulfillments of divine promises and anticipations of far-reaching promises to come.[6]

Jeremiah, Ezekiel and Deutero-Isaiah expected a new David, a new Exodus, a new city of God, *a new covenant*. The old pointed toward the new. Old traditions were constantly being reinterpreted in the light of new contexts, and the prophets freely invest more in one interpretive tradition than in others, as the situation warrants. Von Rad underscores the paradigmatic significance of Jeremiah's new covenant orientation (Jer. 31:31–34) for the ensuing prophetic tradition by pointing out that Jeremiah mysteriously combines elements from the old saving tradition with its radical supersession.[7] Within the Old Testament, a major tradition is *reinterpreted*. The law still plays a significant role, but it has now been placed within the context of a *new* covenant – it will not be like the covenant made with the forefathers, because the LORD will put his law in the minds of the people and write it on their hearts. He will forgive their wickedness and remember their sins no more.

A sense of wonder at the advent of a new event with tremendous significance permeates the New Testament.[8] From the context of Jesus' proclamation, death and resurrection, Old Testament traditions acquired fundamentally new interpretive dimensions in the minds of the New Testament authors.[9] Delbert Hillers, quoting Hebrews 9:11–23, aptly comments: "High priest, tent, blood, sacrifice, covenant: every term here is old, yet each is transmuted. Each has become a way of asserting what happened through Christ."[10]

The Old Testament promise of the eschatological new covenant (Jer. 31:31–34; Ezek. 36:25–28) was oriented *to the future* and to the expectation that God himself would renew the relationship between himself and Israel. Despite the fact that the New Testament speaks about the fulfillment of Old Testament promises in Jesus Christ, the future dimension is still present. There is a dimension of covenant fulfillment which has not yet been realized

---

[6] Von Rad, *Old Testament Theology*, II, 320.

[7] Von Rad, *Old Testament Theology*, II, 324.

[8] Von Rad, *Old Testament Theology*, II, 328.

[9] Von Rad, *Old Testament Theology*, II, 333, notes that tradition history (already inside the Old Testament) has demonstrated that old material can be placed on new ground and in new theological horizons. From a hermeneutical point of view, quite a legitimate transformation happens to Old Testament traditions that are viewed in the light of Jesus Christ.

[10] Hillers, *Covenant: The History of a Biblical Idea* (Baltimore: John Hopkins Press, 1969), 180. Cf. also Luz, "Der alte Bund und der neue Bund," 335–36: "The old covenant and its differentness is mentioned in order to point out the uniqueness of the new ... The past is reverted to in various ways in order to explicate the new, the Christ event."

and still lies in the eschatological future (cf. Rev. 11:19; 21:12–14; note also the "covenant formula" in 21:3[11]).

2. Trajectories for a "theology of a new covenant"

Our discussion of the reinterpretive dynamic expressed by both the Old and New Testament authors invites us to consider how Old and New Testament traditions may be recast to be relevant in a contemporary theological context.

> A vibrant church needs to be in touch with a living confession if it is to avoid having its message become only a 'museum of truths.' A living confession mediates between continuity and change, preserves the core significance of its received theological truth and of the covenant community and makes what is valid from the past relevant to the present.[12]

An overview of the history of the covenant motif reveals this contextualization process in action. In different contexts and with different pastoral intentions,[13] the early Christian authors applied, transmitted and reinterpreted the covenant concept, emphasizing different aspects of the new covenant motif.

What follows is an attempt to lay the groundwork for a contemporary revisioning of the theology of the new covenant based upon an examination of early Christian documents.[14]

---

[11] Rev. 21:3–4: "And I heard a loud voice from the throne saying, 'Now the dwelling of God is with men, and he will live with them. *They will be his people*, and *God himself will be with them and be their God*. He will wipe every tear from their eyes. There will be no more death or mourning or crying or pain, for the old order of things has passed away.'"

[12] "Kurz Formeln des Glaubens I" [Short Statements of Faith I], 69, quoted by Springer, *Neuinterpretation im Alten Testament: Untersucht an den Themenkreisen des Herbstfestes und der Königspsalmen in Israel* (Stuttgart: Katholisches Bibelwerk, 1979), 9.

[13] Cf. the way in which Backhaus, *Der neue Bund und das Werden der Kirche*, 16, includes the pragmatic function of the text in his analysis. Cf. also Gordon, "Studies in the Covenantal Theology of the Epistle to the Hebrews in Light of its Setting," unpublished dissertation (Fuller Theological Seminary, 1979). Backhaus, "Gottes nicht bereuter Bund," 17, asserts: "One has, moreover, to pay attention to the various situational starting points."

[14] Jeanrond, "After Hermeneutics: The Relationship Between Theology and Biblical Studies," in Watson (ed.), *The Open Text: New Directions for Biblical Studies* (London: SCM Press, 1993), 94, 96–97, points out that "the time of the monarchical rule of either formalism or reader-response-criticism is over, and the time of their mutually critical interplay has finally begun ... no reading can be considered appropriate *which*

2.1 The significance of "new" in the expression "new covenant" (the dimension of eschatological newness)

Alluding to Jeremiah 31:31–34, the Lord's Supper tradition (especially in Paul and Luke – see, for example, Luke 22:20; 1 Cor. 11:26) emphasized that a new covenant was established by Jesus' death. In 2 Corinthians 3 Paul claims that the apostles are ministers of a new covenant of glory. Paul elucidates the new covenant inaugurated by Christ's death by describing it as a *new creation* (2 Cor. 5:17). The Epistle to the Hebrews likewise underscores this dimension of newness from a cultic perspective: Jesus as the new and superior high priest. On a more profound level this newness is taken as the reality of the forgiveness of sins.

The concept of newness (καινός) is expressed in the New Testament through a rich semantic backdrop permeated by the *expectation of eschatological salvation*. The idea of an eschatological new covenant (ἡ καινὴ διαθήκη) is explicated through the motifs of the *new creation* (καινὴ κτίσις, 2 Cor. 5:17; Gal. 6:15), the *new person* (cf. καινὸν ἄνθρωπον, Eph. 2:15) and the *new heaven and new earth* (οὐρανὸν καινὸν καὶ γῆν καινήν, Rev. 21:1; cf. Isa. 66:22). The new covenant and the "heavenly Jerusalem" are also closely associated key terms (cf. Gal. 4:21–31; Heb. 12:22–24[15]).

The early post-New Testament Christian authors strongly emphasized the newness of the new covenant. As they understand it, the Christ event inaugurated an eschatologically new order of salvation (cf., for example, Clement of Alexandria *Quis dives salvetur* 3,6). The promise of a new covenant (Jer. 31:31–34) was fulfilled in and through Jesus' crucifixion and the outpouring of the Spirit. Despite its all-surpassing glory (2 Cor. 3:10), there is, however, a *dimension of newness that is still outstanding*: "the new Jerusalem, coming down out of heaven from God." This final closure of the eschatological circle will occur when God's dwelling place is among the people. "They will be his people, and God himself will be with them and be their God" (Rev. 21:3).

---

[14] (Continued) *remains uninvolved with the text*" (italics mine). He underlines the importance of a *theological* dimension in a scientific reading of the Bible and pleads for a new biblical theology where we read the Bible "with a view to doing justice to its complex and at times even contradictory theological potential … [T]heological systems and constructs have at times, in fact most of the time, been used to isolate and emphasize one particular tradition … to the detriment of other equally important … textual perspectives." He concludes: "In view of these developments I wish to propose that we reread the biblical texts with the aim of establishing more fully the diversity of theological reflection in these writings."

[15] We have seen (see 5.3, above) that the contrast between the heavenly character of the one cultic order and the earthly character of the other is an important topic of the Epistle to the Hebrews. Heb. 7:22 speaks of Jesus as guarantee of a *better* covenant. The higher value of the new covenant is of heavenly quality.

2.2 The christocentric emphasis (the dimension of discontinuity)

The newness of the new covenant finds its locus in Christ. The Old Testament tradition of the new covenant is *reinterpreted* in light of the life and death of Christ. As we have noted, this approach is prominently illustrated by the Lord's Supper tradition. Based upon this new covenant concept, early Christians envisioned themselves participating in a new eschatological reality through the saving power of Jesus' death. The christocentric emphasis has a soteriological orientation.

As we have noted, the cultically based new covenant perspective of the Epistle to the Hebrews envisions Christ as the high priest, guarantor, mediator and even testator of a better covenant (Heb. 7:22; 8:6). The parallel with Moses as mediator of the first covenant is evident (cf. also Aphrahat *Dem.* 23,12).[16] New covenant theology in Hebrews is structured around the confession of Christ as the final fulfillment of the cultic heritage of Israel. The glory of this fulfillment is such that it surpasses and replaces the former cultic heritage.

Justin affirms that the new covenant proclaimed by God *is* Christ himself (*Dial.* 51,3). God has made Christ the covenant of the people (Θήσω σε εἰς διαθήκην γένους, *Dial.* 122,3.5). Irenaeus distinguishes four covenants. The decisive fourth covenant is described as "the covenant of the gospel of the Lord Jesus Christ" (τετάρτη δὲ ἡ τοῦ εὐαγγελίου διὰ τοῦ Κυρίου ἡμῶν 'Ιησοῦ Χριστοῦ; *Haer.* 3, 11,8).[17]

Thus a *christocentric newness* lies at the heart of the *discontinuity* between the old and new covenants. Contrasting the covenant of Christ with the Sinai covenant, the author of the Epistle to the Hebrews points to the heavenly and eternal nature of the covenant of Christ and to its saving power. The introduction of the new covenant infers that the old has become obsolete (Heb. 7:11, 19; 8:13; 10:9) and is no longer valid (Heb. 7:18; 10:9). This element of discontinuity should not be taken to indicate extreme supersessionism, however, as the following section indicates.[18]

---

[16] Allison, *The New Moses: A Matthean Typology* (Edinburgh: T&T Clark, 1993), 258, notes the very close link (almost verbal parallels) between the interpretation of the cup (τὸ αἷμά μου τῆς διαθήκης, "this is my blood of the covenant") in the Matthean Lord's Supper tradition and Exodus 24:8 (LXX). He asks: "Does this fact not invite us to imagine a typological correspondence? Through blood Moses was the mediator of the old covenant. Through blood Jesus is the mediator of the new covenant."

[17] Cf. also a letter to the bishop of Rome in which Irenaeus is praised as a "zealot of Christ's covenant" (ζηλωτὴν ὄντα τῆς διαθήκης Χριστοῦ; Eusebius, *Hist. eccl.* V,4, 2 [Lake, *Eusebius*, 444]). See 7.3.4, above.

[18] Cf. how early Christian post-New Testament authors set the new over against the old.

2.3 The theocentric emphasis (the dimension of continuity)

The concept of the new covenant is intimately connected with and founded upon *God's faithfulness*.[19] Justin underlines not only the christocentric dimension of the new covenant but also its theocentric foundation:[20] *God* has promised the establishment of a new covenant (*Dial.* 11,4; 51,3; 67,10), *he* has announced that he will ground a new covenant (34,1; 122,5); according to the *will of the Father* the customs of the old covenant find their end and purpose in Christ. Although Irenaeus emphasizes the eschatological newness of the new covenant, he also notes that one and the same God has made the old as well as the new. The Epistle to the Hebrews also testifies to the *continuity of God's revelation and promises*: "The saving act of Jesus specifically guarantees – in the midst of earthly human discontinuity – God's continuity, and in this way assures the believers of a firm 'anchor' (cf. 3:14; 6:18–20)."[21]

Eberhard Jüngel underscores the supreme importance of God's faithfulness to the entire covenant enterprise, specifically with regard to the context of justification. Apart from a faithful, covenantal God, the message of justification makes no sense. As the one who establishes a covenant with his people, Yahweh reveals himself as the opposite of gods who deal with humankind arbitrarily: "Especially in his covenant this 'agreement making' God demonstrates himself … to be the exact opposite of an arbitrary God."[22]

2.4 The pneumatological emphasis (the eschatological dimension of an internalization of the divine law)

Already in the prophecy of Ezekiel (36:27), the role of the Spirit in the new covenant was cast in an eschatological context. God pours his Spirit into the "new hearts" that he creates in order to enable them to keep his laws.

2 Corinthians 3:6 affirms that God has enabled the apostles to be ministers of a new covenant, which is then interpreted in the context of the Spirit: it is "not of the letter but of the Spirit" (οὐ γράμματος ἀλλὰ πνεύματος).[23] The new covenant, which marks the inception of the end times and introduces the fulfillment of the promises of the prophets, is realized through the ministrations of the Spirit.[24]

---

[19] Cf. Heron, "Bund," 572.

[20] Cf. 7.2, above.

[21] Backhaus, *Der neue Bund und das Werden der Kirche*, 257.

[22] Jüngel, *Das Evangelium von der Rechtfertigung des Gottlosen als Zentrum des christlichen Glaubens: Eine theologische Studie in ökumenischer Absicht* (Tübingen: J. C. B. Mohr [Paul Siebeck], 1999), 33.

[23] Note the frequency with which the Holy Spirit is mentioned in this chapter: vv. 6 (twice), 8, 17 (twice), 18.

[24] Klauck, *2. Korintherbrief*, 37.

The Spirit also plays a significant role in Irenaeus' explication of the concept of the new covenant. "The Spirit ... who also, as Luke says, descended at the day of Pentecost upon the disciples after the Lord's ascension, having power to admit all nations to the entrance of life, and to the opening of the new covenant."[25]

2.5 Universal expansion: A new sociological dimension

In the Lord's Supper tradition, according to Matthew (26:28) and Mark (14:24), Jesus affirms: "This is my blood of the covenant, which is poured out for many (τὸ ἐκχυννόμενον ὑπὲρ πολλῶν)." The phrase "poured out for many" alludes to Isaiah 53:12, where the death of the Servant of God has a dimension of atonement. Although the phrase "the many" was interpreted in the Qumran community to include only the members of that community, this phrase in Isaiah's Servant of God passages cannot be limited only to Israel. The Servant is called "a light for the Gentiles" (cf. Isa. 42:6; 49:7–8). Atonement has a universal scope, and the new covenant has *universal significance*.

This point was of pivotal importance to early Christian authors in their dialogue with the Jews. When discussing the new covenant with Trypho, Justin always emphasizes the universal scope of the new covenant. The function of the new covenant is to enlighten the heathen and, as such, it belongs to *all peoples* who look for divine salvation (*Dial.* 11,4). The "eternal law" and the new covenant is for the *whole world* (*Dial.* 43,1), and for *every people* (*Dial.* 67,10).

In the new covenant, the *sociological function* of the covenant is fundamentally changed: the old ethnic and political divisions are replaced with a universally inclusive perspective. "The 'new covenant' is the one covenant of God extended both soteriologically and sociologically so as to be universal."[26]

2.6 A new law: Internalization, circumcision of the hearts

The concept of the internalization of God's law was already expressed by Jeremiah (31:33): "'This is the covenant I will make with the house of Israel after that time,' declares the LORD. 'I will put my law in their minds and write it on their hearts. I will be their God, and they will be my people.'"

In their discussion with the Jews, early Christian authors such as Aphrahat connected the motif of the circumcision of the heart with the new covenant (cf. Jer. 4:4). In *Dem.* 11,11 he argues that because the covenant of Moses was not kept, God established in the last generation an unchangeable covenant. The circumcision acceptable to God as the mark of this covenant is the circumcision referred to by Jeremiah (4:4): "Circumcise yourselves to the

[25] *Haer.* 3, 17,2.
[26] Backhaus, "Gottes nicht bereuter Bund," 43.

LORD, *circumcise your hearts.*" Those whose hearts have been circumcised are eligible for the baptism of the new covenant: "Those who have been circumcised in their hearts live and are circumcised for a second time in the true Jordan, the baptism for the forgiveness of sins" (*Dem.* 11,11).[27]

In their exposition of the new covenant, some early Christian authors point to parallels between Moses and Jesus. The concept of a new *law* appears synonymously with that of the new *covenant*. In his *Dialogue with Trypho* (11,4, cf. also 34,1; 43,1) Justin affirms that the new law and the new covenant belong to those among all nations who expect the divine salvation. Apart from the covenant established on Mount Horeb, God will establish a new covenant. The new covenant will (according to Justin) reveal which laws have eternal value in God's sight and are suitable for every nation. God has promised to send a new covenant and an eternal law (122,5).

Irenaeus emphasizes the deeper *ethical dimensions* of the new covenant. Those who belong to the new covenant should abstain not only from evil deeds, but also from evil desires. He cites the Lord's words from Matthew 12:36; 5:28 and 5:22 and concludes that we shall be held responsible not only for what we do, but also for our thoughts, for we are people who have experienced the power of *freedom* (cf. *Haer.* 4, 16,5).

The themes of *internalization* and of *a new law* are also common in John's Gospel and the Johannine Epistles, where they reflect the new covenant concept. John 13:34 speaks of a new law: "A new command I give you" ('Εντολὴν[28] καινὴν δίδωμι ὑμῖν). Jesus gives his disciples the "new law" of mutual love as a "covenant instruction."[29] The new law put in their hearts is the new commandment of love (1 John 2:7–8).

The reciprocity of the Johannine emphasis on divine pneumatic immanence resonates with the covenant formula, which is also reciprocal: "God is love. Whoever lives in love lives in God, and God in him" (1 John 4:16). In Johannine theology, the unity of the believer with the Father and the Son is a unity in Spirit and in love. This dynamic is reiterated in a new way, yet it is an integral dimension of both new and old covenant theology. Essential to Yahweh's covenant with his people are: the *close relationship*[30] he has with them

---

[27] Cf. also Irenaeus *Haer.* 4, 25,1: "who [Abraham] did also receive the covenant of circumcision, after that justification by faith which had pertained to him, when *he was yet in uncircumcision*, so that in him both covenants may be prefigured, that he might be the father of all."

[28] 'Εντολή (commandment) and νόμος (law) are synonyms; see Louw and Nida, *Greek-English Lexicon*, I, 426.

[29] Cf. Schnackenburg, *Das Johannesevangelium*, 59.

[30] Cardinal Joseph Ratzinger, "The New Covenant: A Theology of Covenant in the New Testament," *Comm* 22 (1995), 635–51, points out that by establishing a

and their *obedience* of his commandments.[31] These two dimensions of Old Testament covenant theology are interpreted anew in light of John's Christology and pneumatology.

John 15:7 is a variation of the Johannine immanence formula: "If you remain in me and my words remain in you." The concept of relational intimacy and obedience are closely connected to one another. Those who accept Jesus' words accept Jesus himself, as sent by God, and are obliged to keep his words and to put them into practice.

The Johannine statements mentioned above reveal the *ethical dynamic* of the new covenant. This dimension is also addressed by Paul when he affirms that Christians are baptized in the death of Christ in order to live *a new life* (Rom. 6). Here we see God's promise to write the Torah in people's hearts fulfilled.[32] For, as Paul makes clear, the foundation for meeting the ethical demands implicit in living the "new life" is the power and reality of the indwelling *Holy Spirit*.[33]

While John does not speak explicitly about the new covenant, and Paul mentions the covenant concept only a few times, Johannine and Pauline theology both reflect the two themes that lie at the heart of Old Testament covenant theology: the *relational dimension* between God and humankind, and the *ethical dimension of obedience* to God's covenantal will. These two themes are continuously *transmitted and interpreted anew* in the light of Easter and Pentecost.

2.7 New Covenant (καινὴ διαθήκη) and the righteousness of God (δικαιοσύνη θεοῦ)

In our study of the new covenant concept in Paul's letters we observed that covenant (διαθήκη) and righteousness/justification (δικαιόω; δικαίωσις; δικαιοσύνη) belong to the same semantic domain "establish or confirm a relation."[34]

---

[30] (*Continued*) covenant with his people the God of the Bible reveals himself to be "a God-in-relation, and thus in its essence his identity is in opposition to the self-contained God of philosophy" (p. 650).

[31] Especially in the Deuteronomic/Deuteronomistic theology. In Chapter 1 (cf., e.g., 1.2.2.2, above), we examined the relationship between *covenant* and *law*. In the time of Jeremiah, in the midst of Israel's greatest crisis, God's forgiveness opened up the possibility of a new future for his people through his promise to remember their sins no more and to inscribe the Torah on their hearts. Early Christian authors affirm that this new covenant of forgiveness of sins was instituted through the death of Jesus Christ.

[32] Cf. Seebass, "Hat das Alte Testament," 273.

[33] Cf. 11.2.4, above.

[34] Louw and Nida, *Greek-English Lexicon*, 451–53.

Paul affirms in 2 Corinthians 3 that one who is focused on, or bound to, the "letter" of the Mosaic law will not be able to cross over to the life-giving *pneuma*. From the perspective of salvation history, a bridge must be built to overcome the impasse between the disobedience of sin and the life of obedience demanded by the law. This bridge is the "new covenant," which overcomes the powerlessness of the old letter-law through the power of the Spirit.[35] For, as Paul concludes, "the letter kills, but the Spirit gives life" (τὸ γὰρ γράμμα ἀποκτέννει, τὸ δὲ πνεῦμα ζῳοποιεῖ). The new covenant is a covenant of life (2 Cor. 3:6).

In the ensuing sub-pericope (2 Cor. 3:7–11) Paul connects the *new covenant* with the ministry that brings *righteousness* (ἡ διακονία τῆς δικαιοσύνης, 2 Cor. 3:9). According to Paul's message of justification, death and life are the opposite effects of the law and the gospel – "through Jesus Christ the law of the Spirit of life set me free from the law of sin and death" (Rom. 8:2).[36] This realization also stands behind 2 Corinthians 3:6: "He has made us competent as ministers of a new covenant – not of the letter but of the Spirit; for the letter kills, but the Spirit gives life."

The dimension of a "new covenant" may thus be seen to be internal to the concept of the "righteousness of God" (ἡ δικαιοσύνη θεοῦ).[37] Paul actually introduces the new covenant concept in his Epistle to the Romans in the "theme statement" of Romans 1:17[38] by revealing that the "righteousness (δικαιοσύνη) of God is faith from start to finish."[39] The "righteous person (ὁ δίκαιος) by faith" is a person who lives in the reality of the new covenant, through the Spirit (cf. Ezek. 36:26–27).

---

[35] Kertelge, "Buchstabe und Geist," 124. Dautzenberg, "Alter und neuer Bund nach 2 Kor 3," 247, critically questions Paul's antithetic argumentation in this context. He believes that Paul accepts as his starting point contemporary Christian thinking on salvation and negates Jewish positions through his antithetic form of thinking. When characterizing the law as a "letter that kills" (2 Cor. 3:6) and positioning it against the "Spirit that gives life," Paul offends, according to Dautzenberg, not only Jewish piety, focussed in the Torah, but also Christian, Jewish and Hellenistic respect for the Torah and the commandments as regulations following from the covenant. This critique seems unjustified, in my opinion, against the background of Paul's line of argument, as described above.

[36] ὁ γὰρ νόμος τοῦ πνεύματος τῆς ζωῆς ἐν Χριστῷ Ἰησοῦ ἠλευθέρωσέν σε ἀπὸ τοῦ νόμου τῆς ἁμαρτίας καὶ τοῦ θανάτου.

[37] The importance of the Old Testament covenant background for the understanding of the concept of God's righteousness was argued in 4.2.3, above.

[38] This observation has been made by Porter, "The Concept of Covenant in Paul," 282.

[39] This is most probably the meaning of the Greek ἐκ πίστεως εἰς πίστιν (cf. Newman and Nida, *A Translator's Handbook on Paul's Letter to the Romans,* Helps for Translators XIV (Stuttgart: United Bible Societies, 1973), 20.

The insight that the new relationship between God and humanity, established by the death and resurrection of Jesus Christ, is described both in terms of a "new covenant" and in terms of "justification/the righteousness of God" has important consequences for understanding both of these concepts. It clearly implies that covenant (διαθήκη) and justification/righteousness (δικαιόω; δικαίωσις; δικαιοσύνη) have essential components in common. Of course, this statement does not imply that there are components that they do not share. For example, the forensic dimension is a significant feature of the meaning of justification/righteousness (δικαιόω; δικαίωσις; δικαιοσύνη), while it is not prominent in the New Testament understanding of new covenant (καινὴ διαθήκη). However, despite the components of meaning that are unique to each of these terms, the observation that they belong to the same semantic domain leads to significant insights often overlooked in the past.

In his faithfulness and grace God allowed Israel to participate in his "own divine righteousness" by "establishing a covenant, that is, a community of justice between himself and the people of Israel. And as the God who justifies he includes the whole of humanity in this community of justice by taking the sin of the whole world on himself as the founder of the new covenant."[40]

The Protestant Reformation affirmed that the doctrine of justification could best be understood in the light of four exclusives: Christ alone, grace alone, Word alone, faith alone and, above all, God alone.[41] Human work is, therefore, completely excluded from the economy of salvation.

In a similar way, the new covenant message also points to the pivotal role of God. When the people of God experienced the greatest despair, the prophets announced God's gracious, unmerited promise of a new covenant (Jer. 31:31–34). The phrases "grace alone" and "faith alone" are, therefore, equally valid within the context of the Old Testament new covenant message.

During his final meal with his disciples, Jesus said: "This cup is the new covenant in my blood, which is poured out for you" (Luke 22:20). The new covenant reality is, indeed, a reality *extra nos* ("outside ourselves"). In a way identical to that of the dynamic of justification, we can affirm of the new covenant: "In Christ, outside ourselves and beyond our acts of self-determination, we *are*."[42]

---

[40] Jüngel, *Justification: The Heart of the Christian Faith: A Theological Study with an Ecumenical Purpose* (Edinburgh/New York: T&T Clark, 2001), 274.

[41] The significance of this approach for understanding justification is underlined by Jüngel, *Justification*, 149–259.

[42] Jüngel, *Justification*, xi. This basic anthropological affirmation is extended by Jüngel as he points out that the justified exist under two jurisdictions (*simul iustus et peccator*), with primacy accorded to the saving jurisdiction of God in Christ. Created by the saving divine self-manifestation, the Word alone, the life of the justified is

The new covenant is not a covenant of the letter, but of the Spirit; "for the letter kills, but the Spirit gives life" (2 Cor. 3:6). Through the Spirit, believers can follow God's commands and realize the ethical demands of the new covenant (cf. Jer. 31:31–34):

> Therefore, there is now no condemnation for those who are in Christ Jesus, [2] because through Christ Jesus the law of the Spirit of life set me free from the law of sin and death. [3] For what the law was powerless to do in that it was weakened by the sinful nature, God did by sending his own Son in the likeness of sinful man to be a sin offering. And so he condemned sin in sinful man, [4] in order that the righteous requirements of the law might be fully met in us, who do not live according to the sinful nature but according to the Spirit. (Rom. 8:1–4)

New possibilities open up: "The one who is righteous through faith *will live*" (Rom. 1:17; Hab. 2:4). [43] "Therefore, if anyone is in Christ, there is a new creation: The old has gone, the new has come!" (2 Cor. 5:17, TNIV). [44]

3. Conclusion: A new covenant hermeneutic

"Understanding begins … when something addresses us." [45] The new covenant message is a message of a God who speaks and acts. It is the message of a loving, gracious and faithful God, who always does something new.

What relevance does the biblical new covenant message have for Christian theology today? The temporal distance between us and the biblical authors is not primarily "a gulf to be bridged," but a "positive and productive condition enabling understanding. It is … filled with the continuity of custom and tradition, in the light of which everything handed down presents itself to us." [46] The three concluding chapters of this study investigated certain dimensions of the history of the impact/effect (*"Wirkungsgeschichte"*) of the new covenant motif.

The new covenant motif addresses the "ultimate crisis of human existence." [47] The Ephesians are reminded of the time when they were separate

---

[42] (*Continued*) determined at all points by the same Word. Justification is by faith alone. Faith is the passive act in which believers entrust themselves to the saving movement initiated by the Word of God's grace (Jüngel, *Justification*, xii).

[43] Jüngel, *Justification*, 261.

[44] Stuhlmacher, *Reconciliation, Law and Righteousness: Essays in Biblical Theology* (Philadelphia: Fortress Press, 1986), 81, observes that "justification" clearly has the dimension of *new creation*.

[45] Gadamer, *Truth and Method* (New York: Continuum, 2003), 299.

[46] Gadamer, *Truth and Method*, 297.

[47] Horton, *Covenant and Eschatology: The Divine Drama* (Louisville/London: Westminster John Knox, 2002), 181.

from Christ, "excluded from citizenship in Israel and foreigners to the covenants of the promise, without hope and without God in the world" (Eph.
2:12). By accepting the gospel message everything has, however, changed:
"But now in Christ Jesus you who once were far away have been brought near
through the blood of Christ" (Eph. 2:13).

The biblical new covenant message "is not merely a record of past and
future events of redemption, but the medium of our own incorporation into
that history."[48] Through the new covenant message, God bridges the distance
between human despair and the hope of salvation. This message is always new,
exciting and fresh. It is a message of both discontinuity and continuity: through
Christ an eschatologically new era has dawned, and yet there is continuity in
God's faithfulness to his promises. The new covenant is a universal covenant,
including every tribe and language and people and nation (cf. Rev. 5:9). God
has poured out his eschatological Spirit, "in order that the righteous requirements of the law might be fully met in us, who do not live according to the
sinful nature but according to the Spirit" (Rom. 8:4). "*New covenant,*" "*righteousness of God*" and "*new creation*" are intimately connected in New Testament theology. The new covenant message is the message of a new creation (2
Cor. 5:17); it is the message of God's righteousness, "a righteousness that is by
faith from first to last, just as it is written: 'The righteous will live by faith'"
(Rom. 1:17).

---

[48] Horton, *Covenant and Eschatology*, 183.

Bibliography

A Primary sources and translations

ΠΟΛΥΚΑΡΠΟΣ ΣΜΥΡΝΗΣ – ΕΡΜΑΣ – ΠΑΠΙΑΣ – ΑΡΙΣΤΕΙΔΗΣ ΙΟΥΣΤΙΝΟΣ. ΒΙΒΛΙΟΘΗΚΗ ΕΛΛΗΝΩΝ ΠΑΤΕΡΩΝ ΚΑΙ ΕΚΚΛΗΣΙΑΣΤΙΚΩΝ. ΤΟΜΟΣ ΤΡΙΤΟΣ (ΑΘΗΝΑΙ· ΕΚΔΟΣΙΣ ΤΗΣ ΑΠΟΣΤΟΛΙΚΗΣ ΔΙΑΚΟΝΙΑΣ ΤΗΣ ΕΚΚΛΗΣΙΑΣ ΤΗΣ ΕΛΛΑΔΟΣ, 1955)

The Greek New Testament (In cooperation with the Institute for New Testament Textual Research, Münster, Westphalia; Stuttgart: Deutsche Bibelgesellschaft/United Bible Societies, 4th rev. edn, 1994)

Brox, Norbert (trans. and ed.), *Irenäus von Lyon, I–IV*, Fontes Christiani 8/1–4 (Freiburg: Herder, 1993)

Bruns, Peter (trans. and intr.), *Aphrahat: Unterweisungen*, 2 vols., Fontes Christiani 5 (Freiburg: Herder, 1991)

Cohn, L., I. Heinemann and M. Adler (eds.), *Die Werke Philos von Alexandria*, parts III, V and VI, SJHL (Breslau: M. & H. Marcus/Jüdischer Buchverlag Münz, 1919)

Colson, F. H., and G. H. Whitaker (trans. and ed.), *Philo*, 10 vols. (and 2 suppl. vols.), Loeb Classical Library (Cambridge, MA: Harvard University Press; London: William Heinemann, 1981)

Garcia Martinez, Florentino, The Dead Sea Scrolls Translated: The Qumran Texts in English (Leiden: E. J. Brill, 1994)

Goodspeed, Edgar J., *Die ältesten Apologeten: Texte mit kurzen Einleitungen* (Göttingen: Vandenhoeck & Ruprecht, 1984, repr. of 1914)

Haeuser, Philipp, *Des heiligen Philosophen und Martyrers Justinus Dialog mit dem Juden Tryphon* (trans. and annot. with intro.), Bibliothek der Kirchenväter (Kempten & München: Kösel, 1917)

Hall, Stuart G. (trans. and ed.), *Melito of Sardis: "On Pascha" and Fragments*, Oxford Early Christian Texts (Oxford: Clarendon Press, 1979)

Lake, Kirsopp (trans. and ed.), *Eusebius: The Ecclesiastical History*, Loeb Classical Library (London: William Heinemann; Cambridge, MA: Harvard University Press, 1965)

Maier, Johann, *Die Qumran-Essener: Die Texte vom Toten Meer*, 3 vols., UTB für Wissenschaft/Uni-Taschenbücher 1862 und 1863 (München/Basel: Ernst Reinhardt Verlag, 1995)

Mansoor, Menahem, *The Thanksgiving Hymns* (trans. and annot. with intro.), Studies on the Texts of the Desert of Judah, III (Leiden: E.J. Brill, 1961)

Menzies, Allan (ed.), *The Ante-Nicene Fathers*, X (original suppl. to the American edn; Edinburgh: T&T Clark, 1990)

Nestle-Aland, *Novum Testamentum Graece* (Stuttgart: Deutsche Bibelgesellschaft, 26th newly rev. edn [27th rev. edn], 1993)

Osb, Theresia Heither (trans. and intr.), *Origenes Commentarii in Epistulam ad Romanos: Liber Primus, Liber Secundus*, Fontes Christiani 2/1 (Freiburg: Herder, 1990)

Preuschen, Erwin, *Origenes Werke. Vierter Band. Der Johanneskommentar* (Leipzig: J. C. Hinrichs'sche Buchhandlung, 1903)

Rabin, Chaim, *The Zadokite Documents:* I. *The Admonition;* II. *The Laws* (Oxford: Clarendon Press, 2nd edn, 1958)

Rahlfs, Alfred (ed.), *Septuaginta,* 2 vols. (Stuttgart: Privilegierte Württembergische Bibelanstalt, 1935)

Riddle, M. B., "Introductory Notice to the Pseudo-Clementine Literature," in Alexander Roberts and James Donaldson (eds.), *The Ante-Nicene Fathers,* VIII (Edinburgh: T&T Clark, 1989)

Roberts, Alexander, and James Donaldson (eds.), *The Ante-Nicene Fathers,* I, II, VIII (Edinburgh: T&T Clark, 1989)

Schaff, Philip, and Henry Wace (eds.), A Select Library of Nicene and Post-Nicene Fathers of the Christian Church, XIII, Part II: Gregory the Great, Ephraim Syrus, Aphrahat (Grand Rapids: Eerdmans, 1976)

Schneemelcher, Wilhelm (ed.), *New Testament Apocrypha,* II (trans. A. J. B. Higgins et al., ed. R. McL. Wilson; Philadelphia: Westminster Press, 1964)

Stählin, Otto, *Clemens Alexandrinus,* 4 vols., GCS (Leipzig: J. C. Hinrichs'sche Buchhandlung, 2nd edn, 1936)

Stählin, Otto (trans.), *Clemens von Alexandreia,* I–V, Bibliothek der Kirchenvater, Second Series VII (München: Kösel, 1934)

Waitz, Hans, *Die Pseudoklementinen, Homilien und Rekognitionen: Eine quellenkritische Untersuchung,* Texte und Untersuchungen zur Geschichte der altchristlichen Literatur, New series, 10.4 (Leipzig: J. C. Hinrichs'sche Buchhandlung, 1904)

Wengst, Klaus (trans. and intr.), *Didache (Apostellehre), Barnabasbrief, Zweiter Klemensbrief, Schrift an Diognet,* Schriften des Urchristentums, 2nd part (Darmstadt: Wissenschaftliche Buchgesellschaft, 1984)

Wernberg-Møller, P. (trans. and intr.), *The Manual of Discipline: Studies on the Texts of the Desert of Judah,* I (Leiden: E. J. Brill, 1957)

Additional Literature

Abbot, Walter M., S.J. (ed.), *The Documents of Vatican II* (New York: Guild Press; America Press; Association Press, 1966)

Ådna, Jostein, Scott J. Hafemann and Otfried Hofius (eds.), *Evangelium, Schriftauslegung, Kirche: Festschrift für Peter Stuhlmacher zum 65. Geburtstag* (Göttingen: Vandenhoeck & Ruprecht, 1997)

Aland, Kurt, *Studien zur Überlieferung des Neuen Testaments und seines Textes,* Arbeiten zur neutestamentlichen Textforschung 2 (Berlin: Walter de Gruyter, 1967)

Aland, Kurt (ed.), *Synopsis Quattuor Evangeliorum* (Stuttgart: Deutsche Bibelgesellschaft, 15th rev. edn, 1996)

Allison, Dale C., *The New Moses: A Matthean Typology* (Edinburgh: T&T Clark, 1993)

Altaner, Berthold and Alfred Stuiber, *Patrologie: Leben, Schriften und Lehre der Kirchenväter* (Freiburg/Basel/Wien: Herder, 8th rev. and exp. edn, 1978)

Attridge, Harold W., *The Epistle to the Hebrews,* Hermeneia (Philadelphia: Fortress Press, 1989)

Avemarie, Friedrich, and Hermann Lichtenberger (eds.), *Bund und Tora: Zur theologischen Begriffsgeschichte in alttestamentlicher, frühjüdischer und urchristlicher Tradition,* (Wissenschaftliche Untersuchungen zum Neuen Testament 92; Tübingen: J. C. B. Mohr [Paul Siebeck], 1996)

Backhaus, Knut, "Das Bundesmotiv in der frühchristlichen Schwellenzeit: Hebräerbrief, Barnabasbrief, Dialogus cum Tryphone," in Hubert Frankemölle (ed.), *Der ungekündigte Bund? Antworten des Neuen Testaments,* Quaestiones disputatae 172 (Freiburg/Basel/Wien: Herder, 1998), 211–31

—, "Gottes nicht bereuter Bund: Alter und neuer Bund in der Sicht des Frühchristentums," in Rainer Kampling and Thomas Söding (eds.), *Ekklesiologie des Neuen Testaments: Für Karl Kertelge* (Freiburg: Herder, 1996), 33–55

—, "Hat Jesus vom Gottesbund gesprochen?," *TGl* 86 (1996), 343–56

—, *Der neue Bund und das Werden der Kirche: Die Diatheke-Deutung des Hebräerbriefs im Rahmen der frühchristlichen Theologiegeschichte,* Neutestamentliche Abhandlungen (Münster: Aschendorff, 1996)

—, "Rezension: Manuel Vogel, Das Heil des Bundes. Bundestheologie im Frühjudentum und im frühen Christentum," *Biblische Zeitschrift* 41 (1997), 149–51

Bacq, Philippe S.J., *De l'ancienne à la nouvelle Alliance selon S. Irénée* (Paris: Namur, 1978)

Baker, Christopher J., *Covenant and Liberation: Giving New Heart to God's Endangered Family,* European University Studies, Series XXIII, Theology, 411 (Frankfurt am Main/Bern/New York/Paris: Peter Lang, 1991)

Baltzer, Klaus, *Das Bundesformular,* Wissenschaftliche Monographien zum Alten und Neuen Testament 4 (Neukirchen: Neukirchener Verlag, 1960)

Barr, James, The Concept of Biblical Theology: An Old Testament Perspective (London: SCM Press, 1999)

—, *The Semantics of Biblical Language* (Oxford: Oxford University Press, 1967)

—, "Some Old Testament Aspects of Berkhof's 'Christelijk Geloof,'" in E. Flesseman-Van Leer, et al. (eds.), *Weerwoord: Reacties Op Dr H. Berkhof's Christelijk Geloof* (Nijkerk: Callenbach, 1974), 9–19

—, "Some Semantic Notes on the Covenant," in Herbert Donner, Robert Hanhart and Rudolf Smend (eds.), *Beiträge zur Alttestamentlichen Theologie: Festschrift für Walther Zimmerli zum 70. Geburtstag* (Göttingen: Vandenhoeck & Ruprecht, 1977), 23–38

Barth, Karl, *Church Dogmatics* II,2 (Edinburgh: T&T Clark, 1957)

—, *Church Dogmatics* III,1 (Edinburgh: T&T Clark, 1958)

—, *Church Dogmatics* IV,1 (Edinburgh: T&T Clark, 1956)

—, *Church Dogmatics* IV,3 (Edinburgh: T&T Clark, 1961)

—, *Church Dogmatics* IV,4 (Edinburgh: T&T Clark, 1969)

Bauer, Walter, Kurt Aland and Barbara Aland, *Griechisch-deutsches Wörterbuch zu den Schriften des Neuen Testaments und der frühchristlichen Literatur* (Berlin; New York: Walter de Gruyter, 6th comp. new rev. edn, 1988)

Bauer, Walter, William F. Arndt and F. Wilbur Gingrich, *A Greek-English Lexicon of the New Testament and Other Early Christian Literature* (Chicago: University of Chicago Press, 1957)

Becker, Jürgen, "Der Brief an die Galater," in J. Becker, H. Conzelmann and G. Friedrich,
    Die Briefe an die Galater, Epheser, Philipper, Kolosser, Thessalonicher und Philemon, Das
    Neue Testament Deutsch 8 (Göttingen: Vandenhoeck & Ruprecht, 1976)

Behm, Johannes, *Der Begriff ΔΙΑΘΗΚΗ im Neuen Testament* (Leipzig: A. Deichert'sche
    Verlagsbuchhandlung, 1912)

Beker, J. C., *The Triumph of God: The Essence of Paul's Thought* (trans. Loren T.
    Stuckenbruck; Minneapolis: Fortress Press, 1990)

Bellinger, William H., Jr., and William R. Farmer (eds.), *Jesus and the Suffering Servant: Isaiah
    53 and Christian Origins* (Harrisburg, PA: Trinity Press, 1998)

Berger, Klaus, "Kirche II: Neues Testament," in G. Krause and G. Müller (eds.),
    Theologische Realenzyklopädie XVIII (Berlin/New York: Walter de Gruyter, 1989),
    201–18

—, *Theologiegeschichte des Urchristentums: Theologie des Neuen Testaments,* UTB (Tübingen/
    Basel: Francke Verlag, 2nd rev. and exp. edn, 1995)

Betz, Hans Dieter, *Der Galaterbrief: Ein Kommentar zum Brief des Apostels Paulus an die
    Gemeinden in Galatien,* Hermeneia (trans. Sibylle Ann; München: Chr. Kaiser Verlag,
    1988)

Beutler, Johannes, *Habt keine Angst: Die erste johanneische Abschiedsrede (Joh 14),* Stuttgarter
    Bibelstudien 116 (Stuttgart: Verlag Katholisches Bibelwerk, 1984)

Bieringer, R., "Die Gegner des Paulus im 2. Korintherbrief," in R. Bieringer and J.
    Lambrecht (eds.), *Studies on 2 Corinthians,* Bibliotheca ephemeridum theologicarum
    lovaniensium CXII (Leuven: University Press; Uitgeverij Peeters, 1994), 181–221

Billerbeck, Paul, Die Briefe des Neuen Testaments und die Offenbarung Johannis:
    Erläutert   aus   Talmud   und   Midrasch   (München: C.   H.   Beck'sche
    Verlagsbuchhandlung, 5th edn, 1926)

Birdsall, J. Neville, "Problems of the Clementine Literature," in James D. G. Dunn (ed.),
    Jews and Christians: The Parting of the Ways A.D. 70 to 135, Wissenschaftliche
    Untersuchungen zum Neuen Testament 66 (Tübingen: J. C. B. Mohr [Paul Siebeck],
    1992), 347–62

Bishop, Jonathan, *The Covenant: A Reading* (Springfield: Templegate, 1982)

Black, Matthew, "Review Article: The Judean Scrolls, by G. R. Driver, Emeritus Professor
    of Semitic Philology, University of Oxford, Blackwell, Oxford, 1965," *New Testament
    Studies* (1966–67), 81–89

Bockmuehl, Markus, *This Jesus: Martyr, Lord, Messiah* (Edinburgh: T&T Clark, 1994)

Bolyki, J., *Jesu Tischgemeinschaften,* Wissenschaftliche Untersuchungen zum Neuen Testa-
    ment, Second Series 96 (Tübingen: Mohr Siebeck, 1998)

Bornkamm,   Günther,   *Die   Vorgeschichte   des   sogenannten   Zweiten   Korintherbriefes,*
    Sitzungsberichte der Heidelberger Akademie der Wissenschaften, Philosophisch-
    historisch (Heidelberg: Carl Winter Universitätsverlag, 2nd edn, 1965)

Borse, Udo, *Der Brief an die Galater,* Regensburger Neues Testament (Regensburg: Verlag
    Friedrich Pustet, 1984)

Braulik, Georg, "Die Ausdrücke für 'Gesetz' im Buch Deuteronomium," in Georg Braulik
    (ed.), *Studium zur Theologie des Deuteronomiums,* Stuttgarter biblische Aufsatzbände,
    Altes Testament 2 (Stuttgart: Verlag Katholisches Bibelwerk, 1988), 11–38. Also pub-
    lished in *Biblica* 51 (1970), 39–66

Braun, Herbert, *An die Hebräer,* Handbuch zum Neuen Testament 14 (Tübingen: J. C. B.
    Mohr [Paul Siebeck], 1984)

Breytenbach, A. P. B., "Verbond en verbondstekens in die Ou Testament – 'n terreinverkenning,'" *Hervormde Teologiese Studies* 38 (1984), 4–13

Brown, Raymond E., *The Gospel According to John*, 2 vols., Anchor Bible (New York: Doubleday, 1970)

Brox, Norbert, "Juden und Heiden bei Irenäus," *Münchener theologische Zeitschrift* 16 (1965), 89–106

Buchanan, George Wesley, *To the Hebrews*, Anchor Bible (New York: Doubleday, 1972)

Brueggemann, Walter, *The Covenanted Self: Explorations in Law and Covenant* (Minneapolis: Fortress Press, 1999)

Bultmann, Rudolf, "Das Verhältnis der urchristlichen Christusbotschaft zum historischen Jesus," in Erich Dinkler (ed.), *Exegetica: Aufsätze zur Erforschung des Neuen Testaments* (Tübingen: J. C. B. Mohr [Paul Siebeck], 1967), 445–69

—, *Der zweite Brief an die Korinther*, Kritisch-exegetischer Kommentar über das Neue Testament (ed. Erich Dinkler; Göttingen: Vandenhoeck & Ruprecht, 1976)

Busch, Eberhard, "Der eine Gnadenbund Gottes: Karl Barths neue Föderaltheologie," *Theologische Quartalschrift* 176.4 (1996), 341–54

Caird, G. B., *The Gospel of St. Luke*, Pelican Gospel Commentaries (New York: The Seabury Press, 1963)

Campbell, W. S., "Covenant and New Covenant," in G. F. Hawthorne and R. P. Martin (eds.), *Dictionary of Paul and His Letters* (Downers Grove/Leicester: InterVarsity Press, 1993), 179–83

Carleton Paget, James, *The Epistle of Barnabas: Outlook and Background*, Wissenschaftliche Untersuchungen zum Neuen Testament, Second Series 64 (Tübingen: J. C. B. Mohr [Paul Siebeck], 1994)

Chilton, Bruce, "The Kingdom of God in Recent Discussion," in Bruce Chilton and Craig A. Evans (eds.), *Studying the Historical Jesus: Evaluations of the State of Current Research*, New Testament Tools and Studies XIX (Leiden: E. J. Brill, 1994), 255–80

—, *God in Strength: Jesus' Announcement of the Kingdom*, SNTU, Series B, I (Freistadt: Verlag F. Plöchl, 1979)

– and Craig A. Evans (eds.), *Authenticating the Words of Jesus*, New Testament Tools and Studies XXVIII, 1 (Leiden: E. J. Brill, 1999)

Christiansen, Ellen Juhl, *The Covenant in Judaism and Paul: A Study of Ritual Boundaries as Identity Markers*, Arbeiten zur Geschichte des antiken Judentums und des Urchristentums XXVII (Leiden/New York/Köln: E. J. Brill, 1995)

Clements, Ronald E., *Old Testament Theology: A Fresh Approach*, New Foundations Theological Library (Atlanta: John Knox Press, 1978)

Collins, Raymond F., "The Berith-Notion of the Cairo Damascus Document and Its Comparison with the New Testament," *Ephemerides theologicae lovanienses* 39 (1963), 555–94

—, "The Twelve," *Anchor Bible Dictionary* 6 (New York/London/Toronto/Sydney/Auckland: Doubleday, 1992), 670–71

Cranfield, C. E. B., *A Critical and Exegetical Commentary on the Epistle to the Romans*, I, International Critical Commentary (Edinburgh: T&T Clark, 1975)

Crossan, John Dominic, *The Historical Jesus: The Life of a Mediterranean Jewish Peasant* (Edinburgh: T&T Clark, 1991)

Davies, Philip R., *The Damascus Covenant: An Interpretation of the "Damascus Document,"* Journal for the Study of the Old Testament: Supplement Series 25 (Sheffield: JSOT Press, 1983)

Dautzenberg, Gerhard, "Alter und neuer Bund nach 2 Kor 3," in Rainer Kampling (ed.), *"Nun steht aber diese Sache im Evangelium . . .." Zur Frage nach den Anfängen des christlichen Antijudaismus* (Paderborn/München/Wien/Zürich: Ferdinand Schöning, 1999), 53–72

De Oliveira, Anacleto, *Die Diakonie der Gerechtigkeit und der Versöhnung in der Apologie des 2: Korintherbriefes. Analyze und Auslegung von 2 Kor 2,14–4,6; 5,11–6,10,* Neutestamentliche Abhandlungen, New Series 21 (Münster: Aschendorff, 1990)

Deidun, T. J., *New Covenant Morality in Paul,* Analecta biblica 89 (Rome: Biblical Institute Press, 1981)

Delling, Gerhard, "Abendmahl II: Urchristliches Mahl-Verständnis," in *Theologische Realenzyklopädie* I (Berlin/New York: Walter de Gruyter, 1977), 47–58

Drijvers, Han, "Syrian Christianity and Judaism," in Judith Lieu, John North and Tessa Rajak (eds.), *The Jews Among Pagans and Christians in the Roman Empire* (London/New York: Routledge, 1992), 124–46

Duncan, Edward J., *Baptism in the Demonstrationes of Aphraates the Persian Sage,* The Catholic University of America Studies in Christian Antiquity 8 (Washington, DC: The Catholic University of America Press, 1945)

Dunn, James D. G., *The Epistle to the Galatians,* Black's New Testament Commentaries (Peabody, MA: Hendrickson, 1993)

—, *Romans 9 – 16,* Word Biblical Commentary 38B (Dallas: Word Books, 1988)

—, "Who Did Paul Think He Was? A Study of Jewish Christian Identity," *New Testament Studies* 45 (1999), 174–93

—, *The Theology of Paul the Apostle* (Grand Rapids and Cambridge: Eerdmans, 1998)

Dunnill, John, *Covenant and Sacrifice in the Letter to the Hebrews,* Society for New Testament Studies Monograph Series 75 (Cambridge: Cambridge University Press, 1992)

Dyrness, William, *Themes in Old Testament Theology* (Downers Grove, IL: InterVarsity Press; Exeter: Paternoster, 1979)

Eckert, Jost, "Gottes Bundesstiftungen und der neue Bund bei Paulus," in Hubert Frankemölle (ed.), *Der ungekündigte Bund? Antworten des Neuen Testaments,* Quaestiones disputatae 172 (Freiburg/Basel/Wien: Herder, 1998), 135–56

Ehrman, Bart D. (ed. and trans.), *The Apostolic Fathers, Epistle of Barnabas, Papias and Quadratus, Epistle to Diognetus, The Shephard of Hermas,* Loeb Classical Library (Cambridge, MA/London: Harvard University Press, 2003)

Eichrodt, Walther, *Der Prophet Hesekiel: Kapitel 19–48,* Das Alte Testament Deutsch 22.2 (Göttingen: Vandenhoeck & Ruprecht, 3rd edn, 1984)

—, *Theology of the Old Testament,* I (trans. J. A. Barker; London: SCM Press, 1961)

Ellingworth, Paul, *The Epistle to the Hebrews: A Commentary on the Greek Text,* New International Greek Testament Commentary (Grand Rapids: Eerdmans; Carlisle: Paternoster, 1993)

Elliot, James K., "Jerusalem II: Neues Testament," in *Theologische Realenzyklopädie* XVI (Berlin/New York: Walter de Gruyter, 1987), 609–12

Elwell, Walter A., and Robert W. Yarbrough (eds.), *Readings from the First Century World: Primary Sources for New Testament Study,* Encountering Biblical Studies (Grand Rapids: Baker, 1998)

Evans, Craig A., "Authenticating the Activities of Jesus," in Bruce Chilton and Craig A. Evans (eds.), *Authenticating the Activities of Jesus*, New Testament Tools and Studies XXVIII, 2 (Leiden: E. J. Brill, 1999)

—, "Jesus and Zechariah's Messianic Hope," in Bruce Chilton and Craig A. Evans (eds.), *Authenticating the Activities of Jesus*, New Testament Tools and Studies XXVIII, 2 (Leiden: E. J. Brill, 1999)

Fee, Gordon D., *God's Empowering Presence: The Holy Spirit in the Letters of Paul* (Peabody, MA: Hendrickson, 1994)

—, *Paul, the Spirit and the People of God* (Peabody, MA: Hendrickson, 1996)

—, *The First Epistle to the Corinthians*, New International Commentary on the New Testament (Grand Rapids: Eerdmans, 1987)

Feld, Helmut, *Das Verständnis des Abendmahls*, Erträge der Forschung 50 (Darmstadt: Wissenschaftliche Buchgesellschaft, 1976)

Fensham, F. Charles, "Covenant, Promise and Expectation in the Bible," *Theologische Zeitschrift* 23 (1967), 305–22

Fieldsend, John, *Messianic Jews: Challenging Church and Synagogue* (Kent: Marc Olive Press [Monarch Publications], 1993)

Fitzmyer, Joseph A., S.J., *The Gospel According to Luke (X–XXIV)*, Anchor Bible 28A (New York: Doubleday, 1985)

Ford, David F. (ed.), *The Modern Theologians: An Introduction to Christian Theology in the Twentieth Century* (Cambridge, MA/Oxford: Blackwell, 2nd edn, 1997)

Frankemölle, Hubert (ed.), *Der ungekündigte Bund? Antworten des Neuen Testaments* (Quaestiones disputatae 172; Freiburg/Basel/Wien: Herder, 1998)

—, "Kirche/Ekklesiologie: A. Biblisch," in Peter Eicher (ed.), *Neues Handbuch theologischer Grundbegriffe* III (München: Kösel-Verlag, exp. edn, 1991), 104–19

Frey, Jörg, "Die alte und die neue διαθήκη nach dem Hebräerbrief," in Friedrich Avemarie and Hermann Lichtenberger (eds.), *Bund und Tora*, Wissenschaftliche Untersuchungen zum Neuen Testament 92 (Tübingen: J. C. B. Mohr [Paul Siebeck], 1996), 263–310

Friedrich, Johannes, Wolfgang Pöhlmann and Peter Stuhlmacher (eds.), *Rechtfertigung: Festschrift für Ernst Käsemann zum 70. Geburtstag* (Tübingen: J. C. B. Mohr [Paul Siebeck]; Göttingen: Vandenhoeck & Ruprecht, 1976)

Furnish, V. P., *II Corinthians*, Anchor Bible 32A (New York: Doubleday, 1984)

Gadamer, Hans-Georg, *Truth and Method* (trans. rev. J. Weinsheimer and D. G. Marshall; New York: Continuum, 2nd rev. edn, 2003)

Gertz, Jan Christian, "Bund, II: Altes Testament," in *Religion in Geschichte und Gegenwart*, I (Tübingen: J. C. B. Mohr [Paul Siebeck], 4th edn, 1998)

Gese, Hartmut, *Zur biblischen Theologie: Alttestamentliche Vorträge*, Beiträge zur evangelischen Theologie (München: Chr. Kaiser, 1977)

Gesenius, Wilhelm, *Hebräisches und aramäisches Handwörterbuch über das Alte Testament* (ed. Frants Buhl; Berlin/Göttingen/Heidelberg: Springer-Verlag, 1915, repr. 1962)

Gnilka, Joachim, *Der Epheserbrief*, Herders theologischer Kommentar zum Neuen Testament X, 2 (Freiburg/Basel/Wien: Herder, 2nd rev. edn, 1977)

—, *Das Evangelium nach Markus*, Mk 1 – 8,26, Evangelisch-katholischer Kommentar zum Neuen Testament II/1 (Zürich: Benziger; Neukirchen-Vluyn: Neukirchener, 1978)

—, *Das Evangelium nach Markus*, Evangelisch-katholischer Kommentar zum Neuen Testament II/2 (Zürich: Benziger; Neukirchen-Vluyn: Neukirchener, 1979)

—, *Jesus von Nazaret: Botschaft und Geschichte,* Herders theologischer Kommentar zum Neuen Testament, Suppl. III (Freiburg/Basel/Wien: Herder, 1990)

—, *Theologie des Neuen Testaments,* Herders theologischer Kommentar zum Neuen Testament, Suppl. V (Freiburg/Basel/Wien: Herder, 1994)

—, "Wie urteilte Jesus über seinen Tod?," in Karl Kertelge (ed.), *Der Tod Jesu: Deutungen im Neuen Testament,* Quaestiones disputatae 74 (Freiburg/Basel/Wien: Herder, 1976), 13–50

Goeters, J. F. Gerhard, "Föderaltheologie," in G. Krause and G. Müller (eds.), *Theologische Realenzyklopädie* XI (Berlin/New York: Walter de Gruyter, 1983), 246–52

Goppelt, Leonhard, *Theologie des Neuen Testaments: Erster Teil: Jesu Wirken in seiner theologischen Bedeutung. Zweiter Teil: Vielfalt und Einheit des apostolischen Christuszeugnisses* (Göttingen: Vandenhoeck & Ruprecht, 3rd edn, 1985)

Gräbe, Petrus J., "The All-Surpassing Power of God through the Holy Spirit in the Midst of Our Broken Earthly Existence: Perspectives on Paul's Use of δύναμις in 2 Corinthians," *Neotestamentica* 28.1 (1994), 147–56

—, "Δύναμις in the Sense of Power in the Main Pauline Letters" (D.D. Thesis, University of Pretoria, 1990)

—, "Δύναμις in the Sense of Power as a Pneumatological Concept," *Biblische Zeitschrift* 36 (1992), 192–54

—, "Καινὴ διαθήκη in der paulinischen Literatur: Ansätze zu einer paulinischen Ekklesiologie," in Rainer Kampling and Thomas Söding (eds.), *Ekklesiologie des Neuen Testaments: Für Karl Kertelge* (Freiburg: Herder, 1996), 267–87

Gräßer, Erich, *An die Hebräer,* 3 vols, Evangelisch-katholischer Kommentar zum Neuen Testament XVII/1–3 (Zürich: Benziger; Neukirchen-Vluyn: Neukirchener, 1993)

—, "Paulus, der Apostel des neuen Bundes (2 Kor 2,14–4,6)," in L. De Lorenzi (ed.), *Paolo-Ministro del Nuovo Testamento (2 Co 2,14 – 4,16),* Série monographique de Benedictina 9 (Roma: Benedictina Editrice, 1987)

—, *Der Alte Bund im Neuen: Exegetische Studien zur Israelfrage im Neuen Testament,* Wissenschaftliche Untersuchungen zum Neuen Testament 35 (Tübingen: J. C. B. Mohr [Paul Siebeck], 1985)

Green, Joel B., and Scot McKnight (eds.), *Dictionary of Jesus and the Gospels* (Downers Grove/Leicester: InterVarsity Press, 1992)

Groß, Walter, "Der neue Bund in Jer 31 und die Suche nach übergreifenden Bundeskonzeptionen im Alten Testament," *Theologische Quartalschrift* 176.4 (1996), 259–72

—, "Neuer Bund oder erneuerter Bund: Jer 31,31–34 in der jüngsten Diskussion," in B. J. Hilberath and D. Saltler (eds.), *Vorgeschmack: Festschrift für Theodor Schneider* (Mainz: Matthias Grünewald, 1995), 89–114

—, "'Rezeption' in Ex 31,12–17 und Lev 26,39–45: Sprachliche Form und theologisch-konzeptionelle Leistung," in Hubert Frankemölle (ed.), *Der ungekündigte Bund? Antworten des Neuen Testaments,* Quaestiones disputatae 172 (Freiburg/Basel/Wien: Herder, 1998), 44–63

—, *Zukunft für Israel: Alttestamentliche Bundeskonzepte und die aktuelle Debatte um den neuen Bund,* Stuttgarter Bibelstudien 176 (Stuttgart: Verlag Katholisches Bibelwerk, 1998)

—, and Michael Theobald, "Wenn Christen vom neuen Bund reden: Eine riskante Denkfigur auf dem Prüfstand," *Theologische Quartalschrift* 176.4 (1996), 257–58

Gunkel, Hermann, *Genesis* (Göttingen: Vandenhoeck & Ruprecht, 1901).

—, *The Legends of Genesis: The Biblical Saga and History* (trans. W. H. Carruth; New York: Schocken, 1964)

Gutbrod, Karl, *Das Buch vom Lande Gottes: Josua und Richter,* Die Botschaft des Alten Testaments 10.4 (Stuttgart: Calwer Verlag, 1985)

Güttgemanns, E., *Der leidende Apostel und sein Herr,* Forschungen zur Religion und Literatur des Alten und Neuen Testaments 90 (Göttingen: Vandenhoeck & Ruprecht, 1966)

Hafemann, Scott J., *Suffering and the Spirit: An Exegetical Study of II Cor. 2:14–3:3 within the Context of the Corinthian Correspondence,* Wissenschaftliche Untersuchungen zum Neuen Testament, Second Series 19 (Tübingen: J. C. B. Mohr [Paul Siebeck], 1986)

—, *Paul, Moses, and the History of Israel: The Letter/Spirit Contrast and the Argument from Scripture in 2 Corinthians 3,* Wissenschaftliche Untersuchungen zum Neuen Testament 81 (Tübingen: J. C. B. Mohr [Paul Siebeck], 1995)

—, "The Spirit of the New Covenant, the Law and the Temple of God's Presence: Five Theses on Qumran Self-Understanding and the Contours of Paul's Thought," in Jostein Ådna, Scott J. Hafemann and Otfried Hofius (eds.), *Evangelium, Schriftauslegung, Kirche: Festschrift für Peter Stuhlmacher zum 65. Geburtstag* (Göttingen: Vandenhoeck & Ruprecht, 1997)

Hahn, Ferdinand, "Abendmahl, I: Neues Testament," in *Religion in Geschichte und Gegenwart* I (Tübingen: J. C. B. Mohr [Paul Siebeck], 4th rev. edn, 1998)

—, "Abendmahl," in Gert Otto (ed.), *Praktisch Theologisches Handbuch* (Hamburg: Furche, 1970), 25–56

—, "Die alttestamentlichen Motive in der urchristlichen Abendmahlsüberlieferung," *Evangelische Theologie* 27 (1967), 337–74

—, *Christologische Hoheitstitel: Ihre Geschichte im frühen Christentum,* Forschungen zur Religion und Literatur des Alten und Neuen Testaments 83 (Göttingen: Vandenhoeck & Ruprecht, 1963)

—, *Christologische Hoheitstitel: Ihre Geschichte im frühen Christentum,* UTB Für Wissenschaft/ Uni-Taschenbücher (Göttingen: Vandenhoeck & Ruprecht, 5th exp. edn, 1995)

—, Exegetische Beiträge zum ökumenischen Gespräch: Gesammelte Aufsätze (Göttingen: Vandenhoeck & Ruprecht, 1986)

—, "Herrengedächtnis und Herrenmahl bei Paulus," in Ferdinand Hahn (ed.), *Exegetische Beiträge zum ökumenischen Gespräch: Gesammelte Aufsätze,* I (Göttingen: Vandenhoeck & Ruprecht, 1986), 303–14

—, "Das Herrenmahl bei Paulus," in Michael Trowitzsch (ed.), *Paulus, Apostel Jesu Christi: Festschrift für Günter Klein zum 70. Geburtstag* (Tübingen: J. C. B. Mohr [Paul Siebeck], 1998), 23–33

—, "Methodologische Überlegungen zur Rückfrage nach Jesus," in Karl Kertelge (ed.), *Rückfrage nach Jesus,* Quaestiones disputatae 63 (Freiburg/Basel/Wien: Herder, 1974), 11–77

—, "Thesen zur Frage einheitsstiftender Elemente in Lehre und Praxis des urchristlichen Herrenmahls," in Ferdinand Hahn (ed.), *Exegetische Beiträge zum ökumenischen Gespräch: Gesammelte Aufsätze,* I (Göttingen: Vandenhoeck & Ruprecht, 1986), 232–41

—, "Die Verkündigung Jesu und das Osterzeugnis der Jünger," in Bernd Jochen Hilberath and Dorothea Sattler (eds.), *Vorgeschmack: Ökumenische Bemühungen um die Eucharistie: Festschrift für Theodor Schneider* (Mainz: Matthias-Grünewald, 1995), 125–33

—, "Das Verständnis des Opfers im Neuen Testament," in K. Lehmann and E. Schlink (eds.), *Das Opfer Jesu Christi und seine Gegenwart in der Kirche: Klärungen zum*

Opfercharakter des Herrenmahles, Dialog der Kirchen, III (Freiburg: Herder; Göttingen: Vandenhoeck & Ruprecht, 1983), 51–91

—, "Zum Stand der Erforschung des urchristlichen Herrenmahls," *Evangelische Theologie* 35 (1975), 553–63

—, Wenzel Lohff and Günther Bornkamm, *Die Frage nach dem historischen Jesus* (Göttingen: Vandenhoeck & Ruprecht, 2nd rev. edn, 1966)

Hahn, Scott Walker, "A Biblical Theological Study of Covenant Types and Texts in the Old and New Testament" (DPhil Dissertation, Marquette University, Milwaukee, Wisconsin; UMI Microform 9600849, 1995)

Hall, Stuart G., "Melito in the Light of Passover Haggadah," *The Journal of Theological Studies,* New Series XXII (1971), 29–46

Halton, Thomas, "Stylistic Device in Melito, ΠΕΡΙ ΠΑΣΧΑ," in Patrick Granfield and Josef A. Jungmann (eds.), *Kyriakon: Festschrift Johannes Quasten,* I (Münster: Aschendorff, 1970), 249–55

Harrisville, R. A., "The Concept of Newness in the New Testament," *Journal of Biblical Literature* 74 (1955), 69–79

Hasel, Gerhard, *Old Testament Theology: Basic Issues in the Current Debate* (Grand Rapids: Eerdmans, 1972)

Hatina, Thomas R., "Intertextuality and Historical Criticism in New Testament Studies: Is There a Relationship?," *Biblical Interpretation* VII.1 (1999), 28–43

Hegermann, H., "διαθήκη" in Horst Balz and Gerhard Schneider (eds.), *Exegetisches Wörterbuch zum Neuen Testament,* I (Stuttgart: Kohlhammer, 1980), 718–25

Heron, Alasdair I. C., "Bund 3: Dogmatisch," in *Evangelisches Kirchenlexikon,* I (Göttingen: Vandenhoeck & Ruprecht, 1986)

Herrmann, Siegfried, "'Bund' eine Fehlübersetzung von bᵉrīt: Zur Auseinandersetzung mit Ernst Kutsch," in S. Herrmann (ed.), *Gesammelte Studien zur Geschichte und Theologie des Alten Testaments,* Theologische Bücherei: Neudrucke und Berichte aus dem 20. Jahrhundert 75 (München: Chr. Kaiser, 1986), 210–20

Hilberath, Bernd Jochen, and Dorothea Sattler, *Vorgeschmack: Ökumenische Bemühungen um die Eucharistie: Festschrift für Theodor Schneider* (Mainz: Matthias-Grünewald-Verlag, 1995)

Hillers, Delbert R., *Covenant: The History of a Biblical Idea,* Seminars in the History of Ideas (Baltimore: John Hopkins Press, 1969)

Hoegen-Rohls, Christina, *Der nachösterliche Johannes: Die Abschiedsreden als hermeneutischer Schlüssel zum vierten Evangelium,* Wissenschaftliche Untersuchungen zum Neuen Testament, Second Series 84 (Tübingen: J. C. B. Mohr [Paul Siebeck], 1996)

Hofius, Otfried, "Biblische Theologie im Lichte des Hebräerbriefes," in Sigfred Pedersen (ed.), *New Directions in Biblical Theology: Papers of the Aarhus Conference, 16–19 September 1992,* Supplements to Novum Testamentum 76 (Leiden: E. J. Brill, 1994), 108–25

—, "Das Evangelium und Israel: Erwägungen zu Römer 9–11," *Zeitschrift für Theologie und Kirche* 83 (1986), 297–324

—, "Gesetz und Evangelium nach 2. Korinther 3," in Otfried Hofius (ed.), *Paulusstudien,* Wissenschaftliche Untersuchungen zum Neuen Testament 51 (Tübingen: J. C. B. Mohr [Paul Siebeck], 2nd rev. edn, 1994), 75–120

—, "Herrenmahl und Herrenmahlsparadosis," in Otfried Hofius (ed.), *Paulusstudien,* Wissenschaftliche Untersuchungen zum Neuen Testament 51 (Tübingen: J. C. B. Mohr [Paul Siebeck], 1989), 203–40

—, "Das vierte Gottesknechtslied in den Briefen des Neuen Testamentes," *New Testament Studies* 39 (1993), 414–37

Hooker, Morna D., *The Gospel according to St. Mark,* Black's New Testament Commentaries (London: A & C Black, 1991)

—, *Jesus and the Servant: The Influence of the Servant Concept of Deutero-Isaiah in the New Testament* (London: SPCK, 1959)

Horbury, William, "Jewish-Christian Relations in Barnabas and Justin Martyr," in James D. G Dunn (ed.), *Jews and Christians: The Parting of the Ways A.D. 70 to 135*, Wissenschaftliche Untersuchungen zum Neuen Testament 66 (Tübingen: J. C. B. Mohr [Paul Siebeck], 1992), 315–45

Horn, Friedrich Wilhelm, *Das Angeld des Geistes: Studien zur paulinischen Pneumatologie,* Forschungen zur Religion und Literatur des Alten und Neuen Testaments 154 (Göttingen: Vandenhoeck & Ruprecht, 1992)

Horton, Michael S., *Covenant and Eschatology: The Divine Drama* (Louisville/London: Westminster John Knox, 2002)

Hossfeld, Frank-Lothar, "Bund: Im Alten Testament," in *Lexicon für Theologie und Kirche*, II (Freiburg/Basel/Wien: Herder, 3rd rev. edn, 1994)

Hughes, John J., "Hebrews IX 15ff. and Galatians III 15ff.: A Study in Covenant Practice and Procedure" *Novum Testamentum* 21 (1979), 27–96

Hurst, L. D., *The Epistle to the Hebrews: Its Background and Thought*, Society for New Testament Studies Monograph Series 65 (Cambridge: Cambridge University Press, 1990)

Hyldahl, Niels, *Philosophie und Christentum: Eine Interpretation der Einleitung zum Dialog Justins,* Acta theologica danica 9 (Kopenhagen: Prostant Apud Munksgaard, 1966)

Janowski, Bernd, "Er trug unsere Sünden: Jes 53 und die Dramatik der Stellvertretung," in Bernd Janowski and Peter Stuhlmacher (eds.), *Der leidende Gottesknecht: Jesaja 53 und seine Wirkungsgeschichte mit einer Bibliographie zu Jes 53*, Forschungen zum Alten Testament 14 (Tübingen: J. C. B. Mohr [Paul Siebeck], 1996), 27–48

Jaubert, Annie, *La notion d'alliance dans le Judaïsme aux abords de l'ère chrétienne*, Patristica Sorbonensia 6 (Paris: éditions du Seuil, 1963).

Jeanrond, Werner G., "After Hermeneutics: The Relationship between Theology and Biblical Studies," in Francis Watson (ed.), *The Open Text: New Directions for Biblical Studies* (London: SCM Press, 1993), 85–102

Jepsen, Alfred, "Berith: Ein Beitrag zur Theologie der Exilszeit," in A. Kuschke (ed.), *Verbannung und Heimkehr: Beiträge zur Geschichte und Theologie Israels im 6. und 5. Jahrhundert v. Chr. Festschrift für Wilhelm Rudolph* (Tübingen: J. C. B. Mohr [Paul Siebeck], 1962), 161–79

Jeremias, Joachim, *Die Abendmahlsworte Jesu* (Göttingen: Vandenhoeck & Ruprecht, 4th rev. edn, 1967)

—, *Neutestamentliche Theologie,* I: Die Verkündigung Jesu (Gütersloh: Gütersloher Verlagshaus Gerd Mohn, 1971)

Jones, F. Stanley, "The Pseudo-Clementines: A History of Research, Parts I & II," *Second Century* 2 (1982), 1–33; 63–96

Jüngel, Eberhard, "Barth, Karl," in *Theologische Realenzyklopädie* V (Berlin: Walter de Gruyter, 1980)

—, *Das Evangelium von der Rechtfertigung des Gottlosen als Zentrum des christlichen Glaubens: Eine theologische Studie in ökumenischer Absicht* (Tübingen: J. C. B. Mohr [Paul Siebeck], 2nd edn, 1999)

—, *Justification: The Heart of the Christian Faith: A Theological Study with an Ecumenical Purpose* (trans. Jeffrey F. Cayzer; Edinburgh/New York: T&T Clark, 2001)

Kapelrud, Arvid S., "Der Bund in den Qumran-Schriften," in Siegfried Wagner (ed.), *Bibel und Qumran: Beiträge zur Erforschung der Beziehungen zwischen Bibel- und Qumranwissenschaft. Hans Bardtke zum 22.9.1966* (Berlin: Evangelische Haupt-Bibelgesellschaft, 1968), 137–49

Karrer, Martin, "Der Kelch des neuen Bundes: Erwägungen zum Verständnis des Herrenmahls nach 1 Kor 11,23b–25," *Biblische Zeitschrift* 34 (1990), 198–221

Käsemann, Ernst, *An die Römer*, Handbuch zum Neuen Testament 8a (Tübingen: J. C. B. Mohr [Paul Siebeck], 4th edn, 1980)

—, *Paulinische Perspektiven* (Tübingen: J. C. B. Mohr [Paul Siebeck], 2nd rev. edn, 1972)

—, "Anliegen und Eigenart der paulinischen Abendmahlslehre," in E. Käsemann (ed.), *Exegetische Versuche und Besinnungen*, I and II (Göttingen: Vandenhoeck & Ruprecht, 1964), 11–34

—, "Das theologische Problem des Motivs vom Leibe Christi," in E. Käsemann (ed.), *Paulinische Perspektiven* (Tübingen: J. C. B. Mohr [Paul Siebeck], 1969), 178–210

Kaylor, R. D., *Paul's Covenant Community: Jew and Gentile in Romans* (Atlanta: John Knox Press, 1988)

Kennedy, H. A. A., "The Covenant-Conception in the First Epistle of John," *Evangelische Theologie* 28 (1916–17), 23–26

Kertelge, Karl, "Das Abendmahl Jesu im Markusevangelium," in Josef Zmijewski and Ernst Nellessen (eds.), *Begegnung mit dem Wort: Festschrift für Heinrich Zimmermann*, Bonner biblische Beiträge 53 (Bonn: Peter Hanstein, 1980), 67–80

—, "Biblische Theologie im Römerbrief," in Sigfred Pedersen (ed.), *New Directions in Biblical Theology: Papers of the Aarhus Conference, 16–19 September 1992*, Supplements to Novum Testamentum 76 (Leiden: E. J. Brill, 1994), 47–57

—, *The Epistle to the Romans*, New Testament for Spiritual Reading 12 (trans. F. McDonagh; London: Sheed & Ward, 1972)

—, "Buchstabe und Geist nach 2 Kor 3," in James D. G. Dunn (ed.), *Paul and the Mosaic Law: The Third Durham-Tübingen Research Symposium on Earliest Christianity and Judaism*, Wissenschaftliche Untersuchungen zum Neuen Testament 89 (Tübingen: J. C. B. Mohr [Paul Siebeck], 1996), 117–30

—, *Markusevangelium*, Neue Echter Bibel, NT 2 (Würzburg: Echter Verlag, 1994)

—, *Rechtfertigung bei Paulus: Studien zur Struktur und zum Bedeutungsgehalt des paulinischen Rechtfertigungsbegriffs*, Neutestamentliche Abhandlungen, New Series 3 (Münster: Aschendorff, 1967)

—, "Die soteriologischen Aussagen in der urchristlichen Abendmahlsüberlieferung und ihre Beziehung zum geschichtlichen Jesus', *Trierer theologische Zeitschrift* 81 (1972), 193–202

—, "Das Verständnis des Todes Jesu bei Paulus," in Karl Kertelge (ed.), *Grundthemen paulinischer Theologie* (Freiburg/Basel/Wien: Herder, 1991), 62–80

—, "δικαιοσύνη," in Horst Balz and Gerhard Schneider (eds.), *Exegetisches Wörterbuch zum Neuen Testament*, I (Stuttgart: Kohlhammer, 1980), 784–96

Kinzig, Wolfram, "Καινὴ διαθήκη: The Title of the New Testament in the Second and Third Centuries," *Journal of Theological Studies* 45 (1994), 519–44

—, *Novitas Christiana: Die Idee des Fortschritts in der alten Kirche*, Forschungen zur Kirchen und Dogmengeschichte 58 (Göttingen: Vandenhoeck & Ruprecht, 1994)

Kirchschläger, Walter, "'Bund,' in der Herrenmahltradition," in Hubert Frankemölle (ed.), *Der ungekündigte Bund?* Antworten des Neuen Testaments, Quaestiones disputatae 172 (Freiburg/Basel/Wien: Herder, 1998), 117–34

Klaiber, Walter, *Rechtfertigung und Gemeinde: Eine Untersuchung zum paulinischen Kirchenverständnis,* Forschungen zur Religion und Literatur des Alten und Neuen Testaments 127 (Göttingen: Vandenhoeck & Ruprecht, 1982)

Klauck, Hans-Josef, *1. Korintherbrief,* Neue Echter Bibel, NT 7 (Würzburg: Echter Verlag, 3rd edn, 1992)

—, *2. Korintherbrief,* Neue Echter Bibel, NT 8 (Würzburg: Echter Verlag, 3rd edn, 1994)

—, "Die Auswahl der Zwölf (Mk 3,13–19)," in H.-J. Klauck (ed.), *Gemeinde. Amt. Sakrament: Neutestamentliche Perspektive* (Würzburg: Echter Verlag, 1989), 131–36

—, *Der erste Johannesbrief,* Evangelisch-katholischer Kommentar zum Neuen Testament XXIII/1 (Zürich: Benziger; Neukirchen-Vluyn: Neukirchener, 1991)

—, Herrenmahl und hellenistischer Kult: Eine religionsgeschichtliche Untersuchung zum ersten Korintherbrief, Neutestamentliche Abhandlungen, New Series 15, (Münster: Aschendorff, 1982)

Kollmann, Bernd, *Ursprung und Gestalten der frühchristlichen Mahlfeier,* Göttinger theologischer Arbeiten 43 (Göttingen: Vandenhoeck & Ruprecht, 1990)

Kraetzschmar, Richard, *Die Bundesvorstellung im Alten Testament in ihrer geschichtlichen Entwicklung* (Marburg: N. G. Elwert'sche Verlagsbuchhandlung, 1896)

Kraus, Hans-Joachim, "Der erste und der neue Bund: Biblisch-theologische Studie zu Jer 31,31–34: Manfred Josuttis zum 60. Geburtstag," in Christoph Dohmen and Thomas Söding (eds.), *Eine Bibel – zwei Testamente: Positionen biblischer Theologie,* UTB 1893 (Paderborn: Ferdinand Schöningh, 1995), 59–69

Kremer, Jacob, "'Denn der Buchstabe tötet, der Geist aber macht lebendig.' Methodologische und hermeneutische Erwägungen zu 2 Kor 3,6b," in Josef Zmijewski and Ernst Nellessen (eds.), *Begegnung mit dem Wort: Festschrift für Heinrich Zimmermann,* Bonner biblische Beiträge 53 (Bonn: Peter Hanstein, 1980), 219–50

—, *Lukasevangelium,* Neue Echter Bibel, NT 3 (Würzburg: Echter, 1988)

Kutsch, Ernst, "Bund," in *Theologische Realenzyklopädie* VII (Berlin: Walter de Gruyter, 1981), 397–410

—, Neues Testament – Neuer Bund? Eine Fehlübersetzung wird korrigiert (Neukirchen-Vluyn: Neukirchener Verlag, 1978)

—, "בְּרִית Verpflichtung," in E. Jenni and C. Westermann (eds.), *Theologisches Wörterbuch zum Alten Testament,* I (München: Chr. Kaiser, 1971), 339–52

—, *Verheißung und Gesetz: Untersuchungen zum sogenannten "Bund" im Alten Testament,* Beihefte zur Zeitschrift für die alttestamentliche Wissenschaft 131 (Berlin: Walter de Gruyter, 1973)

Lambrecht, Jan, S.J., *Second Corinthians,* Sacra pagina 8 (Collegeville, MN: The Liturgical Press, 1999)

Lamparter, Helmut, *Prophet wider Willen: Der Prophet Jeremia,* Die Botschaft des Alten Testaments 20 (Stuttgart: Calwer Verlag, 1964)

Lane, William L., "Covenant: The Key to Paul's Conflict with Corinth," *Tyndale Bulletin* 33 (1982), 3–29

—, *Hebrews 1 – 8,* Word Biblical Commentary 47A (Dallas: Word Books, 1991)

Lang, Bernhard, "Der Becher als Bundeszeichen: 'Bund' und 'neuer Bund,' in den neutestamentlichen Abendmahlstexten," in Erich Zenger (ed.), *Der Neue*

Bund im Alten, Quaestiones disputatae 146 (Freiburg/Basel/Wien: Herder, 1993), 199–212

Lang, Friedrich, "Abendmahl und Bundesgedanke im Neuen Testament," *Evangelische Theologie* 35 (1975), 524–38

—, *Die Briefe an die Korinther*, Das Neue Testament Deutsch 7 (Göttingen: Vandenhoeck & Ruprecht, 1986)

Lehne, Susanne, *The New Covenant in Hebrews*, Journal for the Study of the New Testament: Supplement Series 44 (Sheffield: Sheffield Academic Press, 1990)

Levin, Christoph, "Rezension: Vogel, Manuel: Das Heil des Bundes," *Theologische Literaturzeitung* 123.3 (1998), 258–60

—, "Rezension: Groß, Walter: Zukunft für Israel," *Zeitschrift für altorientalische und biblische Rechtsgeschichte* 5 (1999), 318–27

—, *Die Verheißung des neuen Bundes in ihrem theologiegeschichtlichen Zusammenhang ausgelegt*, Forschungen zur Religion und Literatur des Alten und Neuen Testaments 137 (Göttingen: Vandenhoeck & Ruprecht, 1985)

Lichtenberger, Hermann, "Alter und neuer Bund," *New Testament Studies* 41 (1995), 400–14

—, "'Bund' in der Abendmhalsüberlieferung," in Friedrich Avemarie and Hermann Lichtenberger (eds.), *Bund und Tora: Zur theologischen Begriffsgeschichte in alttestamentlicher, frühjüdischer und urchristlicher Tradition*, Wissenschaftliche Untersuchungen zum Neuen Testament 92 (Tübingen: J. C. B. Mohr [Paul Siebeck], 1996), 217–28

—, and Ekkehard Stegemann, "Zur Theologie des Bundes in Qumran und im Neuen Testament," *Kirche und Israel* 6/1.91 (1991), 134–46

—, and Armin Lange, "Qumran," in *Theologische Realenzyklopädie* XXVIII (Berlin/New York: Walter de Gruyter, 1997)

—, and Stefan Schreiner, "Der neue Bund in jüdischer Überlieferung," *Theologische Quartalschrift* 176.4 (1996), 272–90

Liddell, H. G., and R. Scott, *A Greek-English Lexicon* (rev. Henry Stuart Jones; Oxford: Clarendon Press, 1968)

Lindemann, Andreas, "Herrschaft Gottes/Reich Gottes IV.2: Herrschaft Gottes bei Jesus und im Urchristentum," in *Theologische Realenzyklopädie* XV (Berlin/New York: Walter de Gruyter, 1986), 200–18

Link, Hans-Georg, "Zur Kreuzestheologie. Gegenwärtige Probleme einer Kreuzestheologie. Ein Bericht über die Herausgebertagung der EvTh (12.–14. Oktober 1972)," *Evangelische Theologie* 33 (1973), 337–45

Lohfink, Norbert, "Der Begriff 'Bund' in der biblischen Theologie," *Theologie und Philosophie* 66 (1991), 161–76

—, "Bundestheologie im Alten Testament: Zum gleichnamigen Buch von Lothar Perlitt," in N. Lohfink (ed.), *Studien zum Deuteronomium und zur deuteronomistischen Literatur I*, Stuttgarter biblische Aufsatzbände, Altes Testament 8 (Stuttgart: Verlag Katholisches Bibelwerk, 1990), 325–61

—, "Bund," in Manfred Görg and Bernhard Lang (eds.), *Neues Bibel-Lexikon* (Zürich: Benziger, 1988), 344–48

—, "Kinder Abrahams aus Steinen: Wird nach dem Alten Testament Israel einst der 'Bund' genommen werden?," in Hubert Frankemölle (ed.), *Der ungekündigte Bund? Antworten des Neuen Testaments*, Quaestiones disputatae 172 (Freiburg/Basel/Wien: Herder, 1998), 17–43

—, Der niemals gekündigte Bund: Exegetische Gedanken zum christlich-jüdischen Dialog (Freiburg: Herder, 1989)

—, "Rezension: Ernest W. Nicholson, 'God and His People: Covenant and Theology in the Old Testament'", *Biblische Zeitschrift* 34 (1990), 296–98

Lohmeyer, Ernst, *Diatheke, ein Beitrag zur Erklärung des neutestamentlichen Begriffs* (Leipzig, 1913)

Lohse, Eduard, "Die alttestamentlichen Bezüge im neutestamentlichen Zeugnis vom Tode Jesu Christi," in *Die Einheit des Neuen Testaments: Exegetische Studien zur Theologie des Neuen Testaments* (Göttingen: Vandenhoeck & Ruprecht, 1973), 111–24

—, *Grundriß der neutestamentlichen Theologie*, Theologische Wissenschaft V (Stuttgart/Berlin/Köln/Mainz: Kohlhammer, 1974)

—, *Die Offenbarung des Johannes*, Das Neue Testament Deutsch 11 (Göttingen: Vandenhoeck & Ruprecht, 1988)

—, "Zion-Jerusalem im nachbiblischen Judentum," in *Theologisches Wörterbuch zum Neuen Testament* VII (1964), 318–38

Longenecker, Bruce W., "Contours of Covenant Theology in the Post-Conversion Paul," in Richard N. Longenecker (ed.), *The Road from Damascus: The Impact of Paul's Conversion on His Life, Thought, and Ministry* (Grand Rapids: Eerdmans, 1997), 125–46

Longenecker, Richard N., *Galatians*, Word Biblical Commentary (Dallas: Word Books, 1990)

Louw, Johannes P., *Semantics of New Testament Greek,* The Society of Biblical Literature Semeia Studies (Philadelphia: Fortress Press, 1982)

—, and Eugene A. Nida (eds.), *Greek-English Lexicon of the New Testament Based on Semantic Domains,* 2 vols. (New York: United Bible Societies, 1988)

Lundbom, Jack R., "New Covenant," in *Anchor Bible Dictionary* IV (New York/London/Toronto: Doubleday, 1992), 1088–94

Luz, Ulrich, "Der alte Bund und der neue Bund bei Paulus und im Hebräerbrief," *Evangelische Theologie* 27 (1967), 318–36

Mach, Michael, "Philo von Alexandrien," in *Theologische Realenzyklopädie* XXVI (Berlin/New York: Walter de Gruyter, 1996)

Maier, Johann, "Bund, IV: Im Judentum," in *Lexicon für Theologie und Kirche*, II (Freiburg/Basel/Wien: Herder, 3rd rev. edn, 1994)

Malatesta, Edward S. J., *Interiority and Covenant: A Study of εἶναι ἐν and μένειν ἐν in the First Letter of Saint John*, Analecta biblica 69 (Rome: Biblical Institute Press, 1978)

Marshall, I. Howard, *The Gospel of Luke,* New International Greek Testament Commentary (Exeter: Paternoster, 1978)

—, *Last Supper and Lord's Supper* (Exeter: Paternoster, 1980)

Martin, Ralph P., *2 Corinthians,* Word Biblical Commentary 40 (Waco, TX: Word Books, 1986)

Martyn, J. Louis, "Apocalyptic Antinomies in Paul's Letter to the Galatians," *New Testament Studies* 31 (1985), 410–24

—, *Galatians,* Anchor Bible (New York: Doubleday, 1997)

Marxsen, Willi, *Das Abendmahl als christologisches Problem* (Gütersloh: Gütersloher Verlagshaus Gerd Mohn, 1963)

März, Claus-Peter, "Bund III: Im Neuen Testament," in *Lexicon für Theologie und Kirche* (Freiburg/Basel/Wien: Herder, 3rd rev. edn, 1994), 785–88

Mayes, A. D. H., and R. B. Salters (eds.), *Covenant as Context: Essays in Honour of E.W. Nicholson* (Oxford: Oxford University Press, 2003)

McCarthy, Dennis, J., *Old Testament Covenant: A Survey of Current Opinions,* Growing Points in Theology (Oxford: Basil Blackwell, 1972)

McCullough, J. C., "Hebrews in Recent Scholarship (Parts 1 & 2)," *Irish Biblical Studies* 16.2 (1994), 66–86; 16.3, 108–20

McKenzie, John L., S.J., *Second Isaiah,* Anchor Bible (New York: Doubleday, 1968)

—, *Covenant:* Understanding Biblical Themes (St. Louis, MO: Chalice, 2000)

McKnight, Edgar V., *What Is Form Criticism?* Guides to Biblical Scholarship New Testament Series (Philadelphia: Fortress Press, 1969)

Méhat, André, "Clemens von Alexandrien," in *Theologische Realenzyklopädie* VIII (Berlin: Walter de Gruyter, 1981)

Mendenhall, George E., "Covenant," in *The Interpreter's Dictionary of the Bible* (Nashville/New York: Abingdon Press, 1962), 714–23

—, and Gary A. Herion, "Covenant," in *Anchor Bible Dictionary* (New York/London/Toronto: Doubleday, 1992), 1179–202

Merklein, Helmut, "Erwägungen zur Überlieferungsgeschichte der neutestamentlichen Abendmahlstraditionen," *Biblische Zeitschrift* 21 (1977), 88–101, 235–44

—, *Jesu Botschaft von der Gottesherrschaft: Eine Skizze,* Stuttgarter Bibelstudien 111 (Stuttgart: Verlag Katholisches Bibelwerk, 1983)

—, "Der (neue) Bund als Thema der paulinischen Theologie," *Theologische Quartalschrift* 176.4 (1996), 290–308

Metzger, Bruce M., *A Textual Commentary on the Greek New Testament* (Stuttgart: Deutsche Bibelgesellschaft; New York: United Bible Societies, 2nd edn, 1994)

Meyer, Ben F., "Appointed Deed, Appointed Doer: Jesus and the Scriptures," in Bruce Chilton and Craig A. Evans (eds.), *Authenticating the Activities of Jesus*, New Testament Tools and Studies XXVIII, 2 (Leiden: E. J. Brill, 1999)

Meyer, H. A. W., *Critical and Exegetical Handbook to the Epistles to the Corinthians* (trans. D. Bannermann and W. P. Dickson; New York: Funk & Wagnalls, 1890)

Morgenthaler, Robert, *Statistik des neutestamentlichen Wortschatzes* (Zürich/Stuttgart: Gotthelf Verlag, 2nd edn, 1972)

Moulton, James H., and George Milligan, *The Vocabulary of the Greek Testament Illustrated from the Papyri and Other Non-Literary Sources* (London: Hodder & Stoughton, 1930)

Murphy-O'Connor, Jerome, "The New Covenant in the Letters of Paul and the Essene Documents," in Maurya P. Horgan and Paul J. Kobelski (eds.), *To Touch the Text: Biblical and Related Studies in Honor of Joseph A. Fitzmyer, S.J.* (New York: Crossroad, 1989), 194–204

—, *The Theology of the Second Letter to the Corinthians,* New Testament Theology (Cambridge: Cambridge University Press, 1991)

Murray, Robert, *Symbols of Church and Kingdom: A Study in Early Syriac Tradition* (Cambridge: Cambridge University Press, 1975)

Mußner, Franz, *Der Galaterbrief,* Herders theologischer Kommentar zum Neuen Testament IX (Freiburg/Basel/Wien: Herder, 5th rev. edn, 1988)

—, "Gottes 'Bund' mit Israel nach Röm 11,27," in Hubert Frankemölle (ed.), *Der ungekündigte Bund? Antworten des Neuen Testaments*, Quaestiones disputatae 172 (Freiburg/Basel/Wien: Herder, 1998), 157–70

—, *Jesus von Nazareth im Umfeld Israels und der Kirche: Gesammelte Aufsätze,* Wissenschaftliche Untersuchungen zum Neuen Testament 111 (ed. Michael Theobald; Tübingen: Mohr Siebeck, 1999)

Nebe, Gottfried, *"Hoffnung" bei Paulus: Elpis und ihre Synonyme im Zusammenhang der Eschatologie,* Studien zur Umwelt des Neuen Testaments 16 (Göttingen: Vandenhoeck & Ruprecht, 1983)

Neef, Heinz-Dieter, "Aspekte alttestamentlicher Bundestheologie," in Friedrich Avemarie and Hermann Lichtenberger (eds.), *Bund und Tora: Zur theologischen Begriffsgeschichte in alttestamentlicher, frühjüdischer und urchristlicher Tradition* (Tübingen: J. C. B. Mohr [Paul Siebeck], 1996), 1–23

Neusner, Jacob, *Aphrahat and Judaism: The Christian-Jewish Argument in Fourth-Century Iran,* Studia post-biblica (Leiden: E. J. Brill, 1971)

Newman, Barclay M., *A Concise Greek-English Dictionary of the New Testament* (London: United Bible Societies, 1971)

—, and Eugene A. Nida, *A Translator's Handbook on Paul's Letter to the Romans,* Helps for Translators XIV (Stuttgart: United Bible Societies, 1973)

Nicholson, Ernest W., "The Covenant Ritual in Exodus XXIV 3–8," *Vetus Testamentum* 32 (1982), 74–86

—, *God and His People: Covenant and Theology in the Old Testament* (Oxford: Clarendon Press, 1986)

Niederwinner, Kurt, *Die Didache,* Kommentar zu den apostolischen Vätern I, Supplement Series of Kritisch-exegetischer Kommentar über das Neue Testament (Göttingen: Vandenhoeck & Ruprecht, 1989)

Noth, Martin, "Das alttestamentliche Bundschließen im Lichte eines Mari-Textes," in M. Noth (ed.), *Gesammelte Studien zum Alten Testament,* Thelogische Bücherei: Neudrucke und Berichte aus dem 20. Jahrhundert 6 (München: Chr. Kaiser, 1966), 142–54

—, *Das zweite Buch Mose, Exodus,* Das Alte Testament Deutsch, 5 (Göttingen: Vandenhoeck & Ruprecht, 1959)

O'Neill, J. C., *Who Did Jesus Think He Was?* Biblical Interpretation Series XI (Leiden/New York/Köln: E. J. Brill, 1995)

Olson, Roger E., *The Story of Christian Theology: Twenty Centuries of Tradition and Reform* (Leicester: InterVarsity Press, 1999)

Otto, Eckart, "Treueid und Gesetz: Die Ursprünge des Deuteronomiums im Horizont neuassyrischen Vertragsrechts," *Zeitschrift für altorientalische und biblische Rechtsgeschichte* 2 (1996), 1–52

—, "Die Ursprünge der Bundestheologie im Alten Testament und im Alten Orient," *Zeitschrift für altorientalische und biblische Rechtsgeschichte* 4 (1998), 1–84

—, "Rezension: H.U. Steymans, Deuteronomium 28 und die adê zur Thronfolgerung Asarhaddons," *Zeitschrift für altorientalische und biblische Rechtsgeschichte* 2 (1996), 214–21

Patsch, Hermann, *Abendmahl und historischer Jesus,* Calwer Theologische Monographien 1 (Stuttgart: Calwer, 1972)

Pawlikowski, John T., "Ein Bund oder zwei Bünde: Zeitgenössische Perspektiven," *Theologische Quartalschrift* 176.4 (1996), 325–40

Perlitt, Lothar, *Bundestheologie im Alten Testament,* Wissenschaftliche Monographien zum Alten und Neuen Testament 36 (Neukirchen-Vluyn: Neukirchener Verlag, 1969)

Pesch, Rudolf, *Das Abendmahl und Jesu Todesverständnis,* Quaestiones disputatae 80 (Freiburg/Basel/Wien: Herder, 1978)

—, *Das Markusevangelium,* II, Herders theologischer Kommentar zum Neuen Testament (Freiburg: Herder, 1980)

Pettegrew, Larry D., *The New Covenant Ministry of the Holy Spirit: A Study in Continuity and Discontinuity* (Lanham/New York/London: University Press of America, 1993)

Pfammater, Josef, *Epheserbrief; Kolosserbrief,* Neue Echter Bibel, NT 10 and 12 (Würzburg: Echter Verlag, 1987)

Plummer, A., *A Critical and Exegetical Commentary on the Second Epistle of St. Paul to the Corinthians,* International Critical Commentary (Edinburgh: T&T Clark, 1915)

Pokorný, Petr, *Der Brief des Paulus an die Epheser,* Theologischer Handkommentar zum Neuen Testament 10,2 (Leipzig: Evangelische Verlagsanstalt, 1992)

Porter, Stanley E., and Jacqueline C. R. de Roo (eds.), *The Concept of the Covenant in the Second Temple Period,* Supplements to the Journal for the Study of Judaism 71 (Leiden/Boston: E. J. Brill, 2003)

Porter, Stanley E., "The Concept of Covenant in Paul," in Stanley E. Porter and Jacqueline C. R. de Roo (eds.), *The Concept of the Covenant in the Second Temple Period,* Supplements to the Journal for the Study of Judaism 71 (Leiden/Boston: E. J. Brill, 2003), 269–85

Preuß, Horst Dietrich, *Theologie des Alten Testaments: Band 1. JHWHs erwählendes und verpflichtendes Handeln* (Stuttgart/Berlin/Köln: Kohlhammer, 1991)

Prostmeier, Ferdinand R., *Der Barnabasbrief,* Kommentar zu den apostolischen Vätern VIII (Göttingen: Vandenhoeck & Ruprecht, 1999)

Pryor, John W., *John: Evangelist of the Covenant People: The Narrative and Themes of the Fourth Gospel* (Downers Grove: InterVarsity Press, 1992)

Radice, Roberto, and David T. Runia, *Philo of Alexandria: An Annotated Bibliography 1937–1986,* Supplements to Vigiliae Christianae VIII (Leiden: E. J. Brill, 1988)

Räisänen, Heikki, "Römer 9–11: Analyze eines geistigen Ringens," in *Aufsteig und Niedergang der römischen Welt* II.25.4 (Berlin: Walter de Gruyter, 1987)

Ratzinger, Cardinal Joseph, "The New Covenant: A Theology of Covenant in the New Testament," *Communio* 22 (1995), 635–51

Rendtorff, Rolf, *Die "Bundesformel": Eine exegetisch-theologische Untersuchung,* Stuttgarter Bibelstudien 160 (Stuttgart: Verlag Katholisches Bibelwerk, 1995)

—, *Canon and Theology,* Overtures to Biblical Theology (trans. and ed. Margaret Kohl; Edinburgh: T&T Clark, 1994)

—, *Theologie des Alten Testaments: Ein kanonischer Entwurf. Band 1: Kanonische Grundlegung* (Neukirchen-Vluyn: Neukirchener Verlag, 1999)

Rengstorf, Karl Heinrich (ed.), *A Complete Concordance to Flavius Josephus* (Leiden: E. J. Brill, 1983)

Ringleben, Joachim, *Wahrhaft auferstanden: Zur Begründung der Theologie des lebendigen Gottes* (Tübingen: Mohr Siebeck, 1998)

Robbins, Vernon K., "Last Meal: Preparation, Betrayal, and Absence (Mark 14:12–15)," in Werner H. Kelber (ed.), *The Passion in Mark* (Philadelphia: Fortress Press, 1976), 21–40

Robinson, James M., and Helmut Koester, *Trajectories through Early Christianity* (Philadelphia: Fortress Press, 1971)

Roloff, Jürgen, "Anfänge der soteriologischen Deutung des Todes Jesu (Mk. X. 45 und Lk. XXII. 27," *New Testament Studies* 19 (1972), 38–64

—, *Neues Testament,* Neukirchener Arbeitsbücher (Neukirchen-Vluyn: Neukirchener Verlag, 1977)

—, *Die Kirche im Neuen Testament,* Grundrisse zum Neuen Testament, Das Neue Testament Deutsch Ergänzungsreihe 10 (Göttingen: Vandenhoeck & Ruprecht, 1993)

Sanders, E. P., *The Historical Figure of Jesus* (London: Penguin, 1993)

—, Paul and Palestinian Judaism: A Comparison of Patterns of Religion (London: SCM Press, 1977)

Sass, Gerhard, "Der alte und der neue Bund bei Paulus," in Klaus Wengst and Gerhard Sass (eds.), *Ja und nein: Christliche Theologie im Angesicht Israels. Festschrift zum 70. Geburtstag von Wolfgang Schrage* (Neukirchen-Vluyn: Neukirchener, 1998), 223–34

Scharbert, Josef, *Exodus,* Neue Echter Bibel AT (Würzburg: Echter Verlag, 1989)

Schenker, Adrian, "Der nie aufgehobene Bund: Exegetische Beobachtungen zu Jer 31,31–34," in Erich Zenger (ed.), *Der neue Bund im Alten: Studien zur Bundestheologie der beiden Testamente,* Quaestiones disputatae 146 (Freiburg/Basel/Wien: Herder, 1993), 85–112

Schmahl, Günther, *Die Zwölf im Markusevangelium: Eine redaktionsgeschichtliche Untersuchung,* Trierer theologische Studien 30 (Trier: Paulinus-Verlag, 1974)

—, "Die erste Bestimmung der Zwölf im Markusevangelium," in Rainer Kampling and Thomas Söding (eds.), *Ekklesiologie des Neuen Testaments: Für Karl Kertelge* (Freiburg/Basel/Wien: Herder, 1996), 134–38

Schmidt, Karl Ludwig, and Martin Buber, "Kirche, Staat, Volk, Judentum: Zwiegespräch im jüdischen Lehrhaus in Stuttgart am 14. Januar 1933," in *Neues Testament – Judentum – Kirche: Kleine Schriften,* Theologische Bücherei: Neudrucke und Berichte aus dem 20. Jahrhundert 69 (München: Chr. Kaiser Verlag, 1981), 149–65

Schnackenburg, Rudolf, *Der Brief an die Epheser,* Evangelisch-katholischer Kommentar zum Neuen Testament X (Zürich: Benziger Verlag; Neukirchen-Vluyn: Neukirchener Verlag, 1982)

—, *Das Johannesevangelium III. Teil,* Herders theologischer Kommentar zum Neuen Testament (Freiburg/Basel/Wien: Herder, 1975)

—, *Die Kirche im Neuen Testament: Ihre Wirklichkeit und theologische Deutung. Ihr Wesen und Geheimnis,* Quaestiones disputatae 14 (Freiburg/Basel/Wien: Herder, 1961)

—, *Neutestamentliche Theologie: Der Stand der Forschung,* Biblische Handbibliothek, I (München: Kösel-Verlag, 1963)

Schnelle, Udo, *Das Evangelium nach Johannes,* Theologischer Handkommentar zum Neuen Testament 4 (Leipzig: Evangelische Verlagsanstalt, new edn, 1998)

Scholtissek, Klaus, *In ihm sein und bleiben: Die Sprache der Immanenz in den johanneischen Schriften,* Herders biblische Studien 21 (Freiburg: Herder, 2000)

Schrage, Wolfgang, *Der Erste Brief an die Korinther,* 1 Kor 6,12–11,16, Evangelisch-katholischer Kommentar zum Neuen Testament VII/2 (Solothurn, Düsseldorf: Benziger; Neukirchen-Vluyn: Neukirchener, 1995)

Schreiber, Rudolf, "Der neue Bund im Spätjudentum und Urchristentum" (Dissertation; Tübingen, 1954)

Schulz, Siegfried, "Zur Rechtfertigung aus Gnaden in Qumran und bei Paulus. Zugleich ein Beitrag zur Form- und Überlieferungsgeschichte der Qumrantexte," *Zeitschrift für Theologie und Kirche* 56 (1959), 155–85

Schürmann, Heinz, *Der Einsetzungsbericht: Lk 22,19–20. II. Teil einer quellenkritischen Untersuchung des lukanischen Abendmahlberichtes Lk 22,7–38*, Neutestamentliche Abhandlungen XX.4 (Münster: Aschendorffsche Verlagsbuchhandlung, 1955)

—, *Jesu ureigener Tod: Exegetische Besinnungen und Ausblick* (Freiburg/Basel/Wien: Herder, 2nd rev. edn, 1975)

—, "Lk 22, 19b–20 als ursprüngliche Textüberlieferung," *Biblica* 32 (1951), 364–92

—, *Der Paschamahlbericht, Lk 22, (7–14.) 15–18, 1. Teil einer quellenkritischen Untersuchung des lukanischen Abendmahlsberichtes, Lk 22,7–38*, Neutestamentliche Abhandlungen (Münster: Aschendorffsche Buchdruckerei, 2nd edn, 1968)

Schweizer, Eduard, "Abendmahl I. Im NT," in *Religion in Geschichte und Gegenwart*, I (Tübingen: J. C. B. Mohr [Paul Siebeck], 3rd rev. edn, 1957)

—, *Das Evangelium nach Lukas*, Das Neue Testament Deutsch 3 (Göttingen: Vandenhoeck & Ruprecht, 1982)

—, "Das Herrenmahl im Neuen Testament," in *Neotestamentica: Deutsche und englische Aufsätze 1951–1963* (Zürich/Stuttgart: Zwingli Verlag, 1963), 344–70

—, *Jesus, das Gleichnis Gottes: Was wissen wir wirklich vom Leben Jesu?* Kleine Vandenhoeck-Reihe 1572 (Göttingen: Vandenhoeck & Ruprecht, 1995)

—, *Neotestamentica: Deutsche und englische Aufsätze 1951–1963* (Zürich/Stuttgart: Zwingli Verlag, 1963)

Schwemer, Anna Maria, "Zum Verhältnis von Diatheke und Nomos in den Schriften der jüdischen Diaspora Ägyptens in hellenistisch-römischer Zeit," in Friedrich Avemarie and Hermann Lichtenberger (eds.), *Bund und Tora: Zur theologischen Begriffsgeschichte in alttestamentlicher, frühjüdischer und urchristlicher Tradition* (Tübingen: J. C. B. Mohr [Paul Siebeck], 1996), 67–109

Seebass, Horst, "Bemerkungen zur 'kleinen Antwort' von Erich Zenger," *Theologische Revue* 90.4 (1994), 277–78

—, "Hat das Alte Testament als Teil der christlichen Bibel für christliche Theologie und Kirchen grundlegende Bedeutung?" *Theologische Revue* 90.4 (1994), 265–74

Seifrid, Mark A., *Justification by Faith: The Origin and Development of a Central Pauline Theme*, Supplements to Novum Testamentum LXVIII (Leiden: E.J. Brill, 1992)

Sekki, Arthur E., *The Meaning of Ruaḥ at Qumran*, Society of Biblical Literature Dissertation Series 110 (Atlanta, GA: Scholars Press, 1989)

Siegert, Folker, "Philon v. Alexandrien," in *Lexikon für Theologie und Kirche*, VIII (Freiburg/Basel/Rome/Wien: Herder, 3rd rev. edn, 1999)

Silva, Moisés, *Biblical Words and their Meanings: An Introduction to Lexical Semantics*, Academie Books (Grand Rapids: Zondervan, 1983)

Simon, Marcel, *Verus Israel: A Study of the Relations between Christians and Jews in the Roman Empire (135–425)*, The Littman Library of Jewish Civilization (trans. H. McKeating; Oxford: Oxford University Press, 1986)

Skarsaune, Oskar, "Justin der Märtyrer," in *Theologische Realenzyklopädie* XVII (Berlin: Walter de Gruyter, 1988)

—, *The Proof from Prophecy: A Study in Justin Martyr's Proof-Text Tradition: Text-Type, Provenance, Theological Profile*, Supplements to Novum Testamentum 56 (Leiden: E. J. Brill, 1987)

Smend, Rudolf, *Die Bundesformel*, ThSt 68 (Zürich: EVZ-Verlag, 1963)

—, *Die Mitte des Alten Testaments*, ThSt 101 (Zürich: EVZ-Verlag, 1970)

Smith, D. Moody, *The Theology of the Gospel of John,* New Testament Theology (Cambridge: Cambridge University Press, 1995)

Söding, Thomas, "Das Mahl des Herrn: Zur Gestalt und Theologie der ältesten nachösterlichen Tradition," in Bernd Jochen Hilberath and Dorothea Sattler (eds.), *Vorgeschmack: Ökumenische Bemühungen um die Eucharistie. Festschrift Theodor Schneider* (Mainz: Matthias Grünewald, 1995), 134–63

—, *Das Wort vom Kreuz: Studien zur paulinischen Theologie,* Wissenschaftliche Untersuchungen zum Neuen Testament 93 (Tübingen: J. C. B. Mohr [Paul Siebeck], 1997)

Sophocles, E. A., *Greek Lexicon of the Roman and Byzantine Periods,* I (New York: Frederick Ungar Publishing, 1887)

Spangenberg, Volker, *Herrlichkeit des neuen Bundes: Die Bestimmung des biblischen Begriffs der "Herrlichkeit" bei Hans Urs von Balthasar,* Wissenschaftliche Untersuchungen zum Neuen Testament, Second Series 55 (Tübingen: J. C. B. Mohr [Paul Siebeck], 1993)

Springer, Simone, *Neuinterpretation im Alten Testament: Untersucht an den Themenkreisen des Herbstfestes und der Königspsalmen in Israel,* Stuttgarter biblische Beiträge (Stuttgart: Katholisches Bibelwerk, 1979)

Stanton, Graham N., *The Gospels and Jesus,* Oxford Bible Series (Oxford/New York/ Toronto: Oxford University Press, 1989)

—, *Gospel Truth? New Light on Jesus and the Gospels* (London: Harper Collins, 1995)

—, *Jesus of Nazareth in New Testament Preaching,* Society for New Testament Studies Monograph Series 27 (Cambridge: Cambridge University Press, 1974)

Steymans, Hans Ulrich, "Eine assyrische Vorlage für Deuteronomium 28,20–44," in Georg Braulik (ed.), *Bundesdokument und Gesetz: Studien zum Deuteronomium,* Herders biblische Studien 4 (Freiburg/Basel/Wien/Barecelona/Rome/New York: Herder, 1995), 119–41

—, *Deuteronomium 28 und die adê zur Thronfolgerung Asarhaddons: Segen und Fluch im Alten Orient und in Israel,* Orbis biblicus et orientalis 145 (Freiburg, Schweitz: Universitätsverlag Freiburg; Göttingen: Vandenhoeck & Ruprecht, 1995)

Stock, P. Klemens, *Boten aus dem Mit-Ihm-Sein,* Analecta biblica 70 (Rome: Biblical Institute Press, 1975)

Stockhausen, Carol Kern, *Moses' Veil and the Glory of the New Covenant: The Exegetical Substructure of II Cor. 3,1–4,6,* Analecta biblica 116 (Roma: Editrice Pontificio Istituto Biblico, 1989)

Strack, Hermann L., and Paul Billerbeck, *Das Evangelium nach Matthäus erläutert aus Talmud und Midrasch,* I (München: C. H. Beck'sche Verlagsbuchhandlung, 3rd edn, 1926)

Strecker, Georg, *Das Judenchristentum in den Pseudoklementinen,* Texte und Untersuchungen 70 (2) (Berlin: Akademie Verlag, 2nd rev. and exp. edn, 1981)

Stuhlmacher, Peter, *Biblische Theologie des Neuen Testaments: Band 1: Grundlegung von Jesus zu Paulus* (Göttingen: Vandenhoeck & Ruprecht, 1992)

—, "Jes 53 in den Evangelien und in der Apostelgeschichte," in Bernd Janowski and Peter Stuhlmacher (eds.), *Der leidende Gottesknecht: Jesaja 53 und seine Wirkungsgeschichte mit einer Bibliographie zu Jes 53,* Forschungen zum Alten Testament 14 (Tübingen: J. C. B. Mohr [Paul Siebeck], 1996), 93–105

—, *Reconciliation, Law and Righteousness: Essays in Biblical Theology* (Philadelphia: Fortress Press, 1986)

Swetnam, James S. J., "A Suggested Interpretation of Hebrews 9,15–18," *Catholic Biblical Quarterly* 27 (1965), 373–90

Talmon, Shemaryahu, "Eschatologie und Geschichte im biblischen Judentum," in R. Schnackenburg (ed.), *Zukunft: Zur Eschatologie bei Juden und Christen*, Schriften der Katholischen Akademie in Bayern 98 (Düsseldorf: Patmos, 1980), 13–50

Theißen, Gerd, and Annette Merz, *Der historische Jesus: Ein Lehrbuch* (Göttingen: Vandenhoeck & Ruprecht, 1996)

Theißen, Gerd, and Dagmar Winter, *Die Kriterienfrage in der Jesusforschung: Vom Differenzkriterium zum Plausibilitätskriterium*, Novum Testamentum et Orbis Antiquus (Freiburg: Universitätsverlag Freiburg; Göttingen: Vandenhoeck & Ruprecht, 1997)

Theobald, Michael, "Zwei Bünde und ein Gottesvolk: Die Bundestheologie des Hebräerbriefs im Horizont des christlich-jüdischen Gesprächs," *Theologische Quartalschrift* 176.4 (1996), 309–25

Thüsing, Wilhelm, "'Laßt uns hinzutreten . . .' (Hebr 10,22). Zur Frage nach dem Sinn der Kulttheologie im Hebräerbrief," in Thomas Söding (ed.), *Studien zur neutestamentlichen Theologie*, Wissenschaftliche Untersuchungen zum Neuen Testament 82 (Tübingen: J. C. B. Mohr [Paul Siebeck], 1995), 184–200

Urbán, Angel, *Barnabae epistulae concordantia*, Concordantia in Patres Apostolicos, Pars IV (Hildesheim/Zürich/New York: Olms-Weidmann, 1996)

Van Aarde, A. G., "Die 'verbondstruktuur,' in die Nuwe Testament – 'n terreinverkenning met die oog op die debat oor die verhouding kinderdoop-verbond," *Hervormde Teologicse Studies* 38.4 (1984), 58–82

Van Unnik, W. C., *La conception de la nouvelle alliance: Littérature et théologie pauliniennes*, Recherches bibliques 5 (Bruges: Desclée, 1960)

Van Unnik, W. C., " Ἡ καινὴ διαθήκη – A Problem in the Early History of the Canon," in F. L. Cross (ed.), *Studia Patristica* IV (Berlin: Akademie-Verlag, 1961), 212–27

Vielhauer, Philipp, *Geschichte der urchristlichen Literatur: Einleitung in das Neue Testament, die Apokryphen und die Apostolischen Väter*, De Gruyter Lehrbuch (Berlin/New York: Walter de Gruyter, 1975)

Vogel, Manuel, *Das Heil des Bundes: Bundestheologie im frühen Christentum*, Texte und Arbeiten zum neutestamentlichen Zeitalter 18 (Tübingen/Basel: A. Francke Verlag, 1996)

Vögtle, Anton, "Grundfragen der Diskussion um das heilsmittlerische Todesverständnis Jesu," in Anton Vögtle (ed.), *Offenbarungsgeschehen und Wirkungsgeschichte: Neutestamentliche Beiträge* (Freiburg/Basel/Wien: Herder, 1985), 141–67

Von Rad, Gerhard, *Das fünfte Buch Mose: Deuteronomium*, Das Alte Testament Deutsch 8 (Göttingen: Vandenhoeck & Ruprecht, 1964)

—, *Theologie des Alten Testaments. 1. Band: Die Theologie der geschichtlichen Überlieferung Israels.* 8. Auflage. Einführung in die evangelische Theologie 1 (München: Chr. Kaiser, 1957)

—, *Old Testament Theology*, 2 vols. (trans. D. M. G. Stalker; London: Oliver and Boyd, 1962, 1965)

Vööbus, Arthur, *History of Ascetism in the Syrian Orient: A Contribution to the History of Culture in the Near East: I: The Origin of Ascetism, Early Monasticism in Persia*, Corpus scriptorium christianorum orientalium (Louvain: Secrétariat du CorpusSCO, 1958)

Vorgrimler, Herbert, "Der ungekündigte Bund: Systematische Aspekte," in Hubert Frankemölle (ed.), *Der ungekündigte Bund? Antworten des Neuen Testaments*, Quaestiones disputatae 172 (Freiburg/Basel/Wien: Herder, 1998), 232–47

Vouga, Francois, *An die Galater*, Handbuch zum Neuen Testament 10 (Tübingen: Mohr Siebeck, 1998)

Vriezen, Th. C., *An Outline of Old Testament Theology* (Oxford: Basil Blackwell, 1958)

Wagner, Volker, "Die Bedeutungswandel von אדשה ברית bei der Ausgestaltung der Abendmahlsworte," *Evangelische Theologie* 35 (1975), 538–63

Wedderburn, A. J. M., "The Body of Christ and Related Concepts in 1 Corinthians," *Scottish Journal of Theology* 24 (1971), 74–96

Weinfeld, M., "ברית," in *Theologisches Wörterbuch zum Alten Testament* (Stuttgart: Kohlhammer, 1973), 781–808

Weir, David A., *The Origins of the Federal Theology in Sixteenth-Century Reformation Thought* (Oxford: Clarendon Press, 1990)

Weiß, Hans-Friedrich, *Der Brief an die Hebräer*, Kritisch-exegetischer Kommentar über das Neue Testament 13 (Göttingen: Vandenhoeck & Ruprecht, 1991)

Weiser, Artur, *Das Buch des Propheten Jeremia: Kapitel 25,15–52,34*, Das Alte Testament Deutsch 21 (Göttingen: Vandenhoeck & Ruprecht, 1955)

Wellhausen, Julius, *Grundrisse zum Alten Testament*, Theologische Bücherei: Neudrucke und Berichte aus dem 20. Jahrhundert 27 (ed. Rudolf Smend; München: Chr. Kaiser, 1965)

—, *Prolegomena zur Geschichte Israels* (Berlin: Druck und Verlag von Georg Reimer, 5th edn, 1899)

Westermann, Claus, *Genesis, II, Genesis 12–36*, Biblischer Kommentar, Altes Testament I/2 (Neukirchen-Vluyn: Neukirchener Verlag, 1981)

—, *Prophetische Heilsworte im Alten Testament*, Forschungen zur Religion und Literatur des Alten und Neuen Testaments 145 (Göttingen: Vandenhoeck & Ruprecht, 1987)

—, *Theologie des Alten Testaments in Grundzügen*, Das Alte Testament Deutsch, Supplement Series VI (Göttingen: Vandenhoeck & Ruprecht, 1978)

Wilckens, Ulrich, *Der Brief an die Römer*, 3 vols., Evangelisch-katholischer Kommentar zum Neuen Testament VI (Zürich: Benziger Verlag; Neukirchen-Vluyn: Neukirchener Verlag, 3rd exp. edn, 1993)

—, *Das Evangelium nach Johannes*, Das Neue Testament Deutsch, Part 4 (Göttingen: Vandenhoeck & Ruprecht, 17th edn, 1998)

Williams, Rowan, "Origenes/Origenismus," in *Theologische Realenzyklopädie* XXV (Berlin/New York: Walter de Gruyter, 1995)

Williamson, Paul, "Review of 'The Covenanted Self,'" *Evangelical Quarterly* 76.3 (2004), 246–47

Wilson, Stephen G., *Related Strangers: Jews and Christians 70–170 C.E.* (Minneapolis: Fortress Press, 1995)

Windisch, Hans, *Der Barnabasbrief*, Handbuch zum Neuen Testament, supplement volume, Die apostolischen Väter III (Tübingen: J. C. B. Mohr [Paul Siebeck], 1920)

Wischmeyer, Oda, "Herrschen als Dienen – Mk 10,41–45," *Zeitschrift für die neutestamentliche Wissenschaft* 90 (1999), 28–44

Wolff, Christian, *Der erste Brief des Paulus an die Korinther, zweiter Teil: Auslegung der Kapitel 8–16*, Theologischer Handkommentar zum Neuen Testament VII/2 (Berlin: Evangelische Verlagsanstalt, 2nd edn, 1982)

—, *Jeremia im Frühjudentum und Urchristentum*, Texte und Untersuchungen 118 (Berlin: Akademie-Verlag, 1976)

Wolff, Hans Walter, *Jesaja 53 im Urchristentum: Die Geschichte der Prophetie 'siehe, es siegt mein Knecht" bis zu Justin* (Bethel bei Bielefeld: Buchdruckerei der Anstalt Bethel, 1942)

Wright, N. T., *The Climax of the Covenant: Christ and the Law in Pauline Theology* (Minneapolis: Fortress Press, 1993)

—, *Who Was Jesus?* (London: SPCK, 1992)

—, *Jesus and the Victory of God: Christian Origins and the Question of God* (London: SPCK, 1996)

Zenger, Erich, "Die Bundestheologie – ein derzeit vernachlässigtes Thema der Bibelwissenschaft und ein wichtiges Thema für das Verhältnis Israel – Kirche," in E. Zenger (ed.), *Der neue Bund im Alten: Zur Bundestheologie der beiden Testamenten* (Quaestiones disputatae 146; Freiburg: Herder, 1993), 13–49

—, "Thesen zu einer Hermeneutik des ersten Testaments nach Auschwitz," in Christoph Dohmen and Thomas Söding (eds.), *Eine Bibel – zwei Testamente: Positionen biblischer Theologie* (UTB 1893; Paderborn: Ferdinand Schöningh, 1995), 143–58

—, "Zum Versuch einer neuen jüdisch-christlichen Bibelhermeneutik: Kleine Antwort auf Horst Seebass," *Theologische Revue* 90.4 (1994), 273–78

Zimmerli, Walther, *Ezechiel*, II, Ezechiel 25–48, Biblischer Kommentar, Altes Testament XIII/2 (Neukirchen-Vluyn: Neukirchener Verlag, 2nd exp. edn, 1979)

—, *Grundriß der alttestamentlichen Theologie*, Theologische Wissenschaft (Stuttgart: Kohlhammer, 1972)

—, "Zum Problem der 'Mitte des Alten Testaments'", *Evangelische Theologie* 35 (1975), 97–118

Scripture Index

Old Testament

Genesis
6:9   6
6:18   6, 17n68
6:22   6
9   5
9:8–17   27
9:9   17n68
9:11   64
9:11–12   17n68
9:11–17   17
9:16   56
9:17   17n68
12:1   24
15   5, 18
15:1   6
15:7–12   21
15:18   18, 22, 27, 63, 64
15:18–21   43
16–21   119n71, 121n80
17   5, 6n19, 9, 21, 27, 44, 56, 189
17:1   63
17:1–5   63
17:1–14   17, 43
17:1–27   6
17:2   17n68, 63, 64
17:4   63, 64
17:6–7   56
17:7   6, 17n68, 37, 39, 41, 56, 204
17:8   37, 39
17:15–22   63
17:18–21   119

17:19   17n68, 39, 64
17:21   17n68, 63, 64
18:18   176
21:22–34   31n113
21:32   12
22:18   176
26:4   176
26:26–31   31n113
26:28   12
26:30–31   17
31:43–55   31n113

Exodus
4:22   188n35
6   44
12–15   47
12:3   106n172
12:14   147
13:3   147
16:10   188
19   20
19–24   20
19–34   54
19:3b–8   20
19:5   6, 7, 43
19:5–6   21, 22
20:2–3   46, 47
20:5a   47
20:13–17a   47
24   18, 80, 134
24:1–11   19
24:3   25, 47
24:3–8   17, 20, 136

24:6b 80
24:6–8 106
24:7 5, 8, 25
24:8 5, 18, 19–20, 78, 79, 80, 103, 104,
    128n18, 133, 136, 138, 208n16
24:9–11 82
24:11 106
24:15b–18 20
24:16 188
27:21 128n18
29:5–46 148
29:45 37, 39
29:45–46 43
31:7 128n18
31:12–17 28
31:16 5
31:17 5
31:18–33:64 3
32–34 20, 47
32:11–13 43
33–34 54
33:1 43
33:13 54n181
33:19 54n181
34 20
34:9 54n181
34:9–10 43, 54
34:10 54n181
34:28 5, 8, 54n181
34:29 5
34:29–35 111
40:34–35 188

Leviticus
11:44–45 44
11:45 37
16 133
22:31–33 44
22:33 37
23:16 49
25:38 37
26 44, 45
26:10 49
26:11 56
26:11–12 148
26:12 37, 39, 44
26:45 37, 44

Numbers
15:41 37
25:13 5, 7, 128n18
28:26 49

Deuteronomy
4 44
4:4 22
4:13 5, 7n22
4:13–14 22
4:20 37
4:23 3, 5, 7
4:31 3, 5
5:2 21
5:15 147
5:33 25
6:44 7
6:4–13 145
6:6–13 145
7:6 37, 41, 44
7:9 3, 5, 21, 44
7:12 3, 5
8:18 3, 5
9:5 62, 64
9:9 5, 17
9:11 5, 17
9:15 5, 17
10:8 5
12–26 47
14:2 37, 41
15:4–5 25
15:7–8 25
16:3 147
16:12 147
17:2 3, 5, 7n22
17:3 3
17:6 136
17:18–19 25
26 38
26:16–19 21, 27, 39
26:17 37
26:17–18 47
26:18 37
26:19 37
27:9 37
28 34, 35, 47
28:9 37

4:4   123n86
4:4–5   121
4:20   118
4:21–31   163, 207
4:21–5:1   117–22
4:24   108, 188n36
4:26   163n59, 169
6:15   143, 207
6:16   196n67

Ephesians
2:5   167
2:11–13   190
2:12   108n1, 190–91, 216
2:13   191, 216
2:14–16   187
2:15   142n1, 143, 207
2:19   121, 163
3:6–7   112
5:8   144

Philippians
2:22   112
3:20   163, 169

Colossians
1:23   112
3:9   143

1 Thessalonians
4:15   72
5:4–5   144

Hebrews
1:1–2   139
1:3   131
2:1   126
2:17   131
3:6   126
3:14   209
4:9   128
4:11   126, 128, 129
4:14   126
4:14–16   126
4:16   126, 129
5:9   128
6:2   136
6:10   126

6:11   126
6:18–20   209
6:19   140
6:19–20   133
6:20   133, 141n67
7:1   127, 128
7:1–28   128
7:11   129, 138, 208
7:12   129, 138
7:16   129
7:18–19   128
7:18   138, 208
7:19   128, 129, 132, 138, 208
7:20–22   127–29, 135
7:22   108, 132, 133, 173, 207n15, 208
7:23–25   129
7:25   128
7:27   133
7:28   128
8:1–6   129
8:1–7   130–32
8:1–13   53
8:1–10:18   129, 133, 135
8:5   122, 132, 133
8:6   108, 128, 129–30, 133, 135, 173, 208
8:6–13   127
8:7   133
8:7–13   130, 131, 135
8:8   78, 108
8:8–9   182n1
8:8–12   129, 131
8:9   108, 131n30, 139
8:10   108, 131
8:8–12   78
8:12   131
8:13   78, 128, 131, 133, 138, 186, 194, 208
9:1–5   132
9:4   108
9:5   188
9:6–7   132
9:7   133, 136
9:8   133
9:9   132, 140
9:10   132
9:11   132
9:11–12   131, 132, 133
9:11–20   133, 135
9:11–23   205

Index of Ancient Sources